SACRED READING

The 2019 Guide to Daily Prayer

"In his apostolic exhortation *The Joy of the Gospel*, Pope Francis invites us to be people of prayer. *Sacred Reading* is an excellent aid in responding to that invitation. This book offers a clear, helpful, and inspirational guide to deepen our love for scripture as we ponder God's Word and live it out in our daily lives."

Most Rev. Robert F. Morneau
Auxiliary Bishop Emeritus of Green Bay

"*Sacred Reading* offers a superb introduction to Ignatian prayer that anyone can use. Too often Ignatian prayer is seen as something reserved only for Jesuits, for people trained in the Spiritual Exercises, or for those who have time for a directed retreat. But this book, created by experts in the traditions of Ignatian prayer, helps the reader encounter Jesus through short scripture passages, inviting questions, and accessible reflections. It's an innovative way to be invited, with gentle wisdom, into meeting Jesus in your prayer."

Rev. James Martin, S.J.

"I encourage anyone looking to deepen their prayer life to spend time learning this ancient practice, and to come to know a God who dances freely in our imaginations if we will but go there with him."

Tim Muldoon
Author of *The Discerning Parent*

"Communion with God increases dramatically as we grow in knowledge of God's Word. For most people the problem is simply getting started: determining where to begin. A most ancient and venerable practice is lectio divina, scripture reading that is meditation and contemplation but also application. *Sacred Reading* is an uncommonly useful tool in really getting into scripture in just this way."

Rev. Michael White and Tom Corcoran
Authors of *Rebuilt*

"In just six simple steps, *Sacred Reading* opens our minds and hearts to scripture in refreshing and profound ways. The daily meditations are clear and concise and yet filled with wisdom and promise. Reading scripture daily is good; reading scripture daily with *Sacred Reading* as your guide is awesome."

Marge Fenelon
Author of *Imitating Mary*

"This guide through the gospel texts of the daily lectionary offers a fully embodied experience that includes the mind, heart, imagination, desire, and behavior. This way of prayerfully reading the gospels as the Spirit-empowered Word of God shows us how to open our lives to be continually formed in Christ."

Stephen J. Binz
Catholic speaker and author of *Transformed by God's Word*

"*Sacred Reading* has become a friend in prayer. I find the format particularly engaging as it inspires me to reflect on the Word of God in a prayerful, practical, and personal way."

Hilda Walter
Administrative Assistant at Gesu Parish
University Heights, Ohio

"*Sacred Reading* is an invaluable companion that helps you cultivate the daily habit of praying with scripture. Learn about God, talk to him, listen to his special message for you, and rest in his presence using the engaging lectio divina format."

Lillian Moore
High school and adult faith-formation catechist
St. Joseph Catholic Church
Honey Creek, Texas

"*Sacred Reading* is an indispensable resource in deepening your prayer and devotional life. Lectio divina will change how you see your relationships—with the Lord, with others, and with yourself. Highly recommended!"

Most Rev. David L. Ricken
Bishop of Green Bay

"This easy-to-use prayer guide is appropriate for teens and adults and provides a wonderful way to enter into the spirit of each day's gospel readings."

Barb Szyszkiewicz
Catholic blogger and editor at *CatholicMom.com*

SACRED READING

The 2019 Guide to
Daily Prayer

Pope's Worldwide
Prayer Network

Ave Maria Press   AVE   Notre Dame, Indiana

Writing Team
Douglas Leonard
William Blazek, S.J.
Richard Buhler, S.J.

Scripture quotations are from *New Revised Standard Version Bible*, copyright ©
1989 National Council of the Churches of Christ in the United States of America.
Used by permission. All rights reserved.

Founded in 1865, Ave Maria Press is a ministry of the United States Province of Holy Cross.

www.avemariapress.com

Paperback: ISBN-13 978-1-59471-855-7

E-book: ISBN-13 978-1-59471-856-4

Cover design by Samantha Watson.

Text design by Dave Scholtes.

Printed and bound in the United States of America.

CONTENTS

INTRODUCTION

It is with great joy that we introduce this 2019 edition of *Sacred Reading*. The Pope's Worldwide Prayer Network—known for so many decades as the Apostleship of Prayer—celebrates its 175th anniversary this year, with a special Papal Mass at St. Peter's Basilica on the Feast of the Most Sacred Heart of Jesus. Thanks be to God for our worldwide network! Thanks be to God for our apostleship!

Who could have anticipated that the Apostleship of Prayer, which began in 1844 in a house of formation for young Jesuits in the south of France, would grow into an international movement spanning ninety-eight countries and four continents? Those young Jesuits in Vals, France, were eager to serve in the foreign missions, yet they grew frustrated with the long, weary years of study and formation. It was at Mass on the Feast of St. Francis Xavier—December 3, 1844—that our founder, Fr. Francis Xavier Gautrelet, S.J., recounted how that great missionary had given his entire life to following Jesus Christ and that those celebrating his memory must do the same. The patron of the universal missions, St. Francis Xavier voyaged as far as the coast of China, passing through many trials and difficulties, entirely committed to service of the Lord. Fr. Gautrelet encouraged his charges to do likewise, not just in foreign lands but also in their own houses of religious formation. He suggested a way of being apostles and missionaries in daily life, uniting everything that they were doing throughout the day with Christ.

One hundred seventy-five years later, the Pope's Worldwide Prayer Network continues to address the challenges facing humanity and assist the mission of the Church. It is our vision, through prayer and work to meet the challenges of the world identified by the pope. His intentions are keys for our prayer and mission. We have a mission: we are apostles in daily life, walking a spiritual path called the "Way of the Heart" and working to serve Christ's mission. Along with the spirit of St. Francis Xavier, we rely on the spirit of our copatroness, St. Thérèse of Lisiuex, herself an Apostleship of Prayer member who desired to pray for the intentions of the Holy Father.

Friends, since 2010, the Apostleship of Prayer has been involved in a deep period of self-examination and, after prayer and reflection, recreated itself as the Pope's Worldwide Prayer Network. In 2015 we launched our new name and logo, and we released our updated digital prayer resources soon thereafter: these include our app, Click to Pray, and the monthly Pope Video, in which the Holy Father personally announces and explains his prayer intention. As with all change, this transformation to a twenty-first century apostolate after one hundred seventy-five years of deeply seated history has not been without sometimes painful growing pains. We thank all our readers and members for their cooperation, patience, and prayers.

This ministry is now a worldwide prayer network, responding to the challenges that confront humanity and the Church's mission as expressed in the pope's monthly intentions. In praying with these intentions, we extend our gaze to the whole world and enter personally into the joys and hopes, the pains and sufferings of our brothers and sisters everywhere.

The reflections in this volume are written by Doug Leonard, our former executive director, and can serve as an excellent adjunct to the Pope's Worldwide Prayer Network's practices of making a daily offering, pausing for recollection at noon, and performing self-examination in the evening. We at the Pope's Worldwide Prayer Network regional offices for Canada and the United States would especially like to thank Fr. Richard Buhler, S.J., of the Manresa Jesuit Retreat House in Convent, Louisiana, for reviewing this work.

Oremus!

Fr. William Blazek, S.J.
Regional Director for US and Canada
Pope's Worldwide Prayer Network

HOW TO USE THIS BOOK

Christians throughout the world are rediscovering a powerful, ancient form of prayer known as sacred reading (*lectio divina*), which invites communion with God through scripture reading and contemplation. What better way to deepen one's friendship with Jesus Christ, the Word of God, than by prayerfully encountering him in the daily gospel reading? This book will set you on a personal prayer journey with Jesus from the start of Advent in December 2018 through the end of Ordinary Time in November 2019: the entire Church year. The Pope's monthly prayer intentions are listed at the beginning of each month for your reference.

Sacred reading is a spiritual practice that, guided by the Holy Spirit, invites you to interact with the words of the daily gospel. As you read and pray this way, you may find—as many others have—that the Lord speaks to you in intimate and surprising ways. The reason for this is simple: as we open our hearts to Jesus, he opens his heart to us.

St. Paul prays beautifully for his readers:

> For this reason I kneel before the Father, from whom every family in heaven and on earth is named, that he may grant you in accord with the riches of his glory to be strengthened with power through his Spirit in the inner self, and that Christ may dwell in your hearts through faith; that you, rooted and grounded in love, may have strength to comprehend with all the holy ones what is the breadth and length and height and depth, and to know the love of Christ that surpasses knowledge, so that you may be filled with all the fullness of God. (Eph 3:14–19)

This book moves you through each day's gospel by prompting you at each step of lectio divina, getting you started with reading, observing, praying, listening, and resolving to act. But most important is your own response to the Word and to the Spirit, for that is how you will grow in your relationship with Jesus. If you are sincerely seeking God, the Holy Spirit will lead you in this process.

The *Sacred Reading* prayer book is intended to guide your prayerful reading during the entire Church year. (Small booklets, suitable for use in parish groups, are also available for Advent and Lent.) Each weekday reflection begins with the date, and some include a reference to the solemnity or feast on that day for which there is a special lectionary gospel reading. When these are indicated, the regular lectionary gospel reading for that day has been replaced with the gospel reading used to celebrate the solemnity or feast. Sunday reflections include both the date and its place in the liturgical calendar; any Sunday reading that includes a reference to a feast day rather than its place in the liturgical calendar uses the gospel reading for the feast day. For the sake of simplicity, other feast days are not cited when their gospel reading has not been used. Due to the length of some gospel readings, some have been shortened. The citation for shortened readings will first show the reading that is included in the book and will then show the citation for the day's complete reading in parentheses.

In prayerful reading of the daily gospels throughout the year—including feast days, days during the high seasons, and days in Ordinary Time—you join your prayers with those of believers all over the world. Each day you will be invited to reflect on the gospel text for the day in six simple but profound steps:

1. Know that God is present with you and ready to converse.

At all times God is everywhere, including where you are in this very moment. The human mind is incapable of fully grasping the mystery of God, but we do know some things about God from scripture. God is the transcendent ground of all being: invisible, eternal, and infinite in power. God is Love, with infinite love for you and me. God is one with and revealed through the Word, Jesus Christ, who became flesh. Through him all things were made, and by him and for him all things subsist. Jesus is the Way, the Truth, and the Life. He says that those who know him also know his Father. Through the Passion, Death, and Resurrection of Jesus, we are reconciled with God. If we believe in Jesus Christ, we become the sons and daughters of Almighty God.

God gives us the Holy Spirit to lead us to truth and understanding. The Holy Spirit also gives us power to live in obedience to the teachings of Jesus. The Holy Spirit draws us to prayer, and works in us as we pray. No wonder we come into God's presence with gladness! All God's ways are good and beautiful. We can get to know God better by encountering God in the Word, which is Jesus himself.

The prayer prompt at the beginning of each day's reading is just that: a prompt, something to get you started. In fact, all the elements in the process of sacred reading are meant to prompt you to your own conversations with God. After reading the prompt, feel free to continue to pray in your own words: respond in your own way, pray in your own way, and hear God speaking to you personally. The goal is to make sacred reading your own prayer time each day.

2. Read the gospel.

The entire Bible is the Word of God, but the gospels (Matthew, Mark, Luke, and John) contain the story of Jesus' life, his teachings, his works, his Passion and Death on the Cross, his Resurrection on the third day, and his Ascension into heaven. Because of this, the Sacred Reading series (the prayer books as well as the seasonal booklets for Advent/Christmas and Lent/Easter) concentrates on praying with the daily gospel readings.

The gospels interpret Jesus' ministry for us. Much more, by the Holy Spirit, we can find in the gospels the very person of Jesus Christ. Prayerful reading of the daily gospel is an opportunity to draw close to the Lord: Father, Son, and Holy Spirit. As we pray with the gospels, we can be transformed by the grace of God, enlightened, strengthened, and moved. Seek to read each day's gospel passage with a complete openness to what God is saying to you. Many who pray with the daily gospel recommend rereading the gospel passage several times.

3. Notice what you think and feel as you read the gospel.

Sacred reading can involve every faculty—mind, heart, emotions, soul, spirit, sensations, imagination, and much more—though usually not all at once. Different passages touch different keys in us. Sometimes we may laugh. Sometimes we may need to stop and worship before we continue. Sometimes we will be puzzled, amazed, stung, abashed, reminded of something lovely, or reminded of something we had wanted to forget.

Seek to feel all of your emotions as you read. Apply your intellect, too. You will confront problems of context and exegesis on a daily basis. That's OK. Sometimes you may experience very little. That's OK, too. God is always at work. Give yourself to the gospel reading and take from it what is there for you each day.

Most important, notice what in particular jumps out at you: it may be a word, a phrase, a character, an image, a pattern, an emotion, a sensation—some arrow to your heart. Whatever it is, pay attention to it, because the Holy Spirit is using it to accomplish something in you.

Sometimes a particular gospel passage repeats during the liturgical year of the Church. To pray through the same gospel passage even on successive days presents no problem whatsoever to your sacred reading. St. Ignatius of Loyola, founder of the Jesuits and author of *The Spiritual Exercises*, actually recommends repeated meditation on passages of scripture. Read in the Spirit, gospel passages have unlimited potential to reveal to us the truths we are ready to receive. The Word of God has boundless power to illuminate and transform the prayerful believer.

4. *Pray as you are led for yourself and others.*

Praying is simply talking with God. Believe God hears you. Believe God will answer you. Believe God knows what you need even before you ask. Jesus says so in Matthew 6:8. Your conversation with God can go far beyond asking for things, though. You may thank, praise, worship, rejoice, mourn, explain, or question, revealing your fears, seeking understanding, or asking forgiveness. Your conversation with God has no limits. God is the ideal conversationalist, and God wants to spend time with you.

Being human, we can't help being self-absorbed, but praying is not just about our own needs. We are often moved by the gospel to pray for others. We will regularly remember our loved ones in prayer. Sometimes we will be led to pray for someone who has hurt us. At other times we will be moved to pray for a class of people in need wherever they are in the world, such as persecuted Christians, refugees, the mentally ill, teachers, the unborn, or the lonely.

We may also pray with the universal Church by praying for the pope's prayer intentions. Those intentions are entrusted to the Pope's Worldwide Prayer Network and are available through its website and its annual and monthly leaflets. You may get your own copy of this year's papal prayer intentions by contacting the Pope's Worldwide Prayer Network, which has more than thirty-five million members worldwide. Jesus asked us to unite in prayer, promising that the Father would grant us whatever we ask in his name, and it is during this time of sacred reading that we take advantage of this invitation to speak with God for ourselves and others.

5. *Listen to Jesus.*

Jesus, the Good Shepherd, speaks to his own sheep, who hear his voice (see Jn 10:27). This listening is a most wonderful time in your prayer experience. The italicized words in this passage are the words I felt impressed upon my heart as I prayed with these readings. I included them in order to help you listen more actively for whatever it is the Lord might be saying to you.

Jesus speaks to all in the gospels, but in *Sacred Reading*, he can now speak exclusively to you. If you wish, write down what he says to you and reread his words during the day. Put all of Jesus' words to you in a folder or keep a spiritual notebook. Believers through the ages have recorded the words of Jesus to them, holy mystics and ordinary believers alike.

It takes faith to hear the voice of Jesus. This faith will grow as you practice listening. Ideally, we will learn to hear what Jesus is saying to us all day long, as we face difficult situations perhaps. Listening to the voice of Jesus is practicing the presence of God. As St. Paul said, "In him we live and move and have our being" (Acts 17:28).

St. Ignatius of Loyola called this conversation with Jesus *colloquy*. That word simply means that two or more people are talking. St. Ignatius even urges us to include the saints in our prayer conversations. We believe in the communion of saints. If you have a patron saint, don't be afraid to talk to him or her. In her autobiography, St. Thérèse of Lisieux, a member of the Apostleship of Prayer, describes how she spoke often with Mary and Joseph, as well as with Jesus.

6. Ask God to show you how to live today.

Pope Benedict XVI commented that sacred reading is not complete without a call to action; something in our praying leads us to do something in our day. Perhaps we find an opportunity to serve, to love, to give, to lead, or to do something good for someone else. Perhaps we find occasion to repent, to forgive, to ask forgiveness, to make amends. Open your heart to anything God might want you to do. Try to keep the conversation with God going all day long.

Asking God to show you how to live is the last step of the *Sacred Reading* prayer time, but that doesn't mean you need to end it here. Keep it going. You may drift off in the presence of God, lose attention, or even fall asleep, but you can come back. God is always present, seeking to love you and to be loved. God is always seeking to lead us to the green pastures. God is our strength, our rock, our ever-present help in time of trouble. God is full of mercy, ready to forgive us again and again. God sees us through very difficult times. God heals us. God gives his life to us constantly. God is our Maker, Father, Mother, Lover, Servant, Savior, and Friend. We know that from the Gospel. He is an inexhaustible spring of blessing and holiness in our innermost selves. The sanctification of our souls is God's work, not our own.

As you read, ask the Holy Spirit to lead you in this process. With genuine faith, open yourself to respond to the Word and the Spirit, and your relationship with Jesus will continue to deepen and grow just as the infant Jesus grew within the womb of the Blessed Mother. This in turn will lead you to share the love of Christ with all those you encounter, just as the Blessed Mother draws all those who encounter her directly to her Son.

The Advent and Christmas Seasons

INTRODUCTION

Advent is all about waiting for Jesus Christ. The gospel readings of Advent make us mindful of three ways we await Jesus: past, present, and future. First, we remember and accompany Mary, Joseph, and the newborn Jesus. Second, we prepare for the celebration of his birth this Christmas so that the day doesn't pass us by with just meaningless words and worthless presents. Third, we anticipate the second coming of Jesus Christ, who will come in power and glory for everyone to see and establish his kingdom of peace and justice upon the earth.

Christ is born, and we follow him in exile and in those joyful early years with the Holy Family. We are blessed, but we are challenged, too, to understand the ways of God and how we personally may understand and respond to them now.

THE POPE'S MONTHLY PRAYER INTENTION FOR DECEMBER 2018

That people, who are involved in the service and transmission of faith, may find in their dialogue with culture a language suited to the conditions of the present time.

Sunday, December 2, 2018
First Sunday of Advent

Know that God is present with you and ready to converse.

Many of us learned as children that God is everywhere. St. Ignatius taught his followers to seek God in all things. So we turn to God's Word, authored by the Holy Spirit, who is One with the Father and the Son, Jesus the Messiah. God is here now, ready to speak to us.

When you are ready, lift your heart to God and receive God in the Word.

Read the gospel: Luke 21:25–28, 34–36.

Jesus said, "There will be signs in the sun, the moon, and the stars, and on the earth distress among nations confused by the roaring of the sea and the waves. People will faint from fear and foreboding of what is coming upon the world, for the powers of the heavens will be shaken. Then they will see 'the Son of Man coming in a cloud' with power and great glory. Now when these things begin to take place, stand up and raise your heads, because your redemption is drawing near. . . .

"Be on guard so that your hearts are not weighed down with dissipation and drunkenness and the worries of this life, and that day does not catch you unexpectedly, like a trap. For it will come upon all who live on the face of the whole earth. Be alert at all times, praying that you may have the strength to escape all these things that will take place, and to stand before the Son of Man."

Notice what you think and feel as you read the gospel.

The gospel asks us to take the long view in our lives, for the ultimate purpose is to live with God forever. In the meantime, we will be buffeted in our daily lives, sometimes terribly and sometimes more gently. Jesus asks us to trust in God's purposes for ourselves and for all people, to stay alert, and to pray.

Pray as you are led for yourself and others.

"I will be patient and alert, Lord, as I trust you to work in my life and with my loved ones. I pray specifically for these . . ." (Continue in your own words.)

Listen to Jesus.

I am glad you have come near to me today, beloved. I will direct your steps as you learn to trust me in everything. What else is Jesus saying to you?

Ask God to show you how to live today.

"Teach me how to listen to you and walk in your presence all day long and for my whole life. Thank you. Amen."

Monday, December 3, 2018

Know that God is present with you and ready to converse.

"Glory to you, Lord. I am grateful for you now. Open me to your holy Word."

Read the gospel: Matthew 8:5–11.

When Jesus entered Capernaum, a centurion came to him, appealing to him and saying, "Lord, my servant is lying at home paralyzed, in terrible distress." And he said to him, "I will come and cure him." The centurion answered, "Lord, I am not worthy to have you come under my roof; but only speak the word, and my servant will be healed. For I also am a man under authority, with soldiers under me; and I say to one, 'Go,' and he goes, and to another, 'Come,' and he comes, and to my slave, 'Do this,' and the slave does it." When Jesus heard him, he was amazed and said to those who followed him, "Truly I tell you, in no one in Israel have I found such faith. I tell you, many will come from east and west and will eat with Abraham and Isaac and Jacob in the kingdom of heaven."

Notice what you think and feel as you read the gospel.

The Roman centurion has all the qualities Jesus loves. It doesn't matter that he is not a Jew. He has faith, he loves his servant, and he is very humble. Jesus says, to our joy, that many from the east and the west will enter the kingdom of heaven.

Pray as you are led for yourself and others.

"Lord, I long to come in to your kingdom with your chosen from every nation. I pray now for people I know who need your healing . . ." (Continue in your own words.)

Listen to Jesus.

Come to me in faith as the centurion did. You will please me and I will give you my life. Pray for others with compassion, for it is the quality of your compassion that makes your prayer powerful. What else is Jesus saying to you?

Ask God to show you how to live today.

"Jesus, your way is so simple, so pure. Give me grace to walk in it today. Thank you. Amen."

Tuesday, December 4, 2018

Know that God is present with you and ready to converse.

"I rejoice in your presence, Almighty God and Father. Let me be filled with your Spirit and your Word."

Read the gospel: Luke 10:21–24.

At that same hour Jesus rejoiced in the Holy Spirit and said, "I thank you, Father, Lord of heaven and earth, because you have hidden these things from the wise and the intelligent and have revealed them to infants; yes, Father, for such was your gracious will. All things have been handed over to me by my Father; and no one knows who the Son is except the Father, or who the Father is except the Son and anyone to whom the Son chooses to reveal him."

Then turning to the disciples, Jesus said to them privately, "Blessed are the eyes that see what you see! For I tell you that many prophets and kings desired to see what you see, but did not see it, and to hear what you hear, but did not hear it."

Notice what you think and feel as you read the gospel.

Jesus prays to his Father, thanking him for revealing the Son to people—not to the wise and intelligent but to infants. Likewise, the Son has power to reveal himself and the Father. We are blessed beyond all we can imagine to have loving knowledge of God.

Pray as you are led for yourself and others.

"Lord, I reject all my pride and come to you as a child. Let me please you in that. I pray also for those you have given me . . ." (Continue in your own words.)

Listen to Jesus.

I love you, my child. Pray for those who do not yet know me. They will come to me. What else is Jesus saying to you?

Ask God to show you how to live today.

"Lord, I humbly ask to know you and the work you have for me each day, this day. I seek to follow you. Amen."

Wednesday, December 5, 2018

Know that God is present with you and ready to converse.

"Lord, you have come to me today to heal and feed me. Thank you."

Read the gospel: Matthew 15:29–37.

After Jesus had left that place, he passed along the Sea of Galilee, and he went up the mountain, where he sat down. Great crowds came to him, bringing with them the lame, the maimed, the blind, the mute, and many others. They put them at his feet, and he cured them, so that the crowd was amazed when they saw the mute speaking, the maimed whole, the lame walking, and the blind seeing. And they praised the God of Israel.

Then Jesus called his disciples to him and said, "I have compassion for the crowd, because they have been with me now for three days and have nothing to eat; and I do not want to send them away hungry, for they might faint on the way." The disciples said to him, "Where are we to get enough bread in the desert to feed so great a crowd?" Jesus asked them, "How many loaves have you?" They said, "Seven, and a few small fish." Then ordering the crowd to sit down on the ground, he took the seven loaves and the fish; and after giving thanks he broke them and gave them to the disciples, and the disciples gave them to the crowds.

And all of them ate and were filled; and they took up the broken pieces left over, seven baskets full.

Notice what you think and feel as you read the gospel.

Those who need healing are brought to the feet of Jesus, and he heals them. The very crowd that brought the lame, the blind, and the mute to Jesus are yet amazed when he heals them. And then, though they don't think to ask for something as simple as food, Jesus knows their needs and provides for them out of love. What are our expectations as we come to Jesus?

Pray as you are led for yourself and others.

"I want to show you faith, Lord—faith to follow you, trusting you for healing and sharing your love with others. I pray now for these . . ." (Continue in your own words.)

Listen to Jesus.

Because you call out to me, I give you healing today, dear disciple. Receive me in your heart. What else is Jesus saying to you?

Ask God to show you how to live today.

"Let me draw near and stay near to you all day, Lord. Help me serve you today. Amen."

Thursday, December 6, 2018

Know that God is present with you and ready to converse.

"Thank you for visiting me as I approach your Word, Lord. I will attend to you."

Read the gospel: Matthew 7:21, 24–27.

Jesus said to his disciples, "Not everyone who says to me, 'Lord, Lord,' will enter the kingdom of heaven, but only one who does the will of my Father in heaven. . . . Everyone then who hears these words of mine and acts on them will be like a wise man who built his house on rock. The rain fell, the floods came, and the winds blew and beat on that house, but it did not fall, because it had been founded on rock. And everyone who hears these words of mine and does not act on them will be like a foolish man who built his house on sand. The rain fell, and the floods came, and the winds blew and beat against that house, and it fell—and great was its fall!"

Notice what you think and feel as you read the gospel.

Jesus says that the Word of God has no saving effect unless the one who hears it acts upon it. It is up to us to speak and act in response to the Word of God. If we do the will of the Father, we will enter the kingdom.

Pray as you are led for yourself and others.

"Jesus, you are my rock; let me build upon you, seeking to do the will of God. Let me serve you and others well . . ." (Continue in your own words.)

Listen to Jesus.

If you rely on me, you will see changes in your life. You will grow stronger in faith, hope, and love, and your service will glorify God. What else is Jesus saying to you?

Ask God to show you how to live today.

"Lord, give me eyes to see you and let me walk with you all day, Lord. I seek to act in your will. Amen."

Friday, December 7, 2018

Know that God is present with you and ready to converse.

"Lord, teach me by your Word today. You are the same yesterday, today, and forever."

Read the gospel: Matthew 9:27–31.

As Jesus went on from there, two blind men followed him, crying loudly, "Have mercy on us, Son of David!" When he entered the house, the blind men came to him; and Jesus said to them, "Do you believe that I am able to do this?" They said to him, "Yes, Lord." Then he touched their eyes and said, "According to your faith let it be done to you." And their eyes were opened. Then Jesus sternly ordered them, "See that no one knows of this." But they went away and spread the news about him throughout that district.

Notice what you think and feel as you read the gospel.

Jesus heals the blind men according to their faith. Because of their faith, their eyes are opened. In their enthusiasm, they fail to obey Jesus, and they tell everyone about him.

Pray as you are led for yourself and others.

"Lord, my own faith is willing but weak. Let me reach out to you with what faith you have given me and seek healing in all the parts needing it. I pray also for the faith of others who need you . . ." (Continue in your own words.)

Listen to Jesus.

Dear servant. I grant you what you ask. Cling to me and know I love you. What else is Jesus saying to you?

Ask God to show you how to live today.

"I resolve today to act upon the faith and love you give me, serving my neighbor. Thank you, Lord. Amen."

Saturday, December 8, 2018
Immaculate Conception of the Blessed Virgin Mary

Know that God is present with you and ready to converse.

"Lord, instruct me by your Word, and let it be done to me accordingly."

Read the gospel: Luke 1:26–38.

In the sixth month the angel Gabriel was sent by God to a town in Galilee called Nazareth, to a virgin engaged to a man whose name was Joseph, of the house of David. The virgin's name was Mary. And he came to her and said, "Greetings, favored one! The Lord is with you." But she was much perplexed by his words and pondered what sort of greeting this might be. The angel said to her, "Do not be afraid, Mary, for you have found favor with God. And now, you will conceive in your womb and bear a son, and you will name him Jesus. He will be great, and will be called the Son of the Most High, and the Lord God will give to him the throne of his ancestor David. He will reign over the house of Jacob forever, and of his kingdom there will be no end." Mary said to the angel, "How can this be, since I am a virgin?" The angel said to her, "The Holy Spirit will come upon you, and the power of the Most High will overshadow you; therefore the child to be born will be holy; he will be called Son of God. And now, your relative Elizabeth in her old age has also conceived a son; and this is the sixth month for her who was said to be barren. For nothing will be impossible with God." Then Mary said, "Here am I, the servant of the Lord; let it be with me according to your word." Then the angel departed from her.

Notice what you think and feel as you read the gospel.

The angel appears to tell Mary what God will do with her. Gabriel does not ask for Mary's permission, but after hearing his words, Mary agrees. She must have barely comprehended the marvelous prophecy, but she has faith and submits to the will of God.

Pray as you are led for yourself and others.

"I bless Mary for her obedience and mildness. Let me have the spirit of our Mother that I may serve others as she did . . ." (Continue in your own words.)

Listen to Jesus.

I thank you for your love for our Mother, mine and yours, for your faith has made you a child of God and a sibling to me. What else is Jesus saying to you?

Ask God to show you how to live today.

"Let me approach today with the simplicity and gentleness of Mary, Lord. Help me to do your will as generously as she did. Amen."

Sunday, December 9, 2018
Second Sunday of Advent

Know that God is present with you and ready to converse.

"Lord, you are present with me in the words John the Baptist proclaimed before your public ministry. Glory to you."

Read the gospel: Luke 3:1–6.

In the fifteenth year of the reign of Emperor Tiberius, when Pontius Pilate was governor of Judea, and Herod was ruler of Galilee, and his brother Philip ruler of the region of Ituraea and Trachonitis, and Lysanias ruler of Abilene, during the high-priesthood of Annas and Caiaphas, the word of God came to John son of Zechariah in the wilderness. He went into all the region around the Jordan, proclaiming a baptism of repentance for the forgiveness of sins, as it is written in the book of the words of the prophet Isaiah,

> "The voice of one crying out in the wilderness:
> 'Prepare the way of the Lord,
>   make his paths straight.
> Every valley shall be filled,

> and every mountain and hill shall be made low,
>   and the crooked shall be made straight,
>   and the rough ways made smooth;
>   and all flesh shall see the salvation of God.'"

Notice what you think and feel as you read the gospel.

The evangelist goes to great pains to locate these events in secular history—he refers to specific worldly authorities to pinpoint place and time—to point out that "the salvation of God" was not just an ethereal prophecy but the concrete, tangible, and real fulfillment of the Old Testament prophecy.

Pray as you are led for yourself and others.

"John spoke the truth to friends and enemies alike. He spoke of you, my Jesus. Let me imitate John in your service . . ." (Continue in your own words.)

Listen to Jesus.

You are seeing the salvation of the Lord, my child, as you turn to me and trust in me. I wash away your sins when you repent. Bear good fruit. Pray for those who need your prayers. What else is Jesus saying to you?

Ask God to show you how to live today.

"My Lord, my Savior. Baptize me with your Holy Spirit that I may have power to serve. Amen."

Monday, December 10, 2018

Know that God is present with you and ready to converse.

"Lord, you have power to forgive sins and to heal. I seek forgiveness and healing through your Word."

Read the gospel: Luke 5:17–26.

One day, while Jesus was teaching, Pharisees and teachers of the law were sitting nearby (they had come from every village of Galilee and Judea and from Jerusalem); and the power of the Lord was with him to heal. Just then some men came, carrying a paralyzed man on a bed. They were trying to bring him in and lay him before Jesus; but finding no way to bring him in because of the crowd, they went up on the roof and let him down with his bed through the tiles into the middle of the crowd in front of Jesus. When he saw their faith, he said, "Friend, your sins are forgiven you." Then the scribes and the Pharisees began to question, "Who is this who is speaking blasphemies? Who can forgive sins but God alone?" When Jesus perceived their questionings, he answered them, "Why do you raise such questions in your hearts? Which is easier, to say, 'Your sins are forgiven you,' or to say, 'Stand up and walk'? But so that you may know that the Son of Man has authority on earth to forgive sins"—he said to the one who was paralyzed—"I say to you, stand up and take your bed and go to your home." Immediately he stood up before them, took what he had been lying on, and went to his home, glorifying God. Amazement seized all of them, and they glorified God and were filled with awe, saying, "We have seen strange things today."

Notice what you think and feel as you read the gospel.

His devoted friends lower the paralyzed man on a bed before Jesus. The Lord forgives the man before the crowd, which included scribes and Pharisees who question his authority to forgive, for only God can forgive sins. Jesus asserts his authority and heals the paralytic, who takes up his bed and goes home, glorifying God. Then all of them, filled with awe, glorify God. Did the scribes and Pharisees join them?

Pray as you are led for yourself and others.

"Lord, I glorify you for your authority to forgive and to heal, for I need both. Make me well in body and soul to serve you and others, including . . ." (Continue in your own words.)

Listen to Jesus.

I receive you, dear child. Turn from sin. I will help you. What else is Jesus saying to you?

Ask God to show you how to live today.

"Jesus, I believe you work wonders every day. Show me how you can use me to help others in need. Let me please you today. Amen."

Tuesday, December 11, 2018

Know that God is present with you and ready to converse.

"Jesus, you are the Word of God. Let me not go astray."

Read the gospel: Matthew 18:12–14.

Jesus asked his disciples, "What do you think? If a shepherd has a hundred sheep, and one of them has gone astray, does he not leave the ninety-nine on the mountains and go in search of the one that went astray? And if he finds it, truly I tell you, he rejoices over it more than over the ninety-nine that never went astray. So it is not the will of your Father in heaven that one of these little ones should be lost."

Notice what you think and feel as you read the gospel.

Jesus and his Father seek and rescue the lost sheep, one by one. God wants to bring all people to him.

Pray as you are led for yourself and others.

"Loving Shepherd, find me. I long to make you happy by being found, redeemed, and returned to the fold. I pray for all the lost sheep . . ." (Continue in your own words.)

Listen to Jesus.

God's love is endless, little one. He saves all the little ones he loves. What else is Jesus saying to you?

Ask God to show you how to live today.

"What can I do to find and feed your sheep, Lord? I offer myself now. Amen."

Wednesday, December 12, 2018
Our Lady of Guadalupe

Know that God is present with you and ready to converse.

"Thank you for your work in the Americas, Lord. Let your Lady continue to turn hearts to you."

Read the gospel: Luke 1:26–38.

In the sixth month the angel Gabriel was sent by God to a town in Galilee called Nazareth, to a virgin engaged to a man whose name was Joseph, of the house of David. The virgin's name was Mary. And he came to her and said, "Greetings, favored one! The Lord is with you." But she was much perplexed by his words and pondered what sort of greeting this might be. The angel said to her, "Do not be afraid, Mary, for you have found favor with God. And now, you will conceive in your womb and bear a son, and you will name him Jesus. He will be great, and will be called the Son of the Most High, and the Lord God will give to him the throne of his ancestor David. He will reign over the house of Jacob for ever, and of his kingdom there will be no end." Mary said to the angel, "How can this be, since I am a virgin?" The angel said to her, "The Holy Spirit will come upon you, and the power of the Most High will overshadow you; therefore the child to be born will be holy; he will be called Son of God. And now, your relative Elizabeth in her old age has also conceived a son; and this is the sixth month for her who was said to be barren. For nothing will be impossible with God." Then Mary said, "Here am I, the servant of the Lord; let it be with me according to your word." Then the angel departed from her.

Notice what you think and feel as you read the gospel.

Is it any wonder that Mary questions the angel Gabriel about the astonishing things God has planned to do for her and through her? In her humility, though, she entrusts herself and her future to God.

Pray as you are led for yourself and others.

"Dear Trinity of Love, I entrust myself to your mighty and holy will. I will not allow myself to be distressed by the threats to my peace in the world. You are Lord, and I give myself and my loved ones to you . . ." (Continue in your own words.)

Listen to Jesus.

Yes, trust me with a peaceful spirit, dear friend and child. Let me operate in your life. I will give you what you need and keep you safe for everlasting life. What else is Jesus saying to you?

Ask God to show you how to live today.

"How may I spread your gospel of peace to others, Lord? Give me the power of your Spirit. Amen."

Thursday, December 13, 2018

Know that God is present with you and ready to converse.

"Jesus, give me ears to hear your Word today. Show me how to follow you."

Read the gospel: Matthew 11:11–15.

Jesus said, "Truly I tell you, among those born of women no one has arisen greater than John the Baptist; yet the least in the kingdom of heaven is greater than he. From the days of John the Baptist until now the kingdom of heaven has suffered violence, and the violent take it by force. For all the prophets and the law prophesied until John came; and if you are willing to accept it, he is Elijah who is to come. Let anyone with ears listen!"

Notice what you think and feel as you read the gospel.

In praising John the Baptist, Jesus unites John's ministry with his own, validating John's baptism and calling his disciples to follow him.

Pray as you are led for yourself and others.

"God, I would rejoice to be the least in your kingdom. Let me come to you, Lord, and lead also those you have given me . . ." (Continue in your own words.)

Listen to Jesus.

I am with you, dear servant. I am leading you. With me you are safe. What else is Jesus saying to you?

Ask God to show you how to live today.

"You are the Messiah, Jesus. I glorify you and thank you for your great promises to me. Make me worthy of your kingdom, starting today. Amen."

Friday, December 14, 2018

Know that God is present with you and ready to converse.

"Jesus, help me to recognize your will for me as I read your Word. Let me receive it as you mean it for me. Teach me now."

Read the gospel: Matthew 11:16–19.

Jesus said, "But to what will I compare this generation? It is like children sitting in the marketplaces and calling to one another,

> 'We played the flute for you, and you did not dance;
> we wailed, and you did not mourn.'

For John came neither eating nor drinking, and they say, 'He has a demon'; the Son of Man came eating and drinking, and they say, 'Look, a glutton and a drunkard, a friend of tax collectors and sinners!' Yet wisdom is vindicated by her deeds."

Notice what you think and feel as you read the gospel.

Jesus considers the contrasting preaching styles of John the Baptist and himself, and he laments those who have rejected both. Some people you just can't please; they will look for problems, because they do not want to come to God.

Pray as you are led for yourself and others.

"Jesus, you speak of wisdom and its connection to one's deeds. Give me the wisdom to do your will, and give those who reject you the wisdom to receive you . . ." (Continue in your own words.)

Listen to Jesus.

I am pleased you ask for wisdom, my child. I am the wisdom of God, and you will find endless wisdom in me. Be patient with yourself and wait patiently for God. I will bless you with wisdom. What else is Jesus saying to you?

Ask God to show you how to live today.

"Thank you for your constant care of me, dear Jesus. I want to cling to you in everything, today, tomorrow, and always. Amen."

Saturday, December 15, 2018

Know that God is present with you and ready to converse.

"God, you reveal yourself to human beings, often in mysterious ways. Lord, open my mind and heart to understand your Word."

Read the gospel: Matthew 17:9–13.

As they were coming down the mountain, Jesus ordered them, "Tell no one about the vision until after the Son of Man has been raised from the dead." And the disciples asked him, "Why, then, do the scribes say that Elijah must come first?" He replied, "Elijah is indeed coming and will restore all things; but I tell you that Elijah has already come, and they did not recognize him, but they did to him whatever they pleased. So also the Son of Man is about to suffer at their hands." Then the disciples understood that he was speaking to them about John the Baptist.

Notice what you think and feel as you read the gospel.

Jesus' disciples question him about what they have just seen: the Transfiguration, when Jesus appeared in glory before them speaking to Moses and Elijah. They speak of some Messianic prophesies foretelling the coming of Elijah before the Messiah. Jesus seems to consider that Elijah has indeed come in the person of John the Baptist, who was killed, and he says that he too will suffer at the hands of the authorities.

Pray as you are led for yourself and others.

"Jesus, you speak of the suffering of the prophets and yourself. As your disciple, I expect to suffer as well, and I seek to accept it with obedience, for I know all things are for my good. I pray also for others who suffer, including . . ." (Continue in your own words.)

Listen to Jesus.

Do not fear suffering, my child. Look to God in all things. What else is Jesus saying to you?

Ask God to show you how to live today.

"As I face my suffering today, Lord, I offer it all for the good of others, especially those who suffer and most especially those who may cause me to suffer. Amen."

Sunday, December 16, 2018
Third Sunday of Advent

Know that God is present with you and ready to converse.

"How wonderful are your ways, God. You are with me now."

Read the gospel: Luke 3:10–18.

And the crowds asked Jesus, "What then should we do?" In reply he said to them, "Whoever has two coats must share with anyone who has none; and whoever has food must do likewise." Even tax collectors came to be baptized, and they asked him, "Teacher, what should we do?" He said to them, "Collect no more than the amount prescribed for you." Soldiers also asked him, "And we, what should we do?" He said to them, "Do not extort money from anyone by threats or false accusation, and be satisfied with your wages."

As the people were filled with expectation, and all were questioning in their hearts concerning John, whether he might be the Messiah, John answered all of them by saying, "I baptize you with water; but one who is more powerful than I is coming; I am not worthy to untie the thong of his sandals. He will baptize you with the Holy Spirit and fire. His winnowing fork is in his hand, to clear his threshing floor and to gather the wheat into his granary; but the chaff he will burn with unquenchable fire."

So, with many other exhortations, he proclaimed the good news to the people.

Notice what you think and feel as you read the gospel.

Jesus teaches the people simple morality, based on justice, generosity, gentleness, and humility. The people are taken with him and his message. Might this be the Messiah John the Baptist spoke of who will baptize with the Holy Spirit and fire?

Pray as you are led for yourself and others.

"Lord, help me to practice morality in my own life. Baptize me with your Holy Spirit and fire so that I may give you glory in my service to you and others . . ." (Continue in your own words.)

Listen to Jesus.

You are right that simplicity is the key to good behavior and a good life. I am with you, dear servant. I send my Spirit upon you as you ask. What else is Jesus saying to you?

Ask God to show you how to live today.

"You are good to me, Lord. Strengthen me to perform my duty to God and others. Let my love for you impel me. Amen."

Monday, December 17, 2018

Know that God is present with you and ready to converse.

"Jesus, you are Son of God and Son of Man. Let me contemplate what it means that you took mortal flesh to confer everlasting life upon us. Open me to your Word, Lord."

Read the gospel: Matthew 1:1–17.

An account of the genealogy of Jesus the Messiah, the son of David, the son of Abraham.

Abraham was the father of Isaac, and Isaac the father of Jacob, and Jacob the father of Judah and his brothers, and Judah the father of Perez and Zerah by Tamar, and Perez the father of Hezron, and Hezron the father of Aram, and Aram the father of Aminadab, and Aminadab the father of Nahshon, and Nahshon the father of Salmon, and Salmon the father of Boaz by Rahab, and Boaz the father of Obed by Ruth, and Obed the father of Jesse, and Jesse the father of King David.

And David was the father of Solomon by the wife of Uriah, and Solomon the father of Rehoboam, and Rehoboam the father of Abijah, and Abijah the father of Asaph, and Asaph the father of Jehoshaphat, and Jehoshaphat the father of Joram, and Joram the father of Uzziah, and Uzziah the father of Jotham, and Jotham the father of Ahaz, and Ahaz the father of Hezekiah, and Hezekiah the father of Manasseh, and Manasseh the father of Amos, and Amos the father of Josiah, and Josiah the father of Jechoniah and his brothers, at the time of the deportation to Babylon.

And after the deportation to Babylon: Jechoniah was the father of Salathiel, and Salathiel the father of Zerubbabel, and Zerubbabel the father of Abiud, and Abiud the father of Eliakim, and Eliakim the father of Azor, and Azor the father of Zadok, and Zadok the father of Achim, and Achim the father of Eliud, and Eliud the father of Eleazar, and Eleazar the father of Matthan, and Matthan the father of Jacob, and Jacob the father of Joseph the husband of Mary, of whom Jesus was born, who is called the Messiah.

So all the generations from Abraham to David are fourteen generations; and from David to the deportation to Babylon, fourteen generations; and from the deportation to Babylon to the Messiah, fourteen generations.

Notice what you think and feel as you read the gospel.

Jesus the man was descended from people good and bad—such are the ways of the Lord in sending his Messiah. He shared our nature, yet he was without sin. Jesus' holiness and divinity in a vessel of flesh are essential for our redemption.

Pray as you are led for yourself and others.

"Lord, thank you for coming to us to save us. You are alive and working among us now. Come to me and save me from my sins. Come to those I pray for . . ." (Continue in your own words.)

Listen to Jesus.

As you come to me in prayer, my beloved, I work to prepare you for the kingdom of God. What else is Jesus saying to you?

Ask God to show you how to live today.

"Lord, inspire me to pray often. Glory to you, Redeemer. Amen."

Tuesday, December 18, 2018

Know that God is present with you and ready to converse.
"You know my heart, Lord. Let it be open now to your Word."

Read the gospel: Matthew 1:18–25.
Now the birth of Jesus the Messiah took place in this way. When his mother Mary had been engaged to Joseph, but before they lived together, she was found to be with child from the Holy Spirit. Her husband Joseph, being a righteous man and unwilling to expose her to public disgrace, planned to dismiss her quietly. But just when he had resolved to do this, an angel of the Lord appeared to him in a dream and said, "Joseph, son of David, do not be afraid to take Mary as your wife, for the child conceived in her is from the Holy Spirit. She will bear a son, and you are to name him Jesus, for he will save his people from their sins." All this took place to fulfill what had been spoken by the Lord through the prophet:

> "Look, the virgin shall conceive and bear a son,
>   and they shall name him Emmanuel,"

which means, "God is with us." When Joseph awoke from sleep, he did as the angel of the Lord commanded him; he took her as his wife, but had no marital relations with her until she had borne a son; and he named him Jesus.

Notice what you think and feel as you read the gospel.
Joseph, a just man betrothed to Mary, here tries to deal with the fact of her pregnancy. He wants to do the right thing. An angel in a dream tells him what is going on and what he should do. Joseph believes and obeys.

Pray as you are led for yourself and others.
"Lord, let me be open to all things that befall me, knowing they come from you. I am your servant, Lord . . ." (Continue in your own words.)

Listen to Jesus.
When you face problems or questions of direction, look to me, my servant. I will guide you into the godly way. What else is Jesus saying to you?

Ask God to show you how to live today.
"Jesus, speak to me always. Let me walk in your Holy Spirit today. Let me hear you more and more. Amen."

Wednesday, December 19, 2018

Know that God is present with you and ready to converse.
"Lord, your Word is true. Let me believe it in my heart, my soul, my mind. Your Spirit is present with me now."

Read the gospel: Luke 1:5–25.

In the days of King Herod of Judea, there was a priest named Zechariah, who belonged to the priestly order of Abijah. His wife was a descendant of Aaron, and her name was Elizabeth. Both of them were righteous before God, living blamelessly according to all the commandments and regulations of the Lord. But they had no children, because Elizabeth was barren, and both were getting on in years.

Once when he was serving as priest before God and his section was on duty, he was chosen by lot, according to the custom of the priesthood, to enter the sanctuary of the Lord and offer incense. Now at the time of the incense-offering, the whole assembly of the people was praying outside. Then there appeared to him an angel of the Lord, standing at the right side of the altar of incense. When Zechariah saw him, he was terrified; and fear overwhelmed him. But the angel said to him, "Do not be afraid, Zechariah, for your prayer has been heard. Your wife Elizabeth will bear you a son, and you will name him John. You will have joy and gladness, and many will rejoice at his birth, for he will be great in the sight of the Lord. He must never drink wine or strong drink; even before his birth he will be filled with the Holy Spirit. He will turn many of the people of Israel to the Lord their God. With the spirit and power of Elijah he will go before him, to turn the hearts of parents to their children, and the disobedient to the wisdom of the righteous, to make ready a people prepared for the Lord." Zechariah said to the angel, "How will I know that this is so? For I am an old man, and my wife is getting on in years." The angel replied, "I am Gabriel. I stand in the presence of God, and I have been sent to speak to you and to bring you this good news. But now, because you did not believe my words, which will be fulfilled in their time, you will become mute, unable to speak, until the day these things occur."

Meanwhile, the people were waiting for Zechariah, and wondered at his delay in the sanctuary. When he did come out, he could not speak to them, and they realized that he had seen a vision in the sanctuary. He kept motioning to them and remained unable to speak. When his time of service was ended, he went to his home.

After those days his wife Elizabeth conceived, and for five months she remained in seclusion. She said, "This is what the Lord has done for me when he looked favorably on me and took away the disgrace I have endured among my people."

Notice what you think and feel as you read the gospel.

While Mary believed Gabriel's announcement and Joseph believed the angel in the dream, Zechariah doubts Gabriel's announcement to him. How could this aged couple conceive a child, even if the child was to be a prophet of the Lord? But Elizabeth becomes pregnant with John the Baptist, who would be the forerunner of the Messiah.

Pray as you are led for yourself and others.

"Lord, fill me with faith as I await your coming. Let me trust in you in all my affairs. In the future with you I have nothing to fear. I pray for those in fear . . ." (Continue in your own words.)

Listen to Jesus.

You are right to trust me, child. I will do marvelous things in your life as you cling to me and seek to walk in all my ways. I love you. What else is Jesus saying to you?

Ask God to show you how to live today.

"Lord, let me, like Elizabeth, humbly and fearlessly proclaim all that God, in his grace, has done for me. Thank you. Amen."

Thursday, December 20, 2018

Know that God is present with you and ready to converse.

"Let me magnify you, my Lord, in the same spirit as your servant Mary."

Read the gospel: Luke 1:26–38.

In the sixth month the angel Gabriel was sent by God to a town in Galilee called Nazareth, to a virgin engaged to a man whose name was Joseph, of the house of David. The virgin's name was Mary. And he came to her and said, "Greetings, favored one! The Lord is with you." But she was much perplexed by his words and pondered what sort of greeting this might be. The angel said to her, "Do not be afraid, Mary, for you have found favor with God. And now, you will conceive in your womb and bear a son, and you will name him Jesus. He will be great, and will be called the Son of the Most High, and the Lord God will give to him the throne of his ancestor David. He will reign over the house of Jacob forever, and of his kingdom there will be no end." Mary said to the angel, "How can this be, since I am a virgin?" The angel said to her, "The Holy Spirit will come upon you, and the power of the Most High will overshadow you; therefore the child to be born will be holy; he will be called Son of God. And now, your relative Elizabeth in her old age has also conceived a son; and this is the sixth month for her who was said to be barren. For nothing will be impossible with God." Then Mary said, "Here am I, the servant of the Lord; let it be with me according to your word." Then the angel departed from her.

Notice what you think and feel as you read the gospel.

The angel emphasizes that Mary will have a child conceived by God. The Holy Spirit will come upon her, the power of the Most High will overshadow her, and the child shall be called the Son of God. Mary must have been amazed, but she consents to God's will.

Pray as you are led for yourself and others.

"Lord, I worship you, for you are Almighty God, though flesh and blood like me. This is a mystery. I rejoice in you . . ." (Continue in your own words.)

Listen to Jesus.

Your trust and your joy in me are gifts I have given you. I am the Master, beloved, and my power shall never fail you neither in this life or the next. You are mine. What else is Jesus saying to you?

Ask God to show you how to live today.

"Give me the strength and the grace, Lord, to be and do all you ask. Today let me look to your power and care. Let me serve you in others. Amen."

Friday, December 21, 2018

Know that God is present with you and ready to converse.

"I rejoice in your presence, Lord. Open my ears to hear your Word, Lord, then let me bless you."

Read the gospel: Luke 1:39–45.

In those days Mary set out and went with haste to a Judean town in the hill country, where she entered the house of Zechariah and greeted

Elizabeth. When Elizabeth heard Mary's greeting, the child leapt in her womb. And Elizabeth was filled with the Holy Spirit and exclaimed with a loud cry, "Blessed are you among women, and blessed is the fruit of your womb. And why has this happened to me, that the mother of my Lord comes to me? For as soon as I heard the sound of your greeting, the child in my womb leapt for joy. And blessed is she who believed that there would be a fulfillment of what was spoken to her by the Lord."

Notice what you think and feel as you read the gospel.

There is great joy in two godly women, both pregnant according to the purposes and power of God. Their love for each other is evident. The Holy Spirit is present in the pregnant women and the infants in their wombs.

Pray as you are led for yourself and others.

"Lord, with Mary and Elizabeth, I rejoice in you. Work your purposes in my life and fill me with praise for you. Do great things with me for your glory and the good of others . . ." (Continue in your own words.)

Listen to Jesus.

I have work for you too, my child, and you will know my joy. You will serve me in love. What else is Jesus saying to you?

Ask God to show you how to live today.

"Help me to do well what you give me to do, Lord. I offer all that I am and all that I have to you. Let God be glorified. Amen."

Saturday, December 22, 2018

Know that God is present with you and ready to converse.

"God, open my heart to praise you. Let me learn praise by your Word."

Read the gospel: Luke 1:46–56.

And Mary said,

> "My soul magnifies the Lord,
>   and my spirit rejoices in God my Savior,
> for he has looked with favor on the lowliness of his servant.
>   Surely, from now on all generations will call me blessed;
> for the Mighty One has done great things for me,
>   and holy is his name.

His mercy is for those who fear him
> from generation to generation.
He has shown strength with his arm;
> he has scattered the proud in the thoughts of their hearts.
He has brought down the powerful from their thrones,
> and lifted up the lowly;
he has filled the hungry with good things,
> and sent the rich away empty.
He has helped his servant Israel,
> in remembrance of his mercy,
according to the promise he made to our ancestors,
> to Abraham and to his descendants forever."

And Mary remained with Elizabeth for about three months and then returned to her home.

Notice what you think and feel as you read the gospel.

Mary praises God for lifting up the lowly and putting down the haughty. God shows mercy to the needy and gathers them; the mighty he scatters.

Pray as you are led for yourself and others.

"Praise to you, O Lord, for you have done and still do what Mary proclaimed in her hymn of praise. Help me to walk in the steps of the lowly, praising you . . ." (Continue in your own words.)

Listen to Jesus.

The joy of the Lord is your strength, beloved. The things that swirl outside and inside need not take away your joy. Share it. What else is Jesus saying to you?

Ask God to show you how to live today.

"Your joy is like no other, Lord. Let me truly rejoice by the power of your Spirit, and I will share your joy with others today. Amen."

Sunday, December 23, 2018
Fourth Sunday of Advent

Know that God is present with you and ready to converse.

"God, as you were present in Mary and Elizabeth, you are also present with me. I glorify you as I read your Word."

Read the gospel: Luke 1:39–45.

In those days Mary set out and went with haste to a Judean town in the hill country, where she entered the house of Zechariah and greeted Elizabeth. When Elizabeth heard Mary's greeting, the child leapt in her womb. And Elizabeth was filled with the Holy Spirit and exclaimed with a loud cry, "Blessed are you among women, and blessed is the fruit of your womb. And why has this happened to me, that the mother of my Lord comes to me? For as soon as I heard the sound of your greeting, the child in my womb leapt for joy. And blessed is she who believed that there would be a fullfilment of what was spoken to her by the Lord."

Notice what you think and feel as you read the gospel.

Elizabeth is aware that her younger cousin, Mary, is pregnant with the Lord. John the Baptist in Elizabeth's womb is already heralding the coming of the Messiah, and Elizabeth blesses Mary.

Pray as you are led for yourself and others.

"Thank you for giving me the example of these holy women who are serving your purposes with such joy and love. Make me like them, Jesus. I pray for joy and love for all those you have given me . . ." (Continue in your own words.)

Listen to Jesus.

I knew you in the womb, child, and I loved you. I will that you may love and serve God and then come into the eternal kingdom. What else is Jesus saying to you?

Ask God to show you how to live today.

"Lord, show me how to live my moments in ways that glorify you and serve others. Walk with me today, my Jesus. Amen."

Monday, December 24, 2018

Know that God is present with you and ready to converse.

"Thank you for being here with me again today. Let me join the raining of praise upon you, Father, Son, and Holy Spirit."

Read the gospel: Luke 1:67–79.

Then his father Zechariah was filled with the Holy Spirit and spoke this prophecy:

"Blessed be the Lord God of Israel,
for he has looked favorably on his people and redeemed
them.
He has raised up a mighty savior for us
in the house of his servant David,
as he spoke through the mouth of his holy prophets from of old,
that we would be saved from our enemies and from the
hand of all who hate us.
Thus he has shown the mercy promised to our ancestors,
and has remembered his holy covenant,
the oath that he swore to our ancestor Abraham,
to grant us that we, being rescued from the hands of our
enemies,
might serve him without fear, in holiness and righteousness
before him all our days.
And you, child, will be called the prophet of the Most High;
for you will go before the Lord to prepare his ways,
to give knowledge of salvation to his people
by the forgiveness of their sins.
By the tender mercy of our God,
the dawn from on high will break upon us,
to give light to those who sit in darkness and in the shadow of
death,
to guide our feet into the way of peace."

Notice what you think and feel as you read the gospel.

Zechariah, who doubted the angel's announcement and was made mute for his unbelief, has seen the light, and he uses his newly restored voice to proclaim the greatness and mercy of God.

Pray as you are led for yourself and others.

"I cannot pray as beautifully as that, Lord, but I join my heart with Zechariah's prayer. Thank you for lifting me and giving me light. I pray for those in darkness . . ." (Continue in your own words.)

Listen to Jesus.

God is the same today as he was when Zechariah prayed, for God is eternal. He dwells in light and holiness. Come to us, beloved. What else is Jesus saying to you?

Ask God to show you how to live today.

"Let my heart be stayed on you all the day long, Lord. Let me reflect upon your high and holy glory. Then I will seek you in humility and service. Amen."

Tuesday, December 25, 2018
The Nativity of the Lord

Know that God is present with you and ready to converse.

"Infant Jesus, I love you. You are God with us. Let me see you in your Word."

Read the gospel: John 1:1–18.

In the beginning was the Word, and the Word was with God, and the Word was God. He was in the beginning with God. All things came into being through him, and without him not one thing came into being. What has come into being in him was life, and the life was the light of all people. The light shines in the darkness, and the darkness did not overcome it.

There was a man sent from God, whose name was John. He came as a witness to testify to the light, so that all might believe through him. He himself was not the light, but he came to testify to the light. The true light, which enlightens everyone, was coming into the world.

He was in the world, and the world came into being through him; yet the world did not know him. He came to what was his own, and his own people did not accept him. But to all who received him, who believed in his name, he gave power to become children of God, who were born, not of blood or of the will of the flesh or of the will of man, but of God.

And the Word became flesh and lived among us, and we have seen his glory, the glory as of a father's only son, full of grace and truth. (John testified to him and cried out, "This was he of whom I said, 'He who comes after me ranks ahead of me because he was before me.'") From his fullness we have all received, grace upon grace. The law indeed was given through Moses; grace and truth came through Jesus Christ. No one has ever seen God. It is God the only Son, who is close to the Father's heart, who has made him known.

Notice what you think and feel as you read the gospel.

John the Evangelist emphasizes the cosmic meaning of the birth of Christ. Jesus, the Messiah, is eternal with God, the very Word of God, equal with

God, the light against the darkness. Humans may choose the light if they are willing to abandon their sins and come to Christ for eternal life.

Pray as you are led for yourself and others.

"Glory and thanks to you, infant Savior. As I come to marvel at you today, I pray for all those in darkness. Let them come to your light . . ." (Continue in your own words.)

Listen to Jesus.

For love of all, I came to bring a blaze of light to the people of the world. Beloved disciple, you share God's mercy when you pray for those in darkness, for there are many who do not know me. What else is Jesus saying to you?

Ask God to show you how to live today.

"So I will continue to pray for those in darkness, Lord. Let me persevere in fervent prayer. Amen."

Wednesday, December 26, 2018

Know that God is present with you and ready to converse.

"Lord, I cling to you in good times and bad. Help me to persevere in faith and service by drawing strength from your Word."

Read the gospel: Matthew 10:17–22.

Jesus said, "Beware of them, for they will hand you over to councils and flog you in their synagogues; and you will be dragged before governors and kings because of me, as a testimony to them and the Gentiles. When they hand you over, do not worry about how you are to speak or what you are to say; for what you are to say will be given to you at that time; for it is not you who speak, but the Spirit of your Father speaking through you. Brother will betray brother to death, and a father his child, and children will rise against parents and have them put to death; and you will be hated by all because of my name. But the one who endures to the end will be saved."

Notice what you think and feel as you read the gospel.

Jesus speaks of the inevitability of rejection and persecution that comes from following him. He tells his disciples to trust God, for God is with them in these trials, and eternal reward will come.

Pray as you are led for yourself and others.

"Be with me when I experience persecution in any form. Lord, I pray for all those who are persecuted, bullied, abused, or belittled for their faith in God . . ." (Continue in your own words.)

Listen to Jesus.

God allows violence against his people, but justice will prevail. In me, your suffering will bear fruit unto eternal life. I have overcome the world. Child, apply yourself to doing good. What else is Jesus saying to you?

Ask God to show you how to live today.

"By your grace, Lord, I will persevere in doing good, even in the face of adversity, seeking peace, and working for justice for all. Amen."

Thursday, December 27, 2018

Know that God is present with you and ready to converse.

"Let me hear and believe your mighty Word, Lord."

Read the gospel: John 20:1a, 2–8.

Early on the first day of the week, while it was still dark, Mary Magdalene came to the tomb and saw that the stone had been removed from the tomb. . . . So she ran and went to Simon Peter and the other disciple, the one whom Jesus loved, and said to them, "They have taken the Lord out of the tomb, and we do not know where they have laid him." Then Peter and the other disciple set out and went towards the tomb. The two were running together, but the other disciple outran Peter and reached the tomb first. He bent down to look in and saw the linen wrappings lying there, but he did not go in. Then Simon Peter came, following him, and went into the tomb. He saw the linen wrappings lying there, and the cloth that had been on Jesus' head, not lying with the linen wrappings but rolled up in a place by itself. Then the other disciple, who reached the tomb first, also went in, and he saw and believed.

Notice what you think and feel as you read the gospel.

We see how the disciples react to Mary Magdalene's announcement of Jesus' empty tomb. They run to the tomb and see the grave, and immediately they believe Jesus has risen from the dead on the third day as he said he would. They would soon see the risen Lord with their own eyes.

Pray as you are led for yourself and others.

"Lord, I too believe you have risen; you abide forever with your Father in heaven in the unity of the Holy Spirit. But you continue your work among us, showing mercy and power on behalf of all, especially the poor and afflicted. Care for them, Lord . . ." (Continue in your own words.)

Listen to Jesus.

I do my work through my faithful servants, beloved. You believe and walk in my light. Trust me. Trust that I am working within you. What else is Jesus saying to you?

Ask God to show you how to live today.

"With you, Lord, I can do anything. I praise you for your mercy to all of us who need you. Amen."

Friday, December 28, 2018
Holy Innocents

Know that God is present with you and ready to converse.

"Lord, you work your will through triumphs and through tragedies. Teach me by your Word."

Read the gospel: Matthew 2:13–18.

An angel of the Lord appeared to Joseph in a dream and said, "Get up, take the child and his mother, and flee to Egypt, and remain there until I tell you; for Herod is about to search for the child, to destroy him." Then Joseph got up, took the child and his mother by night, and went to Egypt, and remained there until the death of Herod. This was to fulfill what had been spoken by the Lord through the prophet, "Out of Egypt I have called my son."

When Herod saw that he had been tricked by the wise men, he was infuriated, and he sent and killed all the children in and around Bethlehem who were two years old or under, according to the time that he had learned from the wise men. Then was fulfilled what had been spoken through the prophet Jeremiah.

Notice what you think and feel as you read the gospel.

While God guides the Holy Family to safety, he allows Herod to slaughter all the young children in and around Bethlehem. Why would he do such a thing? Matthew sees it as the fulfillment of a prophecy of Jeremiah, the Old Testament prophet (see Jer 31:15).

Pray as you are led for yourself and others.

"Let me trust you are also guiding me, Lord. Let me have compassion upon all who suffer, especially the children. Let your love execute justice and mercy, Lord . . ." (Continue in your own words.)

Listen to Jesus.

I do guide you, for you are a child in this holy family of believers. Have no fear of violence. God sees all and will mete out justice and reward. What else is Jesus saying to you?

Ask God to show you how to live today.

"I wish to grow in wisdom to understand the mysterious evil I see in the world. Give me great compassion for victims, Lord, and raise me up for your justice. Thank you. Amen."

Saturday, December 29, 2018

Know that God is present with you and ready to converse.

"Lord, the world long awaited you. Now that you have come, we rejoice. Let me understand your Word and obey it."

Read the gospel: Luke 2:22–35.

When the time came for their purification according to the law of Moses, they brought him up to Jerusalem to present him to the Lord (as it is written in the law of the Lord, "Every firstborn male shall be designated as holy to the Lord"), and they offered a sacrifice according to what is stated in the law of the Lord, "a pair of turtledoves or two young pigeons."

Now there was a man in Jerusalem whose name was Simeon; this man was righteous and devout, looking forward to the consolation of Israel, and the Holy Spirit rested on him. It had been revealed to him by the Holy Spirit that he would not see death before he had seen the Lord's Messiah. Guided by the Spirit, Simeon came into the temple; and when the parents brought in the child Jesus, to do for him what was customary under the law, Simeon took him in his arms and praised God, saying,

> "Master, now you are dismissing your servant in peace,
> according to your word;
> for my eyes have seen your salvation,

which you have prepared in the presence of all peoples,
a light for revelation to the Gentiles
and for glory to your people Israel."

And the child's father and mother were amazed at what was being said about him. Then Simeon blessed them and said to his mother Mary, "This child is destined for the falling and the rising of many in Israel, and to be a sign that will be opposed so that the inner thoughts of many will be revealed—and a sword will pierce your own soul too."

Notice what you think and feel as you read the gospel.

When Jesus is only a few weeks old, can barely lift his own head up, and is still completely dependent on his human parents for survival, they present him at the Temple. Simeon recognizes in this helpless infant the salvation of the entire world.

Pray as you are led for yourself and others.

"Lord, may I too recognize you as I walk through life, and at the end of my life may I give you thanks that I have known you. I pray for those who do not know you . . ." (Continue in your own words.)

Listen to Jesus.

Recognize me in others, my dear one. See me in the faces of children, the poor, the hungry, the sick, the homeless, the imprisoned, the persecuted, and the dying. What else is Jesus saying to you?

Ask God to show you how to live today.

"Only by your grace do I have the power to obey you in this. Yet I resolve to do it. Show me how to obey today. I will trust you for grace. Thank you. Make me more and more a temple of your Spirit. Amen."

Sunday, December 30, 2018
Holy Family

Know that God is present with you and ready to converse.

"Wise Child, I turn to your Word for your Wisdom."

Read the gospel: Luke 2:41–52.

Now every year his parents went to Jerusalem for the festival of the Passover. And when he was twelve years old, they went up as usual for the festival. When the festival was ended and they started to return, the boy Jesus stayed behind in Jerusalem, but his parents did not know it. Assuming that he was in the group of travelers, they went a day's journey. Then they started to look for him among their relatives and friends. When they did not find him, they returned to Jerusalem to search for him. After three days they found him in the temple, sitting among the teachers, listening to them and asking them questions. And all who heard him were amazed at his understanding and his answers. When his parents saw him they were astonished; and his mother said to him, "Child, why have you treated us like this? Look, your father and I have been searching for you in great anxiety." He said to them, "Why were you searching for me? Did you not know that I must be in my Father's house?" But they did not understand what he said to them. Then he went down with them and came to Nazareth, and was obedient to them. His mother treasured all these things in her heart.

And Jesus increased in wisdom and in years, and in divine and human favor.

Notice what you think and feel as you read the gospel.

Mary is hurt by the actions of her adolescent son and confused by his words; she does not fully understand, but she treasures the experiences and the memories.

Pray as you are led for yourself and others.

"As I experience you in my life, Lord, let me build up grateful memories of our time together. Those memories will strengthen my faith and joy to the end of my life . . ." (Continue in your own words.)

Listen to Jesus.

I am with you now and to the end, beloved. Ask me for whatever you want today. What else is Jesus saying to you?

Ask God to show you how to live today.

"Help me stay very close to you every moment of this day. Let me share our moments with others. Amen."

Monday, December 31, 2018

Know that God is present with you and ready to converse.

"You are with me now, mighty Jesus. Let me know you in your Word."

Read the gospel: John 1:1–18.

In the beginning was the Word, and the Word was with God, and the Word was God. He was in the beginning with God. All things came into being through him, and without him not one thing came into being. What has come into being in him was life, and the life was the light of all people. The light shines in the darkness, and the darkness did not overcome it.

There was a man sent from God, whose name was John. He came as a witness to testify to the light, so that all might believe through him. He himself was not the light, but he came to testify to the light. The true light, which enlightens everyone, was coming into the world.

He was in the world, and the world came into being through him; yet the world did not know him. He came to what was his own, and his own people did not accept him. But to all who received him, who believed in his name, he gave power to become children of God, who were born, not of blood or of the will of the flesh or of the will of man, but of God.

And the Word became flesh and lived among us, and we have seen his glory, the glory as of a father's only son, full of grace and truth. (John testified to him and cried out, "This was he of whom I said, 'He who comes after me ranks ahead of me because he was before me.'") From his fullness we have all received, grace upon grace. The law indeed was given through Moses; grace and truth came through Jesus Christ. No one has ever seen God. It is God the only Son, who is close to the Father's heart, who has made him known.

Notice what you think and feel as you read the gospel.

John begins his gospel with this profound description of the Christ, eternal with God yet born in time on earth to bring to all peoples the revelation of the Almighty God of infinite love and mercy. Who can take it in? But this is not just a description. It is a call to open our eyes to the Light of God, to accept God's everlasting Life.

Pray as you are led for yourself and others.

"God, I do not want to miss my moment to know you and love you as you are. Make me truly a child of God and let multitudes come to you . . ." (Continue in your own words.)

Listen to Jesus.

I rejoice in your love, child of God. I hear your prayer and continue to pour out my mercy upon people—more than you can know. I work in a person's heart and soul. What else is Jesus saying to you?

Ask God to show you how to live today.

"You are good to me, Lord. Show me how to be good to others today. Glory to God in the highest. Amen."

THE POPE'S MONTHLY PRAYER INTENTION FOR JANUARY 2019

That young people, especially in Latin America, follow the example of Mary and respond to the call of the Lord to communicate the joy of the Gospel to the world.

Tuesday, January 1, 2019
Blessed Virgin Mary, Mother of God

Know that God is present with you and ready to converse.

"Humble, holy infant, I come with the shepherds in wonder to adore you."

Read the gospel: Luke 2:16–21.

So the shepherds went with haste and found Mary and Joseph, and the child lying in the manger. When they saw this, they made known what had been told them about this child; and all who heard it were amazed at what the shepherds told them. But Mary treasured all these words and pondered them in her heart. The shepherds returned, glorifying and praising God for all they had heard and seen, as it had been told them.

After eight days had passed, it was time to circumcise the child; and he was called Jesus, the name given by the angel before he was conceived in the womb.

Notice what you think and feel as you read the gospel.

The shepherds saw the heavenly host praising God and were directed to the stable by an angel. They find Mary, Joseph, and the infant in the manger. Mary treasures the words of the shepherds and ponders them in her heart. What shall this child become? The shepherds return to their fields, rejoicing in God.

Pray as you are led for yourself and others.

"I praise the works of God in history and in my life. Let God's words and works continue to advance the kingdom. I think of these needs . . ." (Continue in your own words.)

Listen to Jesus.

Dear one, beginning with my birth, I have revealed to humankind the goodness and the glory of God, the Almighty, who offers eternal life to all. Do not despair. I am with you, and God is God. What else is Jesus saying to you?

Ask God to show you how to live today.

"Let me, like the shepherds, come and worship and be near you and then carry your presence with me to proclaim you to the world. Amen."

Wednesday, January 2, 2019

Know that God is present with you and ready to converse.

"You are with me now, Lord. Let me know you in your Word."

Read the gospel: John 1:19–28.

This is the testimony given by John when the Jews sent priests and Levites from Jerusalem to ask him, "Who are you?" He confessed and did not deny it, but confessed, "I am not the Messiah." And they asked him, "What then? Are you Elijah?" He said, "I am not." "Are you the prophet?" He answered, "No." Then they said to him, "Who are you? Let us have an answer for those who sent us. What do you say about yourself?" He said,

> "I am the voice of one crying out in the wilderness,
> 'Make straight the way of the Lord,'"

as the prophet Isaiah said.

Now they had been sent from the Pharisees. They asked him, "Why then are you baptizing if you are neither the Messiah, nor Elijah, nor the prophet?" John answered them, "I baptize with water. Among you stands one whom you do not know, the one who is coming after me; I am not worthy to untie the thong of his sandal." This took place in Bethany across the Jordan where John was baptizing.

Notice what you think and feel as you read the gospel.

John the Baptist is interrogated by the priests and Levites. They are probably worried about the many people who have flocked to his preaching and baptisms. Who is he? He answers with scripture from Isaiah that he is the voice crying in the wilderness to make straight the way of the Lord. He goes on to tell them to expect one greater, even now standing among them. One supposes they were not pleased by his answers.

Pray as you are led for yourself and others.

"God, I look to you this moment. Baptize me with your Spirit that I may love and serve you better, especially in these areas . . ." (Continue in your own words.)

Listen to Jesus.

Child of God, follow me and all will be well with you. I rejoice in your love. What else is Jesus saying to you?

Ask God to show you how to live today.

"How can I straighten the way for you today, Lord? Show me the right path, and use me to fix what is crooked and bent. Amen."

Thursday, January 3, 2019

Know that God is present with you and ready to converse.

"Let me believe and receive the words of your prophets, Lord, for they speak what they know."

Read the gospel: John 1:29–34.

The next day John saw Jesus coming towards him and declared, "Here is the Lamb of God who takes away the sin of the world! This is he of whom I said, 'After me comes a man who ranks ahead of me because he was before me.' I myself did not know him; but I came baptizing with water for this reason, that he might be revealed to Israel." And John testified, "I saw the Spirit descending from heaven like a dove, and it remained on him. I myself did not know him, but the one who sent me to baptize with water said to me, 'He on whom you see the Spirit descend and remain is the one who baptizes with the Holy Spirit.' And I myself have seen and have testified that this is the Son of God."

Notice what you think and feel as you read the gospel.

John recognizes Jesus as the Lamb of God who takes away the sin of the world. He has prophetic knowledge from God that Jesus is destined to be the sacrificial Lamb of God. He certainly knows Jesus ranks ahead of him and existed before him. He testifies that Jesus is the Son of God, because he saw the Spirit descend and remain on him.

Pray as you are led for yourself and others.

"Lamb of God, take away my sins. Fill me with your Holy Spirit, that I may proclaim you . . ." (Continue in your own words.)

Listen to Jesus.

Seek me in the sacraments, dear disciple, and the Spirit will shower you with gifts, and you will bear fruit, giving my gifts to others. What else is Jesus saying to you?

Ask God to show you how to live today.

"Guide me in my giving, doing, and praying today, Lord. Let me give as generously as I have received. Thank you for taking away my sins, Lamb of God. Amen."

Friday, January 4, 2019

Know that God is present with you and ready to converse.

"You have come, Lord. Let me find and love the Lamb of God."

Read the gospel: John 1:35–42.

The next day John again was standing with two of his disciples, and as he watched Jesus walk by, he exclaimed, "Look, here is the Lamb of God!" The two disciples heard him say this, and they followed Jesus. When Jesus turned and saw them following, he said to them, "What are you looking for?" They said to him, "Rabbi" (which translated means Teacher), "where are you staying?" He said to them, "Come and see." They came and saw where he was staying, and they remained with him that day. It was about four o'clock in the afternoon. One of the two who heard John speak and followed him was Andrew, Simon Peter's brother. He first found his brother Simon and said to him, "We have found the Messiah" (which is translated Anointed). He brought Simon to Jesus, who looked at him and said, "You are Simon son of John. You are to be called Cephas" (which is translated Peter).

Notice what you think and feel as you read the gospel.
Jesus' first disciples are drawn to him by the words of John the Baptist.
Jesus does not recruit them but invites them to come and see.

Pray as you are led for yourself and others.
"Lord, let me come and see you. Please know me as your own and let
me be a true disciple that others may also come to you . . ." (Continue
in your own words.)

Listen to Jesus.
*Come, follow me, forsaking all. Set your heart and mind on the will of God. God
will guide you and you will overcome the world and receive eternal life.* What
else is Jesus saying to you?

Ask God to show you how to live today.
"Only by your grace can I follow you purely and truly, Lord. Fill me and
make me new. Amen."

Saturday, January 5, 2019

Know that God is present with you and ready to converse.
"You are present, Lord. Call me to yourself by your Word."

Read the gospel: John 1:43–51.
The next day Jesus decided to go to Galilee. He found Philip and said to
him, "Follow me." Now Philip was from Bethsaida, the city of Andrew
and Peter. Philip found Nathanael and said to him, "We have found him
about whom Moses in the law and also the prophets wrote, Jesus son
of Joseph from Nazareth." Nathanael said to him, "Can anything good
come out of Nazareth?" Philip said to him, "Come and see." When Jesus
saw Nathanael coming towards him, he said of him, "Here is truly an
Israelite in whom there is no deceit!" Nathanael asked him, "Where did
you come to know me?" Jesus answered, "I saw you under the fig tree
before Philip called you." Nathanael replied, "Rabbi, you are the Son
of God! You are the King of Israel!" Jesus answered, "Do you believe
because I told you that I saw you under the fig tree? You will see greater
things than these." And he said to him, "Very truly, I tell you, you will
see heaven opened and the angels of God ascending and descending
upon the Son of Man."

Notice what you think and feel as you read the gospel.

Why is it amazing to Nathanael that Jesus saw him under the fig tree? Yet Jesus didn't just notice him in passing, Jesus saw him, saw his character and his honesty; and Nathanael, in turn, sees something about who Jesus is: the Son of God and the King of Israel.

Pray as you are led for yourself and others.

"Lord, give me the vision to see you and, seeing, to follow you, and let me share your truth with all whom I encounter . . ." (Continue in your own words.)

Listen to Jesus.

Beloved disciple, I see you. Follow me closely and you will be part of the great work of God, the salvation of the world. What else is Jesus saying to you?

Ask God to show you how to live today.

"Open my eyes to your will for me, Lord, especially the knowledge of what to do in situations and opportunities I might miss. Thank you. Amen."

Sunday, January 6, 2019
Epiphany of the Lord

Know that God is present with you and ready to converse.

"Lord, you are Father of the Word, your beloved Son. Let me also adore him by meditating on your Word."

Read the gospel: Matthew 2:1–12.

In the time of King Herod, after Jesus was born in Bethlehem of Judea, wise men from the East came to Jerusalem, asking, "Where is the child who has been born king of the Jews? For we observed his star at its rising, and have come to pay him homage." When King Herod heard this, he was frightened, and all Jerusalem with him; and calling together all the chief priests and scribes of the people, he inquired of them where the Messiah was to be born. They told him, "In Bethlehem of Judea; for so it has been written by the prophet:

'And you, Bethlehem, in the land of Judah,
    are by no means least among the rulers of Judah;

for from you shall come a ruler
    who is to shepherd my people Israel.'"

Then Herod secretly called for the wise men and learned from them the exact time when the star had appeared. Then he sent them to Bethlehem, saying, "Go and search diligently for the child; and when you have found him, bring me word so that I may also go and pay him homage." When they had heard the king, they set out; and there, ahead of them, went the star that they had seen at its rising, until it stopped over the place where the child was. When they saw that the star had stopped, they were overwhelmed with joy. On entering the house, they saw the child with Mary his mother; and they knelt down and paid him homage. Then, opening their treasure-chests, they offered him gifts of gold, frankincense, and myrrh. And having been warned in a dream not to return to Herod, they left for their own country by another road.

Notice what you think and feel as you read the gospel.

Good and evil operate together in this gospel, as the wise men come to pay homage to the infant King and Herod plots to thwart this threat to his power. The kings kneel before the child and give him their precious gifts. Wisely, they do not return to Herod but return home by another road.

Pray as you are led for yourself and others.

"Lord, you have come for all people, any who will say 'yes' to you. Please give all people the chance to receive you . . ." (Continue in your own words.)

Listen to Jesus.

I love your heart for others, my beloved. God is mercy and understands the prison of sin in which the world is locked. But by power he will restore righteousness and peace forever. Trust in God. What else is Jesus saying to you?

Ask God to show you how to live today.

"I want to be part of God's work, Jesus, walking more closely with you. How may I please you today? Amen."

Monday, January 7, 2019

Know that God is present with you and ready to converse.

"Lord, reveal your glory to me. I turn to your Word for light and life."

Read the gospel: Matthew 4:12–17.

Now when Jesus heard that John had been arrested, he withdrew to Galilee. He left Nazareth and made his home in Capernaum by the lake, in the territory of Zebulun and Naphtali, so that what had been spoken through the prophet Isaiah might be fulfilled:

> "Land of Zebulun, land of Naphtali,
>> on the road by the sea, across the Jordan, Galilee of the
>> Gentiles—
> the people who sat in darkness
>> have seen a great light,
> and for those who sat in the region and shadow of death
>> light has dawned."

From that time Jesus began to proclaim, "Repent, for the kingdom of heaven has come near."

Notice what you think and feel as you read the gospel.

Jesus moves from Nazareth to Capernaum to begin his ministry, preaching repentance. He is the light that has come into the land of darkness. He is the Light of the World.

Pray as you are led for yourself and others.

"Shine your light on me, Redeemer, for I am a sinner. Let my greatest longing be to enter the kingdom of heaven so that I may love and praise you forever . . ." (Continue in your own words.)

Listen to Jesus.

Open yourself to me, beloved, and I will fill you with light and dispel all your darkness. What else is Jesus saying to you?

Ask God to show you how to live today.

"I worship you and will walk in the light of your presence today. Let me do something to help someone in need. Amen."

Tuesday, January 8, 2019

Know that God is present with you and ready to converse.

"Bread of Life, Word of God, let me know you in your Word."

Read the gospel: Mark 6:34–44.

As Jesus went ashore, he saw a great crowd; and he had compassion for them, because they were like sheep without a shepherd; and he began to teach them many things. When it grew late, his disciples came to him and said, "This is a deserted place, and the hour is now very late; send them away so that they may go into the surrounding country and villages and buy something for themselves to eat." But he answered them, "You give them something to eat." They said to him, "Are we to go and buy two hundred denarii worth of bread, and give it to them to eat?" And he said to them, "How many loaves have you? Go and see." When they had found out, they said, "Five, and two fish." Then he ordered them to get all the people to sit down in groups on the green grass. So they sat down in groups of hundreds and of fifties. Taking the five loaves and the two fish, he looked up to heaven, and blessed and broke the loaves, and gave them to his disciples to set before the people; and he divided the two fish among them all. And all ate and were filled; and they took up twelve baskets full of broken pieces and of the fish. Those who had eaten the loaves numbered five thousand men.

Notice what you think and feel as you read the gospel.

Jesus feeds a crowd of five thousand with five loaves and two fish, with twelve basketfuls remaining. Out of compassion, he shows his power to provide for the people's need.

Pray as you are led for yourself and others.

"Jesus, I have needs too. Help me to trust you to provide for me. I think of others who also have needs. Feed them, Lord . . ." (Continue in your own words.)

Listen to Jesus.

I came to the world because of the love of my Father. So I come to you today. You have entrusted yourself to me, beloved, and I am trustworthy. What else is Jesus saying to you?

Ask God to show you how to live today.

"Lord, please call others into this wonderful friendship with you. Open the eyes and hearts of those who are closed to you. Let me know what I may do to help. Amen."

Wednesday, January 9, 2019

Know that God is present with you and ready to converse.

"Jesus, break up the hardness of my heart that I may trust in you by the power of your Word."

Read the gospel: Mark 6:45–52.

Immediately Jesus made his disciples get into the boat and go on ahead to the other side, to Bethsaida, while he dismissed the crowd. After saying farewell to them, he went up on the mountain to pray.

When evening came, the boat was out on the lake, and he was alone on the land. When he saw that they were straining at the oars against an adverse wind, he came towards them early in the morning, walking on the lake. He intended to pass them by. But when they saw him walking on the lake, they thought it was a ghost and cried out; for they all saw him and were terrified. But immediately he spoke to them and said, "Take heart, it is I; do not be afraid." Then he got into the boat with them and the wind ceased. And they were utterly astounded, for they did not understand about the loaves, but their hearts were hardened.

Notice what you think and feel as you read the gospel.

The disciples barely have time to accept the miracle that Jesus has performed before he sends them off in the boat. "Who is this man?" they must have asked themselves: "What did he just do?" And here he comes, walking toward them on the surface of the water, and then his presence calms the wind they've been fighting all evening. "Who is this man?" Until they can answer that question, they will be afraid.

Pray as you are led for yourself and others.

"Let your love cast out all fear in me, dear Jesus. Let your love soften my heart in love for others . . ." (Continue in your own words.)

Listen to Jesus.

As you come to know me better, dear disciple, you will lose your fears more and more. You will understand how trustworthy I am. You will be an example to others. What else is Jesus saying to you?

Ask God to show you how to live today.

"Let me hear your voice of consolation and reassurance all day long, Lord. Let me reflect to others your peace and love. Amen."

Thursday, January 10, 2019

Know that God is present with you and ready to converse.
"You are with me, Lord. Let me hear your Good News."

Read the gospel: Luke 4:14–22.

Then Jesus, filled with the power of the Spirit, returned to Galilee, and a report about him spread through all the surrounding country. He began to teach in their synagogues and was praised by everyone.

When he came to Nazareth, where he had been brought up, he went to the synagogue on the sabbath day, as was his custom. He stood up to read, and the scroll of the prophet Isaiah was given to him. He unrolled the scroll and found the place where it was written:

> "The Spirit of the Lord is upon me,
>   because he has anointed me
>   to bring good news to the poor.
> He has sent me to proclaim release to the captives
>   and recovery of sight to the blind,
>   to let the oppressed go free,
> to proclaim the year of the Lord's favor."

And he rolled up the scroll, gave it back to the attendant, and sat down. The eyes of all in the synagogue were fixed on him. Then he began to say to them, "Today this scripture has been fulfilled in your hearing." All spoke well of him and were amazed at the gracious words that came from his mouth. They said, "Is not this Joseph's son?"

Notice what you think and feel as you read the gospel.

Jesus returns to Nazareth and preaches in his home synagogue to people who have known him all his life. They are amazed and say, "Is not this Joseph's son?" Clearly, they are puzzled too.

Pray as you are led for yourself and others.

"Lord, let me not doubt you. Keep my faith fresh and alive. Let me serve all those you have given me . . ." (Continue in your own words.)

Listen to Jesus.

I will continue to teach you as you listen to me and the Word of God. Follow me. What else is Jesus saying to you?

Ask God to show you how to live today.

"Amid doubts and confusions, Lord, I resolve to follow you faithfully today. I glorify you, Teacher. Amen."

Friday, January 11, 2019

Know that God is present with you and ready to converse.

"Jesus, you have power to heal. Help me to come to you for complete healing through the power of your Word."

Read the gospel: Luke 5:12–16.

Once, when Jesus was in one of the cities, there was a man covered with leprosy. When he saw Jesus, he bowed with his face to the ground and begged him, "Lord, if you choose, you can make me clean." Then Jesus stretched out his hand, touched him, and said, "I do choose. Be made clean." Immediately the leprosy left him. And he ordered him to tell no one. "Go," he said, "and show yourself to the priest, and, as Moses commanded, make an offering for your cleansing, for a testimony to them." But now more than ever the word about Jesus spread abroad; many crowds would gather to hear him and to be cured of their diseases. But he would withdraw to deserted places and pray.

Notice what you think and feel as you read the gospel.

The leper seems to doubt whether Jesus will want to heal him, but Jesus reassures him and heals him of his disease. Jesus tells him to tell no one but the priest and to make the prescribed offering. Yet the news about Jesus spread rapidly, so Jesus withdraws to pray.

Pray as you are led for yourself and others.

"Jesus, what is my critical disease? Do you choose to heal me? Show me and heal me. I pray for those who suffer as I do . . ." (Continue in your own words.)

Listen to Jesus.

I do choose to heal you, child. Pray boldly for what you need. I will answer your prayers for yourself and for others. What else is Jesus saying to you?

Ask God to show you how to live today.

"I will obey, Lord, giving thanks to you and offering myself for the good of others. Amen."

Saturday, January 12, 2019

Know that God is present with you and ready to converse.
"Lord, it is common for your people to dispute the truth and the right
way. Let me find simple truth in your Word and adhere to it."

Read the gospel: John 3:22–30.
After this Jesus and his disciples went into the Judean countryside, and
he spent some time there with them and baptized. John also was baptizing at Aenon near Salim because water was abundant there; and people
kept coming and were being baptized—John, of course, had not yet been
thrown into prison.

   Now a discussion about purification arose between John's disciples
and a Jew. They came to John and said to him, "Rabbi, the one who was
with you across the Jordan, to whom you testified, here he is baptizing,
and all are going to him." John answered, "No one can receive anything
except what has been given from heaven. You yourselves are my witnesses that I said, 'I am not the Messiah, but I have been sent ahead of
him.' He who has the bride is the bridegroom. The friend of the bridegroom, who stands and hears him, rejoices greatly at the bridegroom's
voice. For this reason my joy has been fulfilled. He must increase, but I
must decrease."

Notice what you think and feel as you read the gospel.
John's disciples are challenged by Jesus' preaching and baptisms. Who
should they follow? John tells them he is not the Messiah but the one
who goes before the Messiah, not the bridegroom but the friend of the
bridegroom.

Pray as you are led for yourself and others.
"Lord, I thank you for John the Baptist. Give me that kind of humility,
honesty, and courage in my life . . ." (Continue in your own words.)

Listen to Jesus.
*You are right to honor John. You do not err in wanting his virtues. Seek to
practice them. I am with you.* What else is Jesus saying to you?

Ask God to show you how to live today.
"Thank you for the privilege of following you. Lead me forward and
help me serve those in need. Amen."

Sunday, January 13, 2019
Baptism of the Lord

Know that God is present with you and ready to converse.

"I come into your presence, Lord. Renew my baptism by your Word."

Read the gospel: Luke 3:15–16, 21–22.

As the people were filled with expectation, and all were questioning in their hearts concerning John, whether he might be the Messiah, John answered all of them by saying, "I baptize you with water; but one who is more powerful than I is coming; I am not worthy to untie the thong of his sandals. He will baptize you with the Holy Spirit and fire." . . .

Now when all the people were baptized, and when Jesus also had been baptized and was praying, the heaven was opened, and the Holy Spirit descended upon him in bodily form like a dove. And a voice came from heaven, "You are my Son, the Beloved; with you I am well pleased."

Notice what you think and feel as you read the gospel.

Water washes, but fire purifies. John's baptism washes away sins; Jesus burns them to ash in the fire of his love, which is the Holy Spirit.

Pray as you are led for yourself and others.

"I long for the fire of your Holy Spirit, Lord. Let it renew me and renew all the earth . . ." (Continue in your own words.)

Listen to Jesus.

I give you my Spirit, beloved. In you I am well pleased for you have set your heart upon me. Walk in faith, hope, and love. Follow me. What else is Jesus saying to you?

Ask God to show you how to live today.

"By the power of your Spirit, Lord, let me live my life glorifying you. Amen."

Ordinary Time

INTRODUCTION

Ordinary Time is the time of the year in which Christ walks among us, calling us, teaching us, transforming us. Advent, Lent, and the Christmas and Easter seasons are special periods excluded from Ordinary Time. Ordinary Time begins on the Monday following the first Sunday after the Feast of the Epiphany and runs until Ash Wednesday; it then continues on the Monday after Pentecost Sunday and runs until the First Sunday of Advent, which is when the new liturgical year begins.

Ordinary Time is called "ordinary" simply because the weeks are numbered. Like the word "ordinal," the word "ordinary" comes from a Latin word for numbers. Ordinary Time refers to the ordered life of the Church; the gospels of Ordinary Time treat all aspects of Jesus' ministry and sayings more or less in sequence.

Monday, January 14, 2019

Know that God is present with you and ready to converse.

"Lord, I seek you and you have called me. Let me respond to your holy Word."

Read the gospel: Mark 1:14–20.

Now after John was arrested, Jesus came to Galilee, proclaiming the good news of God, and saying, "The time is fulfilled, and the kingdom of God has come near; repent, and believe in the good news."

As Jesus passed along the Sea of Galilee, he saw Simon and his brother Andrew casting a net into the lake—for they were fishermen. And Jesus said to them, "Follow me and I will make you fish for people." And immediately they left their nets and followed him. As he went a little farther, he saw James son of Zebedee and his brother John, who were in their boat mending the nets. Immediately he called them; and they left their father Zebedee in the boat with the hired men, and followed him.

Notice what you think and feel as you read the gospel.

As he begins his ministry, Jesus says "repent and believe." The kingdom of God has come. Then he goes out to choose his first disciples. When he calls, they leave their nets and follow him immediately.

Pray as you are led for yourself and others.

"Lord, let me follow you, too. I repent. I believe. I want to walk with you and serve as you do . . ." (Continue in your own words.)

Listen to Jesus.

Come, my child, for I have much for you to do for love of God and others. Learn from me, and I will give you rest. What else is Jesus saying to you?

Ask God to show you how to live today.

"I am not worthy, but you are my Lord and my God, and I will obey you today. Help me, Jesus. Amen."

Tuesday, January 15, 2019

Know that God is present with you and ready to converse.

"Holy Spirit, testify to my heart about the Son of God. Let me learn and worship God in the reading of the Word."

Read the gospel: Mark 1:21–28.

They went to Capernaum; and when the sabbath came, Jesus entered the synagogue and taught. They were astounded at his teaching, for he taught them as one having authority, and not as the scribes. Just then there was in their synagogue a man with an unclean spirit, and he cried out, "What have you to do with us, Jesus of Nazareth? Have you come to destroy us? I know who you are, the Holy One of God." But Jesus rebuked him, saying, "Be silent, and come out of him!" And the unclean spirit, throwing him into convulsions and crying with a loud voice, came out of him. They were all amazed, and they kept on asking one another, "What is this? A new teaching—with authority! He commands even the unclean spirits, and they obey him." At once his fame began to spread throughout the surrounding region of Galilee.

Notice what you think and feel as you read the gospel.

Jesus shows his authority in his teaching and his command over the unclean spirit, and the people in the synagogue respond to that authority.

Pray as you are led for yourself and others.

"Lord, you speak and act with authority. Command me and I will obey. I put myself in your care . . ." (Continue in your own words.)

Listen to Jesus.

I thank you for your discipleship, dear friend. Let your own authority grow from your closeness to me and your pursuit of God's will. What else is Jesus saying to you?

Ask God to show you how to live today.

"I am so blessed to be yours, Lord. Let me use the authority you've given me to teach others about your power and your goodness. Amen."

Wednesday, January 16, 2019

Know that God is present with you and ready to converse.

"You have all power in heaven and in earth, Jesus, for you are the Lord. I bow to your authority."

Read the gospel: Mark 1:32–39 (Mk 1:29–39).

That evening, at sunset, they brought to Jesus all who were sick or possessed with demons. And the whole city was gathered around the door.

And he cured many who were sick with various diseases, and cast out many demons; and he would not permit the demons to speak, because they knew him.

In the morning, while it was still very dark, he got up and went out to a deserted place, and there he prayed. And Simon and his companions hunted for him. When they found him, they said to him, "Everyone is searching for you." He answered, "Let us go on to the neighboring towns, so that I may proclaim the message there also; for that is what I came out to do." And he went throughout Galilee, proclaiming the message in their synagogues and casting out demons.

Notice what you think and feel as you read the gospel.

Jesus is beginning his ministry of healing and preaching. He rises early to pray. When his disciples find him, he informs them that they must leave to proclaim the message in the neighboring towns because that is what he came to do.

Pray as you are led for yourself and others.

"Jesus, what am I here to do? Let me be your companion in my work and in my prayer. I pray especially for . . ." (Continue in your own words.)

Listen to Jesus.

You are right, beloved. As you draw nearer to me, you will have more power to do good among those I have given you to love and serve. What else is Jesus saying to you?

Ask God to show you how to live today.

"I am willing, Lord. I long to serve others as you direct me. Thank you for your goodness to me. Amen."

Thursday, January 17, 2019

Know that God is present with you and ready to converse.

"Mighty Lord, have mercy on me. I need you in my life. Teach me by your holy Word."

Read the gospel: Mark 1:40–45.

A leper came to Jesus begging him, and kneeling he said to him, "If you choose, you can make me clean." Moved with pity, Jesus stretched out his hand and touched him, and said to him, "I do choose. Be made clean!" Immediately the leprosy left him, and he was made clean. After sternly warning him he sent him away at once, saying to him, "See that you say nothing to anyone; but go, show yourself to the priest, and offer for your cleansing what Moses commanded, as a testimony to them." But he went out and began to proclaim it freely, and to spread the word, so that Jesus could no longer go into a town openly, but stayed out in the country; and people came to him from every quarter.

Notice what you think and feel as you read the gospel.

Because the healed man spreads the word, Jesus' reputation is growing, and people come from all over to see him. He needs to seek out quiet places, yet still people seek him out to ask for healing.

Pray as you are led for yourself and others.

"Son of God, I, too, call to you for healing—for myself and all those you have given me, especially . . ." (Continue in your own words.)

Listen to Jesus.

I bless you for your love of others, my friend. Hold fast to your trust in me. What else is Jesus saying to you?

Ask God to show you how to live today.

"Make me strong in trust, Lord, as I face the difficulties of life. Help me seek you all day long, even while I serve those around me. Amen."

Friday, January 18, 2019

Know that God is present with you and ready to converse.

"I come into your presence, Lord, needing your healing Word."

Read the gospel: Mark 2:1–12.

When Jesus returned to Capernaum after some days, it was reported that he was at home. So many gathered around that there was no longer room for them, not even in front of the door; and he was speaking the word to them. Then some people came, bringing to him a paralyzed man, carried by four of them. And when they could not bring him to Jesus because of the crowd, they removed the roof above him; and after having dug through it, they let down the mat on which the paralytic lay. When Jesus saw their faith, he said to the paralytic, "Son, your sins are forgiven." Now some of the scribes were sitting there, questioning in their hearts, "Why does this fellow speak in this way? It is blasphemy! Who can forgive sins but God alone?" At once Jesus perceived in his spirit that they were discussing these questions among themselves; and he said to them, "Why do you raise such questions in your hearts? Which is easier, to say to the paralytic, 'Your sins are forgiven,' or to say, 'Stand up and take your mat and walk'? But so that you may know that the Son of Man has authority on earth to forgive sins"—he said to the paralytic—"I say to you, stand up, take your mat and go to your home." And he stood up, and immediately took the mat and went out before all of them; so that they were all amazed and glorified God, saying, "We have never seen anything like this!"

Notice what you think and feel as you read the gospel.

Jesus' fame has spread, making it hard to get close to him. He is moved by the faith of those who lower the paralyzed man from the roof. Shocking some of the scribes, he absolves the man of his sins before he heals him. All are amazed.

Pray as you are led for yourself and others.

"Forgive me, Lord, and I shall be healed. In your name and by your command, I forgive those who have sinned against me . . ." (Continue in your own words.)

Listen to Jesus.

Seek me in all you do, dear one. Let nothing come in the way of your drawing near to me and bringing others to me. If you follow me, I will lead you. I am the same today as I ever was, dear one. If you follow me, I will lead you. What else is Jesus saying to you?

Ask God to show you how to live today.

"Thank you, Lord, for your forgiveness. Show me what task you want me to take up today, and where you want me to go. Amen."

Saturday, January 19, 2019

Know that God is present with you and ready to converse.

"Lord, though I am a sinner, you come to me and call me by your Word. Teach me, Jesus."

Read the gospel: Mark 2:13–17.

Jesus went out again beside the lake; the whole crowd gathered around him, and he taught them. As he was walking along, he saw Levi son of

Alphaeus sitting at the tax booth, and he said to him, "Follow me." And he got up and followed him.

And as he sat at dinner in Levi's house, many tax-collectors and sinners were also sitting with Jesus and his disciples—for there were many who followed him. When the scribes of the Pharisees saw that he was eating with sinners and tax-collectors, they said to his disciples, "Why does he eat with tax collectors and sinners?" When Jesus heard this, he said to them, "Those who are well have no need of a physician, but those who are sick; I have come to call not the righteous but sinners."

Notice what you think and feel as you read the gospel.

Jesus calls sinners, even the hated tax collectors, to follow him, and he eats with them in Levi's house. When the scribes and Pharisees complain, Jesus declares his mission is to call not the righteous but sinners.

Pray as you are led for yourself and others.

"Lord, I, too, am in need of you in my life. Have mercy on me . . ." (Continue in your own words.)

Listen to Jesus.

I love the holy soul in every person. If you put yourself in my company, I will wash you and bring you to the glory of my kingdom. What else is Jesus saying to you?

Ask God to show you how to live today.

"Give me your Spirit that I may not judge others in my heart or with my words. Help me to turn to you continuously for mercy. Amen."

Sunday, January 20, 2019
Second Sunday in Ordinary Time

Know that God is present with you and ready to converse.

"Lord, I am your vessel; fill me with your truth."

Read the gospel: John 2:1–11.

On the third day there was a wedding in Cana of Galilee, and the mother of Jesus was there. Jesus and his disciples had also been invited to the wedding. When the wine gave out, the mother of Jesus said to him, "They have no wine." And Jesus said to her, "Woman, what concern is that to you and to me? My hour has not yet come." His mother said to the servants, "Do whatever he tells you." Now standing there were six stone water jars for the Jewish rites of purification, each holding twenty or thirty gallons. Jesus said to them, "Fill the jars with water." And they filled them up to the brim. He said to them, "Now draw some out, and take it to the chief steward." So they took it. When the steward tasted the water that had become wine, and did not know where it came from (though the servants who had drawn the water knew), the steward called the bridegroom and said to him, "Everyone serves the good wine first, and then the inferior wine after the guests have become drunk. But you have kept the good wine until now." Jesus did this, the first of his signs, in Cana of Galilee, and revealed his glory; and his disciples believed in him.

Notice what you think and feel as you read the gospel.
Jesus attends a wedding of friends with his mother and some of his disciples. Mary notices they are short of wine, and Jesus responds with his first miracle, turning six large stone jars of water into fine wine, revealing the perfection and generosity of God.

Pray as you are led for yourself and others.
"Lord, let me drink the wine of your divinity, for that is your very Blood, which transforms me in your image. Let all I think, say, and do give you glory . . ." (Continue in your own words.)

Listen to Jesus.
I give you my Body and Blood freely for the redemption of your immortal soul. You are my servant, my friend, my child, and my sibling. We are family. What else is Jesus saying to you?

Ask God to show you how to live today.
"I am deeply privileged to be a member of your holy family. Help me to show it in my life for the good of others and for your glory. Amen."

Monday, January 21, 2019

Know that God is present with you and ready to converse.
"I rejoice that you are here with me, Jesus. Lift me by your Word."

Read the gospel: Mark 2:18–22.
Now John's disciples and the Pharisees were fasting; and people came and said to Jesus, "Why do John's disciples and the disciples of the

Pharisees fast, but your disciples do not fast?" Jesus said to them, "The wedding guests cannot fast while the bridegroom is with them, can they? As long as they have the bridegroom with them, they cannot fast. The days will come when the bridegroom is taken away from them, and then they will fast on that day.

"No one sews a piece of unshrunk cloth on an old cloak; otherwise, the patch pulls away from it, the new from the old, and a worse tear is made. And no one puts new wine into old wineskins; otherwise, the wine will burst the skins, and the wine is lost, and so are the skins; but one puts new wine into fresh wineskins."

Notice what you think and feel as you read the gospel.

Jesus calls himself the bridegroom, and his presence is reason for joy and feasting. His disciples are the wedding guests, and they will fast only after he is taken away from them. Something new is happening in the world: the bridegroom has come for his bride.

Pray as you are led for yourself and others.

"Jesus, you are doing something new in the world; you are the fulfillment, the overflowing of grace into the world. Give me grace to understand, speak, and honor you, the Bridegroom, in the presence of others . . ." (Continue in your own words.)

Listen to Jesus.

You are my ambassador, dear friend. Although you will not always know how your prayers, words, and actions glorify me before others, persist in good works. What else is Jesus saying to you?

Ask God to show you how to live today.

"Let me live each moment in your presence, Jesus, that my choices may be led by your Spirit. Amen."

Tuesday, January 22, 2019

Know that God is present with you and ready to converse.

"Almighty God, your ways are high above me. I stand before you in awe."

Read the gospel: Mark 2:23–28.

One sabbath Jesus was going through the cornfields; and as they made their way his disciples began to pluck heads of grain. The Pharisees said to him, "Look, why are they doing what is not lawful on the sabbath?" And he said to them, "Have you never read what David did when he and his companions were hungry and in need of food? He entered the house of God, when Abiathar was high priest, and ate the bread of the Presence, which it is not lawful for any but the priests to eat, and he gave some to his companions." Then he said to them, "The sabbath was made for humankind, and not humankind for the sabbath; so the Son of Man is lord even of the sabbath."

Notice what you think and feel as you read the gospel.

While the Pharisees are all about obeying religious rules, Jesus follows the higher call of God, for the Son of Man is Lord even of the Sabbath.

Pray as you are led for yourself and others.

"Jesus, let me always choose you above rules, grace above laws, mercy above judgment. Give me wisdom to discern these things . . ." (Continue in your own words.)

Listen to Jesus.

I fulfill the law. Keep my commandments—love God and all people with all your might. What else is Jesus saying to you?

Ask God to show you how to live today.

"I have far to go in keeping your commandments, Lord. Will you help me today? Amen."

Wednesday, January 23, 2019

Know that God is present with you and ready to converse.

"Lord, break down the hardness in my heart that I may receive your Word of grace and truth."

Read the gospel: Mark 3:1–6.

Again Jesus entered the synagogue, and a man was there who had a withered hand. They watched him to see whether he would cure him on the sabbath, so that they might accuse him. And he said to the man who had the withered hand, "Come forward." Then he said to them, "Is it lawful to do good or to do harm on the sabbath, to save life or to kill?" But they were silent. He looked around at them with anger; he was grieved at their hardness of heart and said to the man, "Stretch out your hand." He stretched it out, and his hand was restored. The Pharisees went out and immediately conspired with the Herodians against him, how to destroy him.

Notice what you think and feel as you read the gospel.

Jesus looks upon the Pharisees with anger, for they are intent upon gathering evidence that he is a law-breaker. Jesus knows their hearts and their thoughts. He silences them with common sense: How can it be unlawful to do good on the Sabbath? They are silent, and Jesus heals the man's hand.

Pray as you are led for yourself and others.

"Lord, do not be angry with me. Heal me by your mercy . . ." (Continue in your own words.)

Listen to Jesus.

Present your wounded and broken parts to me, dear servant, and I will heal you. What else is Jesus saying to you?

Ask God to show you how to live today.

"Thank you, Lord, for the healing you give me. Help me to stretch out my hand to help all your people. Amen."

Thursday, January 24, 2019

Know that God is present with you and ready to converse.

"Lord, master of the universe, you are present everywhere. I thank you for being with me now as I read your Word."

Read the gospel: Mark 3:7–12.

Jesus departed with his disciples to the lake, and a great multitude from Galilee followed him; hearing all that he was doing, they came to him in great numbers from Judea, Jerusalem, Idumea, beyond the Jordan, and the region around Tyre and Sidon. He told his disciples to have a boat ready for him because of the crowd, so that they would not crush him; for he had cured many, so that all who had diseases pressed upon him to touch him. Whenever the unclean spirits saw him, they fell down before him and shouted, "You are the Son of God!" But he sternly ordered them not to make him known.

Notice what you think and feel as you read the gospel.

Everyone wants something from Jesus. The crowd might crush him, so he asks his disciples to ready a boat by which he can escape. All who have diseases press upon him to touch him. Unclean spirits shout, "You are the Son of God!"

Pray as you are led for yourself and others.

"Son of God, I, too, wish to touch you. Let me do so today not only for my good but also for the good of someone else . . ." (Continue in your own words.)

Listen to Jesus.

I bless you for putting others first, my friend. What else is Jesus saying to you?

Ask God to show you how to live today.

"Make me strong in prayer, Lord, for by it I know you and love you. By prayer I cooperate with you to serve others. Amen."

Friday, January 25, 2019
Conversion of Paul

Know that God is present with you and ready to converse.

"Glory to you, Father, Son, and Holy Spirit. Send me forth by your Word."

Read the gospel: Mark 16:15–18.

And Jesus said to them, "Go into all the world and proclaim the good news to the whole creation. The one who believes and is baptized will be saved; but the one who does not believe will be condemned. And these signs will accompany those who believe: by using my name they will cast out demons; they will speak in new tongues; they will pick up snakes in their hands, and if they drink any deadly thing, it will not hurt them; they will lay their hands on the sick, and they will recover."

Notice what you think and feel as you read the gospel.

Jesus sends his disciples into the world with their assignment to proclaim the Good News of the kingdom of heaven. Miraculous signs will reinforce the truth of their message, and God shall protect them in their work.

Pray as you are led for yourself and others.

"Thank you for your clear commission, Jesus. Give me faith to embrace it and trust you as I seek to do your will in the world . . ." (Continue in your own words.)

Listen to Jesus.

If you want me to use you, beloved servant, stay close to me. Seek me every day. What else is Jesus saying to you?

Ask God to show you how to live today.

"I come to you, Jesus. I want to know you well so I can bring salvation to others. Amen."

Saturday, January 26, 2019

Know that God is present with you and ready to converse.

"Jesus, you desire to save and heal all who come to you. I stand before you now."

Read the gospel: Mark 3:20–21.

Jesus went home, and the crowd came together again, so that they could not even eat. When his family heard it, they went out to restrain him, for people were saying, "He has gone out of his mind."

Notice what you think and feel as you read the gospel.

Again we see that Jesus and his disciples are swarmed and imposed upon by the demands of the crowd. Hearing about it, the members of Jesus' family were naturally concerned about him. Some people seriously thought he had gone out of his mind, and Jesus' family wanted to protect him.

Pray as you are led for yourself and others.

"Jesus, help me to be fearless in following you. Who can harm my soul when I am with you? Give my family and friends the wisdom to understand . . ." (Continue in your own words.)

Listen to Jesus.

I am with you always, my beloved, even when following me is difficult. What else is Jesus saying to you?

Ask God to show you how to live today.

"Lord, give me the grace to place my life in your hands. Amen."

Sunday, January 27, 2019
Third Sunday in Ordinary Time

Know that God is present with you and ready to converse.

"I thank you for coming as Messiah, Lord Jesus. Touch me with your Word."

Read the gospel: Luke 4:14–21 (Lk 1:1–4, 4:14–21).

Then Jesus, filled with the power of the Spirit, returned to Galilee, and a report about him spread through all the surrounding country. He began to teach in their synagogues and was praised by everyone.

When he came to Nazareth, where he had been brought up, he went to the synagogue on the sabbath day, as was his custom. He stood up to read, and the scroll of the prophet Isaiah was given to him. He unrolled the scroll and found the place where it was written:

> "The Spirit of the Lord is upon me,
>   because he has anointed me
>   to bring good news to the poor.
> He has sent me to proclaim release to the captives
>   and recovery of sight to the blind,
>   to let the oppressed go free,
> to proclaim the year of the Lord's favor."

And he rolled up the scroll, gave it back to the attendant, and sat down. The eyes of all in the synagogue were fixed on him. Then he began to say to them, "Today this scripture has been fulfilled in your hearing."

Notice what you think and feel as you read the gospel.

Jesus returns home to Nazareth and speaks to people who know him well. After reading a powerful Messianic passage in Isaiah, he courageously announces to them, "Today this scripture has been fulfilled in your hearing." He identifies himself as the Messiah, the anointed one.

Pray as you are led for yourself and others.

"Jesus, this world is still trying to take in who you are. Reveal yourself in our own faithless generation . . ." (Continue in your own words.)

Listen to Jesus.

You are my beloved. Be truth and goodness before others. They will know me through you. What else is Jesus saying to you?

Ask God to show you how to live today.

"Lead me to opportunities to be true and good today, Lord. Open my eyes to possibilities. Thank you. Amen."

Monday, January 28, 2019

Know that God is present with you and ready to converse.

"Almighty God, no one can stand against you. I choose you and embrace your will."

Read the gospel: Mark 3:22–30.

And the scribes who came down from Jerusalem said, "He has Beelzebul, and by the ruler of the demons he casts out demons." And Jesus called them to him, and spoke to them in parables, "How can Satan cast out Satan? If a kingdom is divided against itself, that kingdom cannot stand. And if a house is divided against itself, that house will not be able to stand. And if Satan has risen up against himself and is divided, he cannot stand, but his end has come. But no one can enter a strong man's house and plunder his property without first tying up the strong man; then indeed the house can be plundered.

"Truly I tell you, people will be forgiven for their sins and whatever blasphemies they utter; but whoever blasphemes against the Holy Spirit can never have forgiveness, but is guilty of an eternal sin"—for they had said, "He has an unclean spirit."

Notice what you think and feel as you read the gospel.

The big-city scribes accuse Jesus of casting out demons by the power of the devil; yet Jesus states that his power comes from the Holy Spirit, not from evil spirits. Jesus points out that what they say makes no sense. His analogy of tying up the strong man to plunder his house implies Jesus' power over Satan. His power comes from the Holy Spirit, not from evil spirits.

Pray as you are led for yourself and others.

"Lord, vanquish all evil in me. Give me your Holy Spirit so that I can know and do what is right and good . . ." (Continue in your own words.)

Listen to Jesus.

I breathe my Spirit upon you, dear child, dear friend. Walk with me and do what I do. What else is Jesus saying to you?

Ask God to show you how to live today.

"Let my sights be set exclusively on you, Lord. Help me turn away from all that is not you. Amen."

Tuesday, January 29, 2019

Know that God is present with you and ready to converse.

"Jesus, you invite me into your Holy Family. I come to do your will, Lord."

Read the gospel: Mark 3:31–35.

Then Jesus' mother and his brothers came; and standing outside, they sent to him and called him. A crowd was sitting around him; and they said to him, "Your mother and your brothers and sisters are outside, asking for you." And he replied, "Who are my mother and my brothers?" And looking at those who sat around him, he said, "Here are my mother and my brothers! Whoever does the will of God is my brother and sister and mother."

Notice what you think and feel as you read the gospel.

When his mother and his other kin come to see him, they cannot enter the house for the crowd, so they send Jesus a message that they are there. Jesus uses that moment as an opportunity to show that family relationships are not as important as relationship with God. Those who do God's will, he says, belong to the family of God.

Pray as you are led for yourself and others.

"Jesus, you are generous to me. Let me be a true child of God. Give me love for all in God's family . . ." (Continue in your own words.)

Listen to Jesus.

Those who love are of God, beloved. Practice loving, especially when it is hard. What else is Jesus saying to you?

Ask God to show you how to live today.
"By your grace, Lord, I will love even those I have never loved. Reveal to me my hardness of heart toward others so that you may soften it. Make my heart like yours, Jesus. Amen."

Wednesday, January 30, 2019

Know that God is present with you and ready to converse.
"Lord, let my heart be fruitful ground for the flourishing of your Word."

Read the gospel: Mark 4:2–9 (Mk 4:1–20).
Jesus began to teach them many things in parables, and in his teaching he said to them: "Listen! A sower went out to sow. And as he sowed, some seed fell on the path, and the birds came and ate it up. Other seed fell on rocky ground, where it did not have much soil, and it sprang up quickly, since it had no depth of soil. And when the sun rose, it was scorched; and since it had no root, it withered away. Other seed fell among thorns, and the thorns grew up and choked it, and it yielded no grain. Other seed fell into good soil and brought forth grain, growing up and increasing and yielding thirty and sixty and a hundredfold." And he said, "Let anyone with ears to hear listen!"

Notice what you think and feel as you read the gospel.
In this familiar parable Jesus puts a burden on the hearer of his words to receive them deeply, lest dangers of worldliness or greed or the devil distract us. Those who do receive his Word well will bear much fruit.

Pray as you are led for yourself and others.
"I pray now for all those who do not receive your Word deeply into their hearts. I pray that their eyes will be opened to the Good News and they will believe . . ." (Continue in your own words.)

Listen to Jesus.
You are right to pray for unbelievers. But do not be afraid. All shall be well.
What else is Jesus saying to you?

Ask God to show you how to live today.
"How shall I help people know you as you are, Lord? Show me opportunities. Amen."

Thursday, January 31, 2019

Know that God is present with you and ready to converse.
"Light of the World, illuminate me by your Word."

Read the gospel: Mark 4:21–25.
Jesus said to them, "Is a lamp brought in to be put under the bushel basket, or under the bed, and not on the lampstand? For there is nothing hidden, except to be disclosed; nor is anything secret, except to come to light. Let anyone with ears to hear listen!" And he said to them, "Pay attention to what you hear; the measure you give will be the measure you get, and still more will be given you. For to those who have, more will be given; and from those who have nothing, even what they have will be taken away."

Notice what you think and feel as you read the gospel.
Jesus discloses what seem to be two spiritual laws. The first is that light reveals things, even all hidden or secret things. The second spiritual law has to do with how we give ourselves away. The paradox is that the more we give, the more we receive.

Pray as you are led for yourself and others.
"Lord, banish the darkness within me. Give me your light and let me shine before others. Let me give selflessly to others, that I may be rich in your love . . ." (Continue in your own words.)

Listen to Jesus.
You understand, dear servant. You make me joyful. What else is Jesus saying to you?

Ask God to show you how to live today.
"Where are the dark corners, Lord, in me and in the world? Show me where to go to uncover the light of your generous love. Amen."

THE POPE'S MONTHLY PRAYER INTENTION FOR FEBRUARY 2019

For a generous welcome of the victims of human trafficking, of enforced prostitution, and of violence.

Friday, February 1, 2019

Know that God is present with you and ready to converse.
"Creator of all life, be life in me and let it grow as I receive your Word."

Read the gospel: Mark 4:26–34.

Jesus also said, "The kingdom of God is as if someone would scatter seed on the ground, and would sleep and rise night and day, and the seed would sprout and grow, he does not know how. The earth produces of itself, first the stalk, then the head, then the full grain in the head. But when the grain is ripe, at once he goes in with his sickle, because the harvest has come."

He also said, "With what can we compare the kingdom of God, or what parable will we use for it? It is like a mustard seed, which, when sown upon the ground, is the smallest of all the seeds on earth; yet when it is sown it grows up and becomes the greatest of all shrubs, and puts forth large branches, so that the birds of the air can make nests in its shade."

With many such parables he spoke the word to them, as they were able to hear it; he did not speak to them except in parables, but he explained everything in private to his disciples.

Notice what you think and feel as you read the gospel.

Just as seeds are scattered, grown, and harvested, so too we will grow and be harvested by God when God is ready. The kingdom of God in us starts out small but grows very large.

Pray as you are led for yourself and others

"I open my soul to your seeds, Lord. Let them grow and bear good fruit to your glory . . ." (Continue in your own words.)

Listen to Jesus.

You are mine, beloved, and I am making you beautiful. What else is Jesus saying to you?

Ask God to show you how to live today.

"Plant the seeds of faith, hope, and love in me, Lord, so that I may grow for your kingdom. Amen."

Saturday, February 2, 2019
Presentation of the Lord

Know that God is present with you and ready to converse.

"Lord, you see me waiting for you. I rejoice to see you in my life."

Read the gospel: Luke 2:22–32 (Lk 2:22–40).

When the time came for their purification according to the law of Moses, Joseph and Mary brought Jesus up to Jerusalem to present him to the Lord (as it is written in the law of the Lord, "Every firstborn male shall be designated as holy to the Lord"), and they offered a sacrifice according to what is stated in the law of the Lord, "a pair of turtledoves or two young pigeons."

Now there was a man in Jerusalem whose name was Simeon; this man was righteous and devout, looking forward to the consolation of Israel, and the Holy Spirit rested on him. It had been revealed to him by the Holy Spirit that he would not see death before he had seen the Lord's Messiah. Guided by the Spirit, Simeon came into the temple; and when the parents brought in the child Jesus, to do for him what was customary under the law, Simeon took him in his arms and praised God, saying,

> "Master, now you are dismissing your servant in peace,
>   according to your word;
> for my eyes have seen your salvation,
>   which you have prepared in the presence of all peoples,
> a light for revelation to the Gentiles
>   and for glory to your people Israel."

Notice what you think and feel as you read the gospel.

Mary and Joseph were amazed at the events that transpired when, according to the law of Moses, they presented the infant Jesus in the Temple. A holy man, Simeon, and Anna, a prophetess—both very elderly—have been waiting for the Messiah, and both of them recognize that Jesus is he. They both prophesy of the great things Jesus will do.

Pray as you are led for yourself and others.

"Lord, with Simeon and Anna, I rejoice in your coming to the world and to me. Let me praise you and proclaim your wonders to others . . ." (Continue in your own words.)

Listen to Jesus.

I also rejoice in you, my beloved. I came for you. I will stay with you. Turn your heart to me. What else is Jesus saying to you?

Ask God to show you how to live today.

"Bring to my mind the many times you have blessed me, Lord, and let me glorify you in all I do today. Amen."

Sunday, February 3, 2019
Fourth Sunday in Ordinary Time

Know that God is present with you and ready to converse.

"Jesus, I am among that crowd you are speaking to. Teach me now."

Read the gospel: Luke 4:21–30.

Then Jesus began to say to them, "Today this scripture has been fulfilled in your hearing." All spoke well of him and were amazed at the gracious words that came from his mouth. They said, "Is not this Joseph's son?" He said to them, "Doubtless you will quote to me this proverb, 'Doctor, cure yourself!' And you will say, 'Do here also in your hometown the things that we have heard you did at Capernaum.'" And he said, "Truly I tell you, no prophet is accepted in the prophet's hometown. But the truth is, there were many widows in Israel in the time of Elijah, when the heaven was shut up for three years and six months, and there was a severe famine over all the land; yet Elijah was sent to none of them except to a widow at Zarephath in Sidon. There were also many lepers in Israel in the time of the prophet Elisha, and none of them was cleansed except Naaman the Syrian." When they heard this, all in the synagogue were filled with rage. They got up, drove him out of the town, and led him to the brow of the hill on which their town was built, so that they might hurl him off the cliff. But he passed through the midst of them and went on his way.

Notice what you think and feel as you read the gospel.

Jesus creates controversy when he preaches in his hometown. They want him to do miracles to prove himself as the Messiah. He refuses, refuting them with scripture that shows miracles of healing performed for Gentiles. They are ready to push him off a cliff, but he "passed through the midst of them and went on his way." What gave them pause? Why did they let him go? Did they wonder or have a flicker of faith?

Pray as you are led for yourself and others.

"Lord, I will not test you. I believe in you. I know you will take care of me and those you have given me . . ." (Continue in your own words.)

Listen to Jesus.

I work my will with you through a cooperation of your will, your heart, and my purposes for your life. Do not challenge me or doubt me. Love me. Trust my love for you. What else is Jesus saying to you?

Ask God to show you how to live today.

"Where are the dark corners, Lord, in me and in the world? Show me where to go to uncover the light of your generous love. Amen."

Monday, February 4, 2019

Know that God is present with you and ready to converse.

"Let me be with you Lord, I beg."

Read the gospel: Mark 5:1–20.

They came to the other side of the lake, to the country of the Gerasenes. And when Jesus had stepped out of the boat, immediately a man out of the tombs with an unclean spirit met him. He lived among the tombs; and no one could restrain him anymore, even with a chain; for he had often been restrained with shackles and chains, but the chains he wrenched apart, and the shackles he broke in pieces; and no one had the strength to subdue him. Night and day among the tombs and on the mountains he was always howling and bruising himself with stones. When he saw Jesus from a distance, he ran and bowed down before him; and he shouted at the top of his voice, "What have you to do with me, Jesus, Son of the Most High God? I adjure you by God, do not torment me." For he had said to him, "Come out of the man, you unclean spirit!" Then Jesus asked him, "What is your name?" He replied, "My name is Legion; for we are many." He begged him earnestly not to send them out of the country. Now there on the hillside a great herd of swine was feeding; and the unclean spirits begged him, "Send us into the swine; let us enter them." So he gave them permission. And the unclean spirits came out and entered the swine; and the herd, numbering about two thousand, rushed down the steep bank into the lake, and were drowned in the lake.

The swineherds ran off and told it in the city and in the country. Then people came to see what it was that had happened. They came to Jesus and saw the demoniac sitting there, clothed and in his right mind, the very man who had had the legion; and they were afraid. Those who had seen what had happened to the demoniac and to the swine reported it. Then they began to beg Jesus to leave their neighborhood. As he was getting into the boat, the man who had been possessed by demons begged him that he might be with him. But Jesus refused, and said to him, "Go home to your friends, and tell them how much the Lord has done for you, and what mercy he has shown you." And he went away and began to proclaim in the Decapolis how much Jesus had done for him; and everyone was amazed.

Notice what you think and feel as you read the gospel.

Jesus casts many demons out of a tormented man in a country of the Gentiles. Afterward, the man wishes to follow Jesus, but Jesus directs him to return to his own people and speak to them of the mercy God has shown to him.

Pray as you are led for yourself and others.

"Lord, such is your fearsome power, that even a legion of unclean spirits obeys your authority! Praise to you Lord! . . ." (Continue in your own words.)

Listen to Jesus.

I know the heart of every creature; in me are mercy and justice in equal measure. Come to me, trust in my goodness. What else is Jesus saying to you?

Ask God to show you how to live today.

"Lord, I want to be with you; give me the strength to go where you send me today and to proclaim all you have done for me. Amen."

Tuesday, February 5, 2019

Know that God is present with you and ready to converse.

"Jesus, I need to touch you as you pass by today."

Read the gospel: Mark 5:21–43.

When Jesus had crossed again in the boat to the other side, a great crowd gathered round him; and he was by the lake. Then one of the leaders of the synagogue named Jairus came and, when he saw him, fell at his feet and begged him repeatedly, "My little daughter is at the point of death. Come and lay your hands on her, so that she may be made well, and live." So he went with him.

And a large crowd followed him and pressed in on him. Now there was a woman who had been suffering from hemorrhages for twelve years. She had endured much under many physicians, and had spent all that she had; and she was no better, but rather grew worse. She had heard about Jesus, and came up behind him in the crowd and touched his cloak, for she said, "If I but touch his clothes, I will be made well." Immediately her hemorrhage stopped; and she felt in her body that she was healed of her disease. Immediately aware that power had gone forth from him, Jesus turned about in the crowd and said, "Who touched my clothes?" And his disciples said to him, "You see the crowd pressing in on you; how can you say, 'Who touched me?'" He looked all round to see who had done it. But the woman, knowing what had happened to her, came in fear and trembling, fell down before him, and told him the whole truth. He said to her, "Daughter, your faith has made you well; go in peace, and be healed of your disease."

While he was still speaking, some people came from the leader's house to say, "Your daughter is dead. Why trouble the teacher any further?" But overhearing what they said, Jesus said to the leader of the synagogue, "Do not fear, only believe." He allowed no one to follow him except Peter, James, and John, the brother of James. When they came to the house of the leader of the synagogue, he saw a commotion, people weeping and wailing loudly. When he had entered, he said to them, "Why do you make a commotion and weep? The child is not dead but sleeping." And they laughed at him. Then he put them all outside, and took the child's father and mother and those who were with him, and went in where the child was. He took her by the hand and said to her, "Talitha cum," which means, "Little girl, get up!" And immediately the girl got up and began to walk about (she was twelve years of age). At this they were overcome with amazement. He strictly ordered them that no one should know this, and told them to give her something to eat.

Notice what you think and feel as you read the gospel.

The narrative of the raising of Jairus's daughter from the dead is interrupted by the healing of the woman with hemorrhage. In faith, she touches the hem of Jesus' garment and immediately the hemorrhage stops. Jesus does not seem to be aware of it until it happens. Then she comes to him and he blesses her for her faith. This "little" miracle feels as great as the raising of Jairus's daughter from the dead.

Pray as you are led for yourself and others.

"Lord, nothing is too small for you, nothing too great. Heal me and raise me up to your service . . ." (Continue in your own words.)

Listen to Jesus.

When you speak to me, beloved, you reveal your faith. Pray often, and I will reward your faith with fruitfulness. What else is Jesus saying to you?

Ask God to show you how to live today.

"Forgive me for lapses in prayer and faithfulness, Lord. Let me walk more closely with you today. Amen."

Wednesday, February 6, 2019

Know that God is present with you and ready to converse.

"Lord, let me hear your holy Word afresh and respond with faith."

Read the gospel: Mark 6:1–6.

Jesus left that place and came to his hometown, and his disciples followed him. On the sabbath he began to teach in the synagogue, and many who heard him were astounded. They said, "Where did this man get all this? What is this wisdom that has been given to him? What deeds of power are being done by his hands! Is not this the carpenter, the son of Mary and brother of James and Joses and Judas and Simon, and are not his sisters here with us?" And they took offence at him. Then Jesus said to them, "Prophets are not without honor, except in their hometown, and among their own kin, and in their own house." And he could do no deed of power there, except that he laid his hands on a few sick people and cured them. And he was amazed at their unbelief. Then he went about among the villages teaching.

Notice what you think and feel as you read the gospel.

The people of Jesus' hometown are aware of his wisdom and miracles, but they cannot believe in him because they know his background and his relatives.

Pray as you are led for yourself and others.

"Jesus, let me not take you for granted. Let your mercy be new every morning upon me and upon those I pray for . . ." (Continue in your own words.)

Listen to Jesus.

The more you come to me in faith, beloved, the more you will love me and serve me. What else is Jesus saying to you?

Ask God to show you how to live today.

"I give myself to you today, Lord. Let me rejoice all day in the wonder of your presence. Amen."

Thursday, February 7, 2019

Know that God is present with you and ready to converse.

"Let your Word be light in my heart and soul and mind, O Lord."

Read the gospel: Mark 6:7–13.

Jesus called the twelve and began to send them out two by two, and gave them authority over the unclean spirits. He ordered them to take nothing for their journey except a staff; no bread, no bag, no money in their belts; but to wear sandals and not to put on two tunics. He said to them, "Wherever you enter a house, stay there until you leave the place. If any place will not welcome you and they refuse to hear you, as you leave, shake off the dust that is on your feet as a testimony against them." So they went out and proclaimed that all should repent. They cast out many demons, and anointed with oil many who were sick and cured them.

Notice what you think and feel as you read the gospel.

Jesus instructs his disciples as he sends them out. He gives them spiritual authority and particular advice. They are going out to serve God and others, not themselves.

Pray as you are led for yourself and others.
"Lord, you have sent me too. Let me realize my authority in you. I pray for those I cannot reach . . ." (Continue in your own words.)

Listen to Jesus.
I go before you as you go out, my child, my friend. I give you strength and grace to endure all things and to embrace all things. What else is Jesus saying to you?

Ask God to show you how to live today.
"I trust in your grace, Lord, and not in my own strength. Help me to walk in your way perfectly. Amen."

Friday, February 8, 2019

Know that God is present with you and ready to converse.
"Worldliness blinds a person's eyes to the presence of God in all things. Let me turn away from worldliness and see you in your Word, Lord."

Read the gospel: Mark 6:14–29.
King Herod heard of it, for Jesus' name had become known. Some were saying, "John the baptizer has been raised from the dead; and for this reason these powers are at work in him." But others said, "It is Elijah." And others said, "It is a prophet, like one of the prophets of old." But when Herod heard of it, he said, "John, whom I beheaded, has been raised."

For Herod himself had sent men who arrested John, bound him, and put him in prison on account of Herodias, his brother Philip's wife, because Herod had married her. For John had been telling Herod, "It is not lawful for you to have your brother's wife." And Herodias had a grudge against him, and wanted to kill him. But she could not, for Herod feared John, knowing that he was a righteous and holy man, and he protected him. When he heard him, he was greatly perplexed; and yet he liked to listen to him. But an opportunity came when Herod on his birthday gave a banquet for his courtiers and officers and for the leaders of Galilee. When his daughter Herodias came in and danced, she pleased Herod and his guests; and the king said to the girl, "Ask me for whatever you wish, and I will give it." And he solemnly swore to her, "Whatever you ask me, I will give you, even half of my kingdom." She went out and said to her mother, "What should I ask for?" She replied, "The head of John the baptizer." Immediately she rushed back to the king and requested, "I want you to give me at once the head of John the Baptist on a platter." The king was deeply grieved; yet out of regard for his oaths and for the guests, he did not want to refuse her. Immediately the king sent a soldier of the guard with orders to bring John's head. He went and beheaded him in the prison, brought his head on a platter, and gave it to the girl. Then the girl gave it to her mother. When his disciples heard about it, they came and took his body, and laid it in a tomb.

Notice what you think and feel as you read the gospel.
Herod is a confused man. He has John beheaded because he was drunk with friends at his own birthday party and made a rash promise to his stepdaughter, whose mother manipulates John's gory execution. Herod, though he fears and respects John, kills him anyway.

Pray as you are led for yourself and others.
"Lord, take away from me all darkness of mind. Even when I am perplexed, let your Word enlighten my heart that I may want what you want. Draw my eyes toward you, that I may love you and love my neighbor . . ." (Continue in your own words.)

Listen to Jesus.
Do not be afraid of what others think and say about you because of your devotion to me. You are mine, and I love you. What else is Jesus saying to you?

Ask God to show you how to live today.
"Teach me simplicity, Lord, and humility. Let me seek you first. Amen."

Saturday, February 9, 2019

Know that God is present with you and ready to converse.
"You are my Shepherd, Lord, and you teach me by your Word."

Read the gospel: Mark 6:30–34.
The apostles gathered around Jesus, and told him all that they had done and taught. He said to them, "Come away to a deserted place all by yourselves and rest a while." For many were coming and going, and they had no leisure even to eat. And they went away in the boat to a deserted place by themselves. Now many saw them going and recognized them, and they hurried there on foot from all the towns and arrived ahead of them. As he went ashore, he saw a great crowd; and he had compassion

for them, because they were like sheep without a shepherd; and he began to teach them many things.

Notice what you think and feel as you read the gospel.

As Jesus seeks to escape the crowd by boat, the people anticipate his destination and arrive there before him by land. Is Jesus frustrated? Not at all. He has compassion on them and begins to teach them. He is the Great Shepherd.

Pray as you are led for yourself and others.

"Let me be as you are, Lord, in the midst of events that might frustrate me. Let me operate with your patience and compassion . . ." (Continue in your own words.)

Listen to Jesus.

Accept all things as God's will to work good in your life. I love you and have much to teach you. What else is Jesus saying to you?

Ask God to show you how to live today.

"Thank you, Lord. Thank you for all the things in my life. May I learn from you today, Shepherd. Amen."

Sunday February 10, 2019
Fifth Sunday in Ordinary Time

Know that God is present with you and ready to converse.

"Lord, I need to hear your voice. When I do, help me to obey you."

Read the gospel: Luke 5:1–11.

Once while Jesus was standing beside the lake of Gennesaret, and the crowd was pressing in on him to hear the word of God, he saw two boats there at the shore of the lake; the fishermen had gone out of them and were washing their nets. He got into one of the boats, the one belonging to Simon, and asked him to put out a little way from the shore. Then he sat down and taught the crowds from the boat. When he had finished speaking, he said to Simon, "Put out into the deep water and let down your nets for a catch." Simon answered, "Master, we have worked all night long but have caught nothing. Yet if you say so, I will let down the nets." When they had done this, they caught so many fish that their nets were beginning to break. So they signaled to their partners in the

other boat to come and help them. And they came and filled both boats,
so that they began to sink. But when Simon Peter saw it, he fell down at
Jesus' knees, saying, "Go away from me, Lord, for I am a sinful man!"
For he and all who were with him were amazed at the catch of fish that
they had taken; and so also were James and John, sons of Zebedee, who
were partners with Simon. Then Jesus said to Simon, "Do not be afraid;
from now on you will be catching people." When they had brought their
boats to shore, they left everything and followed him.

Notice what you think and feel as you read the gospel.

Jesus teaches Peter through experience. Peter learns who Jesus is, what
is his power and holiness. It makes Peter realize that he is a sinful man
and unworthy of this relationship with the Messiah, the man who is God.

Pray as you are led for yourself and others.

"Let me be like Peter, humble and broken in your glorious presence. I
offer myself to your service, Lord, for I want to give glory to our Father
in heaven . . ." (Continue in your own words.)

Listen to Jesus.

*I will tell you what to do, for I have placed you here. Follow me in doing the will
of our Father.* What else is Jesus saying to you?

Ask God to show you how to live today.

"I do not want to live my life mechanically, Lord. Show me how to live
intentionally in close friendship with you. Let me begin again today.
Thank you, Savior. Amen."

Monday, February 11, 2019

Know that God is present with you and ready to converse.

"I come into your presence in all my weakness, Lord. Let me touch the
fringe of your cloak."

Read the gospel: Mark 6:53–56.

When Jesus and his disciples had crossed over, they came to land at
Gennesaret and moored the boat. When they got out of the boat, people
at once recognized him, and rushed about that whole region and began
to bring the sick on mats to wherever they heard he was. And wherever he went, into villages or cities or farms, they laid the sick in the

marketplaces, and begged him that they might touch even the fringe of his cloak; and all who touched it were healed.

Notice what you think and feel as you read the gospel.

What a picture of people rushing around to lay their sick before Jesus! Coming to him from villages, cities, or farms, all who touch the fringe of his cloak are healed.

Pray as you are led for yourself and others.

"Jesus, I lay before you now those who need your healing touch, as well as myself. I give you . . ." (Continue in your own words.)

Listen to Jesus.

I hear your prayers, beloved disciple. I know your love for me and for others. Remain in me, and you will bring my healing to others. What else is Jesus saying to you?

Ask God to show you how to live today.

"Give me strength to help those in need, Lord. Allow me to see others with your compassion. Amen."

Tuesday, February 12, 2019

Know that God is present with you and ready to converse.

"Lord, I exult in your presence now. By your Word turn me away from vain and hypocritical practices and let me do instead acts of love."

Read the gospel: Mark 7:1–13.

Now when the Pharisees and some of the scribes who had come from Jerusalem gathered around Jesus, they noticed that some of his disciples were eating with defiled hands, that is, without washing them. (For the Pharisees, and all the Jews, do not eat unless they thoroughly wash their hands, thus observing the tradition of the elders; and they do not eat anything from the market unless they wash it; and there are also many other traditions that they observe, the washing of cups, pots, and bronze kettles.) So the Pharisees and the scribes asked him, "Why do your disciples not live according to the tradition of the elders, but eat with defiled hands?" He said to them, "Isaiah prophesied rightly about you hypocrites, as it is written,

'This people honors me with their lips,

but their hearts are far from me;
in vain do they worship me,
teaching human precepts as doctrines.'

You abandon the commandment of God and hold to human tradition."
Then he said to them, "You have a fine way of rejecting the commandment of God in order to keep your tradition! For Moses said, 'Honor your father and your mother'; and, 'Whoever speaks evil of father or mother must surely die.' But you say that if anyone tells father or mother, 'Whatever support you might have had from me is Corban' (that is, an offering to God)—then you no longer permit doing anything for a father or mother, thus making void the word of God through your tradition that you have handed on. And you do many things like this."

Notice what you think and feel as you read the gospel.
The Pharisees are sticklers for their ritual traditions and expect Jesus and his disciples to observe them, too. But Jesus calls them hypocrites, teaching human precepts as doctrines but not honoring God or God's commandments.

Pray as you are led for yourself and others.
"Lord, I pray for my father and mother today . . ." (Continue in your own words.)

Listen to Jesus.
I have revealed the Spirit that breathes life into the Law. Seek me in scripture and sacrament, and I will fill you with the same Spirit. What else is Jesus saying to you?

Ask God to show you how to live today.
"Today, Lord, let me live out the love that frees us from the law; let me serve you in loving all you love. Amen."

Wednesday, February 13, 2019

Know that God is present with you and ready to converse.
"Almighty Trinity—Father, Son, and Holy Spirit—I place myself here before you and ask for your mercy and grace. I will read your Word."

Read the gospel: Mark 7:14–23.

Then Jesus called the crowd again and said to them, "Listen to me, all of you, and understand: there is nothing outside a person that by going in can defile, but the things that come out are what defile."

When he had left the crowd and entered the house, his disciples asked him about the parable. He said to them, "Then do you also fail to understand? Do you not see that whatever goes into a person from outside cannot defile, since it enters, not the heart but the stomach, and goes out into the sewer?" (Thus he declared all foods clean.) And he said, "It is what comes out of a person that defiles. For it is from within, from the human heart, that evil intentions come: fornication, theft, murder, adultery, avarice, wickedness, deceit, licentiousness, envy, slander, pride, folly. All these evil things come from within, and they defile a person."

Notice what you think and feel as you read the gospel.

Speaking against rules about food and food preparation, Jesus asserts that foods do not defile a person but what comes out of the human heart defiles a person—this is where sin begins.

Pray as you are led for yourself and others.

"Lord, I am not clean. I submit my heart to you for mercy and cleansing. After you cast out the evil from me, fill me with love. Make my heart like yours, Jesus . . ." (Continue in your own words.)

Listen to Jesus.

God asks you to be holy, beloved disciple. Long for it, pray for it, work for it in your life, and you will have joy and bear fruit to the glory of God. What else is Jesus saying to you?

Ask God to show you how to live today.

"I resolve to change my life, Lord, beginning with heart. Pour out your grace upon me so that I may please God with my life. Thank you. Amen."

Thursday, February 14, 2019

Know that God is present with you and ready to converse.

"Your name is mercy, Lord. You love us and care for us every day."

Read the gospel: Mark 7:24–30.

From there Jesus set out and went away to the region of Tyre. He entered a house and did not want anyone to know he was there. Yet he could not escape notice, but a woman whose little daughter had an unclean spirit immediately heard about him, and she came and bowed down at his feet. Now the woman was a Gentile, of Syrophoenician origin. She begged him to cast the demon out of her daughter. He said to her, "Let the children be fed first, for it is not fair to take the children's food and throw it to the dogs." But she answered him, "Sir, even the dogs under the table eat the children's crumbs." Then he said to her, "For saying that, you may go—the demon has left your daughter." So she went home, found the child lying on the bed, and the demon gone.

Notice what you think and feel as you read the gospel.

Jesus surprises us with his response to the woman's request. Perhaps he is annoyed to have been discovered in the house, but more likely he is testing her and making the point that he came to save all of us, not just the Jews. She answers him cleverly, assertively, and for that answer he casts the demon out of her daughter.

Pray as you are led for yourself and others.

"Jesus, I, too, persevere in asking from you what I need. I am concerned about the needs of others and bring these petitions to you now . . ." (Continue in your own words.)

Listen to Jesus.

When you persevere in prayer, my child, you show your faith. Step out in faith, and I will reward you. What else is Jesus saying to you?

Ask God to show you how to live today.

"Lord, give me wisdom to know your will and then the strength to do it. Thank you. Amen."

Friday, February 15, 2019

Know that God is present with you and ready to converse.

"Lord, let my ears be open to your Word and let my mouth sing your praises."

Read the gospel: Mark 7:31–37.

Then Jesus returned from the region of Tyre, and went by way of Sidon towards the Sea of Galilee, in the region of the Decapolis. They brought to him a deaf man who had an impediment in his speech; and they begged him to lay his hand on him. He took him aside in private, away from the crowd, and put his fingers into his ears, and he spat and touched his tongue. Then looking up to heaven, he sighed and said to him, "Ephphatha," that is, "Be opened." And immediately his ears were opened, his tongue was released, and he spoke plainly. Then Jesus ordered them to tell no one; but the more he ordered them, the more zealously they proclaimed it. They were astounded beyond measure, saying, "He has done everything well; he even makes the deaf to hear and the mute to speak."

Notice what you think and feel as you read the gospel.

Jesus takes the deaf man away from the crowd. He seems burdened by all the demands for healing, yet he cures the man of all his infirmities. "Be opened," he tells the deaf man; the man takes his new openness and ability to speak and proclaims Jesus to everyone, and the crowd praises Jesus.

Pray as you are led for yourself and others.

"Lord, you heal me and restore me to joy. I want to proclaim your goodness, that all people may learn to praise you. I pray especially for . . ." (Continue in your own words.)

Listen to Jesus.

I wish to do things through you, beloved. Be open to opportunities for loving service. What else is Jesus saying to you?

Ask God to show you how to live today.

"Make me very sensitive to your bidding, Lord. Give me grace to serve. I praise your holy name. Amen."

Saturday, February 16, 2019

Know that God is present with you and ready to converse.

"Master of the universe, you condescend to be with me, a sinner. Let me grow in love for you by the reading of your Word."

Read the gospel: Mark 8:1–10.

In those days when there was again a great crowd without anything to eat, Jesus called his disciples and said to them, "I have compassion for the crowd, because they have been with me now for three days and have nothing to eat. If I send them away hungry to their homes, they will faint on the way—and some of them have come from a great distance." His disciples replied, "How can one feed these people with bread here in the desert?" He asked them, "How many loaves do you have?" They said, "Seven." Then he ordered the crowd to sit down on the ground; and he took the seven loaves, and after giving thanks he broke them and gave them to his disciples to distribute; and they distributed them to the crowd. They had also a few small fish; and after blessing them, he ordered that these too should be distributed. They ate and were filled; and they took up the broken pieces left over, seven baskets full. Now there were about four thousand people. And he sent them away. And immediately he got into the boat with his disciples and went to the district of Dalmanutha.

Notice what you think and feel as you read the gospel.

Jesus has compassion for the crowd. He knows they are hungry and far from home. His disciples are perplexed by the problem, but Jesus multiplies the loaves and fishes and feeds four thousand.

Pray as you are led for yourself and others.

"Loving Jesus, feed me with yourself, for you are the Bread of Life . . ." (Continue in your own words.)

Listen to Jesus.

Beloved disciple, I love your coming to me, our time together. What else is Jesus saying to you?

Ask God to show you how to live today.

"I wish to do something good for someone else today, Lord. I offer myself to your service. Make of me something more than I am. Amen."

Sunday, February 17, 2019
Sixth Sunday in Ordinary Time

Know that God is present with you and ready to converse.

"God, you sent your only Son to earth to save us from sin and death. Give me the grace to comprehend this great act of love."

Read the gospel: Luke 6:17, 20–26.

Jesus came down with them and stood on a level place, with a great crowd of his disciples and a great multitude of people from all Judea, Jerusalem, and the coast of Tyre and Sidon.

Then he looked up at his disciples and said:

"Blessed are you who are poor,
  for yours is the kingdom of God.
"Blessed are you who are hungry now,
  for you will be filled.
"Blessed are you who weep now,
  for you will laugh.

"Blessed are you when people hate you, and when they exclude you, revile you, and defame you on account of the Son of Man. Rejoice on that day and leap for joy, for surely your reward is great in heaven; for that is what their ancestors did to the prophets.

"But woe to you who are rich,
  for you have received your consolation.
"Woe to you who are full now,
  for you will be hungry.
"Woe to you who are laughing now,
  for you will mourn and weep.

"Woe to you when all speak well of you, for that is what their ancestors did to the false prophets."

Notice what you think and feel as you read the gospel.

Jesus teaches about blessing and woe and our own role in determining what we will experience in life. Though we suffer in our lives, if we trust in Christ, we will receive great consolation and reward in heaven. If we are content on our own in this life, we will not receive God's reward.

Pray as you are led for yourself and others.

"Lord, give me your spiritual attitude toward life. Let me value you most of all and accept what comes. I take consolation in my suffering because of you . . ." (Continue in your own words.)

Listen to Jesus.

I am with you, child, and I gladly adjust your attitude. Be indifferent to circumstance, but attend to your friendship with God. What else is Jesus saying to you?

Ask God to show you how to live today.

"Lord, I hear your words, but I know I often long for comfort rather than to do your will. Please give me your grace when I stray. Amen."

Monday, February 18, 2019

Know that God is present with you and ready to converse.

"Lord, you are not a force I can exploit for my own benefit."

Read the gospel: Mark 8:11–13.

The Pharisees came and began to argue with Jesus, asking him for a sign from heaven, to test him. And he sighed deeply in his spirit and said, "Why does this generation ask for a sign? Truly I tell you, no sign will be given to this generation." And he left them, and getting into the boat again, he went across to the other side.

Notice what you think and feel as you read the gospel.

Jesus has just come from the Decapolis, where he healed the deaf man and fed four thousand people on seven loaves of bread and a couple of fish, and now the Pharisees insist that he prove himself with signs. What exactly are they looking for? And would they accept such a sign if they saw it? He refuses to perform on demand.

Pray as you are led for yourself and others.

"Lord, sometimes I, too, want a sign; sometimes, I need something concrete to hold onto. Help me to see how you sustain me, help me to feel when you heal me, and help me to recognize the incredible miracle that is your care for us . . ." (Continue in your own words.)

Listen to Jesus.

Come to me in faith and live in my love, and you will be a sign for others. What else is Jesus saying to you?

Ask God to show you how to live today.

"I trust in you Lord. Show me how to be your hands and feet for this generation. Amen."

Tuesday, February 19, 2019

Know that God is present with you and ready to converse.

"Lord, you exist, you love, you are here with me now; let me please you by my faith."

Read the gospel: Mark 8:14–21.

Now the disciples had forgotten to bring any bread; and they had only one loaf with them in the boat. And Jesus cautioned them, saying, "Watch out—beware of the yeast of the Pharisees and the yeast of Herod." They said to one another, "It is because we have no bread." And becoming aware of it, Jesus said to them, "Why are you talking about having no bread? Do you still not perceive or understand? Are your hearts hardened? Do you have eyes, and fail to see? Do you have ears, and fail to hear? And do you not remember? When I broke the five loaves for the five thousand, how many baskets full of broken pieces did you collect?" They said to him, "Twelve." "And the seven for the four thousand, how many baskets full of broken pieces did you collect?" And they said to him, "Seven." Then he said to them, "Do you not yet understand?"

Notice what you think and feel as you read the gospel.

When Jesus brings up the yeast of the Pharisees and Herod, the disciples assume he is talking about the fact they forgot to bring bread. He rebukes them for not understanding that he is speaking figuratively. Weak in understanding and weak in faith, they are concerned with worldly things. He reminds them of the miracles multiplying the bread. He wants them to understand that he is Lord.

Pray as you are led for yourself and others.

"Jesus, increase my understanding and my faith. Let me remember the mighty things you have done in my life. Let me be ready to speak of your wonderful ways to all I encounter . . ." (Continue in your own words.)

Listen to Jesus.

Beloved disciple, begin in humble ignorance, but reach out to me in faith. I will teach you the way you should go. What else is Jesus saying to you?

Ask God to show you how to live today.

"Lord, show me how to act upon my small faith so that I can learn how to think, love, pray, and serve as you do. Let this prayer make a positive difference in my day, in my life. Amen."

Wednesday, February 20, 2019

Know that God is present with you and ready to converse.

"Lord, I am blind to your glory. Open my eyes to you and to others."

Read the gospel: Mark 8:22–26.

Jesus and his disciples came to Bethsaida. Some people brought a blind man to him and begged him to touch him. He took the blind man by the hand and led him out of the village; and when he had put saliva on his eyes and laid his hands on him, he asked him, "Can you see anything?" And the man looked up and said, "I can see people, but they look like trees, walking." Then Jesus laid his hands on his eyes again; and he looked intently and his sight was restored, and he saw everything clearly. Then he sent him away to his home, saying, "Do not even go into the village."

Notice what you think and feel as you read the gospel.

The details of Jesus' healing of this blind man are interesting. First he puts his saliva on the man's eyes, lays his hands on the man, and the man's sight is restored partially. He sees people like "trees, walking." Then Jesus lays hands on his eyes again and he is completely healed.

Pray as you are led for yourself and others.

"This healing is so vivid, Lord. Your ways are mysterious, but you do all things well. I pray for my own healing and for the healing of those you have given me . . ." (Continue in your own words.)

Listen to Jesus.

Doing good for others is the secret of joy, my dear servant. Join me in joy. What else is Jesus saying to you?

Ask God to show you how to live today.

"Lord, I aspire to virtue, to walk in your love today. You must fill me with your love and lead me to do good. Let me glorify you in thought, word, and deed. Amen."

Thursday, February 21, 2019

Know that God is present with you and ready to converse.

"Incarnate God, Son of Man, let me know you by your Word."

Read the gospel: Mark 8:27–33.

Jesus went on with his disciples to the villages of Caesarea Philippi; and on the way he asked his disciples, "Who do people say that I am?" And they answered him, "John the Baptist; and others, Elijah; and still others, one of the prophets." He asked them, "But who do you say that I am?" Peter answered him, "You are the Messiah." And he sternly ordered them not to tell anyone about him.

Then he began to teach them that the Son of Man must undergo great suffering, and be rejected by the elders, the chief priests, and the scribes, and be killed, and after three days rise again. He said all this quite openly. And Peter took him aside and began to rebuke him. But turning and looking at his disciples, he rebuked Peter and said, "Get behind me, Satan! For you are setting your mind not on divine things but on human things."

Notice what you think and feel as you read the gospel.

Jesus tests his disciples about his identity. When Peter proclaims him the Messiah, Jesus teaches them that he will have to undergo great suffering, but Peter doesn't understand that.

Pray as you are led for yourself and others.

"Lord, you suffered, died, and rose again so that I might follow you. I unite my sufferings to yours, including . . ." (Continue in your own words.)

Listen to Jesus.

I have liberated you from sin and death, beloved disciple. Your life has profound meaning for yourself and those I have given you. What else is Jesus saying to you?

Ask God to show you how to live today.

"Let me live and work today with my mind tuned to yours, my heart tuned to heaven. Thank you, Savior. Amen."

Friday, February 22, 2019
Chair of Peter

Know that God is present with you and ready to converse.

"Lord, I am stubborn and weak in faith. Come to me and change me with your holy Word."

Read the gospel: Mark 16:13–19.

Later Jesus appeared to the eleven themselves as they were sitting at the table; and he upbraided them for their lack of faith and stubbornness, because they had not believed those who saw him after he had risen. And he said to them, "Go into all the world and proclaim the good news to the whole creation. The one who believes and is baptized will be saved; but the one who does not believe will be condemned. And these signs will accompany those who believe: by using my name they will cast out demons; they will speak in new tongues; they will pick up snakes in their hands, and if they drink any deadly thing, it will not hurt them; they will lay their hands on the sick, and they will recover."

Notice what you think and feel as you read the gospel.

The risen Jesus appears to his disciples knowing they need instructions. "Go into all the world," he says, "and proclaim the good news to the whole creation." They are to be the instruments of God's salvation, and God will be with them.

Pray as you are led for yourself and others.

"Lord, I admit my lack of faith. Come to me, too, and instruct me so that I can go out and do your will . . ." (Continue in your own words.)

Listen to Jesus.

Give your insecurity to me, then your weakness will contribute to my glory, and I will redeem your soul and the souls of those I have given you. What else is Jesus saying to you?

Ask God to show you how to live today.
"Help me to remember often today that you and your kingdom will come with power. Come, Lord Jesus. Amen."

Saturday, February 23, 2019

Know that God is present with you and ready to converse.
"You are the One of whom the prophets spoke, the Christ, the Savior of the world. Let me know you in your glory."

Read the gospel: Mark 9:2–13.
Six days later, Jesus took with him Peter and James and John, and led them up a high mountain apart, by themselves. And he was transfigured before them, and his clothes became dazzling white, such as no one on earth could bleach them. And there appeared to them Elijah with Moses, who were talking with Jesus. Then Peter said to Jesus, "Rabbi, it is good for us to be here; let us make three dwellings, one for you, one for Moses, and one for Elijah." He did not know what to say, for they were terrified. Then a cloud overshadowed them, and from the cloud there came a voice, "This is my Son, the Beloved; listen to him!" Suddenly when they looked around, they saw no one with them anymore, but only Jesus.

As they were coming down the mountain, he ordered them to tell no one about what they had seen, until after the Son of Man had risen from the dead. So they kept the matter to themselves, questioning what this rising from the dead could mean. Then they asked him, "Why do the scribes say that Elijah must come first?" He said to them, "Elijah is indeed coming first to restore all things. How then is it written about the Son of Man, that he is to go through many sufferings and be treated with contempt? But I tell you that Elijah has come, and they did to him whatever they pleased, as it is written about him."

Notice what you think and feel as you read the gospel.
The Transfiguration of Jesus places him in the Jewish historic and prophetic context, for he is speaking with Elijah and Moses. The Father speaks to the three disciples out of a cloud. Jesus predicts his rising from the dead, but his disciples don't understand.

Pray as you are led for yourself and others.

"Lord, some of your promises are so great I cannot take them in. You foretold your own Resurrection, and you promise me that I also shall be raised. Make this promise real to me . . ." (Continue in your own words.)

Listen to Jesus.

I suffered and died in the flesh so that you could take on my glory and join me in everlasting life. I offer you your heart's desire. What else is Jesus saying to you?

Ask God to show you how to live today.

"Lord, I am ready to follow you through suffering to obtain your glorious kingdom. Remind me of that when I experience suffering today. Amen."

Sunday, February 24, 2019
Seventh Sunday in Ordinary Time

Know that God is present with you and ready to converse.

"Jesus, I praise you. Teach me the holiness of God."

Read the gospel: Luke 6:27–38.

Jesus said, "But I say to you that listen, Love your enemies, do good to those who hate you, bless those who curse you, pray for those who abuse you. If anyone strikes you on the cheek, offer the other also; and from anyone who takes away your coat do not withhold even your shirt. Give to everyone who begs from you; and if anyone takes away your goods, do not ask for them again. Do to others as you would have them do to you.

"If you love those who love you, what credit is that to you? For even sinners love those who love them. If you do good to those who do good to you, what credit is that to you? For even sinners do the same. If you lend to those from whom you hope to receive, what credit is that to you? Even sinners lend to sinners, to receive as much again. But love your enemies, do good, and lend, expecting nothing in return. Your reward will be great, and you will be children of the Most High; for he is kind to the ungrateful and the wicked. Be merciful, just as your Father is merciful.

"Do not judge, and you will not be judged; do not condemn, and you will not be condemned. Forgive, and you will be forgiven; give, and it will be given to you. A good measure, pressed down, shaken together, running over, will be put into your lap; for the measure you give will be the measure you get back."

Notice what you think and feel as you read the gospel.

Jesus lays out his extraordinary standards for ordinary morality in those who follow him. He challenges his hearers to love those who hate and abuse them, as he did when he died on the Cross for sinners. He loved those who were hurting him and asked his Father to forgive them. God has rewarded him. God will reward us for doing the same.

Pray as you are led for yourself and others.

"Lord, give me love like yours. Unless you change my heart, I will not be able to love my enemies. By your grace, I beg you, Lord, give me a heart like yours . . ." (Continue in your own words.)

Listen to Jesus.

I pour into you love and mercy, for you have asked for it. I am happy with you. What else is Jesus saying to you?

Ask God to show you how to live today.

"Make me aware today of someone in my life I find it hard to love. Then let me receive love from you for that person. Help me to persevere in that love. Amen."

Monday, February 25, 2019

Know that God is present with you and ready to converse.

"Jesus, you are so good to be present with me now. Let me learn what you want me to learn today in your Word."

Read the gospel: Mark 9:14–29.

When Jesus, Peter, James, and John came to the disciples, they saw a great crowd around them, and some scribes arguing with them. When the whole crowd saw him, they were immediately overcome with awe, and they ran forward to greet him. He asked them, "What are you arguing about with them?" Someone from the crowd answered him, "Teacher, I brought you my son; he has a spirit that makes him unable to speak; and whenever it seizes him, it dashes him down; and he foams and grinds his teeth and becomes rigid; and I asked your disciples to cast it out, but they could not do so." He answered them, "You faithless generation, how much longer must I be among you? How much longer must I put up with you? Bring him to me." And they brought the boy to him. When the spirit saw him, immediately it threw the boy into convulsions, and he fell on the ground and rolled about, foaming at the mouth. Jesus asked the father, "How long has this been happening to him?" And he said, "From childhood. It has often cast him into the fire and into the water, to destroy him; but if you are able to do anything, have pity on us and help us." Jesus said to him, "If you are able!—All things can be done for the one who believes." Immediately the father of the child cried out, "I believe; help my unbelief!" When Jesus saw that a crowd came running together, he rebuked the unclean spirit, saying to it, "You spirit that keep this boy from speaking and hearing, I command you, come out of him, and never enter him again!" After crying out and convulsing him terribly, it came out, and the boy was like a corpse, so that most of them said, "He is dead." But Jesus took him by the hand and lifted him up, and he was able to stand. When he had entered the house, his disciples asked him privately, "Why could we not cast it out?" He said to them, "This kind can come out only through prayer."

Notice what you think and feel as you read the gospel.

The disciples are unable to cast out a violent spirit. Because they tried and failed, perhaps, people are less able to believe that Jesus can heal the boy. Yet the father cries out, "I believe; help my unbelief!"

Pray as you are led for yourself and others.

"Lord, let me know deep within that all things are possible for the one who believes. Help my unbelief, and heal those you have given me. I think of . . ." (Continue in your own words.)

Listen to Jesus.

You are right to ask for faith, dear one. I am pleased to grant your prayer. What would you like me to do for you? What else is Jesus saying to you?

Ask God to show you how to live today.

"Lord, let me focus on the needs of others today and in your power act to provide for them. Amen."

Tuesday, February 26, 2019

Know that God is present with you and ready to converse.

"Lord, speak to my heart by your mighty Word."

Read the gospel: Mark 9:30–37.

Jesus and his disciples went on from there and passed through Galilee. He did not want anyone to know it; for he was teaching his disciples, saying to them, "The Son of Man is to be betrayed into human hands, and they will kill him, and three days after being killed, he will rise again." But they did not understand what he was saying and were afraid to ask him.

Then they came to Capernaum; and when he was in the house he asked them, "What were you arguing about on the way?" But they were silent, for on the way they had argued with one another about who was the greatest. He sat down, called the twelve, and said to them, "Whoever wants to be first must be last of all and servant of all." Then he took a little child and put it among them; and taking it in his arms, he said to them, "Whoever welcomes one such child in my name welcomes me, and whoever welcomes me welcomes not me but the one who sent me."

Notice what you think and feel as you read the gospel.

The disciples are unable to understand Jesus' prediction of his Passion and Resurrection. They are afraid to ask him for an explanation. Instead they argue on the way about who is the greatest, but they are afraid to admit their petty disagreements. He teaches them with the example of the little child.

Pray as you are led for yourself and others.

"Lord, I, too, am obtuse, and I often miss your point or forget it before I can apply it. Let me welcome a little child. Let me be a servant to others . . ." (Continue in your own words.)

Listen to Jesus.

You will find me in that service, my beloved. In the little child, in the poor and the broken, you will find me. What else is Jesus saying to you?

Ask God to show you how to live today.

"Let me see situations in which I can put myself last and give me the grace to do so, Lord. Amen."

Wednesday, February 27, 2019

Know that God is present with you and ready to converse.

"Jesus, by your Word you convey power and authority. Let me understand you well."

Read the gospel: Mark 9:38–40.

John said to Jesus, "Teacher, we saw someone casting out demons in
your name, and we tried to stop him, because he was not following us."
But Jesus said, "Do not stop him; for no one who does a deed of power
in my name will be able soon afterwards to speak evil of me. Whoever
is not against us is for us."

Notice what you think and feel as you read the gospel.

Jesus asks his disciples to show tolerance to those who preach and work
for religious reasons of their own. Whoever is not against us is for us,
he says.

Pray as you are led for yourself and others.

"Lord, give me a greater tolerance for the ways of others. Let me not
judge them, but instead stay focused on my own work for you . . ."
(Continue in your own words.)

Listen to Jesus.

*I am with my people until the end of the age. Though some may err, I will always
be true. Trust me.* What else is Jesus saying to you?

Ask God to show you how to live today.

"I wish to support and respect all your servants, Lord. Give me opportunity to do so. Amen."

Thursday, February 28, 2019

Know that God is present with you and ready to converse.

"Lord, I read in your presence. Let me be comforted and challenged by
your Word as you deem best for me."

Read the gospel: Mark 9:41–50.

Jesus said, "For truly I tell you, whoever gives you a cup of water to drink
because you bear the name of Christ will by no means lose the reward.

"If any of you put a stumbling block before one of these little ones who believe in me, it would be better for you if a great millstone were hung around your neck and you were thrown into the sea. If your hand causes you to stumble, cut it off; it is better for you to enter life maimed than to have two hands and to go to hell, to the unquenchable fire. And if your foot causes you to stumble, cut it off; it is better for you to enter life lame than to have two feet and to be thrown into hell., And if your eye causes you to stumble, tear it out; it is better for you to enter the kingdom of God with one eye than to have two eyes and to be thrown into hell, where their worm never dies, and the fire is never quenched.

"For everyone will be salted with fire. Salt is good; but if salt has lost its saltiness, how can you season it? Have salt in yourselves, and be at peace with one another."

Notice what you think and feel as you read the gospel.

Jesus urges loving actions, promising rewards, and condemns unloving actions, threatening punishment. He uses the shocking metaphor of cutting off a hand or a foot or tearing out an eye if any of those cause us to sin. He asks us to discipline ourselves, remembering what's at stake.

Pray as you are led for yourself and others.

"Lord, give me that hatred for my own sin. Help me root out my complacency and all habits of sin. Salt me with fire, and I shall enter into your kingdom . . ." (Continue in your own words.)

Listen to Jesus.

Gaze upon me, my beloved disciple, and I will show you your own reflection. If you bring your faults to me, I will cleanse you, heal you, and give you new life. What else is Jesus saying to you?

Ask God to show you how to live today.

"Lord, I accept your discipline in my life. Transform what is displeasing to you into what pleases you. Help me to cooperate with you in this. Amen."

THE POPE'S MONTHLY PRAYER INTENTION FOR MARCH 2019

That Christian communities, especially those who are persecuted, feel that they are close to Christ and have their rights respected.

Friday, March 1, 2019

Know that God is present with you and ready to converse.

"Jesus, guide me into your righteousness by your Word. Open my heart to your goodness."

Read the gospel: Mark 10:1–12.

Jesus left that place and went to the region of Judea and beyond the Jordan. And crowds again gathered around him; and, as was his custom, he again taught them.

Some Pharisees came, and to test him they asked, "Is it lawful for a man to divorce his wife?" He answered them, "What did Moses command you?" They said, "Moses allowed a man to write a certificate of dismissal and to divorce her." But Jesus said to them, "Because of your hardness of heart he wrote this commandment for you. But from the beginning of creation, 'God made them male and female. For this reason a man shall leave his father and mother and be joined to his wife, and the two shall become one flesh.' So they are no longer two, but one flesh. Therefore what God has joined together, let no one separate."

Then in the house the disciples asked him again about this matter. He said to them, "Whoever divorces his wife and marries another commits adultery against her; and if she divorces her husband and marries another, she commits adultery."

Notice what you think and feel as you read the gospel.

Jesus responds to the Pharisees' hard question about divorce by affirming a higher morality in marriage than Moses did. He dignifies marriage as the fulfillment of God's purpose in creating man and woman.

Pray as you are led for yourself and others.

"Merciful Lord, you are full of forgiveness when I err or sin. May my heart never harden toward any to whom I have promised my love. Let me keep all my promises . . ." (Continue in your own words.)

Listen to Jesus.

I understand that relationships can be difficult, my child. You may suffer, but you may also find great joy, as God intended. What else is Jesus saying to you?

Ask God to show you how to live today.

"Lord, I do not wish to take any relationship for granted. Give me the wisdom and grace to right any relationship that is faltering. Help me to obey you, Lord. Thank you. Amen."

Saturday, March 2, 2019

Know that God is present with you and ready to converse.

"Jesus, you love the little children. You see yourself in them. Let me learn from your Word."

Read the gospel: Mark 10:13–16.

People were bringing little children to Jesus in order that he might touch them; and the disciples spoke sternly to them. But when Jesus saw this, he was indignant and said to them, "Let the little children come to me; do not stop them; for it is to such as these that the kingdom of God belongs. Truly I tell you, whoever does not receive the kingdom of God as a little child will never enter it." And he took them up in his arms, laid his hands on them, and blessed them.

Notice what you think and feel as you read the gospel.

The disciples seem to think that the children are a distraction from Jesus' serious work. Jesus rebukes them, "indignant," saying that the kingdom of God is populated by the child-like.

Pray as you are led for yourself and others.

"Lord, a child is fun-loving, trusting, open to love. Show me how to be a child of God . . ." (Continue in your own words.)

Listen to Jesus.

I often call you "child" because you come to me trusting and loving me. I bless you for that, dear child. What else is Jesus saying to you?

Ask God to show you how to live today.

"Reveal to me a moment today when I am not thinking and behaving like a trusting child. Lord, I long for your simplicity in loving. Amen."

Sunday, March 3, 2019
Eighth Sunday in Ordinary Time

Know that God is present with you and ready to converse.

"Lord, I wish to draw nearer to you than ever before. Let your sanctifying Word transform my mind and my heart so that I may please you."

Read the gospel: Luke 6:39–45.

Jesus also told them a parable: "Can a blind person guide a blind person? Will not both fall into a pit? A disciple is not above the teacher, but everyone who is fully qualified will be like the teacher. Why do you see the speck in your neighbour's eye, but do not notice the log in your own eye? Or how can you say to your neighbour, 'Friend, let me take out the speck in your eye,' when you yourself do not see the log in your own eye? You hypocrite, first take the log out of your own eye, and then you will see clearly to take the speck out of your neighbor's eye.

"No good tree bears bad fruit, nor again does a bad tree bear good fruit; for each tree is known by its own fruit. Figs are not gathered from thorns, nor are grapes picked from a bramble bush. The good person out of the good treasure of the heart produces good, and the evil person out of evil treasure produces evil; for it is out of the abundance of the heart that the mouth speaks."

Notice what you think and feel as you read the gospel.

Jesus teaches against judging others and urges his audience to avoid hypocrisy. Instead do good from the heart, and you will bear good fruit.

Pray as you are led for yourself and others.

"Lord, I am guilty of judging others, of feeling superior. Forgive me. Let me serve you and others with a humble heart. I pray for those I have judged . . ." (Continue in your own words.)

Listen to Jesus.
I wish to give you peace and absolute confidence in me, your Shepherd. Follow me; I will be the treasure of your heart, and you will bear much fruit. What else is Jesus saying to you?

Ask God to show you how to live today.
"Lead me today, Lord, and help me follow you humbly and fearlessly. Amen."

Monday, March 4, 2019

Know that God is present with you and ready to converse.
"Lord, I turn to you while you are here with me. I ask you to speak to me in your holy Word."

Read the gospel: Mark 10:17–27.
As Jesus was setting out on a journey, a man ran up and knelt before him, and asked him, "Good Teacher, what must I do to inherit eternal life?" Jesus said to him, "Why do you call me good? No one is good but God alone. You know the commandments: 'You shall not murder; You shall not commit adultery; You shall not steal; You shall not bear false witness; You shall not defraud; Honor your father and mother.'" He said to him, "Teacher, I have kept all these since my youth." Jesus, looking at him, loved him and said, "You lack one thing; go, sell what you own, and give the money to the poor, and you will have treasure in heaven; then come, follow me." When he heard this, he was shocked and went away grieving, for he had many possessions.

Then Jesus looked around and said to his disciples, "How hard it will be for those who have wealth to enter the kingdom of God!" And the disciples were perplexed at these words. But Jesus said to them again, "Children, how hard it is to enter the kingdom of God! It is easier for a camel to go through the eye of a needle than for someone who is rich to enter the kingdom of God." They were greatly astounded and said to one another, "Then who can be saved?" Jesus looked at them and said, "For mortals it is impossible, but not for God; for God all things are possible."

Notice what you think and feel as you read the gospel.
The rich young man had obeyed the commandments of Moses, but he is not ready to obey Jesus' higher call to abandon all and follow him.

Jesus calls him because he loves him, but the man is not yet ready to let go of his wealth.

Pray as you are led for yourself and others.

"Lord, I do not know that I am able to abandon everything for you. What I do possess, let me hold it lightly, ready to let it go. I think of these things . . ." (Continue in your own words.)

Listen to Jesus.

I provide for you, beloved disciple. I ask you to be generous with those in need. What else is Jesus saying to you?

Ask God to show you how to live today.

"I am ready to be generous, Lord. Help me identify opportunities to give. Amen."

Tuesday, March 5, 2019

Know that God is present with you and ready to converse.

"Jesus, what treasure do you have for me in your Word today? Let me take it to heart."

Read the gospel: Mark 10:28–31.

Peter began to say to Jesus, "Look, we have left everything and followed you." Jesus said, "Truly I tell you, there is no one who has left house or brothers or sisters or mother or father or children or fields, for my sake and for the sake of the good news, who will not receive a hundredfold now in this age—houses, brothers and sisters, mothers and children, and fields, with persecutions—and in the age to come eternal life. But many who are first will be last, and the last will be first."

Notice what you think and feel as you read the gospel.

Peter frankly asks Jesus what the disciples will gain by leaving everything and following him and proclaiming the Good News. Jesus says everyone who abandons his or her former life will receive great compensation in this lifetime and in the next life.

Pray as you are led for yourself and others.

"Lord, you suggest that denying ourselves and serving you is joy, not deprivation. I have tasted this joy. Let me give you more and serve you

more fully so that I may enjoy your plenty in this life and the next . . ."
(Continue in your own words.)

Listen to Jesus.

Seek out those who love me, and you will have brothers and sisters. Live the Gospel with them, and you will know peace and joy. What else is Jesus saying to you?

Ask God to show you how to live today.

"Lord, I long for close community with those who love and serve you. Lead me among them. Amen."

The Lenten Season

INTRODUCTION

In the gospel, Jesus says his disciples will fast when he, the Bridegroom, is taken from them. We know that Jesus is always with us, but during the season of Lent we honor him in a special way by entering a forty-day period of prayer, fasting, and almsgiving in preparation for the celebration of the Resurrection of the Lord, Easter Sunday. The forty days of Lent correspond to the forty days Jesus prayed and fasted in the desert before beginning his earthly ministry. Lent is a time to allow God to help us become holy, to help us look to the needs of others and minister to those needs, and most of all, to grow in faith, hope, and love, for those virtues are of God, motivating and empowering us to live the Good News.

The season of Lent begins on Ash Wednesday, dividing the cycle of Ordinary Time in the Church year. Sundays in Lent are not counted as fast days. Fast days continue through Holy Saturday, the day before Easter. Lent officially ends on Holy Thursday, the beginning of the Easter Triduum.

Wednesday, March 6, 2019
Ash Wednesday

Know that God is present with you and ready to converse.
"Draw me nearer to yourself in this season of Lent, Lord. Open me fully to your Word."

Read the gospel: Matthew 6:1–6, 16–18.
Jesus said, "Beware of practicing your piety before others in order to be seen by them; for then you have no reward from your Father in heaven.

"So whenever you give alms, do not sound a trumpet before you, as the hypocrites do in the synagogues and in the streets, so that they may be praised by others. Truly I tell you, they have received their reward. But when you give alms, do not let your left hand know what your right hand is doing, so that your alms may be done in secret; and your Father who sees in secret will reward you.

"And whenever you pray, do not be like the hypocrites; for they love to stand and pray in the synagogues and at the street corners, so that they may be seen by others. Truly I tell you, they have received their reward. But whenever you pray, go into your room and shut the door and pray to your Father who is in secret; and your Father who sees in secret will reward you. . . .

"And whenever you fast, do not look dismal, like the hypocrites, for they disfigure their faces so as to show others that they are fasting. Truly I tell you, they have received their reward. But when you fast, put oil on your head and wash your face, so that your fasting may be seen not by others but by your Father who is in secret; and your Father who sees in secret will reward you."

Notice what you think and feel as you read the gospel.
Jesus says to pray, fast, and do good works in secret. When we desire that others think well of us, we tend to become hypocrites; we should trust God for our reward.

Pray as you are led for yourself and others.
"Lord, help me keep secrets. Let me pray, fast, and give alms in secret today. Let me offer this all for the good of others, especially for . . ."
(Continue in your own words.)

Listen to Jesus.
I love when you pray for others, as it draws you closer to my heart. What else
is Jesus saying to you?

Ask God to show you how to live today.
"Lord, I start Lent with great hope. Give me grace to persevere one day
at a time. Amen."

Thursday, March 7, 2019

Know that God is present with you and ready to converse.
"Jesus, you have the words of eternal life. What must I do to inherit
eternal life?"

Read the gospel: Luke 9:22–25.
Jesus said, "The Son of Man must undergo great suffering, and be
rejected by the elders, chief priests, and scribes, and be killed, and on
the third day be raised."

   Then he said to them all, "If any want to become my followers, let
them deny themselves and take up their cross daily and follow me. For
those who want to save their life will lose it, and those who lose their life
for my sake will save it. What does it profit them if they gain the whole
world, but lose or forfeit themselves?"

Notice what you think and feel as you read the gospel.
Jesus predicts his Passion, Death, and Resurrection, then urges his followers to take up their own crosses daily. If we try to save our own lives,
if we hold too tightly to the things of this earth, we will lose them; but
those who let go, who offer their lives for his sake will save them.

Pray as you are led for yourself and others.
"Lord, teach me your way of self-denial, for I long for eternal life with
you. I give you everything, including . . ." (Continue in your own words.)

Listen to Jesus.
*You have nothing to fear, beloved. As long as I am with you, you have everything
you need.* What else is Jesus saying to you?

Ask God to show you how to live today.

"Put me in situations today, Lord, where I can see my choice of saving or losing my life, and let me choose the way of self-denial, not for my sake but for yours. Amen."

Friday, March 8, 2019

Know that God is present with you and ready to converse.

"Father, Son, and Holy Spirit, one Lord, you are present before me in the Spirit and in the Word. I glorify you."

Read the gospel: Matthew 9:14–15.

Then the disciples of John came to Jesus, saying, "Why do we and the Pharisees fast often, but your disciples do not fast?" And Jesus said to them, "The wedding guests cannot mourn as long as the bridegroom is with them, can they? The days will come when the bridegroom is taken away from them, and then they will fast."

Notice what you think and feel as you read the gospel.

Jesus answers the question posed to him by the disciples of John: Why don't your disciples fast? Jesus' answer points to who he is: the Messiah, the Bridegroom. As wedding guests, his disciples cannot fast.

Pray as you are led for yourself and others.

"Jesus, you are always with me, yet I long to look upon your face. With that hope, let me rejoice as I fast, developing hunger for your loveliness . . ." (Continue in your own words.)

Listen to Jesus.

I am the Bridegroom who embraces you and loves you, dear one. What else is Jesus saying to you?

Ask God to show you how to live today.

"Lord, I cannot do much in my own strength and discipline. I depend upon your grace. I thank you for it, Lord. Amen."

Saturday, March 9, 2019

Know that God is present with you and ready to converse.

"Lord, Creator of All, you made humans in the image of God. You know me inside and out. Let me respond to your call."

Read the gospel: Luke 5:27–32.

After this Jesus went out and saw a tax collector named Levi, sitting at the tax booth; and he said to him, "Follow me." And he got up, left everything, and followed him.

Then Levi gave a great banquet for him in his house; and there was a large crowd of tax-collectors and others sitting at the table with them. The Pharisees and their scribes were complaining to his disciples, saying, "Why do you eat and drink with tax collectors and sinners?" Jesus answered, "Those who are well have no need of a physician, but those who are sick; I have come to call not the righteous but sinners to repentance."

Notice what you think and feel as you read the gospel.

Jesus must have known Levi's willingness of heart when he called him, for Levi simply left everything and followed him immediately. Or did Jesus speak with such authority that his invitation was irresistible?

Pray as you are led for yourself and others.

"Lord, I am a sinner. Call me. Levi became Matthew and served you well. What will you make of me? . . ." (Continue in your own words.)

Listen to Jesus.

Beloved, I will make you my lover, more than spouse, friend, sister, or brother. Our work together starts with our love for one another. What else is Jesus saying to you?

Ask God to show you how to live today.

"If I see someone I judge to be a sinner today, let me pray for him or her, knowing that you love that person and call him or her to yourself. Inspire me to speak or act in a loving way toward that person. Amen."

Sunday, March 10, 2019
First Sunday of Lent

Know that God is present with you and ready to converse.

"Lord, here with me now, let me receive your Word, your Spirit, deep into my soul that I may stand in the hour of my temptation."

Read the gospel: Luke 4:1–13.

Jesus, full of the Holy Spirit, returned from the Jordan and was led by the Spirit in the wilderness, where for forty days he was tempted by the devil. He ate nothing at all during those days, and when they were over, he was famished. The devil said to him, "If you are the Son of God, command this stone to become a loaf of bread." Jesus answered him, "It is written, 'One does not live by bread alone.'"

Then the devil led him up and showed him in an instant all the kingdoms of the world. And the devil said to him, "To you I will give their glory and all this authority; for it has been given over to me, and I give it to anyone I please. If you, then, will worship me, it will all be yours." Jesus answered him, "It is written,

> 'Worship the Lord your God,
>   and serve only him.'"

Then the devil took him to Jerusalem, and placed him on the pinnacle of the temple, saying to him, "If you are the Son of God, throw yourself down from here, for it is written,

> 'He will command his angels concerning you,
>   to protect you,'

and

> 'On their hands they will bear you up,
>   so that you will not dash your foot against a stone.'"

Jesus answered him, "It is said, 'Do not put the Lord your God to the test.'" When the devil had finished every test, he departed from him until an opportune time.

Notice what you think and feel as you read the gospel.

Jesus resists all the temptations of the devil, out-dueling him with scripture. The devil betrays what he himself desires, but Jesus desires only to do the will of his Father. We, too, are to live by every word that proceeds from the mouth of God.

Pray as you are led for yourself and others.

"Lord, I wish to live by your Word. In your name, Jesus, give me power over these temptations in my life . . ." (Continue in your own words.)

Listen to Jesus.

I give you power, dear disciple, to do what you cannot do on your own. Receive the Holy Spirit and overcome temptation. What else is Jesus saying to you?

Ask God to show you how to live today.

"Lord, help me to replace sins and temptations with good and lovely things. Let them be my gifts to others. Amen."

Monday, March 11, 2019

Know that God is present with you and ready to converse.

"Lord, I entrust my personal salvation to you. By your Word, help me to serve you and others in my community."

Read the gospel: Matthew 25:31–40 (Mt 25:31–46).

Jesus said, "When the Son of Man comes in his glory, and all the angels with him, then he will sit on the throne of his glory. All the nations will be gathered before him, and he will separate people one from another as a shepherd separates the sheep from the goats, and he will put the sheep at his right hand and the goats at the left. Then the king will say to those at his right hand, 'Come, you that are blessed by my Father, inherit the kingdom prepared for you from the foundation of the world; for I was hungry and you gave me food, I was thirsty and you gave me something to drink, I was a stranger and you welcomed me, I was naked and you gave me clothing, I was sick and you took care of me, I was in prison and you visited me.' Then the righteous will answer him, 'Lord, when was it that we saw you hungry and gave you food, or thirsty and gave you something to drink? And when was it that we saw you a stranger and welcomed you, or naked and gave you clothing? And when was it that we saw you sick or in prison and visited you?' And the king will answer them, 'Truly I tell you, just as you did it to one of the least of these who are members of my family, you did it to me.'"

Notice what you think and feel as you read the gospel.

In Jesus' prophecy of the judgment of the nations, the Son of Man will commend those persons who served the poor and needy, for he identifies with them. The Lord of Judgment will condemn those people who ignored the poor and needy. Ours is the age of redemption and grace.

Pray as you are led for yourself and others.

"Lord, what can I do to serve you in the hungry, poor, homeless, lost, or lonely? Give me eyes to see you . . ." (Continue in your own words.)

Listen to Jesus.

Your love for me will express itself in service to those who suffer. I will show you opportunities, dear disciple. What else is Jesus saying to you?

Ask God to show you how to live today.

"Lord, open my eyes and my heart to opportunities. Let me see you. Thank you. Amen."

Tuesday, March 12, 2019

Know that God is present with you and ready to converse.

"Lord, teach me to pray."

Read the gospel: Matthew 6:7–15.

Jesus said, "When you are praying, do not heap up empty phrases as the Gentiles do; for they think that they will be heard because of their many words. Do not be like them, for your Father knows what you need before you ask him.

"Pray then in this way:

Our Father in heaven,
hallowed be your name.
Your kingdom come.
Your will be done,
on earth as it is in heaven.
Give us this day our daily bread.
And forgive us our debts,
as we also have forgiven our debtors.
And do not bring us to the time of trial,
but rescue us from the evil one.

For if you forgive others their trespasses, your heavenly Father will also forgive you; but if you do not forgive others, neither will your Father forgive your trespasses."

Notice what you think and feel as you read the gospel.

Jesus' great prayer expresses priorities in our relationship with God and others. First we glorify the Father, seeking the kingdom, embracing God's will on earth. Then we ask for bread, the necessities of our lives. We ask God's forgiveness and offer our own forgiveness of others' sins against us. Finally we ask for endurance in difficult times and salvation from evil.

Pray as you are led for yourself and others.

"Jesus, you point out especially our need to forgive others. As I examine my heart, help me forgive these people who have hurt me . . ." (Continue in your own words.)

Listen to Jesus.

The love in your life must often take the form of mercy, my child. Do not judge others. I give you eyes of mercy. What else is Jesus saying to you?

Ask God to show you how to live today.

"Chances are that someone will offend me today, Jesus. Give me grace to forgive that person immediately. Make mercy a habit of my heart. Amen."

Wednesday, March 13, 2019

Know that God is present with you and ready to converse.

"Jesus, speak to me by your Word."

Read the gospel: Luke 11:29–32.

When the crowds were increasing, Jesus began to say, "This generation is an evil generation; it asks for a sign, but no sign will be given to it except the sign of Jonah. For just as Jonah became a sign to the people of Nineveh, so the Son of Man will be to this generation. The queen of the South will rise at the judgment with the people of this generation and condemn them, because she came from the ends of the earth to listen to the wisdom of Solomon, and see, something greater than Solomon is here! The people of Nineveh will rise up at the judgment with this generation and condemn it, because they repented at the proclamation of Jonah, and see, something greater than Jonah is here!"

Notice what you think and feel as you read the gospel.
Jesus deplores those who seek a sign from him. He likens himself to Jonah, who preached repentance; Jesus tells the crowd that he is greater than Jonah, greater even than Solomon, for he is the Son of God.

Pray as you are led for yourself and others.
"Lord, you are here. Let me repent at your command and listen to your wisdom. I open myself to understand what you are saying to me now . . ." (Continue in your own words.)

Listen to Jesus.
I am, beloved disciple, the Son of the Father. My words have the power to save you. I have some things I want you to do. What else is Jesus saying to you?

Ask God to show you how to live today.
"Although I am a sinner, I give myself to you for forgiveness, cleansing, and service today. Let me please you, Blessed Lord. Amen."

Thursday, March 14, 2019

Know that God is present with you and ready to converse.
"Gracious Father, always near me, let me pray well and learn by your Word to do your will."

Read the gospel: Matthew 7:7–12.
Jesus said, "Ask, and it will be given to you; search, and you will find; knock, and the door will be opened for you. For everyone who asks receives, and everyone who searches finds, and for everyone who knocks, the door will be opened. Is there anyone among you who, if your child asks for bread, will give a stone? Or if the child asks for a fish, will give a snake? If you then, who are evil, know how to give good gifts to your children, how much more will your Father in heaven give good things to those who ask him!

"In everything do to others as you would have them do to you; for this is the law and the prophets."

Notice what you think and feel as you read the gospel.
Jesus urges us to ask, search, and knock, requesting from God what we desire. God will give us only good things. Our job? To do to others as we would have them do to us.

Pray as you are led for yourself and others.
"Lord, focus me on what I may do for others. Let me do those things and then return to ask you for the good things I need . . ." (Continue in your own words.)

Listen to Jesus.
It is sweet to be in conversation with you, dear one. Through our intimacy, our friendship will grow into everlasting life in the kingdom of my Father. Desire that. Ask for it. What else is Jesus saying to you?

Ask God to show you how to live today.
"Help me to discern between good things and those things that only appear good. Then let me ask for the good things, Lord. Praise your holy name! Amen."

Friday, March 15, 2019

Know that God is present with you and ready to converse.
"Holy Lord, you are just. Teach me by your Word lest I sin against you or my brother or my sister."

Read the gospel: Matthew 5:20–26.
Jesus said, "For I tell you, unless your righteousness exceeds that of the scribes and Pharisees, you will never enter the kingdom of heaven.

"You have heard that it was said to those of ancient times, 'You shall not murder'; and 'whoever murders shall be liable to judgment.' But I say to you that if you are angry with a brother or sister, you will be liable to judgment; and if you insult a brother or sister, you will be liable to the council; and if you say, 'You fool,' you will be liable to the hell of fire. So when you are offering your gift at the altar, if you remember that your brother or sister has something against you, leave your gift there before the altar and go; first be reconciled to your brother or sister, and then come and offer your gift. Come to terms quickly with your accuser while you are on the way to court with him, or your accuser may hand you over to the judge, and the judge to the guard, and you will be thrown into prison. Truly I tell you, you will never get out until you have paid the last penny."

Notice what you think and feel as you read the gospel.

Jesus raises the standard set by Moses's commandments and asks us to take the first step toward reconciliation even when the other person is angry toward us.

Pray as you are led for yourself and others.

"Lord, who in my life is angry with me, harboring grudges against me, offended by me? Lord, I pray for these . . ." (Continue in your own words.)

Listen to Jesus.

I will give you opportunities to reconcile with those with whom you need to reconcile. Be open to these opportunities so there can be healing. What else is Jesus saying to you?

Ask God to show you how to live today.

"My life is complicated, Lord. Sometimes I feel I drag my sins along with me. Give me hope and strength, Jesus. Amen."

Saturday, March 16, 2019

Know that God is present with you and ready to converse.

"Jesus, risen Lord, I listen to your Word today. "

Read the gospel: Matthew 5:43–48.

Jesus said, "You have heard that it was said, 'You shall love your neighbor and hate your enemy.' But I say to you, Love your enemies and pray for those who persecute you, so that you may be children of your Father in heaven; for he makes his sun rise on the evil and on the good, and sends rain on the righteous and on the unrighteous. For if you love those who love you, what reward do you have? Do not even the tax collectors do the same? And if you greet only your brothers and sisters, what more are you doing than others? Do not even the Gentiles do the same? Be perfect, therefore, as your heavenly Father is perfect."

Notice what you think and feel as you read the gospel.

Again Jesus raises the bar. He calls us to holiness, the very perfection of the heavenly Father. This holiness requires us to love our enemies and our persecutors, just as God does.

Pray as you are led for yourself and others.

"Lord, I am far from your holiness, but I open my heart for your enabling grace. Who is my enemy, who persecutes me? These people will I love . . ." (Continue in your own words.)

Listen to Jesus.

In humility you learn to love those who oppose you. See others with the mercy I give you. What else is Jesus saying to you?

Ask God to show you how to live today.

"Every day is a new chance to obey your Spirit and act in love. Prepare me for those moments today. Let me succeed in loving someone who hates me or hurts me. Amen."

Sunday, March 17, 2019
Second Sunday of Lent

Know that God is present with you and ready to converse.

"Jesus, you were God among us, and your glory was to die for us. Thank you for being with me now as I read your Word."

Read the gospel: Luke 9:28b–36.

Jesus took with him Peter and John and James, and went up on the mountain to pray. And while he was praying, the appearance of his face changed, and his clothes became dazzling white. Suddenly they saw two men, Moses and Elijah, talking to him. They appeared in glory and were speaking of his departure, which he was about to accomplish at Jerusalem. Now Peter and his companions were weighed down with sleep; but since they had stayed awake, they saw his glory and the two men who stood with him. Just as they were leaving him, Peter said to Jesus, "Master, it is good for us to be here; let us make three dwellings, one for you, one for Moses, and one for Elijah"—not knowing what he said. While he was saying this, a cloud came and overshadowed them; and they were terrified as they entered the cloud. Then from the cloud came a voice that said, "This is my Son, my Chosen; listen to him!" When the voice had spoken, Jesus was found alone. And they kept silent and in those days told no one any of the things they had seen.

Notice what you think and feel as you read the gospel.

Peter, James, and John are amazed by Jesus' Transfiguration before them and his meeting with Moses and Elijah. Then the voice from the cloud proclaims the Father's love for the Son and commands that they "listen to him." They are struck speechless by what they've seen and do not tell anyone about it until after the Resurrection.

Pray as you are led for yourself and others.

"Jesus, I believe you are the Son of God, and I put my trust in you. Will you help me do your will? . . ." (Continue in your own words.)

Listen to Jesus.

Lean on my grace, my child, for you are beloved of my Father, too. What else is Jesus saying to you?

Ask God to show you how to live today.

"If I feel your presence with me today, let me praise you and do your will. If I do not feel your presence today, let me praise you and do your will. You are Lord! Amen."

Monday, March 18, 2019

Know that God is present with you and ready to converse.

"Merciful God, I depend on you for repentance, forgiveness, and sanctification."

Read the gospel: Luke 6:36–38.

Jesus said, "Be merciful, just as your Father is merciful.

"Do not judge, and you will not be judged; do not condemn, and you will not be condemned. Forgive, and you will be forgiven; give, and it will be given to you. A good measure, pressed down, shaken together, running over, will be put into your lap; for the measure you give will be the measure you get back."

Notice what you think and feel as you read the gospel.

Jesus commands us to be merciful toward others as God is. He commands us not to judge or condemn, reminding us to forgive and be generous.

Pray as you are led for yourself and others.

"Lord, I see faults in others often. I cannot help but judge. Cleanse me of this judgmental mindset. Give me your true mercy for . . ." (Continue in your own words.)

Listen to Jesus.

I love your sincere efforts to be made new and pleasing to God. You must rely on my grace at every step. As you allow me to work holiness in you, I shall work. What else is Jesus saying to you?

Ask God to show you how to live today.

"Lord, help me to strive to avoid sin and do good today. Pick me up when I fall and put me back on your path by your grace. Amen."

Tuesday, March 19, 2019
Joseph, Husband of Mary

Know that God is present with you and ready to converse.

"Lord, you are high and lifted up in glory even as you are here with me now. I seek your guidance for my life in your Word."

Read the gospel: Matthew 1:16, 18–21, 24a.

Jacob [was] the father of Joseph the husband of Mary, of whom Jesus was born, who is called the Messiah. . . .

Now the birth of Jesus the Messiah took place in this way. When his mother Mary had been engaged to Joseph, but before they lived together, she was found to be with child from the Holy Spirit. Her husband Joseph, being a righteous man and unwilling to expose her to public disgrace, planned to dismiss her quietly. But just when he had resolved to do this, an angel of the Lord appeared to him in a dream and said, "Joseph, son of David, do not be afraid to take Mary as your wife, for the child conceived in her is from the Holy Spirit. She will bear a son, and you are to name him Jesus, for he will save his people from their sins." . . .

When Joseph awoke from sleep, he did as the angel of the Lord commanded him; he took her as his wife.

Notice what you think and feel as you read the gospel.

Joseph heard the guidance from the Lord and obeyed it, even though this guidance was counter to his culture's mores.

Pray as you are led for yourself and others.

"You guide me, Lord, to seek humble obedience that I may do your will and advance the kingdom of God in my life. Lord, I pray for humility and obedience among all who follow you . . ." (Continue in your own words.)

Listen to Jesus.

You will live in joy, my child, as you embrace the role of the obedient servant with all your heart. What else is Jesus saying to you?

Ask God to show you how to live today.

"How may I serve today, Lord? Open my eyes and heart to serving you in others. Thank you for your light, Lord. Amen."

Wednesday, March 20, 2019

Know that God is present with you and ready to converse.

"Lord, let your Word today take my mind off of me and place it on you. Let me hold you in my heart with gratitude and love."

Read the gospel: Matthew 20:17–28.

While Jesus was going up to Jerusalem, he took the twelve disciples aside by themselves, and said to them on the way, "See, we are going up to Jerusalem, and the Son of Man will be handed over to the chief priests and scribes, and they will condemn him to death; then they will hand him over to the Gentiles to be mocked and flogged and crucified; and on the third day he will be raised."

Then the mother of the sons of Zebedee came to him with her sons, and kneeling before him, she asked a favor of him. And he said to her, "What do you want?" She said to him, "Declare that these two sons of mine will sit, one at your right hand and one at your left, in your kingdom." But Jesus answered, "You do not know what you are asking. Are you able to drink the cup that I am about to drink?" They said to him, "We are able." He said to them, "You will indeed drink my cup, but to sit at my right hand and at my left, this is not mine to grant, but it is for those for whom it has been prepared by my Father."

When the ten heard it, they were angry with the two brothers. But Jesus called them to him and said, "You know that the rulers of the Gentiles lord it over them, and their great ones are tyrants over them. It will not be so among you; but whoever wishes to be great among you must be your servant, and whoever wishes to be first among you must be your slave; just as the Son of Man came not to be served but to serve, and to give his life a ransom for many."

Notice what you think and feel as you read the gospel.

The disciples don't really hear Jesus' announcement of his coming Passion, Death, and Resurrection in Jerusalem. They are caught up in their own jockeying for honor and authority. Jesus tells them that the one who would be great must be a servant, a slave, just like the Son of Man.

Pray as you are led for yourself and others.

"I give myself to you and to others today, Lord. I want to serve as you served. Give me the strength to drink from your cup, and guide me . . ." (Continue in your own words.)

Listen to Jesus.

Dearly beloved, I am here to serve you. You wish to be like me in serving others. I will show you how and give you grace to do it. What else is Jesus saying to you?

Ask God to show you how to live today.

"Lord, help me develop a servant's attitude and give me opportunities to serve. I have a new start every day in your grace. Glory to you, Lord. Amen."

Thursday, March 21, 2019

Know that God is present with you and ready to converse.

"Jesus, I live in a world of spirits. Protect me from evil in every form. Let me be with you."

Read the gospel: Luke 16:19–31.

Jesus said to the disciples, "There was a rich man who was dressed in purple and fine linen and who feasted sumptuously every day. And at his gate lay a poor man named Lazarus, covered with sores, who longed to satisfy his hunger with what fell from the rich man's table; even the dogs would come and lick his sores. The poor man died and was carried away by the angels to be with Abraham. The rich man also died and was buried. In Hades, where he was being tormented, he looked up and saw Abraham far away with Lazarus by his side. He called out, 'Father Abraham, have mercy on me, and send Lazarus to dip the tip of his finger in water and cool my tongue; for I am in agony in these flames.' But

Abraham said, 'Child, remember that during your lifetime you received your good things, and Lazarus in like manner evil things; but now he is comforted here, and you are in agony. Besides all this, between you and us a great chasm has been fixed, so that those who might want to pass from here to you cannot do so, and no one can cross from there to us.' He said, 'Then, father, I beg you to send him to my father's house—for I have five brothers—that he may warn them, so that they will not also come into this place of torment.' Abraham replied, 'They have Moses and the prophets; they should listen to them.' He said, 'No, father Abraham; but if someone goes to them from the dead, they will repent.' He said to him, 'If they do not listen to Moses and the prophets, neither will they be convinced even if someone rises from the dead.'"

Notice what you think and feel as you read the gospel.

In this parable, Jesus shows that those who ignore the needs of their fellow people in this life will be judged harshly in the next life.

Pray as you are led for yourself and others.

"Lord, help me see all who are in need. Let me never be blind to those who are less fortunate . . ." (Continue in your own words.)

Listen to Jesus.

Just as I care for you, so you should care for others. In your love of them, you show your love for me. What else is Jesus saying to you?

Ask God to show you how to live today.

"Lord, your love gives me the strength to love all people. Let this knowledge inform all my interactions, Blessed Savior. Amen."

Friday, March 22, 2019

Know that God is present with you and ready to converse.

"Jesus, sometimes people do not understand you; sometimes they do and yet fail to respond. Let me understand your Word and respond."

Read the gospel: Matthew 21:33–41 (Mt 21:33–43, 45–46).

Jesus said, "Listen to another parable. There was a landowner who planted a vineyard, put a fence around it, dug a wine press in it, and built a watchtower. Then he leased it to tenants and went to another country. When the harvest time had come, he sent his slaves to the tenants to collect his produce. But the tenants seized his slaves and beat one, killed another, and stoned another. Again he sent other slaves, more than the first; and they treated them in the same way. Finally he sent his son to them, saying, 'They will respect my son.' But when the tenants saw the son, they said to themselves, 'This is the heir; come, let us kill him and get his inheritance.' So they seized him, threw him out of the vineyard, and killed him. Now when the owner of the vineyard comes, what will he do to those tenants?" They said to him, "He will put those wretches to a miserable death, and lease the vineyard to other tenants who will give him the produce at the harvest time."

Notice what you think and feel as you read the gospel.

In this parable, the tenants wish to exploit the property of the land-owner. They reject all emissaries who assert the landowner's claim on the vineyard. When the landowner sends his son, they kill him. Even Jesus' audiences recognize the injustice in that.

Pray as you are led for yourself and others.

"Jesus, you know people so well. You speak so clearly to us about our nature. I come to you asking for a new nature, the one you suffered and died to give me. I ask for . . ." (Continue in your own words.)

Listen to Jesus.

I am pleased to give you what you ask for, beloved disciple. Come to me often with simple sincerity. What else is Jesus saying to you?

Ask God to show you how to live today.

"Jesus, let me work for you today, pleasing you and leaving the results to you. Let me trust in the power of acting in love even if I do not see results. Amen."

Saturday, March 23, 2019

Know that God is present with you and ready to converse.

"Father, your Son proclaimed your mercy and your greatness to the world. Give me a fresh love for you by his Word."

Read the gospel: Luke 15:11–24 (Lk 15:1–3, 11–32).

Then Jesus said, "There was a man who had two sons. The younger of them said to his father, 'Father, give me the share of the property that will belong to me.' So he divided his property between them. A few days later the younger son gathered all he had and travelled to a distant country, and there he squandered his property in dissolute living. When he had spent everything, a severe famine took place throughout that country, and he began to be in need. So he went and hired himself out to one of the citizens of that country, who sent him to his fields to feed the pigs. He would gladly have filled himself with the pods that the pigs were eating; and no one gave him anything. But when he came to himself he said, 'How many of my father's hired hands have bread enough and to spare, but here I am dying of hunger! I will get up and go to my father, and I will say to him, "Father, I have sinned against heaven and before you; I am no longer worthy to be called your son; treat me like one of your hired hands."' So he set off and went to his father. But while he was still far off, his father saw him and was filled with compassion; he ran and put his arms around him and kissed him. Then the son said to him, 'Father, I have sinned against heaven and before you; I am no longer worthy to be called your son.' But the father said to his slaves, 'Quickly, bring out a robe—the best one—and put it on him; put a ring on his finger and sandals on his feet. And get the fatted calf and kill it, and let us eat and celebrate; for this son of mine was dead and is alive again; he was lost and is found!' And they began to celebrate."

Notice what you think and feel as you read the gospel.

In this great parable, the younger son leaves home to waste time and money in self-indulgence. When he finds misery instead of freedom and pleasure, he returns repentant to his father, who welcomes him with joy.

Pray as you are led for yourself and others.

"Lord, I am a sinner, craving your mercy and love. I am aware that I deserve neither. How many ways can I praise you? . . ." (Continue in your own words.)

Listen to Jesus.

God is always good—do not forget it. Let God's mercy draw you back home. What else is Jesus saying to you?

Ask God to show you how to live today.

"Thank you for your mercy to me, Lord. Let me never forget how you have lifted me out of selfishness to depend on you and serve you all the days of my life. Amen."

Sunday, March 24, 2019
Third Sunday of Lent

Know that God is present with you and ready to converse.
"Jesus, I see great suffering in the world. Give me your light from your Word."

Read the gospel: Luke 13:1–9.

At that very time there were some present who told Jesus about the Galileans whose blood Pilate had mingled with their sacrifices. He asked them, "Do you think that because these Galileans suffered in this way they were worse sinners than all other Galileans? No, I tell you; but unless you repent, you will all perish as they did. Or those eighteen who were killed when the tower of Siloam fell on them—do you think that they were worse offenders than all the others living in Jerusalem? No, I tell you; but unless you repent, you will all perish just as they did."

Then he told this parable: "A man had a fig tree planted in his vineyard; and he came looking for fruit on it and found none. So he said to the gardener, 'See here! For three years I have come looking for fruit on this fig tree, and still I find none. Cut it down! Why should it be wasting the soil?' He replied, 'Sir, let it alone for one more year, until I dig round it and put manure on it. If it bears fruit next year, well and good; but if not, you can cut it down.'"

Notice what you think and feel as you read the gospel.

Jesus tells his hearers not to assume those who suffer in this life are greater sinners than those who do not. Jesus urges repentance to avoid a similar fate as the Galileans who had been killed by Pilate. In his parable about the fruitless tree, Jesus urges effort and patience, in the hope that the tree will yet bear fruit. If it doesn't bear fruit, it will be cut down. God is patient with us, but we are asked to bear fruit.

Pray as you are led for yourself and others.

"Lord, let me not judge those who suffer or attribute their suffering to you. Let me attend to myself and labor for you to bear fruit in my time. I pray now for . . ." (Continue in your own words.)

Listen to Jesus.

See, my child, I have much to teach you. I offer you the opportunity to see others with God's eyes. I love you. Reach out to those who suffer. What else is Jesus saying to you?

Ask God to show you how to live today.

"Lord, thank you for your wisdom. I resolve to obey you. Help me to reach out to those who suffer. Amen."

Monday, March 25, 2019
Annunciation of the Lord

Know that God is present with you and ready to converse.

"Here am I before you, Lord, God of Hosts. Teach me by your Word to do your will."

Read the gospel: Luke 1:26–38.

In the sixth month the angel Gabriel was sent by God to a town in Galilee called Nazareth, to a virgin engaged to a man whose name was Joseph, of the house of David. The virgin's name was Mary. And he came to her and said, "Greetings, favored one! The Lord is with you." But she was much perplexed by his words and pondered what sort of greeting this might be. The angel said to her, "Do not be afraid, Mary, for you have found favor with God. And now, you will conceive in your womb and bear a son, and you will name him Jesus. He will be great, and will be called the Son of the Most High, and the Lord God will give to him the throne of his ancestor David. He will reign over the house of Jacob for ever, and of his kingdom there will be no end." Mary said to the angel, "How can this be, since I am a virgin?" The angel said to her, "The Holy Spirit will come upon you, and the power of the Most High will overshadow you; therefore the child to be born will be holy; he will be called Son of God. And now, your relative Elizabeth in her old age has also conceived a son; and this is the sixth month for her who was said to be barren. For nothing will be impossible with God." Then Mary said, "Here am I, the servant of the Lord; let it be with me according to your word." Then the angel departed from her.

Notice what you think and feel as you read the gospel.

Usually in scripture people who see angels are stricken with fear, yet Mary is not afraid of the angel but perplexed by the greeting and by the prophetic message that she will be the mother of the Son of the Most High God. But her spirit is open and she says yes to the Holy Spirit.

Pray as you are led for yourself and others.

"Mary, I honor you for your willingness to be the Mother of God. I bless you. I ask your prayers, Mother, for these . . ." (Continue in your own words.)

Listen to Jesus.

I love my mother, too, and honor her as you do. She prays for you and all her children. God hears her. What else is Jesus saying to you?

Ask God to show you how to live today.

"Lord, by your grace help me to say yes to your will today. Show me that nothing is impossible with God. Amen."

Tuesday, March 26, 2019

Know that God is present with you and ready to converse.

"Father, let me eat the food your Son, Jesus Christ, gives to me. He is the Word, and he feeds me with himself."

Read the gospel: John 4:5–10, 27–42 (Jn 4:5–42).

So Jesus came to a Samaritan city called Sychar, near the plot of ground that Jacob had given to his son Joseph. Jacob's well was there, and Jesus, tired out by his journey, was sitting by the well. It was about noon.

A Samaritan woman came to draw water, and Jesus said to her, "Give me a drink." (His disciples had gone to the city to buy food.) The Samaritan woman said to him, "How is it that you, a Jew, ask a drink of me, a woman of Samaria?" (Jews do not share things in common with Samaritans.) Jesus answered her, "If you knew the gift of God, and who it is that is saying to you, 'Give me a drink,' you would have asked him, and he would have given you living water." . . .

Just then his disciples came. They were astonished that he was speaking with a woman, but no one said, "What do you want?" or, "Why are you speaking with her?" Then the woman left her water jar and went back to the city. She said to the people, "Come and see a man who told me everything I have ever done! He cannot be the Messiah, can he?" They left the city and were on their way to him.

Meanwhile the disciples were urging him, "Rabbi, eat something." But he said to them, "I have food to eat that you do not know about." So the disciples said to one another, "Surely no one has brought him something to eat?" Jesus said to them, "My food is to do the will of him who sent me and to complete his work. Do you not say, 'Four months more, then comes the harvest'? But I tell you, look around you, and see how the fields are ripe for harvesting. The reaper is already receiving wages and is gathering fruit for eternal life, so that sower and reaper may rejoice together. For here the saying holds true, 'One sows and another reaps.' I sent you to reap that for which you did not labor. Others have labored, and you have entered into their labor."

Many Samaritans from that city believed in him because of the woman's testimony, "He told me everything I have ever done." So when the Samaritans came to him, they asked him to stay with them; and he stayed there for two days. And many more believed because of his word. They said to the woman, "It is no longer because of what you said that we believe, for we have heard for ourselves, and we know that this is truly the Savior of the world."

Notice what you think and feel as you read the gospel.

Jesus is exhausted by his journey, yet instead of satiating his own hunger, he first does the will of his Father, calling sinners to return to him. Instead of slaking his own thirst, he pours out the living water for the Samaritan woman.

Pray as you are led for yourself and others.

"Lord, I too get exhausted on the journey of life. Pour out your living water for me; feed me, and all those you've given me, with a hunger for God's will . . ." (Continue in your own words.)

Listen to Jesus.

This is the journey of faith, dear disciple. Entrust yourself entirely to God, giving up your own will and seeking God's. God will work in your life and bless you. What else is Jesus saying to you?

Ask God to show you how to live today.

"Lord, I abandon all to you today. Take all of me and do with me what you will. I seek your power to do what pleases you. Amen."

Wednesday, March 27, 2019

Know that God is present with you and ready to converse.

"Lord, give me deep understanding of your commandments by your Word."

Read the gospel: Matthew 5:17–19.

Jesus said, "Do not think that I have come to abolish the law or the prophets; I have come not to abolish but to fulfill. For truly I tell you, until heaven and earth pass away, not one letter, not one stroke of a letter, will pass from the law until all is accomplished. Therefore, whoever breaks one of the least of these commandments, and teaches others to do the same, will be called least in the kingdom of heaven; but whoever does them and teaches them will be called great in the kingdom of heaven."

Notice what you think and feel as you read the gospel.

Jesus says he fulfills the law and the prophets and that all they have said will come to pass. Those who break the commandments will be called least in the kingdom, especially those who teach others to break them.

Pray as you are led for yourself and others.

"Lord, let me not abuse the liberty of your law of love, which comprises all of the law and the prophets. Let me understand deeply that God's morality is exacting and I am called to obedience, not for the sake of legality but for the sake of love. Keep me from leading any of these into error . . ." (Continue in your own words.)

Listen to Jesus.

The proper fear of God is to guard yourself and your heart that you may not offend God. If you sin, you may come to the infinite forgiveness I offer. I will wash you white as snow. What else is Jesus saying to you?

Ask God to show you how to live today.

"Lord, I place my sinful self in your hands. Only you can forgive and cleanse me. Give me your Spirit that I may walk in your grace and reflect your grace upon others. Amen."

Thursday, March 28, 2019

Know that God is present with you and ready to converse.

"Lord, I live in a world full of spiritual forces. I seek only you by the Holy Spirit. Let the Spirit illuminate your Word to me."

Read the gospel: Luke 11:14–23.

Now Jesus was casting out a demon that was mute; when the demon had gone out, the one who had been mute spoke, and the crowds were amazed. But some of them said, "He casts out demons by Beelzebul, the ruler of the demons." Others, to test him, kept demanding from him a sign from heaven. But he knew what they were thinking and said to them, "Every kingdom divided against itself becomes a desert, and house falls on house. If Satan also is divided against himself, how will his kingdom stand?—for you say that I cast out the demons by Beelzebul. Now if I cast out the demons by Beelzebul, by whom do your exorcists cast them out? Therefore they will be your judges. But if it is by the finger of God that I cast out the demons, then the kingdom of God has come to you. When a strong man, fully armed, guards his castle, his property is safe. But when one stronger than he attacks him and overpowers him, he takes away his armor in which he trusted and divides his plunder. Whoever is not with me is against me, and whoever does not gather with me scatters."

Notice what you think and feel as you read the gospel.

Seeing his power over evil spirits, some in the crowd accuse Jesus of being in league with Satan, Beelzebul. Jesus repudiates that idea, pointing out that a divided kingdom cannot stand. He describes himself as a man stronger than the strong man, for Jesus exercises the power of God.

Pray as you are led for yourself and others.

"Lord, protect me and those I love from evil. Vanquish evil by your power, and let us all gather with you . . ." (Continue in your own words.)

Listen to Jesus.

Dearest soul, I am your protector. Sometimes you will be opposed by powers greater than yourself. Always turn to me, trusting me and praying for my protection, for there is no power greater than I. What else is Jesus saying to you?

Ask God to show you how to live today.

"Lord, if there is any evil jeopardizing me or those you have given me, direct me to pray. Give me discernment that I may turn to you for all rescue and protection. Thank you, mighty Savior. Amen."

Friday, March 29, 2019

Know that God is present with you and ready to converse.

"Lord, I am here before you, hungry for your Word."

Read the gospel: Mark 12:28–34.

One of the scribes came near and heard them disputing with one another, and seeing that Jesus answered them well, he asked Jesus, "Which commandment is the first of all?" Jesus answered, "The first is, 'Hear, O Israel: the Lord our God, the Lord is one; you shall love the Lord your God with all your heart, and with all your soul, and with all your mind, and with all your strength.' The second is this, 'You shall love your neighbor as yourself.' There is no other commandment greater than these." Then the scribe said to him, "You are right, Teacher; you have truly said that 'he is one, and besides him there is no other'; and 'to love him with all the heart, and with all the understanding, and with all the strength,' and 'to love one's neighbor as oneself,'—this is much more important than all whole burnt offerings and sacrifices." When Jesus saw that he answered wisely, he said to him, "You are not far from the kingdom of God." After that no one dared to ask him any question.

Notice what you think and feel as you read the gospel.

Jesus must have loved the scribe who understood the greatest commandments of the law. Loving God and one's neighbor includes all the commandments of the law and the prophets. Jesus assures the scribe he is "not far" from the kingdom.

Pray as you are led for yourself and others.

"Lord, I embrace your law of love. Fill me with the love in your own heart. Let me love others as you loved the scribe . . ." (Continue in your own words.)

Listen to Jesus.

In love is all your power, dear disciple. Take up your cross and follow me in your journey of love. What else is Jesus saying to you?

Ask God to show you how to live today.

"Lord, if you walk with me, I can bear my cross today. Fill me with love for others so that I may love with your love. I glorify your name, Blessed Savior. Amen."

Saturday, March 30, 2019

Know that God is present with you and ready to converse.

"Lord, I seek your righteousness and your wisdom. By your holy Word, show me how to obtain them."

Read the gospel: Luke 18:9–14.

Jesus also told this parable to some who trusted in themselves that they were righteous and regarded others with contempt: "Two men went up to the temple to pray, one a Pharisee and the other a tax collector. The Pharisee, standing by himself, was praying thus, 'God, I thank you that I am not like other people: thieves, rogues, adulterers, or even like this tax collector. I fast twice a week; I give a tenth of all my income.' But the tax collector, standing far off, would not even look up to heaven, but was beating his breast and saying, 'God, be merciful to me, a sinner!' I tell you, this man went down to his home justified rather than the other; for all who exalt themselves will be humbled, but all who humble themselves will be exalted."

Notice what you think and feel as you read the gospel.

Jesus knows it's human nature to honor oneself. This trait makes us judge others. The sinful tax collector acknowledges his sin to God, while the Pharisee vaunts his own virtues. The tax collector, Jesus says, goes home forgiven. The Pharisee has yet to learn humility.

Pray as you are led for yourself and others.

"God be merciful to me, a sinner! I pray for those who have difficulty repenting . . ." (Continue in your own words.)

Listen to Jesus.

I forgive you, beloved follower. I give you light to recognize your sins in this season. Take it to heart and seek my mercy and cleansing. This is how you grow in the Lord. What else is Jesus saying to you?

Ask God to show you how to live today.

"Lord, I praise you for the greatness of your mercy! Help me to live today both in contrition, knowing my many sins, and in joy and awe at your goodness. Amen."

Sunday, March 31, 2019
Fourth Sunday of Lent

Know that God is present with you and ready to converse.

"Lord, I sometimes wander away from you and your love. Teach me how to return through your Word."

Read the gospel: Luke 15:11–32 (Lk 15:1–3, 11–32).

Then Jesus said, "There was a man who had two sons. The younger of them said to his father, 'Father, give me the share of the property that will belong to me.' So he divided his property between them. A few days later the younger son gathered all he had and travelled to a distant country, and there he squandered his property in dissolute living. When he had spent everything, a severe famine took place throughout that country, and he began to be in need. So he went and hired himself out to one of the citizens of that country, who sent him to his fields to feed the pigs. He would gladly have filled himself with the pods that the pigs were eating; and no one gave him anything. But when he came to himself he said, 'How many of my father's hired hands have bread enough and to spare, but here I am dying of hunger! I will get up and go to my father, and I will say to him, "Father, I have sinned against heaven and before you; I am no longer worthy to be called your son; treat me like one of your hired hands."' So he set off and went to his father. But while he was still far off, his father saw him and was filled with compassion; he ran and put his arms around him and kissed him. Then the son said to him, 'Father, I have sinned against heaven and before you; I am no longer worthy to be called your son.' But the father said to his slaves, 'Quickly, bring out a robe—the best one—and put it on him; put a ring on his finger and sandals on his feet. And get the fatted calf and kill it, and let us eat and celebrate; for this son of mine was dead and is alive again; he was lost and is found!' And they began to celebrate.

"Now his elder son was in the field; and when he came and approached the house, he heard music and dancing. He called one of the slaves and asked what was going on. He replied, 'Your brother has come, and your father has killed the fatted calf, because he has got him back safe and sound.' Then he became angry and refused to go in. His father came out and began to plead with him. But he answered his father, 'Listen! For all these years I have been working like a slave for you, and I have never disobeyed your command; yet you have never given me even a young goat so that I might celebrate with my friends. But when this son of yours came back, who has devoured your property with prostitutes, you killed the fatted calf for him!' Then the father said to him, 'Son, you are always with me, and all that is mine is yours. But we had to celebrate and rejoice, because this brother of yours was dead and has come to life; he was lost and has been found.'"

Notice what you think and feel as you read the gospel.

The Lord tells the great parable about the prodigal son. The lesson is two-fold: let those brought to ruin by their sin return to the merciful Father; let those who have remained with the Father, be merciful in accepting the returning sinner.

Pray as you are led for yourself and others.

"Lord, I enter into your merciful embrace. I rejoice when others return to you. I pray for sinners to come to you now . . ." (Continue in your own words.)

Listen to Jesus.

It is my joy to open your heart, mind, and soul to me, my child. Give yourself to me every day, and I will change your life. What else is Jesus saying to you?

Ask God to show you how to live today.

"Take me by the hand, Lord, bring me back to you, and help me please you today."

THE POPE'S MONTHLY PRAYER INTENTION FOR APRIL 2019

For doctors and their humanitarian collaborators in war zones, who risk their lives to save the lives of others.

Monday, April 1, 2019

Know that God is present with you and ready to converse.

"Lord, let me find you in the darkness of the world and even within my own darkness. You are the Light of the world."

Read the gospel: John 9:1–3, 6–7, 13–41 (Jn 9:1–41)

As Jesus walked along, he saw a man blind from birth. His disciples asked him, "Rabbi, who sinned, this man or his parents, that he was born blind?" Jesus answered, "Neither this man nor his parents sinned; he was born blind so that God's works might be revealed in him. . . ." When he had said this, he spat on the ground and made mud with the saliva and spread the mud on the man's eyes, saying to him, "Go, wash in the pool of Siloam" (which means Sent). Then the man went and washed and came back able to see. . . .

His neighbors brought to the Pharisees the man who had formerly been blind. Now it was a sabbath day when Jesus made the mud and opened his eyes. Then the Pharisees also began to ask him how he had received his sight. He said to them, "He put mud on my eyes. Then I washed, and now I see." Some of the Pharisees said, "This man is not from God, for he does not observe the sabbath." But others said, "How can a man who is a sinner perform such signs?" And they were divided. So they said again to the blind man, "What do you say about him? It was your eyes he opened." He said, "He is a prophet."

The Jews did not believe that he had been blind and had received his sight until they called the parents of the man who had received his sight and asked them, "Is this your son, who you say was born blind? How then does he now see?" His parents answered, "We know that this is our son, and that he was born blind; but we do not know how it is that now he sees, nor do we know who opened his eyes. Ask him; he is of age. He will speak for himself." His parents said this because they were afraid of the Jews; for the Jews had already agreed that anyone who confessed Jesus to be the Messiah would be put out of the synagogue. Therefore his parents said, "He is of age; ask him."

So for the second time they called the man who had been blind, and they said to him, "Give glory to God! We know that this man is a sinner." He answered, "I do not know whether he is a sinner. One thing I do know, that though I was blind, now I see." They said to him, "What did he do to you? How did he open your eyes?" He answered them, "I have told you already, and you would not listen. Why do you want to hear it again? Do you also want to become his disciples?" Then they reviled him, saying, "You are his disciple, but we are disciples of Moses. We know that God has spoken to Moses, but as for this man, we do not know where he comes from." The man answered, "Here is an astonishing thing! You do not know where he comes from, and yet he opened my eyes. We know that God does not listen to sinners, but he does listen to one who worships him and obeys his will. Never since the world began has it been heard that anyone opened the eyes of a person born blind. If this man were not from God, he could do nothing." They answered him, "You were born entirely in sins, and are you trying to teach us?" And they drove him out.

Jesus heard that they had driven him out, and when he found him, he said, "Do you believe in the Son of Man?" He answered, "And who is he, sir? Tell me, so that I may believe in him." Jesus said to him, "You have seen him, and the one speaking with you is he." He said, "Lord, I believe." And he worshiped him. Jesus said, "I came into this world for judgment so that those who do not see may see, and those who do see may become blind." Some of the Pharisees near him heard this and said to him, "Surely we are not blind, are we?" Jesus said to them, "If you were blind, you would not have sin. But now that you say, 'We see,' your sin remains."

Notice what you think and feel as you read the gospel.

This gospel reading is a study of human nature: All are in the dark, in different ways. The disciples don't understand Jesus. The blind man doesn't see anything. His parents can't explain his healing. The Pharisees, blinded by their theology, cannot see past the fact that Jesus breaks the Sabbath according to their laws. Meanwhile, the man restored to sight believes in Jesus, the Messiah.

Pray as you are led for yourself and others.

"Lord, though all the world be wrong, you are right. I believe in you and worship you. As we have a personal relationship, I pray the same for others, especially those in deepest darkness . . ." (Continue in your own words.)

Listen to Jesus.

I cannot do my work in those who deny their sins, beloved disciple. Turn from sin and seek forgiveness, and you will know my joy. What else is Jesus saying to you?

Ask God to show you how to live today.

"What sacrifice can I make today to show my love for you, my gratitude that you are with me, Savior? Amen."

Tuesday, April 2, 2019

Know that God is present with you and ready to converse.

Lord of heaven and earth, stir up my heart to receive your Word today.

Read the gospel: John 5:1–9a, 14–16 (Jn 5:1–16).

After this there was a festival of the Jews, and Jesus went up to Jerusalem.

Now in Jerusalem by the Sheep Gate there is a pool, called in Hebrew Beth-zatha, which has five porticoes. In these lay many invalids—blind, lame, and paralyzed. One man was there who had been ill for thirty-eight years. When Jesus saw him lying there and knew that he had been there a long time, he said to him, "Do you want to be made well?" The sick man answered him, "Sir, I have no one to put me into the pool when the water is stirred up; and while I am making my way, someone else steps down ahead of me." Jesus said to him, "Stand up, take your mat and walk." At once the man was made well, and he took up his mat and began to walk. . . .

Later Jesus found him in the temple and said to him, "See, you have been made well! Do not sin anymore, so that nothing worse happens to you." The man went away and told the Jews that it was Jesus who had made him well. Therefore the Jews started persecuting Jesus, because he was doing such things on the sabbath.

Notice what you think and feel as you read the gospel.

On this Sabbath, Jesus tells the paralyzed man to take up his mat and walk, and the man does so. Some Jews tell the man that it is unlawful for him to carry his mat on the Sabbath, and these Jews start persecuting Jesus for working on the Sabbath.

Pray as you are led for yourself and others.

"How narrow is the human heart, Lord! How easily we reject your free ways of love and allow ourselves to be imprisoned by human rules and expectations. Free us from this sin . . ." (Continue in your own words.)

Listen to Jesus.

If you offer yourself to act upon my love, you, too, will meet opposition. But I will be with you, and I will work through you, dear disciple. What else is Jesus saying to you?

Ask God to show you how to live today.

"Lord, all I ask is to walk in your grace, following you, doing small acts of love. Amen."

Wednesday, April 3, 2019

Know that God is present with you and ready to converse.

"Father, in the unity of the Holy Spirit you are One with your Son, Jesus, who is the everlasting Word. Let me join you in your love."

Read the gospel: John 5:17–24 (Jn 5:17–30).

But Jesus answered them, "My Father is still working, and I also am working." For this reason the Jews were seeking all the more to kill him, because he was not only breaking the sabbath, but was also calling God his own Father, thereby making himself equal to God.

Jesus said to them, "Very truly, I tell you, the Son can do nothing on his own, but only what he sees the Father doing; for whatever the Father does, the Son does likewise. The Father loves the Son and shows him all that he himself is doing; and he will show him greater works than these, so that you will be astonished. Indeed, just as the Father raises the dead and gives them life, so also the Son gives life to whomsoever he wishes. The Father judges no one but has given all judgment to the Son, so that all may honor the Son just as they honor the Father. Anyone who does not honor the Son does not honor the Father who sent him. Very truly, I tell you, anyone who hears my word and believes him who sent me has eternal life, and does not come under judgment, but has passed from death to life."

Notice what you think and feel as you read the gospel.

Some of the Jews want to kill Jesus, not just because he breaks the Sabbath but because he makes himself equal to God by healing, forgiving, raising the dead, and proclaiming that in the end he will judge all humanity. Yet Jesus teaches that he is one with the Father; he does only the Father's will.

Pray as you are led for yourself and others.

"I can imagine how stunned people were to hear your words, Lord. You spoke the truth, but it was too much for many to take in. Open my spirit to humility to receive and believe the truth, your perfect unity with the Father, and your life-giving authority . . ." (Continue in your own words.)

Listen to Jesus.

My work of redemption is both complete and still in process. I did not come to give temporary relief to a fallen people; I came to raise all who trust in me to eternal life with God. Let me work in you, beloved. What else is Jesus saying to you?

Ask God to show you how to live today.

"Jesus, make your saving power real in me. Let me extend it by your grace and guidance to someone else today. I am grateful to you, Blessed Lord. Amen."

Thursday, April 4, 2019

Know that God is present with you and ready to converse.

"Word of God, Savior, Jesus, let me hear your voice today."

Read the gospel: John 5:31–38 (Jn 5:31–47).

Jesus said, "If I testify about myself, my testimony is not true. There is another who testifies on my behalf, and I know that his testimony to me is true. You sent messengers to John, and he testified to the truth. Not that I accept such human testimony, but I say these things so that you may be saved. He was a burning and shining lamp, and you were willing to rejoice for a while in his light. But I have a testimony greater than John's. The works that the Father has given me to complete, the very works that

I am doing, testify on my behalf that the Father has sent me. And the Father who sent me has himself testified on my behalf. You have never heard his voice or seen his form, and you do not have his word abiding in you, because you do not believe him whom he has sent."

Notice what you think and feel as you read the gospel.

Jesus points out the things that identify him as the Messiah, which are not his own evidence but God's. John the Baptist, the mighty works Jesus did, and the scriptures all testify that Jesus is the Messiah. He is telling us that faith is built on the testimony of those we trust. The Jewish elders refused to trust Jesus, so they refused to accept God's own testimony, which was revealed in Jesus' powerful ministry.

Pray as you are led for yourself and others.

"Lord, you are faithful and good. In all matters, I will trust you. I entrust to you especially these . . ." (Continue in your own words.)

Listen to Jesus.

Beloved disciple, trust in me, learn from me, and I will show you the very face of God. What else is Jesus saying to you?

Ask God to show you how to live today.

"Jesus, Word of God, let my actions today bear witness to your goodness and bring you glory. Amen."

Friday, April 5, 2019

Know that God is present with you and ready to converse.

"One God, I am before you, in awe at your wonderful works in the universe, in history, in the salvation of your people. Teach me by your Word."

Read the gospel: John 7:1–2, 10, 25–30.

After this Jesus went about in Galilee. He did not wish to go about in Judea because the Jews were looking for an opportunity to kill him. Now the Jewish festival of Booths was near. . . .

But after his brothers had gone to the festival, then he also went, not publicly but as it were in secret. . . .

Now some of the people of Jerusalem were saying, "Is not this the man whom they are trying to kill? And here he is, speaking openly, but they say nothing to him! Can it be that the authorities really know that this is the Messiah? Yet we know where this man is from; but when the Messiah comes, no one will know where he is from." Then Jesus cried out as he was teaching in the temple, "You know me, and you know where I am from. I have not come on my own. But the one who sent me is true, and you do not know him. I know him, because I am from him, and he sent me." Then they tried to arrest him, but no one laid hands on him, because his hour had not yet come.

Notice what you think and feel as you read the gospel.

As the people of Jerusalem speculate on Jesus' identity as the Messiah, Jesus states in the temple that he has been sent by God, whom they do not know. Jesus is fearless, confident in and surrendered to the will of God, who sent him. They try to arrest him but cannot, because it is God's will that Jesus should continue his ministry at this time; Jesus' arrest will come later.

Pray as you are led for yourself and others.

"Lord, I, too, give myself to your timing and the events you have destined in my life. Let me be true to you and embrace your will . . ." (Continue in your own words.)

Listen to Jesus.

It was my glory to be crucified in shame before men and women, as I did it for love. My Cross is also your glory, dear disciple. Take up your own cross in love and follow me to glory. What else is Jesus saying to you?

Ask God to show you how to live today.

"Let me make a small or great sacrifice in love today, Lord. Let it be to glorify you. I praise the way of the Cross, Jesus. Thank you for teaching me. Amen."

Saturday, April 6, 2019

Know that God is present with you and ready to converse.

"Lord, as I come into your presence let all doubt and disputation die in me, and let me receive the truth of your Word."

Read the gospel: John 7:40–53.

When they heard Jesus' words, some in the crowd said, "This is really the prophet." Others said, "This is the Messiah." But some asked, "Surely the Messiah does not come from Galilee, does he? Has not the scripture said that the Messiah is descended from David and comes from Bethlehem, the village where David lived?" So there was a division in the crowd because of him. Some of them wanted to arrest him, but no one laid hands on him.

Then the temple police went back to the chief priests and Pharisees, who asked them, "Why did you not arrest him?" The police answered, "Never has anyone spoken like this!" Then the Pharisees replied, "Surely you have not been deceived too, have you? Has any one of the authorities or of the Pharisees believed in him? But this crowd, which does not know the law—they are accursed." Nicodemus, who had gone to Jesus before, and who was one of them, asked, "Our law does not judge people without first giving them a hearing to find out what they are doing, does it?" They replied, "Surely you are not also from Galilee, are you? Search and you will see that no prophet is to arise from Galilee."

Notice what you think and feel as you read the gospel.

The people of Jerusalem speak from partial knowledge, and they form their opinions based on self-interest, not regard for the truth. The Pharisees condemn the crowd's ignorance of the law, but Nicodemus points out that they themselves disregard the law in their judgment of Jesus.

Pray as you are led for yourself and others.

"Lord, I can be swept into confusion by all the arguments of my own day. My knowledge is partial, my prejudices hold sway, and I am distracted from having a pure encounter with you. Let me know you and worship you with all my heart . . ." (Continue in your own words.)

Listen to Jesus.

My beloved servant, I give you my heart as you have given me yours. By faith you see me, by love you know me. What else do you ask of me today? What else is Jesus saying to you?

Ask God to show you how to live today.

"Thank you for your wonderful love for me, Lord. Let nothing ever come between us. I humbly ask that I may radiate your love to others today. Amen."

Sunday, April 7, 2019
Fifth Sunday of Lent

Know that God is present with you and ready to converse.

"Jesus, teach me just judgment by your Word."

Read the gospel: John 8:1–11.

Jesus went to the Mount of Olives. Early in the morning he came again to the temple. All the people came to him and he sat down and began to teach them. The scribes and the Pharisees brought a woman who had been caught in adultery; and making her stand before all of them, they said to him, "Teacher, this woman was caught in the very act of committing adultery. Now in the law Moses commanded us to stone such women. Now what do you say?" They said this to test him, so that they might have some charge to bring against him. Jesus bent down and wrote with his finger on the ground. When they kept on questioning him, he straightened up and said to them, "Let anyone among you who is without sin be the first to throw a stone at her." And once again he bent down and wrote on the ground. When they heard it, they went away, one by one, beginning with the elders; and Jesus was left alone with the woman standing before him. Jesus straightened up and said to her, "Woman, where are they? Has no one condemned you?" She said, "No one, sir." And Jesus said, "Neither do I condemn you. Go your way, and from now on do not sin again."

Notice what you think and feel as you read the gospel.

When the scribes and Pharisees bring a woman caught in adultery to Jesus, he teaches them mercy and shows their own sinfulness. In obedience to the law of Moses, they would stone her, but Jesus reminds them they are all sinners. Then Jesus forgives the woman and exhorts her to sin no more.

Pray as you are led for yourself and others.

"Lord, you have fulfilled the law of Moses with plentiful love and mercy. Thank you. Let me love and forgive someone I have been judging . . ." (Continue in your own words.)

Listen to Jesus.

I am glad for your sake that you see that practicing love and mercy are the ways to please God and grow in holiness. You will find happiness in this way. Walk close to me. What else is Jesus saying to you?

Ask God to show you how to live today.

"I resolve to walk with you today, Lord. Use me as you will. I want to serve and please you, but I cannot unless you work through me. Amen."

Monday, April 8, 2019

Know that God is present with you and ready to converse.

"Lord, write on my heart your laws of love. I thank you for your presence here now."

Read the gospel: John 8:12–20.

Again Jesus spoke to them, saying, "I am the light of the world. Whoever follows me will never walk in darkness but will have the light of life." Then the Pharisees said to him, "You are testifying on your own behalf; your testimony is not valid." Jesus answered, "Even if I testify on my own behalf, my testimony is valid because I know where I have come from and where I am going, but you do not know where I come from or where I am going. You judge by human standards; I judge no one. Yet even if I do judge, my judgment is valid; for it is not I alone who judge, but I and the Father who sent me. In your law it is written that the testimony of two witnesses is valid. I testify on my own behalf, and the Father who sent me testifies on my behalf." Then they said to him, "Where is your Father?" Jesus answered, "You know neither me nor my Father. If you knew me, you would know my Father also." He spoke these words while he was teaching in the treasury of the temple, but no one arrested him, because his hour had not yet come.

Notice what you think and feel as you read the gospel.

While the Pharisees are scrupulous in adhering to the Law of Moses, Jesus encourages them to look to the greater law that comes from God, the Father.

Pray as you are led for yourself and others.

"Lord, my heart is quick to judge others who do not follow the letter of the law. By your Spirit, let me seek your forgiveness and let me value obedience to those who honor your higher law." (Continue in your own words.)

Listen to Jesus.

Beloved, you are right to seek holiness by my Spirit, for only in God is it possible to achieve true obedience. What else is Jesus saying to you?

Ask God to show you how to live today.

"Open my eyes and mind that I may see how I can be judgmental. Lord, show me how to put my judgments far from me, case by case. All praise to you, Lord Jesus Christ. Amen."

Tuesday, April 9, 2019

Know that God is present with you and ready to converse.

"Master of the universe, Holy Trinity, One God, I cannot take you in. Take me into yourself. Capture me by your Word."

Read the gospel: John 8:21–30.

Again Jesus said to them, "I am going away, and you will search for me, but you will die in your sin. Where I am going, you cannot come." Then the Jews said, "Is he going to kill himself? Is that what he means by saying, 'Where I am going, you cannot come'?" He said to them, "You are from below, I am from above; you are of this world, I am not of this world. I told you that you would die in your sins, for you will die in your sins unless you believe that I am he." They said to him, "Who are you?" Jesus said to them, "Why do I speak to you at all? I have much to say about you and much to condemn; but the one who sent me is true, and I declare to the world what I have heard from him." They did not understand that he was speaking to them about the Father. So Jesus said, "When you have lifted up the Son of Man, then you will realize that I am he, and that I do nothing on my own, but I speak these things as the Father instructed me. And the one who sent me is with me; he has not left me alone, for I always do what is pleasing to him." As he was saying these things, many believed in him.

Notice what you think and feel as you read the gospel.

Jesus is thinking of his Passion, Death, Resurrection, and Ascension. He exhorts his listeners to believe in him lest they die in their sins. He tells them they will realize who he is when they lift him up on the Cross.

Pray as you are led for yourself and others.

"Lord, I know I am of this world, full of human weakness. Let me believe and come to you. I pray for all those who resist you . . ." (Continue in your own words.)

Listen to Jesus.

Your faithfulness to me touches me, dear friend. You want others to know your peace in knowing me. Our prayers for them have power with our Father. Thank you for praying with me. What else is Jesus saying to you?

Ask God to show you how to live today.

"I offer you all my thoughts, words, deeds, joys, and sorrows this day, that you may count them as a prayer for those you have given me. Keep my mind on you. Amen."

Wednesday, April 10, 2019

Know that God is present with you and ready to converse.

"Jesus, give me your Spirit to know your truth and freedom."

Read the gospel: John 8:31–38 (Jn 8:31–42).

Then Jesus said to the Jews who had believed in him, "If you continue in my word, you are truly my disciples; and you will know the truth, and the truth will make you free." They answered him, "We are descendants of Abraham and have never been slaves to anyone. What do you mean by saying, 'You will be made free'?"

Jesus answered them, "Very truly, I tell you, everyone who commits sin is a slave to sin. The slave does not have a permanent place in the household; the son has a place there forever. So if the Son makes you free, you will be free indeed. I know that you are descendants of Abraham; yet you look for an opportunity to kill me, because there is no place in you for my word. I declare what I have seen in the Father's presence; as for you, you should do what you have heard from the Father."

Notice what you think and feel as you read the gospel.

Jesus declares the truth of his Word: it will make us free from sin, which will allow us to love God the Father.

Pray as you are led for yourself and others.

"Jesus, let me use the freedom you give me to avoid sin. Let me love God and desire to please God in all things. I wish to help others to see the truth of your Word and Person, Jesus . . ." (Continue in your own words.)

Listen to Jesus.

Examine your life, beloved disciple, in the light of my Word and the freedom it gives you. As you give yourself to me, turning from sin, you will rejoice in the love of God. What else is Jesus saying to you?

Ask God to show you how to live today.

"How am I free, Lord? Make me aware of moments of freedom in this day so that I may choose goodness, truth, love, and God. Amen."

Thursday, April 11, 2019

Know that God is present with you and ready to converse.

"You are here with me now, Jesus. You are always with me. Let me know you in your Word and carry you forth into my day by your Spirit."

Read the gospel: John 8:51–59.

Jesus said, "Very truly, I tell you, whoever keeps my word will never see death." The Jews said to him, "Now we know that you have a demon. Abraham died, and so did the prophets; yet you say, 'Whoever keeps my word will never taste death.' Are you greater than our father Abraham, who died? The prophets also died. Who do you claim to be?" Jesus answered, "If I glorify myself, my glory is nothing. It is my Father who glorifies me, he of whom you say, 'He is our God,' though you do not know him. But I know him; if I were to say that I do not know him, I would be a liar like you. But I do know him and I keep his word. Your ancestor Abraham rejoiced that he would see my day; he saw it and was glad." Then the Jews said to him, "You are not yet fifty years old, and have you seen Abraham?" Jesus said to them, "Very truly, I tell you, before Abraham was, I am." So they picked up stones to throw at him, but Jesus hid himself and went out of the temple.

Notice what you think and feel as you read the gospel.

The Jews scorn Jesus' claims of a special relationship with God and his ability to confer eternal life on those who keep his Word. Jesus knows they will turn on him for what seems blasphemy to them, but he is compelled to tell the truth about himself.

Pray as you are led for yourself and others.

"Word of the Father, Light of the World, grant me your Life, your Truth, your Way. I glorify you for your goodness and your generous grace to me and mine . . ." (Continue in your own words.)

Listen to Jesus.

My Father glorified my suffering. I obeyed God for love because God's purposes are all love. Let love operate in your life, child, and God will glorify your suffering as well. What else is Jesus saying to you?

Ask God to show you how to live today.

"I do suffer, Lord, in small and great ways as the days pass. I offer this suffering to our Father for love of those you have given me. Let me love as you do, Jesus. Amen."

Friday, April 12, 2019

Know that God is present with you and ready to converse.

"Jesus, Son of the Father and One with the Father in the unity of the Holy Spirit, lift me to God by your Word."

Read the gospel: John 10:31–39 (Jn 10:31–42).

The Jews took up stones again to stone him. Jesus replied, "I have shown you many good works from the Father. For which of these are you going to stone me?" The Jews answered, "It is not for a good work that we are going to stone you, but for blasphemy, because you, though only a human being, are making yourself God." Jesus answered, "Is it not written in your law, 'I said, you are gods'? If those to whom the word of God came were called 'gods'—and the scripture cannot be annulled—can you say that the one whom the Father has sanctified and sent into the world is blaspheming because I said, 'I am God's Son'? If I am not doing the works of my Father, then do not believe me. But if I do them, even though you do not believe me, believe the works, so that you may know and understand that the Father is in me and I am in the Father." Then they tried to arrest him again, but he escaped from their hands.

Notice what you think and feel as you read the gospel.

Jesus faces stoning by the many who cannot abide the notion that he is God's Son. Jesus appeals to scripture and then to his own mighty works as reasons to believe in him. He affirms again that the Father is in him and he is in the Father. He escapes arrest.

Pray as you are led for yourself and others.

"Lord, what is the difference between those who believe your Word and those who don't? I believe. Help my unbelief. I pray for those who do not believe or who suffer from doubts . . ." (Continue in your own words.)

Listen to Jesus.

Your faith is my gift to you, beloved disciple. Treasure it. Put it to use in your prayers and in your actions. Let it grow and bear fruit. What else is Jesus saying to you?

Ask God to show you how to live today.

"Lord, today when I find myself in a situation in which I may show my faith, let me do so. Let me remember your words and walk in the faith you have given me. Amen."

Saturday, April 13, 2019

Know that God is present with you and ready to converse.

"I am looking for you, Jesus, and ask you to let me find you, know you, and love you in your Word. Speak to me, Lord."

Read the gospel: John 11:45–53 (Jn 11:45–56).

Many of the Jews therefore, who had come with Mary and had seen what Jesus did, believed in him. But some of them went to the Pharisees and told them what he had done. So the chief priests and the Pharisees called a meeting of the council, and said, "What are we to do? This man is performing many signs. If we let him go on like this, everyone will believe in him, and the Romans will come and destroy both our holy place and our nation." But one of them, Caiaphas, who was high priest that year, said to them, "You know nothing at all! You do not understand that it is better for you to have one man die for the people than to have the whole nation destroyed." He did not say this on his own, but being high priest that year he prophesied that Jesus was about to die for the nation, and not for the nation only, but to gather into one the dispersed children of God. So from that day on they planned to put him to death.

Notice what you think and feel as you read the gospel.

Feeling threatened by Jesus' power and growing influence, the Pharisees call a meeting. The chief priest, Caiaphas, suggests that Jesus may make a good scapegoat for the Jewish people; his comment is truer than he realized at the time.

Pray as you are led for yourself and others.

"Jesus, when you hide yourself and show yourself, you are acting in obedience to God, not out of fear of others. Let me be as you were, led only by the will of God. Give me grace to do God's will . . ." (Continue in your own words.)

Listen to Jesus.

Servant of God, I come to you with love this moment, and I will be close to you all day. As you give yourself to God, God's will is done. Follow me. What else is Jesus saying to you?

Ask God to show you how to live today.

"Jesus, you came to earth and changed history. Work with me in my life to change things, that I may hasten the coming of the kingdom of God. Thank you. Amen."

Sunday, April 14, 2019
Palm Sunday of the Lord's Passion

Know that God is present with you and ready to converse.

"Jesus, you are preparing to give yourself to me. Show me how to receive you."

Read the gospel: Luke 22:14–23 (Lk 22:14–23:56).

When the hour came, Jesus took his place at the table, and the apostles with him. He said to them, "I have eagerly desired to eat this Passover with you before I suffer; for I tell you, I will not eat it until it is fulfilled in the kingdom of God." Then he took a cup, and after giving thanks he said, "Take this and divide it among yourselves; for I tell you that from now on I will not drink of the fruit of the vine until the kingdom of God comes." Then he took a loaf of bread, and when he had given thanks, he broke it and gave it to them, saying, "This is my body, which is given for you. Do this in remembrance of me." And he did the same with the cup after supper, saying, "This cup that is poured out for you is the new covenant in my blood. But see, the one who betrays me is with me, and his hand is on the table. For the Son of Man is going as it has been determined, but woe to that one by whom he is betrayed!" Then they began to ask one another which one of them it could be who would do this.

Notice what you think and feel as you read the gospel.

The Passover supper with the Twelve serves as the foundation of the Eucharistic rites we celebrate today. The bread Jesus offers at the Passover supper is his Body; the wine his Blood. We are to receive the bread and wine of the Eucharist in the same faith his disciples did.

Pray as you are led for yourself and others.

"Lord, I do not want to betray you as Judas did or even to deny you as Peter did after you were arrested. I want to come to you and receive you with perfect faith. Let your Eucharist strengthen me, Lord, that I may show your love to others. . ." (Continue in your own words.)

Listen to Jesus.

You are mine, dearest beloved, and I draw you to me. Stay with me, for I have power to bestow holiness and blessing upon you. By them, you will glorify God and help others. Continue in my love. What else is Jesus saying to you?

Ask God to show you how to live today.

"God, remain with me. Let me glorify you in every thought, word, and deed today. Thank you for your Body and Blood, given to me. Amen."

Monday, April 15, 2019

Know that God is present with you and ready to converse.

"Jesus, Word of the Father, enter my heart, mind, soul, and spirit as I read and pray today."

Read the gospel: John 12:1–8 (Jn 12:1–11).

Six days before the Passover Jesus came to Bethany, the home of Lazarus, whom he had raised from the dead. There they gave a dinner for him. Martha served, and Lazarus was one of those at the table with him. Mary took a pound of costly perfume made of pure nard, anointed Jesus' feet, and wiped them with her hair. The house was filled with the fragrance of the perfume. But Judas Iscariot, one of his disciples (the one who was about to betray him), said, "Why was this perfume not sold for three hundred denarii and the money given to the poor?" (He said this not because he cared about the poor, but because he was a thief; he kept the common purse and used to steal what was put into it.) Jesus said, "Leave her alone. She bought it so that she might keep it for the day of my burial. You always have the poor with you, but you do not always have me."

Notice what you think and feel as you read the gospel.

Lazarus, who was raised from the dead, is hosting Jesus, whom Mary symbolically prepares for burial. Jesus embraces the supposed excess of Mary's act, to Judas's disapproval. Yet Jesus reminds him that honoring the Lord and caring for the poor go hand in hand.

Pray as you are led for yourself and others.

"Jesus, I, too, want to honor you, want to fall at your feet in awe and wonder and love . . ." (Continue in your own words.)

Listen to Jesus.

Dear disciple, come to me in the sacraments, honor me with true humility and openness, and love me in all your brothers and sisters. What else is Jesus saying to you?

Ask God to show you how to live today.

"Lord, allow me to glorify you through my words and actions today. Thank you. Amen."

Tuesday, April 16, 2019

Know that God is present with you and ready to converse.

"Jesus, let me know you better so that I may follow you more closely. Teach me by your Word."

Read the gospel: John 13:21–33, 36–38.

After saying this Jesus was troubled in spirit, and declared, "Very truly, I tell you, one of you will betray me." The disciples looked at one another, uncertain of whom he was speaking. One of his disciples—the one whom Jesus loved—was reclining next to him; Simon Peter therefore motioned to him to ask Jesus of whom he was speaking. So while reclining next to Jesus, he asked him, "Lord, who is it?" Jesus answered, "It is the one to whom I give this piece of bread when I have dipped it in the dish." So when he had dipped the piece of bread, he gave it to Judas son of Simon Iscariot. After he received the piece of bread, Satan entered into him. Jesus said to him, "Do quickly what you are going to do." Now no one at the table knew why he said this to him. Some thought that, because Judas had the common purse, Jesus was telling him, "Buy what we need for the festival"; or, that he should give something to the poor. So, after receiving the piece of bread, he immediately went out. And it was night.

When he had gone out, Jesus said, "Now the Son of Man has been glorified, and God has been glorified in him. If God has been glorified in him, God will also glorify him in himself and will glorify him at once. Little children, I am with you only a little longer. You will look for me; and as I said to the Jews so now I say to you, 'Where I am going, you cannot come.'" . . .

Simon Peter said to him, "Lord, where are you going?" Jesus answered, "Where I am going, you cannot follow me now; but you will follow afterwards." Peter said to him, "Lord, why can I not follow you now? I will lay down my life for you." Jesus answered, "Will you lay down your life for me? Very truly, I tell you, before the cock crows, you will have denied me three times."

Notice what you think and feel as you read the gospel.

Jesus begins the evening of the Passover troubled by his impending betrayal, but when Judas leaves to betray him, Jesus speaks of glory and his departure to a place they cannot come. Peter protests, but Jesus predicts his denial.

Pray as you are led for yourself and others.

"Lord, I have denied you, and I'm sorry. But I ask you to let me follow you, dying to myself and forsaking all for you . . ." (Continue in your own words.)

Listen to Jesus.

If I am the love of your life, if you give your whole heart to me, I will guide you in my path of service. Will you suffer? Yes. But you will also share my glory. What else is Jesus saying to you?

Ask God to show you how to live today.

"Help me to get my eyes off of myself, Lord, and look upon you, the crucified and risen King of Glory. I praise your holy name. Amen."

Wednesday, April 17, 2019

Know that God is present with you and ready to converse.
"Lord, I have been close to you, and you are with me now. Keep me from all betrayal; let me never turn away from you."

Read the gospel: Matthew 26:14–25.
Then one of the twelve, who was called Judas Iscariot, went to the chief priests and said, "What will you give me if I betray him to you?" They paid him thirty pieces of silver. And from that moment he began to look for an opportunity to betray him.

On the first day of Unleavened Bread the disciples came to Jesus, saying, "Where do you want us to make the preparations for you to eat the Passover?" He said, "Go into the city to a certain man, and say to him, 'The Teacher says, My time is near; I will keep the Passover at your house with my disciples.'" So the disciples did as Jesus had directed them, and they prepared the Passover meal.

When it was evening, he took his place with the twelve; and while they were eating, he said, "Truly I tell you, one of you will betray me." And they became greatly distressed and began to say to him one after another, "Surely not I, Lord?" He answered, "The one who has dipped his hand into the bowl with me will betray me. The Son of Man goes as it is written of him, but woe to that one by whom the Son of Man is betrayed! It would have been better for that one not to have been born." Judas, who betrayed him, said, "Surely not I, Rabbi?" He replied, "You have said so."

Notice what you think and feel as you read the gospel.
Judas, though he had traveled with Jesus, heard his preaching, seen his miracles, and was given a position of trust, agrees to betray Jesus to the chief priests for money. Judas shows that all people are subject to temptation, no matter their experiences or status.

Pray as you are led for yourself and others.
"Lord, let me never forget that I am weak, easily tempted to value things other than you. Forgive me for my weakness, love me and let me do what pleases you . . ." (Continue in your own words.)

Listen to Jesus.

I do love you, my dear child. Open yourself in all your failure and weakness to me. I understand. I will wash and heal you and make you strong. What else is Jesus saying to you?

Ask God to show you how to live today.

"I need you, Lord. Today I need you to see well, to love well, to speak well, and to do well. Thank you. Amen."

Thursday, April 18, 2019
Holy Thursday

Know that God is present with you and ready to converse.

"Jesus, Son of the Father, you show me how you live by your Word. Let your lessons be bound to my heart."

Read the gospel: John 13:2b–15 (Jn 13:1–15).

And during supper Jesus, knowing that the Father had given all things into his hands, and that he had come from God and was going to God, got up from the table, took off his outer robe, and tied a towel around himself. Then he poured water into a basin and began to wash the disciples' feet and to wipe them with the towel that was tied around him. He came to Simon Peter, who said to him, "Lord, are you going to wash my feet?" Jesus answered, "You do not know now what I am doing, but later you will understand." Peter said to him, "You will never wash my feet." Jesus answered, "Unless I wash you, you have no share with me." Simon Peter said to him, "Lord, not my feet only but also my hands and my head!" Jesus said to him, "One who has bathed does not need to wash, except for the feet, but is entirely clean. And you are clean, though not all of you." For he knew who was to betray him; for this reason he said, "Not all of you are clean."

After he had washed their feet, had put on his robe, and had returned to the table, he said to them, "Do you know what I have done to you? You call me Teacher and Lord—and you are right, for that is what I am. So if I, your Lord and Teacher, have washed your feet, you also ought to wash one another's feet. For I have set you an example, that you also should do as I have done to you."

Notice what you think and feel as you read the gospel.

Jesus teaches by example that the greatest ones will wash the feet of those they serve. Not just in the washing of the feet but throughout his ministry Jesus served others.

Pray as you are led for yourself and others.

"How shall I put your lesson into action, Lord? Help me reach the people I intend to serve, including . . ." (Continue in your own words.)

Listen to Jesus.

Find great joy in humble service, but do not glorify yourself, and you will follow my commands. What else is Jesus saying to you?

Ask God to show you how to live today.

"Give me the skill, Jesus, to serve others without embarrassing them or striking a false pose of humility. Amen."

Friday, April 19, 2019
Good Friday

Know that God is present with you and ready to converse.

"Lord, I come to you on this day with awe and trembling. You willingly went to your death for love of me."

Read the gospel: John 18:1–19:42.

After Jesus had spoken these words, he went out with his disciples across the Kidron valley to a place where there was a garden, which he and his disciples entered. Now Judas, who betrayed him, also knew the place, because Jesus often met there with his disciples. So Judas brought a detachment of soldiers together with police from the chief priests and the Pharisees, and they came there with lanterns and torches and weapons. Then Jesus, knowing all that was to happen to him, came forward and asked them, "For whom are you looking?" They answered, "Jesus of Nazareth." Jesus replied, "I am he." Judas, who betrayed him, was standing with them. When Jesus said to them, "I am he," they stepped back and fell to the ground. Again he asked them, "For whom are you looking?" And they said, "Jesus of Nazareth." Jesus answered, "I told you that I am he. So if you are looking for me, let these men go." This was to fulfill the word that he had spoken, "I did not lose a single one of those whom you gave me." Then Simon Peter, who had a sword, drew it, struck the high priest's slave, and cut off his right ear. The slave's name was Malchus. Jesus said to Peter, "Put your sword back into its sheath. Am I not to drink the cup that the Father has given me?"

So the soldiers, their officer, and the Jewish police arrested Jesus and bound him. First they took him to Annas, who was the father-in-law of Caiaphas, the high priest that year. Caiaphas was the one who had advised the Jews that it was better to have one person die for the people.

Simon Peter and another disciple followed Jesus. Since that disciple was known to the high priest, he went with Jesus into the courtyard of the high priest, but Peter was standing outside at the gate. So the other disciple, who was known to the high priest, went out, spoke to the woman who guarded the gate, and brought Peter in. The woman said to Peter, "You are not also one of this man's disciples, are you?" He said, "I am not." Now the slaves and the police had made a charcoal fire because it was cold, and they were standing round it and warming themselves. Peter also was standing with them and warming himself.

Then the high priest questioned Jesus about his disciples and about his teaching. Jesus answered, "I have spoken openly to the world; I have always taught in synagogues and in the temple, where all the Jews come together. I have said nothing in secret. Why do you ask me? Ask those who heard what I said to them; they know what I said." When he had said this, one of the police standing nearby struck Jesus on the face, saying, "Is that how you answer the high priest?" Jesus answered, "If I have spoken wrongly, testify to the wrong. But if I have spoken rightly, why do you strike me?" Then Annas sent him bound to Caiaphas the high priest.

Now Simon Peter was standing and warming himself. They asked him, "You are not also one of his disciples, are you?" He denied it and said, "I am not." One of the slaves of the high priest, a relative of the man whose ear Peter had cut off, asked, "Did I not see you in the garden with him?" Again Peter denied it, and at that moment the cock crowed.

Then they took Jesus from Caiaphas to Pilate's headquarters. It was early in the morning. They themselves did not enter the headquarters, so as to avoid ritual defilement and to be able to eat the Passover. So Pilate went out to them and said, "What accusation do you bring against this man?" They answered, "If this man were not a criminal, we would not have handed him over to you." Pilate said to them, "Take him yourselves and judge him according to your law." The Jews replied, "We are not permitted to put anyone to death." (This was to fulfill what Jesus had said when he indicated the kind of death he was to die.)

Then Pilate entered the headquarters again, summoned Jesus, and asked him, "Are you the King of the Jews?" Jesus answered, "Do you ask this on your own, or did others tell you about me?" Pilate replied, "I am not a Jew, am I? Your own nation and the chief priests have handed you over to me. What have you done?" Jesus answered, "My kingdom is not from this world. If my kingdom were from this world, my followers would be fighting to keep me from being handed over to the Jews. But as it is, my kingdom is not from here." Pilate asked him, "So you are a king?" Jesus answered, "You say that I am a king. For this I was born, and for this I came into the world, to testify to the truth. Everyone who belongs to the truth listens to my voice." Pilate asked him, "What is truth?"

After he had said this, he went out to the Jews again and told them, "I find no case against him. But you have a custom that I release someone for you at the Passover. Do you want me to release for you the King of the Jews?" They shouted in reply, "Not this man, but Barabbas!" Now Barabbas was a bandit.

Then Pilate took Jesus and had him flogged. And the soldiers wove a crown of thorns and put it on his head, and they dressed him in a purple robe. They kept coming up to him, saying, "Hail, King of the Jews!" and striking him on the face. Pilate went out again and said to them, "Look, I am bringing him out to you to let you know that I find no case against him." So Jesus came out, wearing the crown of thorns and the purple robe. Pilate said to them, "Here is the man!" When the chief priests and the police saw him, they shouted, "Crucify him! Crucify him!" Pilate said to them, "Take him yourselves and crucify him; I find no case against him." The Jews answered him, "We have a law, and according to that law he ought to die because he has claimed to be the Son of God."

Now when Pilate heard this, he was more afraid than ever. He entered his headquarters again and asked Jesus, "Where are you from?" But Jesus gave him no answer. Pilate therefore said to him, "Do you refuse to speak to me? Do you not know that I have power to release you, and power to crucify you?" Jesus answered him, "You would have no power over me unless it had been given you from above; therefore the one who handed me over to you is guilty of a greater sin." From then on Pilate tried to release him, but the Jews cried out, "If you release this man, you are no friend of the emperor. Everyone who claims to be a king sets himself against the emperor."

When Pilate heard these words, he brought Jesus outside and sat on the judge's bench at a place called The Stone Pavement, or in Hebrew Gabbatha. Now it was the day of Preparation for the Passover; and it was about noon. He said to the Jews, "Here is your King!" They cried out, "Away with him! Away with him! Crucify him!" Pilate asked them,

"Shall I crucify your King?" The chief priests answered, "We have no king but the emperor." Then he handed him over to them to be crucified.

So they took Jesus; and carrying the cross by himself, he went out to what is called The Place of the Skull, which in Hebrew is called Golgotha. There they crucified him, and with him two others, one on either side, with Jesus between them. Pilate also had an inscription written and put on the cross. It read, "Jesus of Nazareth, the King of the Jews." Many of the Jews read this inscription, because the place where Jesus was crucified was near the city; and it was written in Hebrew, in Latin, and in Greek. Then the chief priests of the Jews said to Pilate, "Do not write, 'The King of the Jews,' but, 'This man said, I am King of the Jews.'" Pilate answered, "What I have written I have written." When the soldiers had crucified Jesus, they took his clothes and divided them into four parts, one for each soldier. They also took his tunic; now the tunic was seamless, woven in one piece from the top. So they said to one another, "Let us not tear it, but cast lots for it to see who will get it." This was to fulfill what the scripture says,

"They divided my clothes among themselves,
   and for my clothing they cast lots."
And that is what the soldiers did.

Meanwhile, standing near the cross of Jesus were his mother, and his mother's sister, Mary the wife of Clopas, and Mary Magdalene. When Jesus saw his mother and the disciple whom he loved standing beside her, he said to his mother, "Woman, here is your son." Then he said to the disciple, "Here is your mother." And from that hour the disciple took her into his own home.

After this, when Jesus knew that all was now finished, he said (in order to fulfill the scripture), "I am thirsty." A jar full of sour wine was standing there. So they put a sponge full of the wine on a branch of hyssop and held it to his mouth. When Jesus had received the wine, he said, "It is finished." Then he bowed his head and gave up his spirit.

Since it was the day of Preparation, the Jews did not want the bodies left on the cross during the sabbath, especially because that sabbath was a day of great solemnity. So they asked Pilate to have the legs of the crucified men broken and the bodies removed. Then the soldiers came and broke the legs of the first and of the other who had been crucified with him. But when they came to Jesus and saw that he was already dead, they did not break his legs. Instead, one of the soldiers pierced his side with a spear, and at once blood and water came out. (He who saw this has testified so that you also may believe. His testimony is true, and he knows that he tells the truth.) These things occurred so that the scripture might be fulfilled, "None of his bones shall be broken." And again another passage of scripture says, "They will look on the one whom they have pierced."

After these things, Joseph of Arimathea, who was a disciple of Jesus, though a secret one because of his fear of the Jews, asked Pilate to let him take away the body of Jesus. Pilate gave him permission; so he came and removed his body. Nicodemus, who had at first come to Jesus by night, also came, bringing a mixture of myrrh and aloes, weighing about a hundred pounds. They took the body of Jesus and wrapped it with the spices in linen cloths, according to the burial custom of the Jews. Now there was a garden in the place where he was crucified, and in the garden there was a new tomb in which no one had ever been laid. And so, because it was the Jewish day of Preparation, and the tomb was nearby, they laid Jesus there.

Notice what you think and feel as you read the gospel.

How brave Jesus was throughout that horrible ordeal, his betrayal, torture, and death! In the end, blood and water flowed out of his pierced side, emblematic of our entering into redemption through the blood of his sacrifice and in Baptism by his Church.

Pray as you are led for yourself and others.

"Jesus, I am not worthy, but you died for love of me. Let me be washed clean of all sin by your blood. Let me thank you and glorify you this moment . . ." (Continue in your own words.)

Listen to Jesus.

My child, I love you now as I loved you then. Do you love me? What else is Jesus saying to you?

Ask God to show you how to live today.

"Lord, I am burdened and broken by my own crosses, even today. Give me your courage and your heart to journey today until the end. Amen."

Saturday, April 20, 2019
Holy Saturday

Know that God is present with you and ready to converse.

"Jesus, you live. Live in me and guide me by your Word."

Read the gospel: Luke 24:1–12.

But on the first day of the week, at early dawn, the women came to the tomb, taking the spices that they had prepared. They found the stone rolled away from the tomb, but when they went in, they did not find the body. While they were perplexed about this, suddenly two men in dazzling clothes stood beside them. The women were terrified and bowed their faces to the ground, but the men said to them, "Why do you look for the living among the dead? He is not here, but has risen. Remember how he told you, while he was still in Galilee, that the Son of Man must be handed over to sinners, and be crucified, and on the third day rise again." Then they remembered his words, and returning from the tomb, they told all this to the eleven and to all the rest. Now it was Mary Magdalene, Joanna, Mary the mother of James, and the other women with them who told this to the apostles. But these words seemed to them an idle tale, and they did not believe them. But Peter got up and ran to the tomb; stooping and looking in, he saw the linen cloths by themselves; then he went home, amazed at what had happened.

Notice what you think and feel as you read the gospel.

The women are the first to know and believe Jesus is alive. They understood. They worshipped. They obeyed.

Pray as you are led for yourself and others.

"Lord, strengthen my faith in the miracle of your Resurrection. Let it be so real to me that the living Jesus becomes the center of my life. Let others see you through me . . ." (Continue in your own words.)

Listen to Jesus.

I take care of you, beloved. Trust in me. Let others know you do. Ask me for whatever you need. What else is Jesus saying to you?

Ask God to show you how to live today.

"Show me how to recognize you, worship you, and obey you today. I need you, Lord. Amen."

Sunday, April 21, 2019
Easter Sunday

Know that God is present with you and ready to converse.

"Risen Lord, you have revealed yourself to many. Reveal yourself to me."

Read the gospel: Luke 24:13–35.

Now on that same day two of them were going to a village called Emmaus, about seven miles from Jerusalem, and talking with each other about all these things that had happened. While they were talking and discussing, Jesus himself came near and went with them, but their eyes were kept from recognizing him. And he said to them, "What are you discussing with each other while you walk along?" They stood still, looking sad. Then one of them, whose name was Cleopas, answered him, "Are you the only stranger in Jerusalem who does not know the things that have taken place there in these days?" He asked them, "What things?" They replied, "The things about Jesus of Nazareth, who was a prophet mighty in deed and word before God and all the people, and how our chief priests and leaders handed him over to be condemned to death and crucified him. But we had hoped that he was the one to redeem Israel. Yes, and besides all this, it is now the third day since these things took place. Moreover, some women of our group astounded us. They were at the tomb early this morning, and when they did not find his body there, they came back and told us that they had indeed seen a vision of angels who said that he was alive. Some of those who were with us went to the tomb and found it just as the women had said; but they did not see him." Then he said to them, "Oh, how foolish you are, and how slow of heart to believe all that the prophets have declared! Was it not necessary that the Messiah should suffer these things and then enter into his glory?" Then beginning with Moses and all the prophets, he interpreted to them the things about himself in all the scriptures.

As they came near the village to which they were going, he walked ahead as if he were going on. But they urged him strongly, saying, "Stay with us, because it is almost evening and the day is now nearly over." So he went in to stay with them. When he was at the table with them, he took bread, blessed and broke it, and gave it to them. Then their eyes were opened, and they recognized him; and he vanished from their sight. They said to each other, "Were not our hearts burning within us while he was talking to us on the road, while he was opening the scriptures to us?" That same hour they got up and returned to Jerusalem; and they found the eleven and their companions gathered together. They were saying, "The Lord has risen indeed, and he has appeared to Simon!" Then they told what had happened on the road, and how he had been made known to them in the breaking of the bread.

Notice what you think and feel as you read the gospel.

Why are the disciples in this story going to Emmaus? Perhaps they're confused, disheartened, scared, so they're going home. Jesus comes to them, though they don't recognize it's him; he walks alongside them, explains things to them. His words give them comfort, and they ask him to stay with them. And when he breaks the bread and feeds them, suddenly they see him—everything is made clear and bright. In his words he has given them courage, and in the bread he has given them strength, and they jump up that moment and run back to Jerusalem, back to the ministry to which Jesus calls all Christians.

Pray as you are led for yourself and others.

"The world has never seen such a miracle as your Resurrection, Lord. Alleluia! Fill me with knowledge of you, sustain me, that I may hurry to do your will . . ." (Continue in your own words.)

Listen to Jesus.

I will walk alongside you, dear one. With me you will do well, and those around you will notice. What else is Jesus saying to you?

Ask God to show you how to live today.

"I would like to help others believe in you, Lord. Let me see the opportunities to say and do things that reveal you. You are one with Almighty God, Father, Son, and Holy Spirit. Amen."

The Easter Season

INTRODUCTION

Easter is the greatest feast of the Church year because it celebrates the victory of Jesus Christ over sin and death, a victory not just for himself but for all who believe in him. Jesus is the pioneer who leads us into eternal life. "Just as in Adam all die," wrote St. Paul, "so in Christ all will come to life again. . . . Christ the first fruits and then, at his coming, all those who belong to him" (1 Cor 15:22–23). In the risen Christ, we are reconciled with God now and forever.

Our hearts and minds may wonder at the great mystery of resurrection. In the gospels, we read how the disciples received the amazing news that Jesus was not dead but lives. At first, many of them are skeptical, but they come to believe as Jesus shows himself to them again and again. For modern readers, their skepticism that turns to faith helps us to believe in this greatest of all miracles.

The season ends with Pentecost, the descent of the Holy Spirit to empower the disciples of Jesus to carry on his great work. The Spirit is given to us, too, as is the work. Let us pray the gospels of this season with joy and thanksgiving.

Monday, April 22, 2019

Know that God is present with you and ready to converse.
"Jesus, where are you? Why do I worry? You are here. I will not be afraid."

Read the gospel: Matthew 28:8–15.
So the women left the tomb quickly with fear and great joy, and ran to tell his disciples. Suddenly Jesus met them and said, "Greetings!" And they came to him, took hold of his feet, and worshiped him. Then Jesus said to them, "Do not be afraid; go and tell my brothers to go to Galilee; there they will see me."

While they were going, some of the guard went into the city and told the chief priests everything that had happened. After the priests had assembled with the elders, they devised a plan to give a large sum of money to the soldiers, telling them, "You must say, 'His disciples came by night and stole him away while we were asleep.' If this comes to the governor's ears, we will satisfy him and keep you out of trouble." So they took the money and did as they were directed. And this story is still told among the Jews to this day.

Notice what you think and feel as you read the gospel.
The empty tomb fills Mary Magdalene and the other Mary with fear and great joy. What were they afraid of? What were they joyful about?

Pray as you are led for yourself and others.
"Lord, the world is full of lies and is lost without God. I pray that your truth and Resurrection be revealed to all, that they may come to believe in you, know you, and be saved. I think of certain people who need you . . ." (Continue in your own words.)

Listen to Jesus.
Dear disciple, love as I love. People of every time shall know this truth: I am Lord. Pray for the coming of my kingdom. What else is Jesus saying to you?

Ask God to show you how to live today.
"I desire to live according to my faith today, Jesus, seeing situations as you do and doing what you would do. Help me to do that, Jesus. Amen."

Tuesday, April 23, 2019

Know that God is present with you and ready to converse.
"Risen Lord, you have been waiting for me here. Tell me what I need to know today."

Read the gospel: John 20:11–18.
But Mary stood weeping outside the tomb. As she wept, she bent over to look into the tomb; and she saw two angels in white, sitting where the body of Jesus had been lying, one at the head and the other at the feet. They said to her, "Woman, why are you weeping?" She said to them, "They have taken away my Lord, and I do not know where they have laid him." When she had said this, she turned round and saw Jesus standing there, but she did not know that it was Jesus. Jesus said to her, "Woman, why are you weeping? For whom are you looking?" Supposing him to be the gardener, she said to him, "Sir, if you have carried him away, tell me where you have laid him, and I will take him away." Jesus said to her, "Mary!" She turned and said to him in Hebrew, "Rabbouni!" (which means Teacher). Jesus said to her, "Do not hold on to me, because I have not yet ascended to the Father. But go to my brothers and say to them, 'I am ascending to my Father and your Father, to my God and your God.'" Mary Magdalene went and announced to the disciples, "I have seen the Lord"; and she told them that he had said these things to her.

Notice what you think and feel as you read the gospel.
Mary is privileged to see and speak with the risen Jesus, whom she loves so much. He sends a message to the disciples through her: "I am ascending to my Father and your Father, to my God and your God." In his Resurrection, Jesus opens the way for us to share his relationship with our Father.

Pray as you are led for yourself and others.
"Father in heaven, give me understanding to walk with you as a trusting child, for you have my life in your loving hand and will lead me all the way. Let me strengthen others on the way . . ." (Continue in your own words.)

Listen to Jesus.
Lean on my Word every day, and I will accompany you hour by hour. What else is Jesus saying to you?

Ask God to show you how to live today.

"I love being present with you like this, Lord. Help me to find you during the distractions of my day. Teach me to abide in you. Amen."

Wednesday, April 24, 2019

Know that God is present with you and ready to converse.

"Lord, open my eyes to you, to your truth, to your Word."

Read the gospel: Luke 24:13–35.

Now on that same day two of them were going to a village called Emmaus, about seven miles from Jerusalem, and talking with each other about all these things that had happened. While they were talking and discussing, Jesus himself came near and went with them, but their eyes were kept from recognizing him. And he said to them, "What are you discussing with each other while you walk along?" They stood still, looking sad. Then one of them, whose name was Cleopas, answered him, "Are you the only stranger in Jerusalem who does not know the things that have taken place there in these days?" He asked them, "What things?" They replied, "The things about Jesus of Nazareth, who was a prophet mighty in deed and word before God and all the people, and how our chief priests and leaders handed him over to be condemned to death and crucified him. But we had hoped that he was the one to redeem Israel. Yes, and besides all this, it is now the third day since these things took place. Moreover, some women of our group astounded us. They were at the tomb early this morning, and when they did not find his body there, they came back and told us that they had indeed seen a vision of angels who said that he was alive. Some of those who were with us went to the tomb and found it just as the women had said; but they did not see him." Then he said to them, "Oh, how foolish you are, and how slow of heart to believe all that the prophets have declared! Was it not necessary that the Messiah should suffer these things and then enter into his glory?" Then beginning with Moses and all the prophets, he interpreted to them the things about himself in all the scriptures.

As they came near the village to which they were going, he walked ahead as if he were going on. But they urged him strongly, saying, "Stay with us, because it is almost evening and the day is now nearly over." So he went in to stay with them. When he was at the table with them, he took bread, blessed and broke it, and gave it to them. Then their eyes were opened, and they recognized him; and he vanished from their sight.

They said to each other, "Were not our hearts burning within us while he was talking to us on the road, while he was opening the scriptures to us?" That same hour they got up and returned to Jerusalem; and they found the eleven and their companions gathered together. They were saying, "The Lord has risen indeed, and he has appeared to Simon!" Then they told what had happened on the road, and how he had been made known to them in the breaking of the bread.

Notice what you think and feel as you read the gospel.

I have felt my heart burning within me as I read the scriptures. I know this is the power of the Holy Spirit, to recognize Truth even when it is shrouded in high mystery. The Lord is risen indeed!

Pray as you are led for yourself and others.

"Let your Truth be food and drink to me, Jesus Christ. Reign over me and those I love and pray for . . ." (Continue in your own words.)

Listen to Jesus.

I love you, beloved. I will increase your faith and strengthen you in wisdom and grace as you seek me and pray. Come to me often. What else is Jesus saying to you?

Ask God to show you how to live today.

"Jesus, when I forget you during the day, come to me, open my eyes to your presence, feed me with the bread of life. Amen."

Thursday, April 25, 2019

Know that God is present with you and ready to converse.

"If I saw you here with me, Jesus, I would be afraid. Give me eyes to see you, a mind to understand, and a heart full of your peace."

Read the gospel: Luke 24:35–48.

Then they told what had happened on the road, and how Jesus had been made known to them in the breaking of the bread.

While they were talking about this, Jesus himself stood among them and said to them, "Peace be with you." They were startled and terrified, and thought that they were seeing a ghost. He said to them, "Why are you frightened, and why do doubts arise in your hearts? Look at my hands and my feet; see that it is I myself. Touch me and see; for a ghost does not have flesh and bones as you see that I have." And when he had said this, he showed them his hands and his feet. While in their joy they were disbelieving and still wondering, he said to them, "Have you anything here to eat?" They gave him a piece of broiled fish, and he took it and ate in their presence.

Then he said to them, "These are my words that I spoke to you while I was still with you—that everything written about me in the law of Moses, the prophets, and the psalms must be fulfilled." Then he opened their minds to understand the scriptures, and he said to them, "Thus it is written, that the Messiah is to suffer and to rise from the dead on the third day, and that repentance and forgiveness of sins is to be proclaimed in his name to all nations, beginning from Jerusalem. You are witnesses of these things."

Notice what you think and feel as you read the gospel.

Look at his hands and his feet, still bearing the imprint of the nails of the Cross. Touch him and see. He is alive. All that is written about him is true, and all shall be fulfilled.

Pray as you are led for yourself and others.

"I cling to your promise of forgiveness, Lord. For by your Cross and Resurrection you have set me free. I pray for those who need forgiveness today, that they may repent and turn to you for everlasting life . . ." (Continue in your own words.)

Listen to Jesus.

Loving God is a daily act. Love me all the time. Give me your fears, your doubts. Give me those who need me every day. We are walking and working side by side. What else is Jesus saying to you?

Ask God to show you how to live today.

"I cannot know what will happen in my life today, but I want to face it in your company, Lord. You will help me do that. Thank you. Amen."

Friday, April 26, 2019

Know that God is present with you and ready to converse.

"I know you are with me always, Lord, but I do not always recognize you. Let me do so now."

Read the gospel: John 21:1–14.

After these things Jesus showed himself again to the disciples by the Sea of Tiberias; and he showed himself in this way. Gathered there together were Simon Peter, Thomas called the Twin, Nathanael of Cana in Galilee, the sons of Zebedee, and two others of his disciples. Simon Peter said to them, "I am going fishing." They said to him, "We will go with you." They went out and got into the boat, but that night they caught nothing.

Just after daybreak, Jesus stood on the beach; but the disciples did not know that it was Jesus. Jesus said to them, "Children, you have no fish, have you?" They answered him, "No." He said to them, "Cast the net to the right side of the boat, and you will find some." So they cast it, and now they were not able to haul it in because there were so many fish. That disciple whom Jesus loved said to Peter, "It is the Lord!" When Simon Peter heard that it was the Lord, he put on some clothes, for he was naked, and jumped into the lake. But the other disciples came in the boat, dragging the net full of fish, for they were not far from the land, only about a hundred yards off.

When they had gone ashore, they saw a charcoal fire there, with fish on it, and bread. Jesus said to them, "Bring some of the fish that you have just caught." So Simon Peter went aboard and hauled the net ashore, full of large fish, a hundred and fifty-three of them; and though there were so many, the net was not torn. Jesus said to them, "Come and have breakfast." Now none of the disciples dared to ask him, "Who are you?" because they knew it was the Lord. Jesus came and took the bread and gave it to them, and did the same with the fish. This was now the third time that Jesus appeared to the disciples after he was raised from the dead.

Notice what you think and feel as you read the gospel.

How did Jesus look after his Resurrection? His disciples have difficulty recognizing him as he appears to them in different ways in different places. Here he cooks them breakfast on the shore.

Pray as you are led for yourself and others.

"Jesus, feed me, too. Feed me with the truth of your Resurrection, mighty Lord and King. Let me give to you all my circumstances. Let me entrust to you all those you have given me . . ." (Continue in your own words.)

Listen to Jesus.

I will provide for all your needs, dear friend, for you have placed your trust in me. What else is Jesus saying to you?

Ask God to show you how to live today.

"How shall I behave, Lord? Now that I have seen you with eyes of faith, show me how to be in this world. How may I glorify you, Jesus, my Rock and my Redeemer? Amen."

Saturday, April 27, 2019

Know that God is present with you and ready to converse.

"The reality of your Resurrection takes time to sink into one's being. Banish my doubts with your presence, Lord Jesus."

Read the gospel: Mark 16:9–15.

Now after Jesus rose early on the first day of the week, he appeared first to Mary Magdalene, from whom he had cast out seven demons. She went out and told those who had been with him, while they were mourning and weeping. But when they heard that he was alive and had been seen by her, they would not believe it.

After this he appeared in another form to two of them, as they were walking into the country. And they went back and told the rest, but they did not believe them.

Later he appeared to the eleven themselves as they were sitting at the table; and he upbraided them for their lack of faith and stubbornness, because they had not believed those who saw him after he had risen. And he said to them, "Go into all the world and proclaim the good news to the whole creation."

Notice what you think and feel as you read the gospel.

Jesus tells those who have been slow to believe to go into all the world and proclaim the Good News to all. Even when we doubt, he sends us with a message of faith to others.

Pray as you are led for yourself and others.

"Lord, send me. Even today, let me be a messenger of your love and your truth. Let me walk and speak in your power, Lord, and by your Spirit. Though I doubt myself, let me trust in you. I give you . . ." (Continue in your own words.)

Listen to Jesus.
You are blessed to believe in me. Your heart aches for those who still have not come to me. I join you in praying for them. With God all things are possible. What else is Jesus saying to you?

Ask God to show you how to live today.
"Give me the right words to say at the right time, Lord. Give me work to do and let me do it with you. Amen."

Sunday, April 28, 2019
Second Sunday of Easter

Know that God is present with you and ready to converse.
"Breathe your holy truth upon me, Lord, as I read your Word. I seek your blessing. I seek you, Son of God."

Read the gospel: John 20:19–23, 30–31 (Jn 20:19–31).
When it was evening on that day, the first day of the week, and the doors of the house where the disciples had met were locked for fear of the Jews, Jesus came and stood among them and said, "Peace be with you." After he said this, he showed them his hands and his side. Then the disciples rejoiced when they saw the Lord. Jesus said to them again, "Peace be with you. As the Father has sent me, so I send you." When he had said this, he breathed on them and said to them, "Receive the Holy Spirit. If you forgive the sins of any, they are forgiven them; if you retain the sins of any, they are retained." . . .

Now Jesus did many other signs in the presence of his disciples, which are not written in this book. But these are written so that you may come to believe that Jesus is the Messiah, the Son of God, and that through believing you may have life in his name.

Notice what you think and feel as you read the gospel.
Jesus breathes on his disciples and tells them to receive the Holy Spirit, then he sends them out to continue his work on earth. We, too, are sent to do the work of the Father.

Pray as you are led for yourself and others.
"Lord, you know I am weak and flawed, yet I offer myself entirely to you. Give me your Holy Spirit that I may serve you well. I am a sinner

restored to grace by your power, Lord. Let me be a vessel of grace for others . . ." (Continue in your own words.)

Listen to Jesus.

You are right to rely on me. Do not be afraid. I have work for you only you can do. I love you. What else is Jesus saying to you?

Ask God to show you how to live today.

"I resolve to lean on the Lord today with my heart open to him. Let my eyes be open to see the Lord in others. Amen."

Monday, April 29, 2019

Know that God is present with you and ready to converse.

"Who has seen the wind? Who can control the Spirit of God? I am here with you now, Spirit of Christ. Do with me what you will."

Read the gospel: John 3:1–8.

Now there was a Pharisee named Nicodemus, a leader of the Jews. He came to Jesus by night and said to him, "Rabbi, we know that you are a teacher who has come from God; for no one can do these signs that you do apart from the presence of God." Jesus answered him, "Very truly, I tell you, no one can see the kingdom of God without being born from above." Nicodemus said to him, "How can anyone be born after having grown old? Can one enter a second time into the mother's womb and be born?" Jesus answered, "Very truly, I tell you, no one can enter the kingdom of God without being born of water and Spirit. What is born of the flesh is flesh, and what is born of the Spirit is spirit. Do not be astonished that I said to you, 'You must be born from above.' The wind blows where it chooses, and you hear the sound of it, but you do not know where it comes from or where it goes. So it is with everyone who is born of the Spirit."

Notice what you think and feel as you read the gospel.

Becoming a child of God requires a spiritual birth. We must be born from above. It is not our doing but God's.

Pray as you are led for yourself and others.

"Lord, I often strive be great through my own efforts. Let me allow you to transform me and guide me by your Spirit. I wish to do your will, Lord . . ." (Continue in your own words.)

Listen to Jesus.

I will that you worship God in Spirit and in Truth, dear follower. Ask me for the grace you need. Look around you and see what we can do together. What else is Jesus saying to you?

Ask God to show you how to live today.

"Whatever happens today, Lord, I surrender to you in trust. I know that you work in all circumstances, that nothing is more than I can manage with your help. I am yours, Jesus. Amen."

Tuesday, April 30, 2019

Know that God is present with you and ready to converse.

"Jesus, let me read your Word in the light of the Holy Spirit, that I might learn what I most need. Thank you, Jesus."

Read the gospel: John 3:7b–15.

Jesus said, "Do not be astonished that I said to you, 'You must be born from above.' The wind blows where it chooses, and you hear the sound of it, but you do not know where it comes from or where it goes. So it is with everyone who is born of the Spirit." Nicodemus said to him, "How can these things be?" Jesus answered him, "Are you a teacher of Israel, and yet you do not understand these things?

"Very truly, I tell you, we speak of what we know and testify to what we have seen; yet you do not receive our testimony. If I have told you about earthly things and you do not believe, how can you believe if I tell you about heavenly things? No one has ascended into heaven except the one who descended from heaven, the Son of Man. And just as Moses lifted up the serpent in the wilderness, so must the Son of Man be lifted up, that whoever believes in him may have eternal life."

Notice what you think and feel as you read the gospel.

Jesus speaks in response to sincere questions from Nicodemus, telling him that it requires faith to understand his words and God's ways. The divine is not limited by human understanding—have faith first, and understanding will follow. Jesus prophesies his own death, something Nicodemus will not forget.

Pray as you are led for yourself and others.

"Give me that simple faith, Lord, for I long to live as you command. Give me the awareness that this is a serious age and souls are at stake. I pray for these people . . ." (Continue in your own words.)

Listen to Jesus.

Life is short, my dear child. You believe and wish to serve me and those I have put in your life. I am with you in this. What else is Jesus saying to you?

Ask God to show you how to live today.

"Do not let me create barriers to you by my own ways of thinking, Lord. Help me to entrust myself to your mysterious power. Let me do your will and give glory to God! Amen."

THE POPE'S MONTHLY PRAYER INTENTION FOR MAY 2019

That the Church in Africa, through the commitment of its members, may be the seed of unity among her peoples and a sign of hope for this continent.

Wednesday, May 1, 2019
Joseph the Worker

Know that God is present with you and ready to converse.

"Lord, let not unbelief creep in because of my familiarity with you and your Word. I long to grow in faith and love."

Read the gospel: Matthew 13:54–58.

He came to his hometown and began to teach the people in their synagogue, so that they were astounded and said, "Where did this man get this wisdom and these deeds of power? Is not this the carpenter's son? Is not his mother called Mary? And are not his brothers James and Joseph and Simon and Judas? And are not all his sisters with us? Where then did this man get all this?" And they took offence at him. But Jesus said to them, "Prophets are not without honor except in their own country and in their own house." And he did not do many deeds of power there, because of their unbelief.

Notice what you think and feel as you read the gospel.

Jesus is not well received in his hometown. They are amazed by his preaching and teaching, because they know him as the son of Joseph, the carpenter, not as the Messiah.

Pray as you are led for yourself and others.

"Lord, I pray for all those who doubt you. Let us all turn toward you with fresh faith, for you require faith from your followers . . ." (Continue in your own words.)

Listen to Jesus.

I am here with you always. Come to me with an open heart each day, and I will reveal myself to you more and more. What else is Jesus saying to you?

Ask God to show you how to live today.

"Let my eyes be fixed upon you, Lord, and let me walk in faith all day. Amen."

Thursday, May 2, 2019

Know that God is present with you and ready to converse.

"You have come down from heaven for me, Lord. Thank you."

Read the gospel: John 3:31–36.

The one who comes from above is above all; the one who is of the earth belongs to the earth and speaks about earthly things. The one who comes from heaven is above all. He testifies to what he has seen and heard, yet no one accepts his testimony. Whoever has accepted his testimony has certified this, that God is true. He whom God has sent speaks the words of God, for he gives the Spirit without measure. The Father loves the Son and has placed all things in his hands. Whoever believes in the Son has eternal life; whoever disobeys the Son will not see life, but must endure God's wrath.

Notice what you think and feel as you read the gospel.

God is true, and Jesus speaks the words of God. God is all truth, all love, and all life. In him we have eternal life.

Pray as you are led for yourself and others.

"What blessedness you give to me, dear Lord. Pour out your Spirit and renew the earth. Kindle hearts with love for God, for you alone are worthy of worship . . ." (Continue in your own words.)

Listen to Jesus.

I quicken hearts like yours to hunger for God, in whom is infinite perfection. When you feel the need to pray, it is I calling you, my beloved disciple. What else is Jesus saying to you?

Ask God to show you how to live today.

"Teach me obedience to you, Jesus. Reveal to me whatever is not pleasing to you and give me your Spirit to obey you well. Glory be to the Father, the Son, and the Holy Spirit. Amen."

Friday, May 3, 2019
Sts. Philip and James, Apostles

Know that God is present with you and ready to converse.

"Jesus, you yourself are the great sign from God. You are the Lord of glory. Come in."

Read the gospel: John 14:6–14.

Jesus said to him, "I am the way, and the truth, and the life. No one comes to the Father except through me. If you know me, you will know my Father also. From now on you do know him and have seen him."

Philip said to him, "Lord, show us the Father, and we will be satisfied." Jesus said to him, "Have I been with you all this time, Philip, and you still do not know me? Whoever has seen me has seen the Father. How can you say, 'Show us the Father'? Do you not believe that I am in the Father and the Father is in me? The words that I say to you I do not speak on my own; but the Father who dwells in me does his works. Believe me that I am in the Father and the Father is in me; but if you do not, then believe me because of the works themselves. Very truly, I tell you, the one who believes in me will also do the works that I do and, in fact, will do greater works than these, because I am going to the Father. I will do whatever you ask in my name, so that the Father may be glorified in the Son. If in my name you ask me for anything, I will do it."

Notice what you think and feel as you read the gospel.

Jesus identifies with his Father, saying that if we know him, we know his Father. He encourages his followers to pray to the Father in his name.

Pray as you are led for yourself and others.

"Lord, I pray in your holy name for those you place on my heart, especially. . ." (Continue in your own words.)

Listen to Jesus.

In your love for others, you reveal your love for me and give glory to the Father. What else is Jesus saying to you?

Ask God to show you how to live today.

"So many hearts long for your love, Lord. Let me be a conduit of your grace."

Saturday, May 4, 2019

Know that God is present with you and ready to converse.

"You are with me, Lord. What have I to fear?"

Read the gospel: John 6:16–21.

When evening came, Jesus' disciples went down to the lake, got into a boat, and started across the lake to Capernaum. It was now dark, and Jesus had not yet come to them. The lake became rough because a strong wind was blowing. When they had rowed about three or four miles, they saw Jesus walking on the lake and coming near the boat, and they were terrified. But he said to them, "It is I; do not be afraid." Then they wanted to take him into the boat, and immediately the boat reached the land towards which they were going.

Notice what you think and feel as you read the gospel.

Jesus is off by himself praying while the disciples are rowing toward Capernaum in the dark. The waters are rough, but what seems to scare the disciples is the sight of Jesus walking toward them on the lake. He calms their fears.

Pray as you are led for yourself and others.

"Jesus, sometimes I sail in rough seas. Come to me and calm my fears . . ."
(Continue in your own words.)

Listen to Jesus.

Tell me all that frightens you, my child. Tell me all your concerns for others as well. Then receive my peace and my reassurance that all shall be well. What else is Jesus saying to you?

Ask God to show you how to live today.

"Hold me in your peace today especially as I deal with rough matters. Prince of Peace, keep me in your presence all day long. Amen."

Sunday, May 5, 2019
Third Sunday of Easter

Know that God is present with you and ready to converse.

"Lord, I rejoice in your presence this moment. Let me know you better by your Word."

Read the gospel: John 21:1–14 (Jn 21:1–19).

After these things Jesus showed himself again to the disciples by the Sea of Tiberias; and he showed himself in this way. Gathered there together were Simon Peter, Thomas called the Twin, Nathanael of Cana in Galilee, the sons of Zebedee, and two others of his disciples. Simon Peter said to them, "I am going fishing." They said to him, "We will go with you." They went out and got into the boat, but that night they caught nothing.

Just after daybreak, Jesus stood on the beach; but the disciples did not know that it was Jesus. Jesus said to them, "Children, you have no fish, have you?" They answered him, "No." He said to them, "Cast the net to the right side of the boat, and you will find some." So they cast it, and now they were not able to haul it in because there were so many fish. That disciple whom Jesus loved said to Peter, "It is the Lord!" When Simon Peter heard that it was the Lord, he put on some clothes, for he was naked, and jumped into the lake. But the other disciples came in the boat, dragging the net full of fish, for they were not far from the land, only about a hundred yards off.

When they had gone ashore, they saw a charcoal fire there, with fish on it, and bread. Jesus said to them, "Bring some of the fish that you have just caught." So Simon Peter went aboard and hauled the net

ashore, full of large fish, a hundred and fifty-three of them; and though
there were so many, the net was not torn. Jesus said to them, "Come and
have breakfast." Now none of the disciples dared to ask him, "Who are
you?" because they knew it was the Lord. Jesus came and took the bread
and gave it to them, and did the same with the fish. This was now the
third time that Jesus appeared to the disciples after he was raised from
the dead.

Notice what you think and feel as you read the gospel.

After his Resurrection, Jesus appears to his disciples, showing them
where to fish. After they surprisingly catch a great many large fish, Peter
recognizes Jesus, and Jesus prepares breakfast for them all on the beach.
Then he tests Peter, asking him three times if he loves him. Peter says
yes, and Jesus orders him to feed his sheep.

Pray as you are led for yourself and others.

"Let me show you my love, Lord. I stand ready and willing to feed your
flock. Lord, may those near and far believe in you, know you, and love
you . . ." (Continue in your own words.)

Listen to Jesus.

*I want to share my life with all humanity. I give it to those who follow me. You
may share it with others.* What else is Jesus saying to you?

Ask God to show you how to live today.

"Make a difference in my day, Lord. Let me move someone with your
love. Amen."

Monday, May 6, 2019

Know that God is present with you and ready to converse.

"It is human to take blessings for granted. Lord, wake me up to your
wonderful works in my life."

Read the gospel: John 6:22–29.

The next day the crowd that had stayed on the other side of the lake saw
that there had been only one boat there. They also saw that Jesus had not
got into the boat with his disciples, but that his disciples had gone away
alone. Then some boats from Tiberias came near the place where they
had eaten the bread after the Lord had given thanks. So when the crowd

saw that neither Jesus nor his disciples were there, they themselves got into the boats and went to Capernaum looking for Jesus.

When they found him on the other side of the lake, they said to him, "Rabbi, when did you come here?" Jesus answered them, "Very truly, I tell you, you are looking for me, not because you saw signs, but because you ate your fill of the loaves. Do not work for the food that perishes, but for the food that endures for eternal life, which the Son of Man will give you. For it is on him that God the Father has set his seal." Then they said to him, "What must we do to perform the works of God?" Jesus answered them, "This is the work of God, that you believe in him whom he has sent."

Notice what you think and feel as you read the gospel.

The people whom Jesus miraculously fed follow him across the lake. Jesus criticizes those followers who stay near him just for earthly food. He promises eternal life and divine sustenance for those who do the work of God: believing in the One whom God sent.

Pray as you are led for yourself and others.

"Lord, I believe that you are who you say you are. I want to follow you; sustain me, body and soul, so that I may do your work here on earth . . ." (Continue in your own words.)

Listen to Jesus.

You are in my service, beloved. Do your work humbly and faithfully. God is with you. What else is Jesus saying to you?

Ask God to show you how to live today.

"Show me the work you want me to do today, Lord, and give me the grace to do it. Amen."

Tuesday, May 7, 2019

Know that God is present with you and ready to converse.

"Jesus, I hunger for God. Give me the bread of heaven today."

Read the gospel: John 6:30–35.

So the crowd said to Jesus, "What sign are you going to give us then, so that we may see it and believe you? What work are you performing? Our ancestors ate the manna in the wilderness; as it is written, 'He gave them bread from heaven to eat.'" Then Jesus said to them, "Very truly, I tell you, it was not Moses who gave you the bread from heaven, but it is my Father who gives you the true bread from heaven. For the bread of God is that which comes down from heaven and gives life to the world." They said to him, "Sir, give us this bread always."

Jesus said to them, "I am the bread of life. Whoever comes to me will never be hungry, and whoever believes in me will never be thirsty."

Notice what you think and feel as you read the gospel.

People in the crowd want Jesus to prove himself a prophet by a sign as Moses did with the manna in the wilderness. Jesus says that he himself is the true bread from heaven.

Pray as you are led for yourself and others.

"Jesus, you nourish me with the bread of your Word and with your Body and Blood in the Eucharist. Thank you for giving yourself to me. I offer you myself in response. How may I serve you? . . ." (Continue in your own words.)

Listen to Jesus.

There is joy and freedom in giving yourself to me. I will take care of you. You and I may become very close. What else is Jesus saying to you?

Ask God to show you how to live today.

"Thank you for being my food and drink, Lord. Send me out to do your will. Amen."

Wednesday, May 8, 2019

Know that God is present with you and ready to converse.

"Lord, let me know you by the reading of your Word. Let me give you my love and worship."

Read the gospel: John 6:35–40.

Jesus said to them, "I am the bread of life. Whoever comes to me will never be hungry, and whoever believes in me will never be thirsty. But I said to you that you have seen me and yet do not believe. Everything that the Father gives me will come to me, and anyone who comes to me I will never drive away; for I have come down from heaven, not to do my own will, but the will of him who sent me. And this is the will of him who sent me, that I should lose nothing of all that he has given me, but raise it up on the last day. This is indeed the will of my Father, that all who see the Son and believe in him may have eternal life; and I will raise them up on the last day."

Notice what you think and feel as you read the gospel.
Jesus is one with the Father and promises eternal life to all those who believe in him. He will raise us up on the last day.

Pray as you are led for yourself and others.
"Jesus, I ask in your name for the salvation of the world and the coming of your kingdom. Let the whole earth glorify your name . . ." (Continue in your own words.)

Listen to Jesus.
I hear your prayers, and I will do what you ask. Believe in me with all your heart, and you will see great good come upon you and those for whom you pray. What else is Jesus saying to you?

Ask God to show you how to live today.
"Give me the faith I need to pray and act in your name, Lord. I want to do all for the glory of God. Amen."

Thursday, May 9, 2019

Know that God is present with you and ready to converse.
"Father, you have drawn me to Jesus, the very Word of God before me."

Read the gospel: John 6:44–51.
Jesus said, "No one can come to me unless drawn by the Father who sent me; and I will raise that person up on the last day. It is written in the prophets, 'And they shall all be taught by God.' Everyone who has heard and learned from the Father comes to me. Not that anyone has seen the Father except the one who is from God; he has seen the Father. Very truly, I tell you, whoever believes has eternal life. I am the bread of life. Your ancestors ate the manna in the wilderness, and they died. This is the bread that comes down from heaven, so that one may eat of it and not die. I am the living bread that came down from heaven. Whoever eats of this bread will live for ever; and the bread that I will give for the life of the world is my flesh."

Notice what you think and feel as you read the gospel.

Jesus says those who come to him are drawn by the Father, and those who believe will have eternal life. The "food that endures for eternal life," the life-giving bread of heaven, is his very flesh.

Pray as you are led for yourself and others.

"Jesus, your promise is great; your words are true. Let me understand and act upon them. Your Father draws me to you . . ." (Continue in your own words.)

Listen to Jesus.

You shall be taught by God, dear one, for you are coming to me. In me is life for you and all you pray for. What else is Jesus saying to you?

Ask God to show you how to live today.

"Let me remember today that in you is life. Let me remain in you, Jesus, and live forever. Amen."

Friday, May 10, 2019

Know that God is present with you and ready to converse.

"Lord, let me read your Word with eyes of faith. I long to know you and to understand all the truth you have for me."

Read the gospel: John 6:52–59.

The Jews then disputed among themselves, saying, "How can this man give us his flesh to eat?" So Jesus said to them, "Very truly, I tell you, unless you eat the flesh of the Son of Man and drink his blood, you have no life in you. Those who eat my flesh and drink my blood have eternal life, and I will raise them up on the last day; for my flesh is true food and my blood is true drink. Those who eat my flesh and drink my blood abide in me, and I in them. Just as the living Father sent me, and I live because of the Father, so whoever eats me will live because of me. This is the bread that came down from heaven, not like that which your ancestors ate, and they died. But the one who eats this bread will live for ever." He said these things while he was teaching in the synagogue at Capernaum.

Notice what you think and feel as you read the gospel.

Those who listen to Jesus cannot understand how he can give them his flesh to eat. Jesus repeats in very literal terms that one must eat his flesh and drink his blood to abide in him and have everlasting life.

Pray as you are led for yourself and others.

"Jesus, let me receive your Body and Blood in the Eucharist with growing faith and appreciation. I pray for all who cannot receive the truth of this gospel . . ." (Continue in your own words.)

Listen to Jesus.

Child, do you see that my devotion to you is total? I give you all of myself. What else is Jesus saying to you?

Ask God to show you how to live today.

"Lord, I am following you. I want to give as you give. I ask that your life flow through me to others today. Amen."

Saturday, May 11, 2019

Know that God is present with you and ready to converse.

"Lord, you challenge me by your Word, but I have nowhere else to go for truth and life. Let me receive it now."

Read the gospel: John 6:60–69.

When many of Jesus' disciples heard it, they said, "This teaching is difficult; who can accept it?" But Jesus, being aware that his disciples were complaining about it, said to them, "Does this offend you? Then what if you were to see the Son of Man ascending to where he was before? It is the spirit that gives life; the flesh is useless. The words that I have spoken to you are spirit and life. But among you there are some who do not believe." For Jesus knew from the first who were the ones that did not believe, and who was the one that would betray him. And he said, "For this reason I have told you that no one can come to me unless it is granted by the Father."

Because of this many of his disciples turned back and no longer went about with him. So Jesus asked the twelve, "Do you also wish to go away?" Simon Peter answered him, "Lord, to whom can we go? You have the words of eternal life. We have come to believe and know that you are the Holy One of God."

Notice what you think and feel as you read the gospel.

Jesus asks his disciples to believe in mysteries—that he himself is the bread of heaven, that he is one with the Father, that he will ascend to his Father, and that the Spirit alone gives life, eternal life. Overwhelmed by his teaching, some turn back; others accept the difficulty because they acknowledge him as the Messiah.

Pray as you are led for yourself and others

"Jesus, with your help I will not turn back. You ask for great faith and great commitment. Increase both in me. Father, draw me into Jesus. I pray also for . . ." (Continue in your own words.)

Listen to Jesus.

Great work is being done in your spirit as you seek me and contemplate my words. They are the words of eternal life for you, my beloved disciple. Keep following me. What else is Jesus saying to you?

Ask God to show you how to live today.

"I have chosen life, Lord. I am all in with you. Purify me that I may be truly single-minded in my devotion to you and to your work on earth. I offer myself again, Lord. Use me. Amen."

Sunday, May 12, 2019
Fourth Sunday of Easter

Know that God is present with you and ready to converse.

"Dear Lord, let me read and understand all that you have for me here today."

Read the gospel: John 10:27–30.

Jesus said, "My sheep hear my voice. I know them, and they follow me. I give them eternal life, and they will never perish. No one will snatch them out of my hand. What my Father has given me is greater than all else, and no one can snatch it out of the Father's hand. The Father and I are one."

Notice what you think and feel as you read the gospel.

Jesus uses a figure of speech to describe himself in relation to us. He is the shepherd who knows his sheep and is known by them, and they follow him. Just as a shepherd guards his sheep from wolves, Jesus guides and guards us from sin.

Pray as you are led for yourself and others.

"Let me follow you alone, Lord, and not strangers or thieves. Thank you for the life you give me. Thank you for your holy Word that transforms me from within. I pray that others may know you and enter your pasture . . ." (Continue in your own words.)

Listen to Jesus.

I speak to hearts in many ways. I gather my sheep and I do it well. You may trust me with your life and with the lives of those I have given you. What else is Jesus saying to you?

Ask God to show you how to live today.

"Let me take what you show me in the spirit and bring it to practical uses in this day-to-day world of matter and practicality. I thank you for your faithful care for me and all those you have given me. Amen."

Monday, May 13, 2019

Know that God is present with you and ready to converse.

"Who is here with me? It is you, Lord. Always you. Alleluia."

Read the gospel: John 10:1–10.

Jesus said, "Very truly, I tell you, anyone who does not enter the sheepfold by the gate but climbs in by another way is a thief and a bandit. The one who enters by the gate is the shepherd of the sheep. The gatekeeper opens the gate for him, and the sheep hear his voice. He calls his own sheep by name and leads them out. When he has brought out all his own, he goes ahead of them, and the sheep follow him because they know his voice. They will not follow a stranger, but they will run from him because they do not know the voice of strangers." Jesus used this figure of speech with them, but they did not understand what he was saying to them.

So again Jesus said to them, "Very truly, I tell you, I am the gate for the sheep. All who came before me are thieves and bandits; but the sheep did not listen to them. I am the gate. Whoever enters by me will be saved, and will come in and go out and find pasture. The thief comes only to steal and kill and destroy. I came that they may have life, and have it abundantly."

Notice what you think and feel as you read the gospel.

Jesus is both the rightful shepherd and the gate that keeps the sheep safe. His own sheep will always recognize him, and he will save them.

Pray as you are led for yourself and others.

"Jesus, I come into your fold and listen to your voice. I pray for those who have wandered away from you or who are afraid to enter . . ." (Continue in your own words.)

Listen to Jesus.

Rely on me, my beloved, and I will keep you safe at all times. As you abide in me, you will know me more and more. You may pray for those you love with confidence. I love them, too. What else is Jesus saying to you?

Ask God to show you how to live today.

"Jesus, you do so much for me and mine that I long to do something for you. Give me work that pleases you. Amen."

Tuesday, May 14, 2019

Know that God is present with you and ready to converse.

"Jesus, as I read your Word, give me your Spirit of understanding and faith."

Read the gospel: John 10:22–26 (Jn 10:22–30).

At that time the festival of the Dedication took place in Jerusalem. It was winter, and Jesus was walking in the temple, in the portico of Solomon. So the Jews gathered around him and said to him, "How long will you keep us in suspense? If you are the Messiah, tell us plainly." Jesus answered, "I have told you, and you do not believe. The works that I do in my Father's name testify to me; but you do not believe, because you do not belong to my sheep."

Notice what you think and feel as you read the gospel.

Jesus admits to being the Messiah, but they keep asking because they do not believe. Those who do believe, and who follow him, will never perish. They are safe with him, for he is the shepherd of his sheep. Those who believe are a gift to him from his Father, and he and his Father are one.

Pray as you are led for yourself and others.

"You promise me eternal life; you have already given it to me. Let me treasure that life and rest in my security. You are my security, Lord. I love you . . ." (Continue in your own words.)

Listen to Jesus.

I love you, child. My Father has drawn you to me. You hear my voice. What else is Jesus saying to you?

Ask God to show you how to live today.

"Jesus, let me hear your voice often as I go about my day. And let me obey you completely. Give me grace to obey you always. Amen."

Wednesday, May 15, 2019

Know that God is present with you and ready to converse.

"Jesus, you speak the Word of your Father. Save me."

Read the gospel: John 12:44–50.

Then Jesus cried aloud: "Whoever believes in me believes not in me but in him who sent me. And whoever sees me sees him who sent me. I have come as light into the world, so that everyone who believes in me should not remain in the darkness. I do not judge anyone who hears my words and does not keep them, for I came not to judge the world, but to save the world. The one who rejects me and does not receive my word has a judge; on the last day the word that I have spoken will serve as judge, for I have not spoken on my own, but the Father who sent me has himself given me a commandment about what to say and what to speak. And I know that his commandment is eternal life. What I speak, therefore, I speak just as the Father has told me."

Notice what you think and feel as you read the gospel.

Jesus proclaims that he is one with the Father, that he comes as light into the world, and that he brings salvation, not judgment. On the last day the word he has spoken will judge all people.

Pray as you are led for yourself and others.

"Jesus, let your light continue to shine in our darkness. I pray for those in darkness. Let them come into your marvelous light . . ." (Continue in your own words.)

Listen to Jesus.

Your life and all history are very brief. All the time that ever was or will be cannot fill up eternity. You walk in time toward eternal life, my child. Follow me. What else is Jesus saying to you?

Ask God to show you how to live today.

"Keep my eyes and mind on heavenly things, Lord. Let me do what is good today. Amen."

Thursday, May 16, 2019

Know that God is present with you and ready to converse.

"Jesus, let me hear, learn, and know you in your Word."

Read the gospel: John 13:16–20.

Jesus said, "Very truly, I tell you, servants are not greater than their master, nor are messengers greater than the one who sent them. If you know these things, you are blessed if you do them. I am not speaking of all of you; I know whom I have chosen. But it is to fulfill the scripture, 'The one who ate my bread has lifted his heel against me.' I tell you this now, before it occurs, so that when it does occur, you may believe that I am he. Very truly, I tell you, whoever receives one whom I send receives me; and whoever receives me receives him who sent me."

Notice what you think and feel as you read the gospel.

Jesus says we are blessed if we do the things we know from him. As his servants, we are to do what Jesus did and serve others. This is the will of the Father.

Pray as you are led for yourself and others.

"Lord, I resolve to do what you would have me do. I place myself and my day in your hands to do with whatever you will. Let me do your work . . ." (Continue in your own words.)

Listen to Jesus.

Whatever you do for love of me and for love of others is a great thing. Do not be discouraged that your deeds are small or ordinary. Do them with love and you shall be as I am. What else is Jesus saying to you?

Ask God to show you how to live today.

"Master, help me receive those you send to me, and let me be sent to those you wish to receive you. Give me wisdom to do this. I glorify you, Lord. Amen."

Friday, May 17, 2019

Know that God is present with you and ready to converse.

"Jesus, I seek God: Father, Son, and Holy Spirit. I seek God now in your Word."

Read the gospel: John 14:1–6.

Jesus said, "Do not let your hearts be troubled. Believe in God, believe also in me. In my Father's house there are many dwelling-places. If it were not so, would I have told you that I go to prepare a place for you? And if I go and prepare a place for you, I will come again and will take you to myself, so that where I am, there you may be also. And you know the way to the place where I am going." Thomas said to him, "Lord, we do not know where you are going. How can we know the way?" Jesus said to him, "I am the way, and the truth, and the life. No one comes to the Father except through me."

Notice what you think and feel as you read the gospel.

Jesus speaks peace to his troubled disciples. He is going away so he can return and bring them to himself in his Father's house. Thomas questions him further, and Jesus assures Thomas that he is the way, the truth, and the life.

Pray as you are led for yourself and others.

"Jesus, thank you for your reassurances. I long for your Father's house. May I dwell with God forever with all those you have given me . . ." (Continue in your own words.)

Listen to Jesus.

All those in your life, I have given you. Look upon each one with love as I look upon you. Do unto them what I would do. What else is Jesus saying to you?

Ask God to show you how to live today.

"Jesus, you challenge me to love and to act upon that love. My love is imperfect. Strengthen me to love others as you love and to do for others what you would do. Amen."

Saturday, May 18, 2019

Know that God is present with you and ready to converse.

"Jesus, you are my way to God. Let me know you through your Word and your Spirit."

Read the gospel: John 14:7–14.

Jesus said, "If you know me, you will know my Father also. From now on you do know him and have seen him."

Philip said to him, "Lord, show us the Father, and we will be satisfied." Jesus said to him, "Have I been with you all this time, Philip, and you still do not know me? Whoever has seen me has seen the Father. How can you say, 'Show us the Father'? Do you not believe that I am in the Father and the Father is in me? The words that I say to you I do not speak on my own; but the Father who dwells in me does his works. Believe me that I am in the Father and the Father is in me; but if you do not, then believe me because of the works themselves. Very truly, I tell you, the one who believes in me will also do the works that I do and, in fact, will do greater works than these, because I am going to the Father. I will do whatever you ask in my name, so that the Father may be glorified in the Son. If in my name you ask me for anything, I will do it."

Notice what you think and feel as you read the gospel.

Jesus wants his disciples to know his Father, for he and his Father are one, and he speaks for his Father. The ones who believe in him will do the works he does and pray as he does, in the power and the glory of the Father.

Pray as you are led for yourself and others.

"Lord, thank you for the power of prayer in your name. I pray for these needs and these people . . ." (Continue in your own words.)

Listen to Jesus.

I hear your prayers and thank you for them. By prayer you are doing my works and glorifying my Father. You will know the power of your prayers. What else is Jesus saying to you?

Ask God to show you how to live today.

"Let me see you and know you today in others, Lord, and do what you want me to do for them. Let me do it as unto you. Amen."

Sunday, May 19, 2019
Fifth Sunday of Easter

Know that God is present with you and ready to converse.

"Lord, speak to my heart and soul with power, that I may love you and do your holy will."

Read the gospel: John 13:31–33a, 34–35.

Jesus said, "Now the Son of Man has been glorified, and God has been glorified in him. If God has been glorified in him, God will also glorify him in himself and will glorify him at once. Little children, I am with you only a little longer. You will look for me; and as I said to the Jews so now I say to you, 'Where I am going, you cannot come.' . . . I give you a new commandment, that you love one another. Just as I have loved you, you also should love one another. By this everyone will know that you are my disciples, if you have love for one another."

Notice what you think and feel as you read the gospel.

Jesus is ready to die for those he has loved, for this is the proof of love. He commands his disciples to love one another as he has loved, for that will be the proof to the world that we are his disciples.

Pray as you are led for yourself and others.

"Lord, grant me the love for others that you command of me. Guide my prayers for those you have given me . . ." (Continue in your own words.)

Listen to Jesus.

I rejoice in your obedience, my dear one. What else is Jesus saying to you?

Ask God to show you how to live today.
"I believe in you, Lord, and I offer myself to do the works that you do. Be my companion today, Jesus. Amen."

Monday, May 20, 2019

Know that God is present with you and ready to converse.
"Holy Spirit, author of the Word of God, teach me what I need to know. Quicken me."

Read the gospel: John 14:21–26.
Jesus said, "They who have my commandments and keep them are those who love me; and those who love me will be loved by my Father, and I will love them and reveal myself to them." Judas (not Iscariot) said to him, "Lord, how is it that you will reveal yourself to us, and not to the world?" Jesus answered him, "Those who love me will keep my word, and my Father will love them, and we will come to them and make our home with them. Whoever does not love me does not keep my words; and the word that you hear is not mine, but is from the Father who sent me.

"I have said these things to you while I am still with you. But the Advocate, the Holy Spirit, whom the Father will send in my name, will teach you everything, and remind you of all that I have said to you."

Notice what you think and feel as you read the gospel.
Jesus says he will reveal himself to those who love him. If we love him, we obey him, and he and the Father will love us and make their home with us.

Pray as you are led for yourself and others.
"Lord, be the reality of my life. Help me love and obey you, for I long to know you and to be the dwelling place of God. Holy Spirit, work in me . . ." (Continue in your own words.)

Listen to Jesus.
The love I put in your heart is for you and for others, my child. I will remind you today that the love of God is the way and the destination. Follow me. What else is Jesus saying to you?

Ask God to show you how to live today.

"I give myself to your love, Lord Jesus Christ. I give myself to your truth, Holy Spirit. Father in heaven, I glorify you and come to do your will. Amen."

Tuesday, May 21, 2019

Know that God is present with you and ready to converse.

"Lord, I open my heart to your Word of peace. Fill me with your love."

Read the gospel: John 14:27–31a.

Jesus said, "Peace I leave with you; my peace I give to you. I do not give to you as the world gives. Do not let your hearts be troubled, and do not let them be afraid. You heard me say to you, 'I am going away, and I am coming to you.' If you loved me, you would rejoice that I am going to the Father, because the Father is greater than I. And now I have told you this before it occurs, so that when it does occur, you may believe. I will no longer talk much with you, for the ruler of this world is coming. He has no power over me; but I do as the Father has commanded me, so that the world may know that I love the Father. Rise, let us be on our way."

Notice what you think and feel as you read the gospel.

Jesus tells his disciples he is going away to the Father and he is also coming back to them. He says he does what his Father commands so the world may know that he loves his Father.

Pray as you are led for yourself and others.

"Lord, I love the Father, too, and wish to do what he commands of me. Shower me and those you have given me with faith, hope, and love . . ." (Continue in your own words.)

Listen to Jesus.

Beloved child, you are precious to me. Come to me often and we shall become very close. Rise, let us be on our way. What else is Jesus saying to you?

Ask God to show you how to live today.

"Lord, I am following. By your grace, I shall walk in your peace today. Amen."

Wednesday, May 22, 2019

Know that God is present with you and ready to converse.

"You seek me constantly, Lord. I turn my attention from myself to you now. What do you ask of me, Lord?"

Read the gospel: John 15:1–8.

Jesus said, "I am the true vine, and my Father is the vinegrower. He removes every branch in me that bears no fruit. Every branch that bears fruit he prunes to make it bear more fruit. You have already been cleansed by the word that I have spoken to you. Abide in me as I abide in you. Just as the branch cannot bear fruit by itself unless it abides in the vine, neither can you unless you abide in me. I am the vine, you are the branches. Those who abide in me and I in them bear much fruit, because apart from me you can do nothing. Whoever does not abide in me is thrown away like a branch and withers; such branches are gathered, thrown into the fire, and burned. If you abide in me, and my words abide in you, ask for whatever you wish, and it will be done for you. My Father is glorified by this, that you bear much fruit and become my disciples."

Notice what you think and feel as you read the gospel.

Jesus is the vine and we are the branches bearing fruit. The Father removes the unfruitful branches and prunes the fruitful ones to bear more fruit. If we abide in him, the true vine, we will bear much fruit and so glorify the Father.

Pray as you are led for yourself and others.

"Lord, I would be more fruitful. I offer myself for pruning. I place all my trust in you. May I glorify the Lord by my life . . ." (Continue in your own words.)

Listen to Jesus.

We abide in each other, you and I. Give yourself entirely to me, and you will bring glory to the Father. What else is Jesus saying to you?

Ask God to show you how to live today.

"Lord, give me the gift of prayer. Let me pray as you would have me pray, and let others be blessed by my prayers. I want to bear fruit to the glory of God. Thank you for letting me serve, Lord. Amen."

Thursday, May 23, 2019

Know that God is present with you and ready to converse.
"My desire is to abide in your love, Jesus. Teach me how to do that."

Read the gospel: John 15:9–11.
Jesus said, "As the Father has loved me, so I have loved you; abide in my love. If you keep my commandments, you will abide in my love, just as I have kept my Father's commandments and abide in his love. I have said these things to you so that my joy may be in you, and that your joy may be complete."

Notice what you think and feel as you read the gospel.
Loving—abiding in God's love—is not primarily an emotion; it is obedience to the commandments of love. It is in doing acts of love that we know the joy of God.

Pray as you are led for yourself and others.
"Open my eyes to your commandments, Lord, that I may walk in them. Let my obedience prove my love for you. Let me abide in your love. I pray that others may also know the joy of abiding in your love . . ." (Continue in your own words.)

Listen to Jesus.
Just as my peace is not the peace of the world, so my joy is far above what the world can give you. I give you my peace and my joy, for you serve me. What else is Jesus saying to you?

Ask God to show you how to live today.
"Lord, I thank you for your blessings. You have given me so many. Give me the blessing of serving others as you do, giving them peace and joy. Amen."

Friday, May 24, 2019

Know that God is present with you and ready to converse.
"Teach me your commandments, Lord, that I may obey and abide in you."

Read the gospel: John 15:12–17.

Jesus said, "This is my commandment, that you love one another as I have loved you. No one has greater love than this, to lay down one's life for one's friends. You are my friends if you do what I command you. I do not call you servants any longer, because the servant does not know what the master is doing; but I have called you friends, because I have made known to you everything that I have heard from my Father. You did not choose me but I chose you. And I appointed you to go and bear fruit, fruit that will last, so that the Father will give you whatever you ask him in my name. I am giving you these commands so that you may love one another."

Notice what you think and feel as you read the gospel.

Jesus commands us to love one another as he loves us. What is love? What is the greatest love? To lay down one's life for one's friends, as he did. We are his friends, so let us also love one another in thought, word, and deed.

Pray as you are led for yourself and others.

"Lord, I rejoice to be your friend and that you have appointed me to go and bear fruit that will last. I pray in your name to the Father for these people . . ." (Continue in your own words.)

Listen to Jesus.

I am teaching you the mystery of true love. Love like mine is full of power to do good in the world, though the world will not understand it. Do what I command you: love one another. What else is Jesus saying to you?

Ask God to show you how to live today.

"You would not give me a commandment I could not keep. But, Jesus, only by your Holy Spirit can I love others as you love them. Give me grace to love and to pray. Amen."

Saturday, May 25, 2019

Know that God is present with you and ready to converse.

"Jesus, you came into the world to take us out of this world. Teach me what that means."

Read the gospel: John 15:18–21.

Jesus said, "If the world hates you, be aware that it hated me before it hated you. If you belonged to the world, the world would love you as its own. Because you do not belong to the world, but I have chosen you out of the world—therefore the world hates you. Remember the word that I said to you, 'Servants are not greater than their master.' If they persecuted me, they will persecute you; if they kept my word, they will keep yours also. But they will do all these things to you on account of my name, because they do not know him who sent me."

Notice what you think and feel as you read the gospel.

The world is hostile to Jesus Christ and his followers. What they did to him they will do to us. They will hate us. We belong to Christ, not to the world. That is a hard truth.

Pray as you are led for yourself and others.

"Lord, strengthen me against persecution. Let me be bold in your Spirit and walk in love, even loving those who hate me. I pray for . . ." (Continue in your own words.)

Listen to Jesus.

It is impossible to love your enemies, your persecutors, in your own power. I give you my love, which perseveres through hatred and persecution. As you follow me and do my work, you will experience rejection, but I will never leave you. What else is Jesus saying to you?

Ask God to show you how to live today.

"Lord, remove all fear from me. Please let me walk in full confidence of your love and protection, even when I face hostility. Let me be blameless as you were and suffer nobly as you did, praying for them. Amen."

Sunday, May 26, 2019
Sixth Sunday of Easter

Know that God is present with you and ready to converse.

"Eternal Word of God, impress upon me the profound truths of your way. Give me ears to hear."

Read the gospel: John 14:23–29.

Jesus said, "Those who love me will keep my word, and my Father will love them, and we will come to them and make our home with them. Whoever does not love me does not keep my words; and the word that you hear is not mine, but is from the Father who sent me.

"I have said these things to you while I am still with you. But the Advocate, the Holy Spirit, whom the Father will send in my name, will teach you everything, and remind you of all that I have said to you. Peace I leave with you; my peace I give to you. I do not give to you as the world gives. Do not let your hearts be troubled, and do not let them be afraid. You heard me say to you, 'I am going away, and I am coming to you.' If you loved me, you would rejoice that I am going to the Father, because the Father is greater than I. And now I have told you this before it occurs, so that when it does occur, you may believe."

Notice what you think and feel as you read the gospel.

Jesus exhorts his disciples to be one in love as he and the Father are one in love. If we do, the world will know we are his.

Pray as you are led for yourself and others.

"What greater gift could you have given us, Lord? Let me appreciate your love more and more. Let others come to you and know your love . . ." (Continue in your own words.)

Listen to Jesus.

Your power to act and to pray comes from God, beloved disciple. Abandon yourself to God—loving, obeying, and praying. What else is Jesus saying to you?

Ask God to show you how to live today.

"I give myself to you, Lord. How may I love, obey, and pray? I want to serve you all day long. Amen."

Monday, May 27, 2019

Know that God is present with you and ready to converse.

"What have you to say to me today, Lord? Open me up to receive your Word in the depths of my being."

Read the gospel: John 15:26–16:4a.

Jesus said, "When the Advocate comes, whom I will send to you from the Father, the Spirit of truth who comes from the Father, he will testify on my behalf. You also are to testify because you have been with me from the beginning.

"I have said these things to you to keep you from stumbling. They will put you out of the synagogues. Indeed, an hour is coming when those who kill you will think that by doing so they are offering worship to God. And they will do this because they have not known the Father or me. But I have said these things to you so that when their hour comes you may remember that I told you about them.

"I did not say these things to you from the beginning, because I was with you."

Notice what you think and feel as you read the gospel.

Jesus wants to keep his disciples from stumbling after he is gone, for the time of their persecution is coming.

Pray as you are led for yourself and others.

"Lord, send me your Spirit that I may testify on your behalf. Give me the grace to persevere even if people reject me. Let me remember what you say to me today . . ." (Continue in your own words.)

Listen to Jesus.

Trust the Holy Spirit to be your Advocate and Teacher. You can walk in that truth without fear. What else is Jesus saying to you?

Ask God to show you how to live today.

"How do I testify to those who have not known the Father or you, Jesus? Give me wisdom and courage today as I seek to share your love. Amen."

Tuesday, May 28, 2019

Know that God is present with you and ready to converse.

"Jesus, speak to me today. I need your Spirit and your Truth."

Read the gospel: John 16:5–11.

Jesus said, "But now I am going to him who sent me; yet none of you asks me, 'Where are you going?' But because I have said these things to you, sorrow has filled your hearts. Nevertheless, I tell you the truth: it is to your advantage that I go away, for if I do not go away, the Advocate will not come to you; but if I go, I will send him to you. And when he comes, he will prove the world wrong about sin and righteousness and judgment: about sin, because they do not believe in me; about righteousness, because I am going to the Father and you will see me no longer; about judgment, because the ruler of this world has been condemned."

Notice what you think and feel as you read the gospel.

Jesus promises his disciples that the Advocate will come to them, and he prophesies what the Advocate will accomplish: the Holy Spirit will prove the world wrong about sin, righteousness, and judgment.

Pray as you are led for yourself and others.

"Lord, the fulfillment of the mission of the Holy Spirit is yet to come. May your Spirit renew the face of the earth; may your Spirit gather your people into God. I think of . . ." (Continue in your own words.)

Listen to Jesus.

I abide in joy with my Father, but I am not far off from you, beloved. Ask for my Holy Spirit to replace all your sorrow with enduring joy. What else is Jesus saying to you?

Ask God to show you how to live today.

"Lord, I need your Holy Spirit to live well for you. I abandon myself to the Spirit to do in me and through me what is pleasing to God. Amen."

Wednesday, May 29, 2019

Know that God is present with you and ready to converse.

"Holy Spirit, declare to me by your Word all the truth I need, for I long to know, love, and serve God."

Read the gospel: John 16:12–15.

Jesus said, "I still have many things to say to you, but you cannot bear them now. When the Spirit of truth comes, he will guide you into all the truth; for he will not speak on his own, but will speak whatever he hears, and he will declare to you the things that are to come. He will glorify me, because he will take what is mine and declare it to you. All that the Father has is mine. For this reason I said that he will take what is mine and declare it to you."

Notice what you think and feel as you read the gospel.

Knowledge of God, Jesus makes clear, can come to us only by the Holy Spirit, for the Spirit is one with the Father and the Son.

Pray as you are led for yourself and others.

"Lord, raise me above earthly knowledge and give me godly knowledge by your Spirit, for it is my desire to know you as I am known by you. In your power, Lord, I pray for . . ." (Continue in your own words.)

Listen to Jesus.

By the Spirit, you recognize truth. The Spirit can declare to you the deep wisdom of God, and you will know God more and more. What else is Jesus saying to you?

Ask God to show you how to live today.

"Thank you, Jesus, for the gift of your Spirit. Let me receive all you have for me and let me glorify the Father, the Son, and the Holy Spirit in all I think, say, and do today. Amen."

Thursday, May 30, 2019

The ecclesiastical provinces of Boston, Hartford, New York, Newark, Omaha, and Philadelphia have retained the celebration of the Solemnity of the Ascension of the Lord to this day, while all other ecclesiastical provinces of the United States of America have transferred this Solemnity to the following Sunday, June 2, 2019. In those archdioceses and dioceses, Thursday, May 30, 2019, is observed as an Easter Weekday.

Know that God is present with you and ready to converse.

"I cannot see you, Lord, but you have promised to be here with me. I take you at your Word."

Read the gospel: John 16:16–20.

Jesus said, "A little while, and you will no longer see me, and again a little while, and you will see me." Then some of his disciples said to one another, "What does he mean by saying to us, 'A little while, and you will no longer see me, and again a little while, and you will see me'; and 'Because I am going to the Father'?" They said, "What does he mean by this 'a little while'? We do not know what he is talking about." Jesus knew that they wanted to ask him, so he said to them, "Are you discussing among yourselves what I meant when I said, 'A little while, and you will no longer see me, and again a little while, and you will see me'? Very truly, I tell you, you will weep and mourn, but the world will rejoice; you will have pain, but your pain will turn into joy."

Notice what you think and feel as you read the gospel.

Jesus is preparing his disciples for his Death and Resurrection. He tells them the truth, but they cannot imagine what he means. They will no longer see him in a little while, and then they will? He seems to be speaking in riddles again when he says they will mourn but the world will rejoice and then their pain will turn to joy. Something unheard of is about to happen, and they will be firsthand witnesses.

Pray as you are led for yourself and others.

"Jesus, the events of my own life are often hard to make sense of. Sometimes you allow things to happen that seem contrary to the way things should go. Help me to trust in your loving providence, knowing that all things work together for good for those who love God . . ." (Continue in your own words.)

Listen to Jesus.

Yes, you may trust me with everything: your life, your loved ones, your work, your health. When things seem to go bad for you, look to me, for your redemption is near. What else is Jesus saying to you?

Ask God to show you how to live today.

"Jesus, let me be patient and grateful to you in both hardship and blessing. You are Lord. Let me praise you all day long. Amen."

Friday, May 31, 2019
Visitation of the Blessed Virgin Mary

Know that God is present with you and ready to converse.

"I am blessed that the Word of my Lord comes to me."

Read the gospel: Luke 1:39–56.

In those days Mary set out and went with haste to a Judean town in the hill country, where she entered the house of Zechariah and greeted Elizabeth. When Elizabeth heard Mary's greeting, the child leapt in her womb. And Elizabeth was filled with the Holy Spirit and exclaimed with a loud cry, "Blessed are you among women, and blessed is the fruit of your womb. And why has this happened to me, that the mother of my Lord comes to me? For as soon as I heard the sound of your greeting, the child in my womb leapt for joy. And blessed is she who believed that there would be a fulfillment of what was spoken to her by the Lord."

And Mary said,

> "My soul magnifies the Lord,
>   and my spirit rejoices in God my Savior,
> for he has looked with favor on the lowliness of his servant.
>   Surely, from now on all generations will call me blessed;
> for the Mighty One has done great things for me,
>   and holy is his name.
> His mercy is for those who fear him
>   from generation to generation.
> He has shown strength with his arm;
>   he has scattered the proud in the thoughts of their hearts.
> He has brought down the powerful from their thrones,
>   and lifted up the lowly;
> he has filled the hungry with good things,
>   and sent the rich away empty.
> He has helped his servant Israel,
>   in remembrance of his mercy,
> according to the promise he made to our ancestors,
>   to Abraham and to his descendants for ever."

And Mary remained with her for about three months and then returned to her home.

Notice what you think and feel as you read the gospel.

After the angel tells her that she is to be the Mother of God, Mary visits her cousin Elizabeth, who is also miraculously pregnant. They rejoice together in the Holy Spirit, recognizing the role each will play in fulfilling God's promise of a Messiah. Mary's prayer reflects God's mercy to the poor and weak.

Pray as you are led for yourself and others.

"Lord, even in the midst of life's difficulties, let me praise you for your goodness, let me be open to receive your blessings, and let me share your joy with everyone you have given me . . ." (Continue in your own words.)

Listen to Jesus.

Model yourself on my Mother, the most beautiful of God's creatures. Emulate her joyful humility, her receptivity, her trust in the Father, and you will likewise be blessed. What else is Jesus saying to you?

Ask God to show you how to live today.

"Lord, place the image of your Blessed Mother in my mind today, that in all my actions I may imitate her and thus draw closer to you. Amen."

THE POPE'S MONTHLY PRAYER INTENTION FOR JUNE 2019

That priests, through the modesty and humility of their lives, commit themselves actively to a solidarity with those who are most poor.

Saturday, June 1, 2019

Know that God is present with you and ready to converse.

"I come with joy into your presence, Lord. You are calling me to yourself, healing me by your Word."

Read the gospel: John 16:23b–28.

Jesus said, "Very truly, I tell you, if you ask anything of the Father in my name, he will give it to you. Until now you have not asked for anything in my name. Ask and you will receive, so that your joy may be complete.

"I have said these things to you in figures of speech. The hour is coming when I will no longer speak to you in figures, but will tell you plainly of the Father. On that day you will ask in my name. I do not say to you that I will ask the Father on your behalf; for the Father himself loves you, because you have loved me and have believed that I came from God. I came from the Father and have come into the world; again, I am leaving the world and am going to the Father."

Notice what you think and feel as you read the gospel.

How many times in these readings from John has Jesus reminded his disciples that if they ask anything of the Father in his name, he will give it to them? Here he says it again. Why should they pray to the Father? So their joy may be complete.

Pray as you are led for yourself and others.

"Father, thank you for your Son, Jesus. I ask that I, and all those you have given me, may respond with love to his great love for us. That will complete my joy . . ." (Continue in your own words.)

Listen to Jesus.

My Father is Love. God is the power behind the mysteries of creation and salvation. My Father loves you as he loves me. I love you, too. What else is Jesus saying to you?

Ask God to show you how to live today.

"Knowing of your love for me, I wish to love others, especially those who need a kindness or a favor. Place me in those situations, Lord, and give me grace to share your love. Amen."

Sunday, June 2, 2019
Ascension of the Lord

Know that God is present with you and ready to converse.

"Risen Lord, you are with us always, even to the end of the age. Raise me up to do your will."

Read the gospel: Luke 24:46–53.

And Jesus said to them, "Thus it is written, that the Messiah is to suffer and to rise from the dead on the third day, and that repentance and forgiveness of sins is to be proclaimed in his name to all nations, beginning from Jerusalem. You are witnesses of these things. And see, I am sending upon you what my Father promised; so stay here in the city until you have been clothed with power from on high."

Then he led them out as far as Bethany, and, lifting up his hands, he blessed them. While he was blessing them, he withdrew from them and was carried up into heaven. And they worshiped him, and returned to Jerusalem with great joy; and they were continually in the temple blessing God.

Notice what you think and feel as you read the gospel.

Jesus sends out his disciples to preach the Good News, but he tells them that first they are to wait to be clothed with power from on high. Then they follow him out toward Bethany, receive a final blessing, and watch him be carried up into heaven. It gives them great joy.

Pray as you are led for yourself and others.

"Jesus, you are with your Father in heaven. I long to join you there. But first let me be obedient to your commandments, loving and serving others. Give me the power of your Holy Spirit to serve you in a way that glorifies God . . ." (Continue in your own words.)

Listen to Jesus.

I am with you, beloved disciple, as I was with my first disciples. I ask you to continue my work in the ways I show you. Draw near to me and I will guide you in the way. What else is Jesus saying to you?

Ask God to show you how to live today.

"I am just one weak person, Lord. I depend on you to lead me and help me do what pleases you. Thank you for being with me today. Amen."

Monday, June 3, 2019

Know that God is present with you and ready to converse.

"Who is with me now, here to strengthen and guide me? It is you, Jesus Christ, conqueror of the world."

Read the gospel: John 16:29–33.

Jesus' disciples said, "Yes, now you are speaking plainly, not in any figure of speech! Now we know that you know all things, and do not need to have anyone question you; by this we believe that you came from God." Jesus answered them, "Do you now believe? The hour is coming, indeed it has come, when you will be scattered, each one to his home, and you will leave me alone. Yet I am not alone because the Father is with me. I have said this to you, so that in me you may have peace. In the world you face persecution. But take courage; I have conquered the world!"

Notice what you think and feel as you read the gospel.

Just when the disciples get comfortable with his messages, Jesus disrupts their complacency by telling them that they will be scattered. They will face persecution in the world, but he has conquered the world. How were they to understand that? He would soon be crucified by the world.

Pray as you are led for yourself and others.

"Lord, disrupt my complacency today and prepare me for what is to come. Let me be vigilant, too, for all those you have given me. I pray for . . ." (Continue in your own words.)

Listen to Jesus.

Ask me for peace, dear one; ask me for courage. I gladly give you whatever you need on your journey to my eternal kingdom. What else is Jesus saying to you?

Ask God to show you how to live today.

"Every day is another challenge, my Jesus. Let me turn and face each difficulty with peaceful courage, knowing you have overcome the world. You are at my side. Amen."

Tuesday, June 4, 2019

Know that God is present with you and ready to converse.

"Jesus, Savior, Mighty God, let me know you and love you better through the power of the Word."

Read the gospel: John 17:1–11a.

After Jesus had spoken these words, he looked up to heaven and said, "Father, the hour has come; glorify your Son so that the Son may glorify you, since you have given him authority over all people, to give eternal life to all whom you have given him. And this is eternal life, that they may know you, the only true God, and Jesus Christ whom you have sent. I glorified you on earth by finishing the work that you gave me to do. So now, Father, glorify me in your own presence with the glory that I had in your presence before the world existed.

"I have made your name known to those whom you gave me from the world. They were yours, and you gave them to me, and they have kept your word. Now they know that everything you have given me is from you; for the words that you gave to me I have given to them, and they have received them and know in truth that I came from you; and they have believed that you sent me. I am asking on their behalf; I am not asking on behalf of the world, but on behalf of those whom you gave me, because they are yours. All mine are yours, and yours are mine; and I have been glorified in them. And now I am no longer in the world, but they are in the world, and I am coming to you. Holy Father, protect them in your name that you have given me, so that they may be one, as we are one."

Notice what you think and feel as you read the gospel.

Jesus' prayer declares that what is most important is that his followers know the Father, the only true God, and God's Son. Now all who believe in him belong to the Father. Jesus prays for their protection, that they may be one as God is one.

Pray as you are led for yourself and others.

"Lord, I embrace the mysteries of oneness: God is one and God's worshipers are united by his love. I pray that many, many souls may join this blessed unity. For it is the nature of love to give the good it has to others. I pray for . . ." (Continue in your own words.)

Listen to Jesus.

Do you wish to please me, beloved? See others through my eyes. Do not place limits on what you can do for those in need. What else is Jesus saying to you?

Ask God to show you how to live today.

"Jesus, let my hands serve you today. Thank you for giving me life to do what pleases you, Lord. I worship you and glorify you for your great goodness. Amen."

Wednesday, June 5, 2019

Know that God is present with you and ready to converse.

"Lord, living is not always easy. We struggle. We turn to you for protection, for your truth in your Word."

Read the gospel: John 17:11b–19.

Jesus said, "And now I am no longer in the world, but they are in the world, and I am coming to you. Holy Father, protect them in your name that you have given me, so that they may be one, as we are one. While I was with them, I protected them in your name that you have given me. I guarded them, and not one of them was lost except the one destined to be lost, so that the scripture might be fulfilled. But now I am coming to you, and I speak these things in the world so that they may have my joy made complete in themselves. I have given them your word, and the world has hated them because they do not belong to the world, just as I do not belong to the world. I am not asking you to take them out of the world, but I ask you to protect them from the evil one. They do not belong to the world, just as I do not belong to the world. Sanctify them in the truth; your word is truth. As you have sent me into the world, so I have sent them into the world. And for their sakes I sanctify myself, so that they also may be sanctified in truth."

Notice what you think and feel as you read the gospel.

Jesus prays to the Father for his protection over those who believe in him. We need protection because of the evil in the world. He prays that we be sanctified in God's truth.

Pray as you are led for yourself and others.

"Lord, protect all those I love. Let them know your truth. I pray for those you have given me . . ." (Continue in your own words.)

Listen to Jesus.

I grant you the protection you ask, beloved servant. Trust me with yourself and all those you love. You are strong in my truth. What else is Jesus saying to you?

Ask God to show you how to live today.

"Lord, I am lifted high by your blessings and goodness. Help me to pass on this all-consuming love. Amen."

Thursday, June 6, 2019

Know that God is present with you and ready to converse.

"Father, let me join Jesus as he prays for those you have given him. Let his prayer also be for those you have given me."

Read the gospel: John 17:20–26.

Jesus said, "I ask not only on behalf of these, but also on behalf of those who will believe in me through their word, that they may all be one. As you, Father, are in me and I am in you, may they also be in us, so that the world may believe that you have sent me. The glory that you have given me I have given them, so that they may be one, as we are one, I in them and you in me, that they may become completely one, so that the world may know that you have sent me and have loved them even as you have loved me. Father, I desire that those also, whom you have given me, may be with me where I am, to see my glory, which you have given me because you loved me before the foundation of the world.

"Righteous Father, the world does not know you, but I know you; and these know that you have sent me. I made your name known to them, and I will make it known, so that the love with which you have loved me may be in them, and I in them."

Notice what you think and feel as you read the gospel.

As we are one in God, like Jesus, we know that we have been loved before the foundation of the world. That love is in us.

Pray as you are led for yourself and others.

"Lord, let me desire to be one with all who love you. Let me pray and work for unity, for that is your sign to those who do not yet believe. I pray for . . ." (Continue in your own words.)

Listen to Jesus.

The world is full of strife and selfishness, dear disciple—have no part in those. Cling to me and my promises with faith, hope, and love. What else is Jesus saying to you?

Ask God to show you how to live today.

"Draw me to you today, Lord, and use me to draw the world to yourself. Let me see your glory in every moment, let me see you in everyone I meet. Amen."

Friday, June 7, 2019

Know that God is present with you and ready to converse.

"Master, I invite you into my day and my prayers. Let me draw near to you and listen to your words with my heart."

Read the gospel: John 21:15–19.

When they had finished breakfast, Jesus said to Simon Peter, "Simon son of John, do you love me more than these?" He said to him, "Yes, Lord; you know that I love you." Jesus said to him, "Feed my lambs." A second time he said to him, "Simon son of John, do you love me?" He said to him, "Yes, Lord; you know that I love you." Jesus said to him, "Tend my sheep." He said to him the third time, "Simon son of John, do you love me?" Peter felt hurt because he said to him the third time, "Do you love me?" And he said to him, "Lord, you know everything; you know that I love you." Jesus said to him, "Feed my sheep. Very truly, I tell you, when you were younger, you used to fasten your own belt and to go wherever you wished. But when you grow old, you will stretch out your hands, and someone else will fasten a belt around you and take you where you do not wish to go." (He said this to indicate the kind of death by which he would glorify God.) After this he said to him, "Follow me."

Notice what you think and feel as you read the gospel.

Jesus commissions Peter to feed his sheep as the natural result of Peter's love for the Lord. Then he predicts Peter's death at the hands of men. Peter would follow his beloved Lord to martyrdom.

Pray as you are led for yourself and others.

"As you asked Peter to lay down his life for your sheep and for the glory of God, you ask us to die to self and to worldly desires, Lord. That is the necessary condition to receive and give your love. Remove from me all fear of death and dying. Give me confidence that I am coming to you. I pray for those I know who are sick or dying . . ." (Continue in your own words.)

Listen to Jesus.

Death for those who love me is a transition to a better place and even a better self, my child. In eternity, we will share our love and joy. In the Eucharist, I give you a foretaste of that love and joy. Receive me and lose your fears. What else is Jesus saying to you?

Ask God to show you how to live today.

"Feed me today, Lord, to prepare me for eternity with you and to enable me to feed your lambs and tend your sheep here on earth. Amen."

Saturday, June 8, 2019

Know that God is present with you and ready to converse.

"Master of the Universe, your will is shrouded, your ways far above our ways. Reveal to me what I need to know to love and serve you."

Read the gospel: John 21:20–25.

Peter turned and saw the disciple whom Jesus loved following them; he was the one who had reclined next to Jesus at the supper and had said, "Lord, who is it that is going to betray you?" When Peter saw him, he said to Jesus, "Lord, what about him?" Jesus said to him, "If it is my will that he remain until I come, what is that to you? Follow me!" So the rumor spread in the community that this disciple would not die. Yet Jesus did not say to him that he would not die, but, "If it is my will that he remain until I come, what is that to you?"

This is the disciple who is testifying to these things and has written them, and we know that his testimony is true. But there are also many other things that Jesus did; if every one of them were written down, I suppose that the world itself could not contain the books that would be written.

Notice what you think and feel as you read the gospel.

Jesus does not reveal how or when that other disciple (John, the writer of today's gospel) will die. John ends his testimony affirming the truth of what he has written, even though it is only a partial account of the many things Jesus did.

Pray as you are led for yourself and others.

"Lord, much of your life remains unknown, especially your early life. My future life remains unknown. Let me be faithful to you until the end. I pray now for . . ." (Continue in your own words.)

Listen to Jesus.

No one alive knows the wisdom of God, but when you see God you will know as you are known. What else is Jesus saying to you?

Ask God to show you how to live today.

"Let me realize how much I do not know, Lord, that I may all the more trust and rely upon you, day by day, hour by hour. I glorify the ways of God Almighty. Amen."

Sunday, June 9, 2019
Pentecost Sunday

Know that God is present with you and ready to converse.

"Holy Spirit, God with me now, open to me the Word and impress it upon me."

Read the gospel: John 20:19–23.

When it was evening on that day, the first day of the week, and the doors of the house where the disciples had met were locked for fear of the Jews,

Jesus came and stood among them and said, "Peace be with you." After he said this, he showed them his hands and his side. Then the disciples rejoiced when they saw the Lord. Jesus said to them again, "Peace be with you. As the Father has sent me, so I send you." When he had said this, he breathed on them and said to them, "Receive the Holy Spirit. If you forgive the sins of any, they are forgiven them; if you retain the sins of any, they are retained."

Notice what you think and feel as you read the gospel.

The risen Jesus mysteriously appears in the locked room where the disciples had met for fear of the Jews. He gives them his peace and shows them his wounds. As they rejoice, he commissions them to continue to do his works—breathing on them and saying, "Receive the Holy Spirit."

Pray as you are led for yourself and others.

"Jesus, you were crucified because you proclaimed yourself equal to God, able to forgive sins. Then you gave that power to people. I pray for forgiveness for myself and all those you have given me. Wash us all of our sins . . ." (Continue in your own words.)

Listen to Jesus.

Do you hold unforgiven any sins against you, beloved disciple? First forgive with all your heart, and you, too, will be forgiven and blessed by God. What else is Jesus saying to you?

Ask God to show you how to live today.

"As I go through my day, Lord, and all my days, let me understand and practice the power of forgiveness. Whom may I forgive? Amen."

Ordinary Time

INTRODUCTION

The second period of Ordinary Time begins immediately after Pentecost. The Holy Spirit has fallen upon the disciples while they prayed in the upper room. For the disciples, Pentecost was even more transforming than Easter, for the Holy Spirit gave them, as Jesus had promised, power to carry the Good News to every nation on earth. So began the age of grace.

Our own journeys are similarly wrapped up with Christ's command to follow him every day. This is our own time of grace as we seek to do his work in today's world. By praying with the Word of God in this season, we may discover how we, too, can serve the Master. The last Sunday of Ordinary Time is the Feast of Christ the King, whose coming and kingdom we await.

Monday, June 10, 2019

Know that God is present with you and ready to converse.

"Jesus, I rejoice in your continuous presence. What have you to teach me today by your holy Word?"

Read the gospel: Matthew 5:1–12.

When Jesus saw the crowds, he went up the mountain; and after he sat down, his disciples came to him. Then he began to speak, and taught them, saying:

"Blessed are the poor in spirit, for theirs is the kingdom of heaven.

"Blessed are those who mourn, for they will be comforted.

"Blessed are the meek, for they will inherit the earth.

"Blessed are those who hunger and thirst for righteousness, for they will be filled.

"Blessed are the merciful, for they will receive mercy.

"Blessed are the pure in heart, for they will see God.

"Blessed are the peacemakers, for they will be called children of God.

"Blessed are those who are persecuted for righteousness' sake, for theirs is the kingdom of heaven.

"Blessed are you when people revile you and persecute you and utter all kinds of evil against you falsely on my account. Rejoice and be glad, for your reward is great in heaven, for in the same way they persecuted the prophets who were before you."

Notice what you think and feel as you read the gospel.

Jesus teaches the crowd his secrets to happiness. Practice poverty of spirit, meekness, mercy, purity, and be ready to be persecuted for righteousness' sake. Mourn, hunger and thirst for righteousness, make peace, and rejoice to be reviled for your faith and work on behalf of Jesus Christ.

Pray as you are led for yourself and others.

"Lord, I am unworthy, but you generously share with me the secrets of true blessedness. You show me how to do your will. Help me do it, Lord, for love of you and those you have given me . . ." (Continue in your own words.)

Listen to Jesus.

God can use you for his purposes, child. I can use even your weaknesses to serve others. Do not fear your weakness. Give it to me. What else is Jesus saying to you?

Ask God to show you how to live today.

"Jesus, you allowed yourself to be weak before the cruel power of people, yet in your suffering and dying you were victorious, reconciling sinful humanity with God. Help me understand how my own weakness can serve others today. Thank you, Lord. Amen."

Tuesday, June 11, 2019

Know that God is present with you and ready to converse.

"Lord, enlighten this one who seeks to know and love you."

Read the gospel: Matthew 5:13–16.

Jesus said, "You are the salt of the earth; but if salt has lost its taste, how can its saltiness be restored? It is no longer good for anything, but is thrown out and trampled under foot.

"You are the light of the world. A city built on a hill cannot be hidden. No one after lighting a lamp puts it under the bushel basket, but on the lampstand, and it gives light to all in the house. In the same way, let your light shine before others, so that they may see your good works and give glory to your Father in heaven."

Notice what you think and feel as you read the gospel.

Jesus affirms the crowds listening to him, calling them the salt of the earth and light of the world. He is the Light of the World, yet he identifies himself with the motley lost people desperate for salvation. They have found their Savior.

Pray as you are led for yourself and others.

"Jesus, you are so good to those who have no hope but you. I myself am among them. Let me please you, Lord, by loving you and others. I pray for all those who seek you . . ." (Continue in your own words.)

Listen to Jesus.

I shall come again in power and glory to gather my own into my kingdom. Prepare your heart, my beloved. What else is Jesus saying to you?

Ask God to show you how to live today.

"Teach me simplicity and truthfulness, Lord, in all I do. Let me find your lessons in the circumstances of my day so that I may please you. Amen."

Wednesday, June 12, 2019

Know that God is present with you and ready to converse.

"Word of the Father, you speak the truth. Let me revere your Word and take it to heart right now."

Read the gospel: Matthew 5:17–19.

Jesus said, "Do not think that I have come to abolish the law or the prophets; I have come not to abolish but to fulfill. For truly I tell you, until heaven and earth pass away, not one letter, not one stroke of a letter, will pass from the law until all is accomplished. Therefore, whoever breaks one of the least of these commandments, and teaches others to do the same, will be called least in the kingdom of heaven; but whoever does them and teaches them will be called great in the kingdom of heaven."

Notice what you think and feel as you read the gospel.

Jesus affirms the Word of God, speaking of the Old Testament scriptures. These words shall be fulfilled, so we must consider the books of the prophets as part of our own gospel. Jesus fulfills the Old Testament.

Pray as you are led for yourself and others.

"Lord, God of the prophets and Father of Jesus, the Messiah promised by the prophets, give me proper appreciation for your truth. I pray for those who resist you . . ." (Continue in your own words.)

Listen to Jesus.

Those who hunger for truth will find it. Those who seek God find God. All shall be well. What else is Jesus saying to you?

Ask God to show you how to live today.

"For the time until all is accomplished, Lord, let me focus my efforts on my own journey, and let me be a help to others in their journey to you. Let me hunger after your goodness and truth, whatever it may cost me. Amen."

Thursday, June 13, 2019

Know that God is present with you and ready to converse.

"Lord, you train me in the way that I should go. Command me by your holy Word."

Read the gospel: Matthew 5:20–26.

Jesus said, "For I tell you, unless your righteousness exceeds that of the scribes and Pharisees, you will never enter the kingdom of heaven.

"You have heard that it was said to those of ancient times, 'You shall not murder'; and 'whoever murders shall be liable to judgment.' But I say to you that if you are angry with a brother or sister, you will be liable to judgment; and if you insult a brother or sister, you will be liable to the council; and if you say, 'You fool,' you will be liable to the hell of fire. So when you are offering your gift at the altar, if you remember that your brother or sister has something against you, leave your gift there before the altar and go; first be reconciled to your brother or sister, and then come and offer your gift. Come to terms quickly with your accuser while you are on the way to court with him, or your accuser may hand you over to the judge, and the judge to the guard, and you will be thrown into prison. Truly I tell you, you will never get out until you have paid the last penny."

Notice what you think and feel as you read the gospel.

Preaching to ordinary people, Jesus sets a high standard of holiness. Our righteousness must exceed that of the scribes and Pharisees. We must not murder, but, more, we must not be angry against a brother or sister. We must go to them and reconcile, for this is the way of Jesus' love.

Pray as you are led for yourself and others.

"Lord, I pray for your righteousness, which I cannot obtain without you. Give me your grace and a heart for your commandments of love for God and for one another . . ." (Continue in your own words.)

Listen to Jesus.

This is why I say that the kingdom of God is already among you. Dear disciple, my kingdom is a world of perfect love. Enter it here and now. What else is Jesus saying to you?

Ask God to show you how to live today.

"Jesus, I do love God and others, but my love is not perfect. Help me to love with your heart and to remain in your love. Amen."

Friday, June 14, 2019

Know that God is present with you and ready to converse.
"Lord, your Word is a mystery. Let me read it in the light of the Holy Spirit, who inspired it."

Read the gospel: Matthew 5:27–32.
Jesus said, "You have heard that it was said, 'You shall not commit adultery.' But I say to you that everyone who looks at a woman with lust has already committed adultery with her in his heart. If your right eye causes you to sin, tear it out and throw it away; it is better for you to lose one of your members than for your whole body to be thrown into hell. And if your right hand causes you to sin, cut it off and throw it away; it is better for you to lose one of your members than for your whole body to go into hell.

"It was also said, 'Whoever divorces his wife, let him give her a certificate of divorce.' But I say to you that anyone who divorces his wife, except on the ground of unchastity, causes her to commit adultery; and whoever marries a divorced woman commits adultery."

Notice what you think and feel as you read the gospel.
Jesus identifies not just adultery but also lust in the heart as sinful. He condemns divorce and exhorts his hearers to practice perfect marital fidelity.

Pray as you are led for yourself and others.
"God, your salvation is a work-in-progress in us. Let my progress in the faith be your work. I pray in the same way for these . . ." (Continue in your own words.)

Listen to Jesus.
This is the season of God's mercy and grace, my child. But the time is coming when God will judge each one with perfect justice. What else is Jesus saying to you?

Ask God to show you how to live today.
"Let me extend mercy to others today, for I wish to place myself under your mercy, Lord. I praise you for your mercy, loving Father. Amen."

Saturday, June 15, 2019

Know that God is present with you and ready to converse.

"Jesus, I seek your simplicity. Teach me what you would have me do. Jesus, I seek you in your Word."

Read the gospel: Matthew 5:33–37.

Jesus said, "Again, you have heard that it was said to those of ancient times, 'You shall not swear falsely, but carry out the vows you have made to the Lord.' But I say to you, Do not swear at all, either by heaven, for it is the throne of God, or by the earth, for it is his footstool, or by Jerusalem, for it is the city of the great King. And do not swear by your head, for you cannot make one hair white or black. Let your word be 'Yes, Yes' or 'No, No'; anything more than this comes from the evil one."

Notice what you think and feel as you read the gospel.

Jesus continues his moral teaching of the crowds gathered on the mountain to hear him. He forbids swearing falsely in God's name, urging simple yeses and nos.

Pray as you are led for yourself and others.

"Lord, with your help I will forsake complication and adopt a straightforward manner of thinking and speaking. Give me your integrity. I pray for all those who are ensnared in lies . . ." (Continue in your own words.)

Listen to Jesus.

Think and speak always as though you are in the presence of the Lord God, for you are. Bring all your thoughts to me, lay your words at my feet; let the love of God at all times guard your mind and your lips. What else is Jesus saying to you?

Ask God to show you how to live today.

"Give me wisdom today, Lord, in speaking to all I encounter. Let me not sin but glorify you and help others. Amen."

Sunday, June 16, 2019
Holy Trinity

Know that God is present with you and ready to converse.

"Jesus, you have the Word of salvation. Guide me into all truth by your Spirit."

Read the gospel: John 16:12–15.

Jesus said, "I still have many things to say to you, but you cannot bear them now. When the Spirit of truth comes, he will guide you into all the truth; for he will not speak on his own, but will speak whatever he hears, and he will declare to you the things that are to come. He will glorify me, because he will take what is mine and declare it to you. All that the Father has is mine. For this reason I said that he will take what is mine and declare it to you."

Notice what you think and feel as you read the gospel.

Jesus speaks in a familiar way about the Trinity of God: Father, Son, and Holy Spirit. The Spirit will guide us all to truth.

Pray as you are led for yourself and others.

"Lord, I pray earnestly today for the work of the Holy Spirit. Touch hearts, Spirit, and renew the whole earth. I pray for all who need you . . ." (Continue in your own words.)

Listen to Jesus.

I continue to send my Spirit into the world, and I invite all to come to me for life. Do not be afraid to speak of me today. What else is Jesus saying to you?

Ask God to show you how to live today.

"Let me be part of your invitation to love and eternal life, Lord. Let me pray for those who need you today. By the power of your Spirit, let me speak of your goodness without fear. Amen."

Monday, June 17, 2019

Know that God is present with you and ready to converse.

"Lord, I know you want what is best for me. I seek your virtue, now and forever. Teach me by your Word."

Read the gospel: Matthew 5:38–42.

Jesus said, "You have heard that it was said, 'An eye for an eye and a tooth for a tooth.' But I say to you, Do not resist an evildoer. But if anyone strikes you on the right cheek, turn the other also; and if anyone wants to sue you and take your coat, give your cloak as well; and if anyone forces you to go one mile, go also the second mile. Give to everyone who begs from you, and do not refuse anyone who wants to borrow from you."

Notice what you think and feel as you read the gospel.

The Lord teaches against retaliation and revenge. This is part of the righteousness of his followers. We are to be kind to those who abuse us and generous to those who ask anything from us.

Pray as you are led for yourself and others.

"Lord, give me your meekness. Let me observe your peace in all my relationships. I pray for those who are angry with others . . ." (Continue in your own words.)

Listen to Jesus.

I love to give you my view of things, dear disciple. Your love for another is never wasted. Your acts of love will always bear fruit for good. Trust in me. What else is Jesus saying to you?

Ask God to show you how to live today.

"Open my eyes to your view of things, Lord. Sometimes I glimpse your heart of love for all. Let me be in the world today as you were in the world, Jesus. Thank you. Amen."

Tuesday, June 18, 2019

Know that God is present with you and ready to converse.

"Let me learn from you about love by the light of your Word, Lord."

Read the gospel: Matthew 5:43–48.

Jesus said, "You have heard that it was said, 'You shall love your neighbour and hate your enemy.' But I say to you, Love your enemies and pray for those who persecute you, so that you may be children of your Father in heaven; for he makes his sun rise on the evil and on the good, and sends rain on the righteous and on the unrighteous. For if you love those who love you, what reward do you have? Do not even the tax collectors do the same? And if you greet only your brothers and sisters, what more are you doing than others? Do not even the Gentiles do the same? Be perfect, therefore, as your heavenly Father is perfect."

Notice what you think and feel as you read the gospel.

Jesus broadens and deepens his call to love. He insists that his Father demands holiness, which is perfect love for all, neighbors and enemies alike.

Pray as you are led for yourself and others.

"Jesus, let me not neglect the working of your grace within me. Let me learn to love as you do, to the glory of God, the Father . . ." (Continue in your own words.)

Listen to Jesus.

Beloved, love is a gift of God, for all love is God's love. Let it magnify in you life through your thoughts, words, and deeds. What else is Jesus saying to you?

Ask God to show you how to live today.

"You challenge me every day, Lord, to do something good. With your help, I shall do something loving today. Stay with me, Jesus. I thank you, praise you, and worship you, my King. Amen."

Wednesday, June 19, 2019

Know that God is present with you and ready to converse.

"Lord, often in your Word you are forceful and commanding. Let me receive your Word in holy fear."

Read the gospel: Matthew 6:1–6, 16–18.

Jesus said, "Beware of practicing your piety before others in order to be seen by them; for then you have no reward from your Father in heaven.

"So whenever you give alms, do not sound a trumpet before you, as the hypocrites do in the synagogues and in the streets, so that they may be praised by others. Truly I tell you, they have received their reward. But when you give alms, do not let your left hand know what your right hand is doing, so that your alms may be done in secret; and your Father who sees in secret will reward you.

"And whenever you pray, do not be like the hypocrites; for they love to stand and pray in the synagogues and at the street corners, so that they may be seen by others. Truly I tell you, they have received their reward. But whenever you pray, go into your room and shut the door and pray to your Father who is in secret; and your Father who sees in secret will reward you. . . .

"And whenever you fast, do not look dismal, like the hypocrites, for they disfigure their faces so as to show others that they are fasting. Truly I tell you, they have received their reward. But when you fast, put oil on your head and wash your face, so that your fasting may be seen not by others but by your Father who is in secret; and your Father who sees in secret will reward you."

Notice what you think and feel as you read the gospel.

Jesus preaches against hypocrisy in all our religious practices. He says to do our almsgiving, praying, and fasting in secret, and God will reward us.

Pray as you are led for yourself and others.

"Lord, give me grace to search my heart for hypocrisy and remove it. Root out all my sin and renew me in grace. I pray also for those you have given me . . ." (Continue in your own words.)

Listen to Jesus.

I ask you to do your best, child, just for today. Remember that I am always near and you may touch my hand whenever you need me. What else is Jesus saying to you?

Ask God to show you how to live today.

"I need you, Lord, more than I know as I get distracted by the business of the day. Let me find those secret moments to reach out to you. Amen."

Thursday, June 20, 2019

Know that God is present with you and ready to converse.

"Lord, teach me by your Word. You are here now to lead me on your way."

Read the gospel: Matthew 6:7–15.

Jesus said, "When you are praying, do not heap up empty phrases as the Gentiles do; for they think that they will be heard because of their many words. Do not be like them, for your Father knows what you need before you ask him.

"Pray then in this way:

Our Father in heaven,
  hallowed be your name.
  Your kingdom come.
  Your will be done,
    on earth as it is in heaven.
  Give us this day our daily bread.
  And forgive us our debts,
    as we also have forgiven our debtors.
  And do not bring us to the time of trial,
    but rescue us from the evil one.

For if you forgive others their trespasses, your heavenly Father will also forgive you; but if you do not forgive others, neither will your Father forgive your trespasses."

Notice what you think and feel as you read the gospel.

Jesus teaches his disciples a simple yet profound prayer. He emphasizes forgiveness, for as we forgive we will be forgiven.

Pray as you are led for yourself and others.

"I pray this prayer from the heart for myself and others: Our Father who art in heaven, hallowed be thy name . . ." (Continue in your own words.)

Listen to Jesus.

At every occasion, forgive others. All need forgiveness, and this is the healing of God. Be part of it, beloved. What else is Jesus saying to you?

Ask God to show you how to live today.

"Who do I need to forgive today, Jesus? Or whose forgiveness do I need to ask? Heal my heart, so that I can offer your forgiveness and work to heal a difficult relationship today. Amen."

Friday, June 21, 2019

Know that God is present with you and ready to converse.

"Lord, I come into your presence looking for love and light, longing to learn from you. Teach me."

Read the gospel: Matthew 6:19–23.

Jesus said, "Do not store up for yourselves treasures on earth, where moth and rust consume and where thieves break in and steal; but store up for yourselves treasures in heaven, where neither moth nor rust consumes and where thieves do not break in and steal. For where your treasure is, there your heart will be also.

"The eye is the lamp of the body. So, if your eye is healthy, your whole body will be full of light; but if your eye is unhealthy, your whole body will be full of darkness. If then the light in you is darkness, how great is the darkness!"

Notice what you think and feel as you read the gospel.

Jesus instructs his followers to store up the treasures of heaven, spiritual treasures, rather than set our hearts on earthly things. He urges us to look toward the light, the truth of God.

Pray as you are led for yourself and others.

"Lord, thank you for shedding your light upon me. I ask you to remove all darkness and greed from my heart, and I pray for those who walk in darkness . . ." (Continue in your own words.)

Listen to Jesus.

There is no true happiness in sin, my child. Darkness is sin. Seek the light of God, today and every day, in holiness, truth, and pure worship. What else is Jesus saying to you?

Ask God to show you how to live today.

"Lord, guide me into your perpetual light. Let me help to light others' ways. Amen."

Saturday, June 22, 2019

Know that God is present with you and ready to converse.

"Lord, write your Word upon my heart. Let it teach me how to grow nearer to you and please you. You are here to teach me now."

Read the gospel: Matthew 6:24–34.

Jesus said, "No one can serve two masters; for a slave will either hate the one and love the other, or be devoted to the one and despise the other. You cannot serve God and wealth.

"Therefore I tell you, do not worry about your life, what you will eat or what you will drink, or about your body, what you will wear. Is not life more than food, and the body more than clothing? Look at the birds of the air; they neither sow nor reap nor gather into barns, and yet your heavenly Father feeds them. Are you not of more value than they? And can any of you by worrying add a single hour to your span of life? And why do you worry about clothing? Consider the lilies of the field, how they grow; they neither toil nor spin, yet I tell you, even Solomon in all his glory was not clothed like one of these. But if God so clothes the grass of the field, which is alive today and tomorrow is thrown into the oven, will he not much more clothe you—you of little faith? Therefore do not worry, saying, 'What will we eat?' or 'What will we drink?' or 'What will we wear?' For it is the Gentiles who strive for all these things; and indeed your heavenly Father knows that you need all these things. But strive first for the kingdom of God and his righteousness, and all these things will be given to you as well.

"So do not worry about tomorrow, for tomorrow will bring worries of its own. Today's trouble is enough for today."

Notice what you think and feel as you read the gospel.

Jesus exhorts us to seek God and God's righteousness, and God will take care of us. Do not worry about your life. Do not worry about tomorrow. Trust God. God will take care of you.

Pray as you are led for yourself and others.

"Lord, how often do I worry? Teach me to set aside the worry when it comes over me and to place my life in your loving care. I have far to go, Lord. I pray also for those you have given me . . ." (Continue in your own words.)

Listen to Jesus.

The Holy Spirit searches hearts, my beloved. We reward your faith and trust in God. What else is Jesus saying to you?

Ask God to show you how to live today.

"Search my heart as often as you wish, Lord. Let me walk simply by faith in you, my Good Shepherd, doing the work you set before me each day and trusting you for everything. Amen."

Sunday, June 23, 2019
Body and Blood of Christ

Know that God is present with you and ready to converse.

"When you are ready, open yourself to the Word of God, for this is the Bread of Life."

Read the gospel: Luke 9:11b–17.

When the crowds found out about it, they followed Jesus; and he welcomed them, and spoke to them about the kingdom of God, and healed those who needed to be cured.

The day was drawing to a close, and the twelve came to him and said, "Send the crowd away, so that they may go into the surrounding villages and countryside, to lodge and get provisions; for we are here in a deserted place." But he said to them, "You give them something to eat." They said, "We have no more than five loaves and two fish—unless we are to go and buy food for all these people." For there were about five thousand men. And he said to his disciples, "Make them sit down in groups of about fifty each." They did so and made them all sit down. And taking the five loaves and the two fish, he looked up to heaven, and blessed and broke them, and gave them to the disciples to set before the crowd. And all ate and were filled. What was left over was gathered up, twelve baskets of broken pieces.

Notice what you think and feel as you read the gospel.

Jesus feeds the five thousand with only a few loaves and fishes. He is the Bread of Life. He provides for us in our daily lives, and he promises that those who eat his Body and drink his Blood abide in him and live forever.

Pray as you are led for yourself and others.

"Lord, let me receive your Body and Blood with faith in your promises, for I long to abide with you forever. I pray for those who do not yet believe your words . . ." (Continue in your own words.)

Listen to Jesus.

As I am Bread for others, dear follower, so are you. Draw near to me often, and I shall use you. What else is Jesus saying to you?

Ask God to show you how to live today.

"Lord, I offer you my day and my whole life. Use me as you will, but be with me in the work. I do not want to be striving vainly by my own efforts without you. Amen."

Monday, June 24, 2019
Nativity of John the Baptist

Know that God is present with you and ready to converse.

"You guide your saints, Lord, and show them what to do. What shall I do?"

Read the gospel: Luke 1:57–66, 80.

Now the time came for Elizabeth to give birth, and she bore a son. Her neighbors and relatives heard that the Lord had shown his great mercy to her, and they rejoiced with her.

On the eighth day they came to circumcise the child, and they were going to name him Zechariah after his father. But his mother said, "No; he is to be called John." They said to her, "None of your relatives has this name." Then they began motioning to his father to find out what name he wanted to give him. He asked for a writing tablet and wrote, "His name is John." And all of them were amazed. Immediately his mouth was opened and his tongue freed, and he began to speak, praising God. Fear came over all their neighbors, and all these things were talked about throughout the entire hill country of Judea. All who heard them pondered them and said, "What then will this child become?" For, indeed, the hand of the Lord was with him. . . .

The child grew and became strong in spirit, and he was in the wilderness until the day he appeared publicly to Israel.

Notice what you think and feel as you read the gospel.

This gospel gives us a glimpse of the community of Elizabeth and Zechariah and their reactions at the birth and naming of their son, John. The neighbors must have wondered when Zachariah regained his power of speech by naming their child; they must wonder what this boy will become.

Pray as you are led for yourself and others.

"Lord, John led souls to you, the Lamb of God. I come to you now. I pray for these people you have given me . . ." (Continue in your own words.)

Listen to Jesus.

My cousin John announced my coming, and they killed him for it. You have the freedom to follow me even to your death, for in me you will not fear death. I am your protection. What else is Jesus saying to you?

Ask God to show you how to live today.

"Let me live humbly and fearlessly today in you, Lord, as John did. Give me courage to walk close to you. Amen."

Tuesday, June 25, 2019

Know that God is present with you and ready to converse.

"Heavenly Father, I seek the path of life that leads to you. Let me learn the way by the Word of your Son."

Read the gospel: Matthew 7:6, 12–14.

Jesus said, "Do not give what is holy to dogs; and do not throw your pearls before swine, or they will trample them under foot and turn and maul you. . . . In everything do to others as you would have them do to you; for this is the law and the prophets.

"Enter through the narrow gate; for the gate is wide and the road is easy that leads to destruction, and there are many who take it. For the gate is narrow and the road is hard that leads to life, and there are few who find it."

Notice what you think and feel as you read the gospel.

Jesus urges simplicity and decisiveness, even if it means turning away from others who do not understand. Do unto others what you would have them do to you. Come in by the narrow gate, and expect the road to be hard, for this is the road to life.

Pray as you are led for yourself and others.

"Lord, I earnestly seek your narrow way. Give me grace and strength to find it and walk in it. I entrust you with my life and the lives of those you have given me . . ." (Continue in your own words.)

Listen to Jesus.

I am the way. Seek me out; spend time with me. I love you, and I will lead you home to the Father. What else is Jesus saying to you?

Ask God to show you how to live today.
"Jesus, when I struggle on the way, remind me of what you are teaching me now. Help me to be faithful in all things. Amen."

Wednesday, June 26, 2019

Know that God is present with you and ready to converse.
"Lord, you understand the human heart. You know me better than I know myself. Guide me by your Word."

Read the gospel: Matthew 7:15–20.
Jesus said, "Beware of false prophets, who come to you in sheep's clothing but inwardly are ravenous wolves. You will know them by their fruits. Are grapes gathered from thorns, or figs from thistles? In the same way, every good tree bears good fruit, but the bad tree bears bad fruit. A good tree cannot bear bad fruit, nor can a bad tree bear good fruit. Every tree that does not bear good fruit is cut down and thrown into the fire. Thus you will know them by their fruits."

Notice what you think and feel as you read the gospel.
Jesus warns us against false prophets, people who disguise themselves in piety and goodness but are really governed by their own selfish wants. You will know them by their fruits, he says. We must be patient in our assessment of people until we see the fruits of their actions and words.

Pray as you are led for yourself and others.
"Let me receive your wisdom, Lord. Keep me safe from those leaders who would hurt me or those I love . . ." (Continue in your own words.)

Listen to Jesus.
One bears good fruit in simplicity and love, my child. There is great joy in dropping all pretense before others and being who you are. What else is Jesus saying to you?

Ask God to show you how to live today.
"Let me speak and live in your truth, Lord. Holy Spirit, I need your light and your strength in this. Thank you. Amen."

Thursday, June 27, 2019

Know that God is present with you and ready to converse.

"Praise to you, Lord God of Hosts. Let my heart be converted anew by your holy Word."

Read the gospel: Matthew 7:21–29.

Jesus said, "Not everyone who says to me, 'Lord, Lord,' will enter the kingdom of heaven, but only one who does the will of my Father in heaven. On that day many will say to me, 'Lord, Lord, did we not prophesy in your name, and cast out demons in your name, and do many deeds of power in your name?' Then I will declare to them, 'I never knew you; go away from me, you evildoers.'

"Everyone then who hears these words of mine and acts on them will be like a wise man who built his house on rock. The rain fell, the floods came, and the winds blew and beat on that house, but it did not fall, because it had been founded on rock. And everyone who hears these words of mine and does not act on them will be like a foolish man who built his house on sand. The rain fell, and the floods came, and the winds blew and beat against that house, and it fell—and great was its fall!"

Now when Jesus had finished saying these things, the crowds were astounded at his teaching, for he taught them as one having authority, and not as their scribes.

Notice what you think and feel as you read the gospel.

Jesus urges us not to be complacent in our faith in his salvation. Salvation is a process, a way of life. We should build the houses of our lives upon rock, upon him, so that we may withstand the storms.

Pray as you are led for yourself and others.

"Lord, let me never take you for granted. Let me always be seeking you and your righteousness. Let me build upon the solid rock. Let me offer haven to others who are struggling . . ." (Continue in your own words.)

Listen to Jesus.

I look to your heart, beloved servant. Let your heart be set on me in all you think, do, and say. There is safety in loving God in truth. What else is Jesus saying to you?

Ask God to show you how to live today.

"Lord, walking with you is sometimes difficult. Help me hear and do what pleases you today. I can do all things with you. Amen."

Friday, June 28, 2019
Sacred Heart of Jesus

Know that God is present with you and ready to converse.

"Father, you reveal your truths not to the wise but to infants. I am a child before you today."

Read the gospel: Luke 15:3–7.

So Jesus told this parable: "Which one of you, having a hundred sheep and losing one of them, does not leave the ninety-nine in the wilderness and go after the one that is lost until he finds it? When he has found it, he lays it on his shoulders and rejoices. And when he comes home, he calls together his friends and neighbors, saying to them, 'Rejoice with me, for I have found my sheep that was lost.' Just so, I tell you, there will be more joy in heaven over one sinner who repents than over ninety-nine righteous people who need no repentance."

Notice what you think and feel as you read the gospel.

This is the heart of Jesus, to seek and save those who are lost and return them to his flock. He rejoices in our salvation.

Pray as you are led for yourself and others.

"I seek rest in your fold, Lord. I rejoice in you. I begin by praying for others who are wandering away from you . . ." (Continue in your own words.)

Listen to Jesus.

You are mine, dear child and friend. You may know perfect peace in me. Share it with others. What else is Jesus saying to you?

Ask God to show you how to live today.

"I believe your promises to me. Make my heart like your heart, Lord, so that I may find rest for my soul and do as you do. Amen."

Saturday, June 29, 2019
Sts. Peter and Paul, Apostles

Know that God is present with you and ready to converse.

"Lord, are the Messiah, the Holy One of God. Let me hear you in your Word."

Read the gospel: Matthew 16:13–19.

Now when Jesus came into the district of Caesarea Philippi, he asked his disciples, "Who do people say that the Son of Man is?" And they said, "Some say John the Baptist, but others Elijah, and still others Jeremiah or one of the prophets." He said to them, "But who do you say that I am?" Simon Peter answered, "You are the Messiah, the Son of the living God." And Jesus answered him, "Blessed are you, Simon son of Jonah! For flesh and blood has not revealed this to you, but my Father in heaven. And I tell you, you are Peter, and on this rock I will build my church, and the gates of Hades will not prevail against it. I will give you the keys of the kingdom of heaven, and whatever you bind on earth will be bound in heaven, and whatever you loose on earth will be loosed in heaven."

Notice what you think and feel as you read the gospel.

Peter doesn't hesitate to say that Jesus is the Messiah, the Son of the living God. Jesus commends Peter's forceful pronouncement, and he tells him that he is the rock upon which he will build his Church.

Pray as you are led for yourself and others.

"Lord, let me be one with your Church, one with those who follow you as you will. I pray for all the leaders of your Church and for those who follow . . ." (Continue in your own words.)

Listen to Jesus.

You are a child of the Father, a member of the holy family and the kingdom of heaven. Even small things you do in God are great things. What else is Jesus saying to you?

Ask God to show you how to live today.

"Give me something small to do for someone today, Lord, for I would like to do something great for you. Amen."

Sunday, June 30, 2019
Thirteenth Sunday in Ordinary Time

Know that God is present with you and ready to converse.

"Lord, you demand commitment of your followers. Strengthen me through your Word."

Read the gospel: Luke 9:51–62.

When the days drew near for Jesus to be taken up, he set his face to go to Jerusalem. And he sent messengers ahead of him. On their way they entered a village of the Samaritans to make ready for him; but they did not receive him, because his face was set towards Jerusalem. When his disciples James and John saw it, they said, "Lord, do you want us to command fire to come down from heaven and consume them?" But he turned and rebuked them. Then they went on to another village.

As they were going along the road, someone said to him, "I will follow you wherever you go." And Jesus said to him, "Foxes have holes, and birds of the air have nests; but the Son of Man has nowhere to lay his head." To another he said, "Follow me." But he said, "Lord, first let me go and bury my father." But Jesus said to him, "Let the dead bury their own dead; but as for you, go and proclaim the kingdom of God." Another said, "I will follow you, Lord; but let me first say farewell to those at my home." Jesus said to him, "No one who puts a hand to the plough and looks back is fit for the kingdom of God."

Notice what you think and feel as you read the gospel.

Jesus commits to his final journey to Jerusalem. Many are challenged to follow him; he warns them of the difficulties, and he does not abide excuses for delay.

Pray as you are led for yourself and others.

"Lord, I have determined to follow you all my life. Let my eyes and heart be always on you, and I will trust you to direct my steps. I pray for those who are wavering in their faith . . ." (Continue in your own words.)

Listen to Jesus.

I set you free by my truth, dear disciple. As you walk in my way, you will see my truth ever more clearly. Trust me. What else is Jesus saying to you?

Ask God to show you how to live today.
"I am ready to walk with you today, Lord. How may I show you that I trust you? Amen."

THE POPE'S MONTHLY PRAYER INTENTION FOR JULY 2019

That those who administer justice may work with integrity, and that the injustice which prevails in the world may not have the last word.

Monday, July 1, 2019

Know that God is present with you and ready to converse.
"Lord, you will come again to judge the living and the dead. Teach me about judgment."

Read the gospel: Matthew 8:18–22.
Now when Jesus saw great crowds around him, he gave orders to go over to the other side. A scribe then approached and said, "Teacher, I will follow you wherever you go." And Jesus said to him, "Foxes have holes, and birds of the air have nests; but the Son of Man has nowhere to lay his head." Another of his disciples said to him, "Lord, first let me go and bury my father." But Jesus said to him, "Follow me, and let the dead bury their own dead."

Notice what you think and feel as you read the gospel.
Jesus has advice for would-be followers: his way is hard and all-consuming. It's almost as if he is discouraging would-be followers—but no, what he wants is that his followers have their eyes open and their resolution firm.

Pray as you are led for yourself and others.

"Let me be strong in my choice to follow you, Lord. Let me draw close to you with my heart and honor you with all my words and actions. Help me to love others as you do . . ." (Continue in your own words.)

Listen to Jesus.

I want you to steel your heart for battle against the forces of the world, the flesh, and the devil, my child. But I am with you, strong to save. Do your best to rely on me. I am with you to the end. What else is Jesus saying to you?

Ask God to show you how to live today.

"You are the strength of my life, Lord. How may I strengthen someone else today? Amen."

Tuesday, July 2, 2019

Know that God is present with you and ready to converse.

"Lord, I have fears in my life. Let your Word bring me peace today."

Read the gospel: Matthew 8:23–27.

And when Jesus got into the boat, his disciples followed him. A gale arose on the lake, so great that the boat was being swamped by the waves; but he was asleep. And they went and woke him up, saying, "Lord, save us! We are perishing!" And he said to them, "Why are you afraid, you of little faith?" Then he got up and rebuked the winds and the sea; and there was a dead calm. They were amazed, saying, "What sort of man is this, that even the winds and the sea obey him?"

Notice what you think and feel as you read the gospel.

Jesus is napping while the disciples' boat all but sinks. In fear for their lives, they awaken him, yet he chides them for lack of faith. Jesus, the Word who created the winds and the sea, is with them, and his word of authority saves them.

Pray as you are led for yourself and others.

"Almighty Savior, let me abide in your saving power every day. I pray for those who are in danger now . . ." (Continue in your own words.)

Listen to Jesus.

I value your perseverance, beloved. Stay with me through thick and thin and you will have peace in your life. Though you may weep for a time, you will have joy in the morning. What else is Jesus saying to you?

Ask God to show you how to live today.

"Thank you for being with me, Lord, and calming the storm of my anxieties. I pray today for faithfulness in your service. Amen."

Wednesday, July 3, 2019
St. Thomas, Apostle

Know that God is present with you and ready to converse.

"God, you are present with me in times of tranquility and in times of danger. You are here with me now. Hallowed be your name."

Read the gospel: John 20:24–29.

But Thomas (who was called the Twin), one of the twelve, was not with them when Jesus came. So the other disciples told him, "We have seen the Lord." But he said to them, "Unless I see the mark of the nails in his hands, and put my finger in the mark of the nails and my hand in his side, I will not believe."

A week later his disciples were again in the house, and Thomas was with them. Although the doors were shut, Jesus came and stood among them and said, "Peace be with you." Then he said to Thomas, "Put your finger here and see my hands. Reach out your hand and put it in my side. Do not doubt but believe." Thomas answered him, "My Lord and my God!" Jesus said to him, "Have you believed because you have seen me? Blessed are those who have not seen and yet have come to believe."

Notice what you think and feel as you read the gospel.

After his Resurrection, Jesus appears to his disciples, but Thomas is not among them. When Thomas hears their report, he is skeptical; he demands physical proof. When Jesus appears to them again, he speaks to Thomas and shows his wounds for examination, and Thomas believes with passion. Yet Jesus praises those who believe without seeing.

Pray as you are led for yourself and others.

"Lord, I have not seen you, but I seek the blessedness of faith in you. Pour out your Spirit upon the world that many more may come to you . . ." (Continue in your own words.)

Listen to Jesus.

Beloved, you cannot see the Holy Spirit at work, but the Spirit is moving all over the world. Whoever comes to me, I will preserve for the everlasting kingdom of God. What else is Jesus saying to you?

Ask God to show you how to live today.

"Let me feel your presence with me today, help me recognize the effects of the Spirit active in the world, and let me be your hands and feet and heart in the world today, that others may come to believe in you. Amen."

Thursday, July 4, 2019

Know that God is present with you and ready to converse.

"Father, I come to you for forgiveness and healing through your Word."

Read the gospel: Matthew 9:1–8.

And after getting into a boat Jesus crossed the water and came to his own town.

    And just then some people were carrying a paralyzed man lying on a bed. When Jesus saw their faith, he said to the paralytic, "Take heart, son; your sins are forgiven." Then some of the scribes said to themselves, "This man is blaspheming." But Jesus, perceiving their thoughts, said, "Why do you think evil in your hearts? For which is easier, to say, 'Your sins are forgiven,' or to say, "Stand up and walk'? But so that you may know that the Son of Man has authority on earth to forgive sins"—he then said to the paralytic—"Stand up, take your bed and go to your home." And he stood up and went to his home. When the crowds saw it, they were filled with awe, and they glorified God, who had given such authority to human beings.

Notice what you think and feel as you read the gospel.

Jesus loves to see the faith of the friends of the paralytic man, and he forgives the man's sins. The onlooking scribes are scandalized by his presumption, because only God can forgive sins. Jesus says he has the authority to do so, and then the crowds glorify God.

Pray as you are led for yourself and others.

"Lord, let me glorify you too, for you are my redeemer, my healer. I love you. I pray for all those who seek you . . ." (Continue in your own words.)

Listen to Jesus.

Pray, and do not fear, for I am with you. I have overcome the world. What else is Jesus saying to you?

Ask God to show you how to live today.

"I offer myself to you today, Lord, to pray for those who seek you. Give them faith. Amen."

Friday, July 5, 2018

Know that God is present with you and ready to converse.

"Lord of Love, you call me to yourself by your Word. I come, for you have the words of eternal life."

Read the gospel: Matthew 9:9–13.

As Jesus was walking along, he saw a man called Matthew sitting at the tax booth; and he said to him, "Follow me." And he got up and followed him.

And as he sat at dinner in the house, many tax collectors and sinners came and were sitting with him and his disciples. When the Pharisees saw this, they said to his disciples, "Why does your teacher eat with tax collectors and sinners?" But when he heard this, he said, "Those who are well have no need of a physician, but those who are sick. Go and learn what this means, 'I desire mercy, not sacrifice.' For I have come to call not the righteous but sinners."

Notice what you think and feel as you read the gospel.

Jesus calls an unlikely person to follow him—Matthew, the tax collector. The Pharisees criticize him for associating with a known sinner and for eating at his house. But Jesus orders them to learn and take to heart God's desire for mercy.

Pray as you are led for yourself and others.

"To show your mercy, Lord, is to sacrifice something: material wealth, the good opinion of others, personal time. Show me what it is I'm clinging to that is preventing me from sharing your perfect love and mercy, and free me from it, so that I may bring your mercy to all I encounter today, especially . . ." (Continue in your own words.)

Listen to Jesus.

Always first remember that you have received great mercy, first recall that I love you; then I will go with you and together we will call my beloved sinners. What else is Jesus saying to you?

Ask God to show you how to live today.

"Dwell in me today, Lord, and give me your eyes to see and love all your people. Let your presence in me draw all sinners closer to you. Amen."

Saturday, July 6, 2019

Know that God is present with you and ready to converse.

"Lord, you are doing something new in the world. Fill me with your Word; I am listening, Jesus."

Read the gospel: Matthew 9:14–17.

Then the disciples of John came to Jesus, saying, "Why do we and the Pharisees fast often, but your disciples do not fast?" And Jesus said to them, "The wedding guests cannot mourn as long as the bridegroom is with them, can they? The days will come when the bridegroom is taken away from them, and then they will fast. No one sews a piece of unshrunk cloth on an old cloak, for the patch pulls away from the cloak, and a worse tear is made. Neither is new wine put into old wineskins; otherwise, the skins burst, and the wine is spilled, and the skins are destroyed; but new wine is put into fresh wineskins, and so both are preserved."

Notice what you think and feel as you read the gospel.

Jesus answers questions from the disciples of John about fasting, explaining that his disciples do not fast now but they will after he leaves them. He speaks of bringing something new to the world, new wine.

Pray as you are led for yourself and others.

"Lord Jesus, beloved Bridegroom, you are with us, yet we await your coming. You come to patch this broken world, yet you fashion the world anew. Help me to understand and accept your words; make me new and fill me with the wine of your Word . . ." (Continue in your own words.)

Listen to Jesus.

Rely on my wisdom, trust in my love, and I will refresh your soul. What else is Jesus saying to you?

Ask God to show you how to live today.

"Lord, give me true humility, teach me wisdom, and I will give praise and thanks to you all day long. Amen."

Sunday, July 7, 2019
Fourteenth Sunday in Ordinary Time

Know that God is present with you and ready to converse.

"Lord, you are here with me too. Give me grace to respond to your holy Word."

Read the gospel: Luke 10:10–12, 17–20 (Lk 10:1–12, 17–20).

Jesus said, "But whenever you enter a town and they do not welcome you, go out into its streets and say, 'Even the dust of your town that clings to our feet, we wipe off in protest against you. Yet know this: the kingdom of God has come near.' I tell you, on that day it will be more tolerable for Sodom than for that town." . . .

The seventy returned with joy, saying, "Lord, in your name even the demons submit to us!" He said to them, "I watched Satan fall from heaven like a flash of lightning. See, I have given you authority to tread on snakes and scorpions, and over all the power of the enemy; and nothing will hurt you. Nevertheless, do not rejoice at this, that the spirits submit to you, but rejoice that your names are written in heaven."

Notice what you think and feel as you read the gospel.

Jesus sends out the seventy to proclaim the Good News and directs them to trust God and deal honorably in all they do. They return rejoicing that they had power even over demons in their preaching. But Jesus tells them to rejoice not because of their power but because of their relationship with God.

Pray as you are led for yourself and others.

"Lord, I rejoice that my name is written in heaven, that your blood has signed my name. I long to live my whole life in you, so I can serve others . . ." (Continue in your own words.)

Listen to Jesus.

Your time of service is short, beloved disciple. Use it to do what good you can do, and your time of reward will be eternal. What else is Jesus saying to you?

Ask God to show you how to live today.

"Whom may I welcome today, Lord? To whom may I speak of your goodness and mercy? I offer myself to your service because I love you. Amen."

Monday, July 8, 2019

Know that God is present with you and ready to converse.

"Almighty God, you are invisible Spirit. Jesus Christ, you are God and a man who walked on the earth, but I have never seen you either. Let me see you in the Word you have spread before me today."

Read the gospel: Matthew 9:18–26.

While Jesus was saying these things to them, suddenly a leader of the synagogue came in and knelt before him, saying, "My daughter has just died; but come and lay your hand on her, and she will live." And Jesus got up and followed him, with his disciples. Then suddenly a woman who had been suffering from hemorrhages for twelve years came up behind him and touched the fringe of his cloak, for she said to herself, "If I only touch his cloak, I will be made well." Jesus turned, and seeing her he said, "Take heart, daughter; your faith has made you well." And instantly the woman was made well. When Jesus came to the leader's house and saw the flute players and the crowd making a commotion, he said, "Go away; for the girl is not dead but sleeping." And they laughed at him. But when the crowd had been put outside, he went in and took her by the hand, and the girl got up. And the report of this spread throughout that district.

Notice what you think and feel as you read the gospel.

On his way to raise the girl from death, Jesus heals a woman who had suffered from hemorrhages for twelve years. She had not asked him for healing, she just had faith that if she could touch his cloak she would be made well. Jesus commends her faith, and then, despite mocking and disbelieving laughter, he raises the little girl from death as if she had been merely sleeping.

Pray as you are led for yourself and others.

"Jesus, increase my faith in you, for I want to please you. I pray for . . ."
(Continue in your own words.)

Listen to Jesus.

I give you what you pray for, my dear child. I am happy to grant your prayers.
What else is Jesus saying to you?

Ask God to show you how to live today.

"Help me to walk steadfast in faith today. Reveal to me my doubts and
transform them into greater faith. Thank you, Jesus. Amen."

Tuesday, July 9, 2019

Know that God is present with you and ready to converse.

"Lord, you have found me today needing you and afraid of many things.
I need assurance of your strong hand in my life. Calm me, Lord, and set
me straight."

Read the gospel: Matthew 9:32–38.

After they had gone away, a demoniac who was mute was brought to
Jesus. And when the demon had been cast out, the one who had been
mute spoke; and the crowds were amazed and said, "Never has anything
like this been seen in Israel." But the Pharisees said, "By the ruler of the
demons he casts out the demons."

Then Jesus went about all the cities and villages, teaching in their
synagogues, and proclaiming the good news of the kingdom, and curing every disease and every sickness. When he saw the crowds, he had
compassion for them, because they were harassed and helpless, like
sheep without a shepherd. Then he said to his disciples, "The harvest is
plentiful, but the laborers are few; therefore ask the Lord of the harvest
to send out laborers into his harvest."

Notice what you think and feel as you read the gospel.

Jesus works to cast out demons and heals every disease and sickness. He
has compassion for the crowds, seeing them as sheep without a shepherd.

Pray as you are led for yourself and others.

"Have compassion on me, too, Lord. Be my Good Shepherd and let me follow those you have sent. I pray for the Lord to send more laborers into the harvest . . ." (Continue in your own words.)

Listen to Jesus.

When you are distressed, dear disciple, come to me and spend time with me, sharing all that troubles you, every detail. I will hear it and lead you in the way. What else is Jesus saying to you?

Ask God to show you how to live today.

"Lord, I am ready to walk with you today. I worship and adore you, Jesus, and wish to glorify God as it pleases you. Amen."

Wednesday, July 10, 2019

Know that God is present with you and ready to converse.

"Lord, before you created the universe you chose me. I live in a fallen world of sin. Rescue me."

Read the gospel: Matthew 10:1–7.

Then Jesus summoned his twelve disciples and gave them authority over unclean spirits, to cast them out, and to cure every disease and every sickness. These are the names of the twelve apostles: first, Simon, also known as Peter, and his brother Andrew; James son of Zebedee, and his brother John; Philip and Bartholomew; Thomas and Matthew the tax collector; James son of Alphaeus, and Thaddaeus; Simon the Cananaean, and Judas Iscariot, the one who betrayed him.

These twelve Jesus sent out with the following instructions: "Go nowhere among the Gentiles, and enter no town of the Samaritans, but go rather to the lost sheep of the house of Israel. As you go, proclaim the good news, 'The kingdom of heaven has come near.'"

Notice what you think and feel as you read the gospel.

Jesus names his twelve apostles and sends them out to proclaim the Good News.

Pray as you are led for yourself and others.

"Lord, I am willing to go out and do your work. I now pray for these . . ." (Continue in your own words.)

Listen to Jesus.
Child, I will go with you. What else is Jesus saying to you?

Ask God to show you how to live today.
"I give myself to you, Lord; teach me to walk in your way. You will defend me and keep me safe. Amen."

Thursday, July 11, 2019

Know that God is present with you and ready to converse.
"Lord, when I come to you I don't always know what I need or what I want. I know you will give me what is best."

Read the gospel: Matthew 10:7–15.
Jesus said, "As you go, proclaim the good news, 'The kingdom of heaven has come near.' Cure the sick, raise the dead, cleanse the lepers, cast out demons. You received without payment; give without payment. Take no gold, or silver, or copper in your belts, no bag for your journey, or two tunics, or sandals, or a staff; for laborers deserve their food. Whatever town or village you enter, find out who in it is worthy, and stay there until you leave. As you enter the house, greet it. If the house is worthy, let your peace come upon it; but if it is not worthy, let your peace return to you. If anyone will not welcome you or listen to your words, shake off the dust from your feet as you leave that house or town. Truly I tell you, it will be more tolerable for the land of Sodom and Gomorrah on the day of judgment than for that town."

Notice what you think and feel as you read the gospel.
Jesus instructs his disciples as he sends them out. He knows not everyone will accept their Good News. But they are to keep moving and preaching and healing.

Pray as you are led for yourself and others.
"Lord, I rejoice in your Good News. Let it be known throughout the world—and here in my community. Now lead me as I pray . . ." (Continue in your own words.)

Listen to Jesus.

I know your heart, my child. I know every part of you, and I love you. I work in you to make you holy that you may be worthy of eternal life with God. What else is Jesus saying to you?

Ask God to show you how to live today.

"Jesus, work in me as you see fit. Then be with me as I seek to serve others and let them know your power to forgive sins and to heal. Amen."

Friday, July 12, 2019

Know that God is present with you and ready to converse.

"Lord, your Word is truth. Give me strength to live it out in the world."

Read the gospel: Matthew 10:16–23.

Jesus said, "See, I am sending you out like sheep into the midst of wolves; so be wise as serpents and innocent as doves. Beware of them, for they will hand you over to councils and flog you in their synagogues; and you will be dragged before governors and kings because of me, as a testimony to them and the Gentiles. When they hand you over, do not worry about how you are to speak or what you are to say; for what you are to say will be given to you at that time; for it is not you who speak, but the Spirit of your Father speaking through you. Brother will betray brother to death, and a father his child, and children will rise against parents and have them put to death; and you will be hated by all because of my name. But the one who endures to the end will be saved. When they persecute you in one town, flee to the next; for truly I tell you, you will not have gone through all the towns of Israel before the Son of Man comes."

Notice what you think and feel as you read the gospel.

Jesus lets his followers know that their lives will not be easy as they do his work. They will be hated and betrayed, persecuted, tried, jailed, and put to death. He exhorts them to endure, for he will come again to establish his kingdom.

Pray as you are led for yourself and others.

"Lord, your way is hard. Give me the grace to endure and to encourage all your sons and daughters journeying through this world . . ." (Continue in your own words.)

Listen to Jesus.

I call people of all kinds, at all times, and everywhere. I have called you, dear disciple. Follow me. There is work only you can do. What else is Jesus saying to you?

Ask God to show you how to live today.

"Give me the work you have for me, Lord. Give me grace to do it well and faithfully because I desire to please you and glorify you by my life. Amen."

Saturday, July 13, 2019

Know that God is present with you and ready to converse.

"Lord, prepare me to hear your Word whispering in my heart."

Read the gospel: Matthew 10:24–33.

Jesus said, "A disciple is not above the teacher, nor a slave above the master; it is enough for the disciple to be like the teacher, and the slave like the master. If they have called the master of the house Beelzebul, how much more will they malign those of his household!

"So have no fear of them; for nothing is covered up that will not be uncovered, and nothing secret that will not become known. What I say to you in the dark, tell in the light; and what you hear whispered, proclaim from the housetops. Do not fear those who kill the body but cannot kill the soul; rather fear him who can destroy both soul and body in hell. Are not two sparrows sold for a penny? Yet not one of them will fall to the ground unperceived by your Father. And even the hairs of your head are all counted. So do not be afraid; you are of more value than many sparrows.

"Everyone therefore who acknowledges me before others, I also will acknowledge before my Father in heaven; but whoever denies me before others, I also will deny before my Father in heaven."

Notice what you think and feel as you read the gospel.

Jesus comforts his followers, letting them know that despite their rejection, they are beloved by God and in God's care. They are to fearlessly proclaim God to the world.

Pray as you are led for yourself and others.

"Lord, you speak love to the depths of my heart. Give me the courage to shout your love from the rooftops . . ." (Continue in your own words.)

Listen to Jesus.

What are you afraid of, beloved? Why do you hold back? Bring that fear to me; throw it into the burning fire of my love for all creation. What else is Jesus saying to you?

Ask God to show you how to live today.

"Today, Lord, let me be aware of the constant outpouring of your grace; let me not try to hoard it and hold it secret in my heart; let it flood through me and out into the world. Amen."

Sunday, July 14, 2019
Fifteenth Sunday in Ordinary Time

Know that God is present with you and ready to converse.

"Jesus, write your commandment on my heart."

Read the gospel: Luke 10:25–37.

Just then a lawyer stood up to test Jesus. "Teacher," he said, "what must I do to inherit eternal life?" He said to him, "What is written in the law? What do you read there?" He answered, "You shall love the Lord your God with all your heart, and with all your soul, and with all your strength, and with all your mind; and your neighbor as yourself." And he said to him, "You have given the right answer; do this, and you will live."

But wanting to justify himself, he asked Jesus, "And who is my neighbor?" Jesus replied, "A man was going down from Jerusalem to Jericho, and fell into the hands of robbers, who stripped him, beat him, and went away, leaving him half dead. Now by chance a priest was going down that road; and when he saw him, he passed by on the other side. So likewise a Levite, when he came to the place and saw him, passed by on the other side. But a Samaritan while traveling came near him; and when he saw him, he was moved with pity. He went to him and bandaged his wounds, having poured oil and wine on them. Then he put him on his own animal, brought him to an inn, and took care of him. The next day he took out two denarii, gave them to the innkeeper, and said, 'Take care of him; and when I come back, I will repay you whatever more you spend.' Which of these three, do you think, was a neighbor to the man who fell into the hands of the robbers?" He said, "The one who showed him mercy." Jesus said to him, "Go and do likewise."

Notice what you think and feel as you read the gospel.

Jesus tells the parable of the good Samaritan to answer the question, "Who is our neighbor?" Who is it we are to love and to serve, even at expense to ourselves? Everyone. Love costs us, but it is our richest treasure. It lets us be like God.

Pray as you are led for yourself and others.

"I was created to know and love you, Lord. Draw me by your love so I may love others. I wait for you, Lord . . ." (Continue in your own words.)

Listen to Jesus.

Before the universe was created, you were in my heart. What else is Jesus saying to you?

Ask God to show you how to live today.

"Teach me to walk in your gentleness, Jesus, and with your humble heart let me serve others. Amen."

Monday, July 15, 2019

Know that God is present with you and ready to converse.

"God of Peace, help me to understand the world I live in. Teach me by your Word."

Read the gospel: Matthew 10:34–11:1.

Jesus said, "Do not think that I have come to bring peace to the earth; I have not come to bring peace, but a sword.

> For I have come to set a man against his father,
> and a daughter against her mother,
> and a daughter-in-law against her mother-in-law;
> and one's foes will be members of one's own household.

Whoever loves father or mother more than me is not worthy of me; and whoever loves son or daughter more than me is not worthy of me; and whoever does not take up the cross and follow me is not worthy of me. Those who find their life will lose it, and those who lose their life for my sake will find it.

"Whoever welcomes you welcomes me, and whoever welcomes me welcomes the one who sent me. Whoever welcomes a prophet in the name of a prophet will receive a prophet's reward; and whoever welcomes a righteous person in the name of a righteous person will receive the reward of the righteous; and whoever gives even a cup of cold water to one of these little ones in the name of a disciple—truly I tell you, none of these will lose their reward."

Now when Jesus had finished instructing his twelve disciples, he went on from there to teach and proclaim his message in their cities.

Notice what you think and feel as you read the gospel.

Jesus announces that his Gospel will cause violence among people. He tells his followers that they must love him more than they love their own families. Because the disciples belong to him, those who welcome and care for them will be rewarded.

Pray as you are led for yourself and others.

"Lord, in a violent world, I put you first. Let me be a person of peace and love. Let me welcome and serve others who serve you. Touch my heart with love, Lord, and touch others . . ." (Continue in your own words.)

Listen to Jesus.

When you ask me for love, I give it to you. Keep asking, for the world will drain your love. What else is Jesus saying to you?

Ask God to show you how to live today.

"I want to accomplish what pleases you, precious Lord. Give me the grace to keep my eyes set on you, for the cross I bear today will be a joy if I bear it for your sake. Amen."

Tuesday, July 16, 2019

Know that God is present with you and ready to converse.

"I am here with you, Lord. I come to do your will. Open my heart to your Word."

Read the gospel: Matthew 11:20–24.

Then Jesus began to reproach the cities in which most of his deeds of power had been done, because they did not repent. "Woe to you, Chorazin! Woe to you, Bethsaida! For if the deeds of power done in you had been done in Tyre and Sidon, they would have repented long ago in sackcloth and ashes. But I tell you, on the day of judgment it will be more tolerable for Tyre and Sidon than for you. And you, Capernaum,

> will you be exalted to heaven?
> No, you will be brought down to Hades.

For if the deeds of power done in you had been done in Sodom, it would have remained until this day. But I tell you that on the day of judgment it will be more tolerable for the land of Sodom than for you."

Notice what you think and feel as you read the gospel.

Jesus pronounces judgment upon the cities that reject him as Messiah, comparing those cities to Tyre, Sidon, and Sodom, evil cities of the Old Testament.

Pray as you are led for yourself and others.

"Jesus, just judge, have mercy on sinners, because they don't know what they are doing. They are in darkness without you. Please enlighten them and turn their hearts to you. I pray also for . . ." (Continue in your own words.)

Listen to Jesus.

Sin is real, and I died to save all from sin and death. What else is Jesus saying to you?

Ask God to show you how to live today.

"Lord, every day you perform great works in my life; open my eyes that I may see them and give you praise and glory. Amen."

Wednesday, July 17, 2019

Know that God is present with you and ready to converse.

"Almighty God, you yourself are the kingdom of heaven and you have drawn near to me. Speak to me by your Word."

Read the gospel: Matthew 11:25–27.

At that time Jesus said, "I thank you, Father, Lord of heaven and earth, because you have hidden these things from the wise and the intelligent and have revealed them to infants; yes, Father, for such was your gracious will. All things have been handed over to me by my Father; and no one knows the Son except the Father, and no one knows the Father except the Son and anyone to whom the Son chooses to reveal him."

Notice what you think and feel as you read the gospel.

Jesus speaks of how we come to know God. Not through wisdom or intelligence, he says, but through the revelation of the Father. The Son is in constant, eternal, and loving communion with the Father. We are invited into that communion.

Pray as you are led for yourself and others.

"Lord Jesus Christ, Son of the eternal Father, you are present with your Church, with your followers, and with me. Thank you. I pray for all those whose needs only you know . . ." (Continue in your own words.)

Listen to Jesus.

Come to me humbly and simply in prayer, and I will reveal the Father to you, so that you can bring our truth to the world. What else is Jesus saying to you?

Ask God to show you how to live today.

"Lord, whenever I am perplexed or troubled today, whenever I encounter a need, let me turn to you for wisdom; guide my words and actions that I, too, may reveal you. Amen."

Thursday, July 18, 2019

Know that God is present with you and ready to converse.

"Unchanging God, you make all things new through your Son, our Lord Jesus Christ. Renew me by your Word."

Read the gospel: Matthew 11:28–30.

Jesus said, "Come to me, all you that are weary and are carrying heavy burdens, and I will give you rest. Take my yoke upon you, and learn from me; for I am gentle and humble in heart, and you will find rest for your souls. For my yoke is easy, and my burden is light."

Notice what you think and feel as you read the gospel.

Jesus, gentle and humble of heart, calls us to take his yoke upon ourselves. By doing so we lose our own weariness and burdens. We find rest for our souls, for his yoke is easy and light. We exchange the troubles of this world for the yoke of Christ's perfect love.

Pray as you are led for yourself and others.

"Lord, I am not worthy of you, but I thank you for loving me and transforming me to your image. Give me the love I need to serve you bravely, selflessly, and honestly. I pray for these people . . ." (Continue in your own words.)

Listen to Jesus.

Beloved disciple, I work through you. You are working, but it is I who am bringing in the harvest and gathering the fruit of your efforts. Do not be discouraged by what seem like small results. I do all things well. What else is Jesus saying to you?

Ask God to show you how to live today.

"Lord, I give you all that I am and all that I have, for you to use as you see fit today. Give me your heart for the good of others. Amen."

Friday, July 19, 2019

Know that God is present with you and ready to converse.

"Lord Jesus, feed me with the Word of God."

Read the gospel: Matthew 12:1–8.

At that time Jesus went through the grainfields on the sabbath; his disciples were hungry, and they began to pluck heads of grain and to eat. When the Pharisees saw it, they said to him, "Look, your disciples are doing what is not lawful to do on the sabbath." He said to them, "Have you not read what David did when he and his companions were hungry? He entered the house of God and ate the bread of the Presence, which it was not lawful for him or his companions to eat, but only for the priests. Or have you not read in the law that on the sabbath the priests in the temple break the sabbath and yet are guiltless? I tell you, something greater than the temple is here. But if you had known what this means, 'I desire mercy and not sacrifice,' you would not have condemned the guiltless. For the Son of Man is lord of the sabbath."

Notice what you think and feel as you read the gospel.

Jesus uses scripture to argue against the Pharisees who judge him and his disciples for picking corn and eating it on the Sabbath. He tells them he is greater than the temple in Jerusalem, where the priests do work on the

Sabbath. He is greater than manmade religious rules. He reminds them what God spoke through a prophet: "I desire mercy and not sacrifice."

Pray as you are led for yourself and others.

"Jesus, you are the Lord of the Universe, which was created for you and by you. You desire mercy. Give me mercy for those whom I encounter today . . ." (Continue in your own words.)

Listen to Jesus.

The world longs for mercy, dear disciple. I will teach you mercy for those you encounter, and I am already doing so. What else is Jesus saying to you?

Ask God to show you how to live today.

"Lord, make me an instrument of your mercy. How may I be mercy in my own world? Amen."

Saturday, July 20, 2019

Know that God is present with you and ready to converse.

"Lord, make yourself known to me in your Word."

Read the gospel: Matthew 12:14–21.

But the Pharisees went out and conspired against Jesus, how to destroy him.

When Jesus became aware of this, he departed. Many crowds followed him, and he cured all of them, and he ordered them not to make him known. This was to fulfill what had been spoken through the prophet Isaiah:

> "Here is my servant, whom I have chosen,
>   my beloved, with whom my soul is well pleased.
> I will put my Spirit upon him,
>   and he will proclaim justice to the Gentiles.
> He will not wrangle or cry aloud,
>   nor will anyone hear his voice in the streets.
> He will not break a bruised reed
>   or quench a smouldering wick
> until he brings justice to victory.
>   And in his name the Gentiles will hope."

Notice what you think and feel as you read the gospel.

Jesus, in his meekness, fulfills the Messianic prophesies of Isaiah, yet he will bring justice to victory throughout all the world. He remains our only hope.

Pray as you are led for yourself and others.

"Lord, such is your power that you can cure all ills, yet you seek no glory for yourself. Help me to follow in your footsteps, caring quietly for those around me, especially . . ." (Continue in your own words.)

Listen to Jesus.

When you serve humbly for my sake, gentle disciple, you proclaim my justice, and I am well pleased. What else is Jesus saying to you?

Ask God to show you how to live today.

"Show me what I can do today, Lord, to heal the bruised reed, rekindle the smoldering wick, and bring your justice to victory in the world. Amen."

Sunday, July 21, 2019
Sixteenth Sunday in Ordinary Time

Know that God is present with you and ready to converse.

"Jesus, I seek to be ever closer to you as I listen to your voice in your Word."

Read the gospel: Luke 10:38–42.

Now as they went on their way, Jesus entered a certain village, where a woman named Martha welcomed him into her home. She had a sister named Mary, who sat at the Lord's feet and listened to what he was saying. But Martha was distracted by her many tasks; so she came to him and asked, "Lord, do you not care that my sister has left me to do all the work by myself? Tell her then to help me." But the Lord answered her, "Martha, Martha, you are worried and distracted by many things; there is need of only one thing. Mary has chosen the better part, which will not be taken away from her."

Notice what you think and feel as you read the gospel.

Jesus gently takes Mary's side after Martha's complaint that Mary is not helping her with the many tasks that need doing. Mary has preferred to sit at Jesus' feet and listen to his teaching. Besides, she wants to be near to the one she loves so much. Jesus calls Mary's choice the "better part."

Pray as you are led for yourself and others.

"Lord, let me choose the better part, too. Let me hear your Word, and let it be deeply rooted in me . . ." (Continue in your own words.)

Listen to Jesus.

You are blessed, my child. I plant my Word in you; let it grow and your blessing shall flow to others. What else is Jesus saying to you?

Ask God to show you how to live today.

"I thank you, Lord, for calling me your child, for that is what I long to be. Simplify me, that I may see and hear and understand only you. Amen."

Monday, July 22, 2019
St. Mary Magdalene

Know that God is present with you and ready to converse.

"Lord, what would you have me learn from you today? Be present for me in your Word."

Read the gospel: John 20:1–2, 11–18.

Early on the first day of the week, while it was still dark, Mary Magdalene came to the tomb and saw that the stone had been removed from the tomb. So she ran and went to Simon Peter and the other disciple, the one whom Jesus loved, and said to them, "They have taken the Lord out of the tomb, and we do not know where they have laid him." . . .

But Mary stood weeping outside the tomb. As she wept, she bent over to look into the tomb; and she saw two angels in white, sitting where the body of Jesus had been lying, one at the head and the other at the feet. They said to her, "Woman, why are you weeping?" She said to them, "They have taken away my Lord, and I do not know where they have laid him." When she had said this, she turned round and saw Jesus standing there, but she did not know that it was Jesus. Jesus said to her, "Woman, why are you weeping? For whom are you looking?" Supposing him to be the gardener, she said to him, "Sir, if you have carried him away, tell me where you have laid him, and I will take him away." Jesus said to her, "Mary!" She turned and said to him in Hebrew, "Rabbouni!" (which means Teacher). Jesus said to her, "Do not hold on to me, because

I have not yet ascended to the Father. But go to my brothers and say to them, 'I am ascending to my Father and your Father, to my God and your God.'" Mary Magdalene went and announced to the disciples, "I have seen the Lord"; and she told them that he had said these things to her.

Notice what you think and feel as you read the gospel.

The risen Jesus chooses to reveal himself first to Mary Magdalene, who hurries to tell the apostles of the stone moved away from the tomb. Jesus chooses to honor her above even Peter and John, implying that Jesus does not consider her any less worthy than his apostles.

Pray as you are led for yourself and others.

"Lord, reveal yourself to me, for I love you. I offer myself to you. Strengthen me in my inner self to follow you . . ." (Continue in your own words.)

Listen to Jesus.

Following me, dear disciple, is not easy—but it is easy. I ask you for everything, but I give you everything, too. As you give me yourself, I give you myself. Walk with me. What else is Jesus saying to you?

Ask God to show you how to live today.

"Let me walk today in the awareness that you are in me and I am in you. Let me be a blessing to those you have given me. Amen."

Tuesday, July 23, 2019

Know that God is present with you and ready to converse.

"Holy Trinity, God Almighty, you have accepted me into your holy family. I thank you for your Word."

Read the gospel: Matthew 12:46–50.

While Jesus was still speaking to the crowds, his mother and his brothers were standing outside, wanting to speak to him. Someone told him, "Look, your mother and your brothers are standing outside, wanting to speak to you." But to the one who had told him this, Jesus replied, "Who is my mother, and who are my brothers?" And pointing to his disciples, he said, "Here are my mother and my brothers! For whoever does the will of my Father in heaven is my brother and sister and mother."

Notice what you think and feel as you read the gospel.

Jesus makes it clear that he belongs to the family of people who do God's will. While that does not exclude his own kin, it does include all who believe in him and follow him, doing good.

Pray as you are led for yourself and others.

"Lord, I am part of several communities. Let me be one of those who hears you and obeys you for the good of the whole community. I pray for these . . ." (Continue in your own words.)

Listen to Jesus.

Listen to me and do the will of my Father, and you will be my family, and I will send you out to draw others into our family; I want to gather them to myself, for I love sinners and long to show them mercy. What else is Jesus saying to you?

Ask God to show you how to live today.

"Lord, make me a true child of God. Let me join with those who do your will. May your goodness spread over all the earth. Amen."

Wednesday, July 24, 2019

Know that God is present with you and ready to converse.

"God, you are here to draw me into love and knowledge of yourself. Let your Word grow and bear fruit in me."

Read the gospel: Matthew 13:1–9.

That same day Jesus went out of the house and sat beside the sea. Such great crowds gathered around him that he got into a boat and sat there, while the whole crowd stood on the beach. And he told them many things in parables, saying: "Listen! A sower went out to sow. And as he sowed, some seeds fell on the path, and the birds came and ate them up. Other seeds fell on rocky ground, where they did not have much soil, and they sprang up quickly, since they had no depth of soil. But when the sun rose, they were scorched; and since they had no root, they withered away. Other seeds fell among thorns, and the thorns grew up and choked them. Other seeds fell on good soil and brought forth grain, some a hundredfold, some sixty, some thirty. Let anyone with ears listen!"

Notice what you think and feel as you read the gospel.

Jesus' famous parable demonstrates that not all who hear the Word of God receive it deeply into their hearts and minds. He is the sower, but the germination, growth, and fruitfulness of the seed he spreads depends on the soil into which it falls. The soil is the hearts of people. Good soil will yield much fruit.

Pray as you are led for yourself and others.

"I open my heart to your Word, Jesus, and I offer myself for loving service of all I encounter. I pray for all those who hear your Word . . ." (Continue in your own words.)

Listen to Jesus.

Beloved, you can know God and love God more and more. I give you that gift, a gift unto eternity. What else is Jesus saying to you?

Ask God to show you how to live today.

"Lord, I receive what you give me, though I cannot comprehend it. Increase my capacity for your love moment by moment, hour by hour. Amen."

Thursday, July 25, 2019
St. James, Apostle

Know that God is present with you and ready to converse.

"Jesus, you welcome me as your child. I seek your goodness in your Word. I listen, Lord."

Read the gospel: Matthew 20:20–28.

Then the mother of the sons of Zebedee came to him with her sons, and kneeling before him, she asked a favor of him. And he said to her, "What do you want?" She said to him, "Declare that these two sons of mine will sit, one at your right hand and one at your left, in your kingdom." But Jesus answered, "You do not know what you are asking. Are you able to drink the cup that I am about to drink?" They said to him, "We are able." He said to them, "You will indeed drink my cup, but to sit at my right hand and at my left, this is not mine to grant, but it is for those for whom it has been prepared by my Father."

When the ten heard it, they were angry with the two brothers. But Jesus called them to him and said, "You know that the rulers of the

Gentiles lord it over them, and their great ones are tyrants over them. It will not be so among you; but whoever wishes to be great among you must be your servant, and whoever wishes to be first among you must be your slave; just as the Son of Man came not to be served but to serve, and to give his life a ransom for many."

Notice what you think and feel as you read the gospel.

The mother of the sons of Zebedee asks Jesus to exalt her two sons when they come into his kingdom. Jesus tells her that he cannot promise it, because the honor she asks is his Father's choice. They must drink the cup of suffering as he does. They are ready to do that. The other disciples resent the sons of Zebedee. Jesus teaches them all that to be great you must be the servant of all.

Pray as you are led for yourself and others.

"Lord, give me your gentle, humble heart. I seek to be servant of all because I wish to be like you . . ." (Continue in your own words.)

Listen to Jesus.

My servant is motivated by love, love for God and love for others. This is where you will find glory. What else is Jesus saying to you?

Ask God to show you how to live today.

"Teach me to drink your cup, Lord. Let me come to you morning, noon, and night, loving you and loving others. Amen."

Friday, July 26, 2019

Know that God is present with you and ready to converse.

"Without your Spirit, Lord, people misunderstand your purposes. Thank you for being present with me now as I receive your Word."

Read the gospel: Matthew 13:18–23.

Jesus said, "Hear then the parable of the sower. When anyone hears the word of the kingdom and does not understand it, the evil one comes and snatches away what is sown in the heart; this is what was sown on the path. As for what was sown on rocky ground, this is the one who hears the word and immediately receives it with joy; yet such a person has no root, but endures only for a while, and when trouble or persecution arises on account of the word, that person immediately falls away. As for what was sown among thorns, this is the one who hears the word, but the cares of the world and the lure of wealth choke the word, and it yields nothing. But as for what was sown on good soil, this is the one who hears the word and understands it, who indeed bears fruit and yields, in one case a hundredfold, in another sixty, and in another thirty."

Notice what you think and feel as you read the gospel.

Jesus explains the spiritual meaning of the parable of the sower. The devil, troubles, cares of the world, and greed for wealth can steal away the Word from the heart of a person, and that person will bear no fruit.

Pray as you are led for yourself and others.

"Lord, let me rejoice in your Word, and let it grow steadily within me. How shall I bear fruit to your glory? . . ." (Continue in your own words.)

Listen to Jesus.

Cultivate my Word in you: feed it with the sacraments, practice virtue, and weed out vice. I will shower you with my grace and breathe my Spirit upon you, and you will bear fruit to the glory of the Father. What else is Jesus saying to you?

Ask God to show you how to live today.

"Breathe yourself into all I do today, Lord. Let me bear your fruits—charity, generosity, joy, gentleness, peace, faithfulness, patience, modesty, kindness, self-control, goodness, and chastity—as gifts to the world. Amen."

Saturday, July 27, 2019

Know that God is present with you and ready to converse.

"Jesus, you are present. May your harvest come soon."

Read the gospel: Matthew 13:24–30.

Jesus put before them another parable: "The kingdom of heaven may be compared to someone who sowed good seed in his field; but while everybody was asleep, an enemy came and sowed weeds among the wheat, and then went away. So when the plants came up and bore grain, then the weeds appeared as well. And the slaves of the householder came and said to him, 'Master, did you not sow good seed in your field? Where, then, did these weeds come from?' He answered, 'An enemy has done this.' The slaves said to him, 'Then do you want us to go and gather them?' But he replied, 'No; for in gathering the weeds you would uproot the wheat along with them. Let both of them grow together until the harvest; and at harvest time I will tell the reapers, Collect the weeds first and bind them in bundles to be burned, but gather the wheat into my barn.'"

Notice what you think and feel as you read the gospel.

Jesus tells another parable about a sower of seed, but this one has a different point. The sower sows good seed, but an enemy comes by night and sows weeds in the same field. His servants ask whether they should pluck out the weeds, but the master tells them to let them go. At harvest time the wheat will be separated from the weeds: the wheat will go to the barns, the weeds to the fire. God is patient, and in the end he will judge all people.

Pray as you are led for yourself and others.

"Lord, your justice waits. I both long for it and fear it. I pray for those who have not received your Word and come to faith . . ." (Continue in your own words.)

Listen to Jesus.

Throw your whole self, daily, into the fire of my love. I will purify you and save you for eternal life with me, and you will bring my love to the world. What else is Jesus saying to you?

Ask God to show you how to live today.

"Let me more fully grasp your call to justice and just actions, Jesus. If I can really obey you, I will find ways to work for justice in this world and in my community. Amen."

Sunday, July 28, 2019
Seventeenth Sunday in Ordinary Time

Know that God is present with you and ready to converse.

"Word of God, I have confidence that you will lead me into the truth I need; the Holy Spirit is here to teach me."

Read the gospel: Luke 11:1–13.

Jesus was praying in a certain place, and after he had finished, one of his disciples said to him, "Lord, teach us to pray, as John taught his disciples." He said to them, "When you pray, say:

Father, hallowed be your name.
> Your kingdom come.
> Give us each day our daily bread.
> And forgive us our sins,
>> for we ourselves forgive everyone indebted to us.
> And do not bring us to the time of trial."

And he said to them, "Suppose one of you has a friend, and you go to him at midnight and say to him, 'Friend, lend me three loaves of bread; for a friend of mine has arrived, and I have nothing to set before him.' And he answers from within, 'Do not bother me; the door has already been locked, and my children are with me in bed; I cannot get up and give you anything.' I tell you, even though he will not get up and give him anything because he is his friend, at least because of his persistence he will get up and give him whatever he needs.

"So I say to you, Ask, and it will be given to you; search, and you will find; knock, and the door will be opened for you. For everyone who asks receives, and everyone who searches finds, and for everyone who knocks, the door will be opened. Is there anyone among you who, if your child asks for a fish, will give a snake instead of a fish? Or if the child asks for an egg, will give a scorpion? If you then, who are evil, know how to give good gifts to your children, how much more will the heavenly Father give the Holy Spirit to those who ask him!"

Notice what you think and feel as you read the gospel.

Jesus teaches his disciples to pray and tells them by parables that persisting in prayer is the secret of answered prayer. Ask and it will be given to you, he says. The loving Father gives only good gifts to his children. The best gift is the Holy Spirit.

Pray as you are led for yourself and others.

"Lord, teach me to pray worthily. I entrust myself to your care. I also entrust to you those you have given me . . ." (Continue in your own words.)

Listen to Jesus.

Be patient, beloved disciple. I grant you what you ask. Pray and work as I show you. What else is Jesus saying to you?

Ask God to show you how to live today.

"You bless me with your Spirit, Jesus. How may I walk in it as I join you in this work? Amen."

Monday, July 29, 2019
St. Martha

Know that God is present with you and ready to converse.

"Jesus, let your words, familiar or new, flame into my heart and transform me. Make of me what you will."

Read the gospel: John 11:19–27.

Many of the Jews had come to Martha and Mary to console them about their brother. When Martha heard that Jesus was coming, she went and met him, while Mary stayed at home. Martha said to Jesus, "Lord, if you had been here, my brother would not have died. But even now I know that God will give you whatever you ask of him." Jesus said to her, "Your brother will rise again." Martha said to him, "I know that he will rise again in the resurrection on the last day." Jesus said to her, "I am the resurrection and the life. Those who believe in me, even though they die, will live, and everyone who lives and believes in me will never die. Do you believe this?" She said to him, "Yes, Lord, I believe that you are the Messiah, the Son of God, the one coming into the world."

Notice what you think and feel as you read the gospel.

Jesus arrives at the home of Martha and Mary after their brother Lazarus has died. He consoles Martha by telling her that her brother will rise again. Martha says she knows that he will rise on the last day. Jesus foreshadows what he is going to do, calling himself "the resurrection and the life." She believes he is the Messiah, the Son of God.

Pray as you are led for yourself and others.

"Let me keep your Resurrection and life foremost in my mind and heart, Lord. I seek to move from this life to your life. Even now, Lord, live in me, that I may never die. Make me pleasing to you, fit to serve in your name . . ." (Continue in your own words.)

Listen to Jesus.

I give you my life, beloved disciple. I am preparing you for eternal life with God, who is holy. What else is Jesus saying to you?

Ask God to show you how to live today.

"Lord, let me walk in your life today, confident of your work in me, always attentive to your leadership. Amen."

Tuesday, July 30, 2019

Know that God is present with you and ready to converse.

"Lord of heaven and earth, give me a heart to understand what you have for me today. Nourish me with the bread of your Word."

Read the gospel: Matthew 13:36–43.

Then Jesus left the crowds and went into the house. And his disciples approached him, saying, "Explain to us the parable of the weeds of the field." He answered, "The one who sows the good seed is the Son of Man; the field is the world, and the good seed are the children of the kingdom; the weeds are the children of the evil one, and the enemy who sowed them is the devil; the harvest is the end of the age, and the reapers are angels. Just as the weeds are collected and burned up with fire, so will it be at the end of the age. The Son of Man will send his angels, and they will collect out of his kingdom all causes of sin and all evildoers, and they will throw them into the furnace of fire, where there will be weeping and gnashing of teeth. Then the righteous will shine like the sun in the kingdom of their Father. Let anyone with ears listen!"

Notice what you think and feel as you read the gospel.

Jesus explains the parable of the sower who finds his field has been sown with weeds by an enemy; we need to be paying attention to his explanation.

Pray as you are led for yourself and others.

"Lord, I wish to come into your kingdom. Let me be watchful in my service of you and others. I offer myself to you for the good of others, especially . . ." (Continue in your own words.)

Listen to Jesus.

I rejoice in your prayers, beloved. I love you and also those I have given you. Continue to pray and to serve in the joy I give you. What else is Jesus saying to you?

Ask God to show you how to live today.

"Jesus, you give my life meaning and purpose. Keep me tuned to that as I fulfill my duties today. All for you, Lord. Amen."

Wednesday, July 31, 2019

Know that God is present with you and ready to converse.
"Lord, let me listen to your Word. Let it take root in me."

Read the gospel: Matthew 13:44–46.
Jesus said, "The kingdom of heaven is like treasure hidden in a field, which someone found and hid; then in his joy he goes and sells all that he has and buys that field.

"Again, the kingdom of heaven is like a merchant in search of fine pearls; on finding one pearl of great value, he went and sold all that he had and bought it."

Notice what you think and feel as you read the gospel.
These two brief parables tell us that the kingdom of heaven is a found treasure and a pearl of great value. Those who find the kingdom of heaven sell all they have to possess it.

Pray as you are led for yourself and others.
"You offer me the kingdom, Lord. Let me give up all I have that I may receive it. Let me cling only to you and this blessed hope . . ." (Continue in your own words.)

Listen to Jesus.
Pray for the coming of God's kingdom. Pray that souls come to receive the kingdom. What else is Jesus saying to you?

Ask God to show you how to live today.
"Lord, I offer myself to you today for the work of the kingdom. By your grace I shall do my work well today, even the most menial tasks. Amen."

THE POPE'S MONTHLY PRAYER INTENTION FOR AUGUST 2019

That families, through their life of prayer and love, become ever more clearly schools of true human growth.

Thursday, August 1, 2019

Know that God is present with you and ready to converse.

"Lord, how mysterious is the working of your Word! I wish to know the secrets of the kingdom, how to enter it. Instruct me now."

Read the gospel: Matthew 13:47–53.

Jesus said, "Again, the kingdom of heaven is like a net that was thrown into the sea and caught fish of every kind; when it was full, they drew it ashore, sat down, and put the good into baskets but threw out the bad. So it will be at the end of the age. The angels will come out and separate the evil from the righteous and throw them into the furnace of fire, where there will be weeping and gnashing of teeth.

"Have you understood all this?" They answered, "Yes." And he said to them, "Therefore every scribe who has been trained for the kingdom of heaven is like the master of a household who brings out of his treasure what is new and what is old." When Jesus had finished these parables, he left that place.

Notice what you think and feel as you read the gospel.

Jesus compares the judgment at the end of time to a net full of fish, both good and bad. The good are retained and the bad are discarded. And the kingdom shall contain treasure old and new.

Pray as you are led for yourself and others.

"Lord, your words of truth are my treasure. Help me to understand, and help also those you have given me . . ." (Continue in your own words.)

Listen to Jesus.

It is your task not to judge but to be judged. Do not give up on people, even those who scorn me or are indifferent to what I have to say. Pray for them, and love them as I love them. What else is Jesus saying to you?

Ask God to show you how to live today.

"Let me see the world and the people in it with eyes of hope, Lord. Thank you for showing me your kingdom. Amen."

Friday, August 2, 2019

Know that God is present with you and ready to converse.

"Open your Word to me, Lord. You are with me now to give me what I need. Thank you."

Read the gospel: Matthew 13:54–58.

He came to his hometown and began to teach the people in their synagogue, so that they were astounded and said, "Where did this man get this wisdom and these deeds of power? Is not this the carpenter's son? Is not his mother called Mary? And are not his brothers James and Joseph and Simon and Judas? And are not all his sisters with us? Where then did this man get all this?" And they took offence at him. But Jesus said to them, "Prophets are not without honor except in their own country and in their own house." And he did not do many deeds of power there, because of their unbelief.

Notice what you think and feel as you read the gospel.

Jesus impresses the people of his hometown with his knowledge and wisdom, but they know him too well. They know his family. Jesus notes that a prophet is without honor in his own country, and because of their unbelief, he does very few miracles among them.

Pray as you are led for yourself and others.

"I myself can discount your power or your Word. Prepare my heart to hear and understand your Word, Lord. Let it show me your power . . ." (Continue in your own words.)

Listen to Jesus.

Believe in me, beloved, and I will perform great works in and through you, and you will bear witness to the power of God. What else is Jesus saying to you?

Ask God to show you how to live today.

"Teach me how to walk in the proper fear of the Lord, not trusting myself but in all things consulting you. Let me lose myself to find you. I glorify you, king of heaven. Amen."

Saturday, August 3, 2019

Know that God is present with you and ready to converse.

"I turn to your Word, my God, that my faith, hope, and love may grow by it. All those things come from you."

Read the gospel: Matthew 14:1–12.

At that time Herod the ruler heard reports about Jesus; and he said to his servants, "This is John the Baptist; he has been raised from the dead, and for this reason these powers are at work in him." For Herod had arrested John, bound him, and put him in prison on account of Herodias, his brother Philip's wife, because John had been telling him, "It is not lawful for you to have her." Though Herod wanted to put him to death, he feared the crowd, because they regarded him as a prophet. But when Herod's birthday came, the daughter of Herodias danced before the company, and she pleased Herod so much that he promised on oath to grant her whatever she might ask. Prompted by her mother, she said, "Give me the head of John the Baptist here on a platter." The king was grieved, yet out of regard for his oaths and for the guests, he commanded it to be given; he sent and had John beheaded in the prison. The head was brought on a platter and given to the girl, who brought it to her mother. His disciples came and took the body and buried it; then they went and told Jesus.

Notice what you think and feel as you read the gospel.

This passage shows a deep understanding of Herod's twisted mind. When he hears of Jesus, he guiltily thinks it is John the Baptist—whom he had had killed because of his wife's manipulation—risen from the dead. Herod makes Jesus and his work about himself.

Pray as you are led for yourself and others.

"Lord, I pray for those who are corrupt in their power, lust, and violence. Let them repent and make amends. Comfort their victims . . ." (Continue in your own words.)

Listen to Jesus.

So it has ever been, that the wicked inflict suffering upon the innocent and the good. I hate their evil deeds, and I come with sure justice. What else is Jesus saying to you?

Ask God to show you how to live today.

"Lord, what can I do today to help those who suffer unjustly at the hands of evildoers? I offer my service. Amen."

Sunday, August 4, 2019
Eighteenth Sunday in Ordinary Time

Know that God is present with you and ready to converse.

"Your Word is a treasure. I am ready to hear your Word and draw nearer to you."

Read the gospel: Luke 12:13–21.

Someone in the crowd said to him, "Teacher, tell my brother to divide the family inheritance with me." But he said to him, "Friend, who set me to be a judge or arbitrator over you?" And he said to them, "Take care! Be on your guard against all kinds of greed; for one's life does not consist in the abundance of possessions." Then he told them a parable: "The land of a rich man produced abundantly. And he thought to himself, 'What should I do, for I have no place to store my crops?' Then he said, 'I will do this: I will pull down my barns and build larger ones, and there I will store all my grain and my goods. And I will say to my soul, Soul, you have ample goods laid up for many years; relax, eat, drink, be merry.' But God said to him, 'You fool! This very night your life is being demanded of you. And the things you have prepared, whose will they be?' So it is with those who store up treasures for themselves but are not rich towards God."

Notice what you think and feel as you read the gospel.

Jesus preaches against greed by the parable of the rich man who dies at the height of his prosperity. Be rich toward God, not earthly treasures.

Pray as you are led for yourself and others.

"Sometimes I worry about wealth and possessions, as if I do not have enough. Forgive me, Jesus. Lord, let me rejoice to possess your treasure, yourself. Keep my eyes on you, Jesus. I pray now for those who suffer from greed . . ." (Continue in your own words.)

Listen to Jesus.

If you wish to be rich toward God, then you must pray. I give you precious souls to pray for. Give them to me as often as I put it into your heart. This is great service for the kingdom of God. What else is Jesus saying to you?

Ask God to show you how to live today.

"Prayer is my gate to you, Lord, and the only wealth I need. Prayer is our ongoing friendship. Keep me in prayer all day, dear Jesus. Amen."

Monday, August 5, 2019

Know that God is present with you and ready to converse.

"Lord, your Word has power when received in your Spirit. I call upon the Holy Spirit to quicken your Word in me."

Read the gospel: Matthew 14:13–21.

Now when Jesus heard this, he withdrew from there in a boat to a deserted place by himself. But when the crowds heard it, they followed him on foot from the towns. When he went ashore, he saw a great crowd; and he had compassion for them and cured their sick. When it was evening, the disciples came to him and said, "This is a deserted place, and the hour is now late; send the crowds away so that they may go into the villages and buy food for themselves." Jesus said to them, "They need not go away; you give them something to eat." They replied, "We have nothing here but five loaves and two fish." And he said, "Bring them here to me." Then he ordered the crowds to sit down on the grass. Taking the five loaves and the two fish, he looked up to heaven, and blessed and broke the loaves, and gave them to the disciples, and the disciples gave them to the crowds. And all ate and were filled; and they took up what was left over of the broken pieces, twelve baskets full. And those who ate were about five thousand men, besides women and children.

Notice what you think and feel as you read the gospel.

Jesus feeds the crowd of five thousand with five loaves and two fish, and twelve basketfuls remain after everyone has eaten. He provided for their need out of compassion. He showed his power to provide for the material needs of the people following him.

Pray as you are led for yourself and others.

"Jesus, I have needs too. Help me to trust you to provide for me. I think of others who also have needs. Feed them, Lord . . ." (Continue in your own words.)

Listen to Jesus.

I came to people in response to the love of my Father. So I come to you today. You have entrusted yourself to me, beloved, and I am trustworthy. What else is Jesus saying to you?

Ask God to show you how to live today.

"Lord, please call others into this wonderful friendship with you. Open the eyes and hearts of those who are closed to you. Let me know what I may do to help. Amen."

Tuesday, August 6, 2019
Transfiguration of the Lord

Know that God is present with you and ready to converse.

"Jesus, you are God's Chosen One. Let me hear your voice now as I pray with this gospel."

Read the gospel: Luke 9:28b–36.

Now about eight days after these sayings Jesus took with him Peter and John and James, and went up on the mountain to pray. And while he was praying, the appearance of his face changed, and his clothes became dazzling white. Suddenly they saw two men, Moses and Elijah, talking to him. They appeared in glory and were speaking of his departure, which he was about to accomplish at Jerusalem. Now Peter and his companions were weighed down with sleep; but since they had stayed awake, they saw his glory and the two men who stood with him. Just as they were leaving him, Peter said to Jesus, "Master, it is good for us to be here; let us make three dwellings, one for you, one for Moses, and one for Elijah"—not knowing what he said. While he was saying this, a cloud came and overshadowed them; and they were terrified as they entered the cloud. Then from the cloud came a voice that said, "This is my Son, my Chosen; listen to him!" When the voice had spoken, Jesus was found alone. And they kept silent and in those days told no one any of the things they had seen.

Notice what you think and feel as you read the gospel.

Jesus takes Peter, James, and John up the mountain. They had probably accompanied Jesus up the mountain before to keep him company while he prayed, so they settle in for a nap. Then suddenly they see Jesus, transfigured, speaking with Moses and Elijah, the greatest of the prophets, about his approaching Passion. The disciples are confused and amazed; Peter starts babbling; and then they hear the voice of God from out of the cloud. Any doubts they may have had about Jesus are banished; still, the events of the day strike them speechless.

Pray as you are led for yourself and others.

"Your friendship and kindness are inconceivably great gifts, yet in your sweet familiarity, I can lose sight of your power and majesty. Let me be aware of both, today, Lord . . ." (Continue in your own words.)

Listen to Jesus.

You will find in my Cross both my love and my power. Seek me there; join me there, and you will know both in equal measure. What else is Jesus saying to you?

Ask God to show you how to live today.

"Lord, keep the image of your Cross, your glory, ever before me today, and let me proclaim that glory in my words and actions. Amen."

Wednesday, August 7, 2019

Know that God is present with you and ready to converse.

"Renew in me the joy of my salvation as I attend to your Word, Lord God."

Read the gospel: Matthew 15:21–28.

Jesus left that place and went away to the district of Tyre and Sidon. Just then a Canaanite woman from that region came out and started shouting, "Have mercy on me, Lord, Son of David; my daughter is tormented by a demon." But he did not answer her at all. And his disciples came and urged him, saying, "Send her away, for she keeps shouting after us." He answered, "I was sent only to the lost sheep of the house of Israel." But she came and knelt before him, saying, "Lord, help me." He answered, "It is not fair to take the children's food and throw it to the dogs." She said, "Yes, Lord, yet even the dogs eat the crumbs that fall from their masters' table." Then Jesus answered her, "Woman, great is your faith! Let it be done for you as you wish." And her daughter was healed instantly.

Notice what you think and feel as you read the gospel.

Why does Jesus not grant the woman's request immediately? He helped many who were not Israelites. What do her actions and responses tell us? She shows humility, in her kneeling before him and in her response to his initial refusal. She shows courage and persistence, for she counters his argument and continues to ask for what she needs. But above all, she shows great faith, and it is her faith in Jesus that is rewarded.

Pray as you are led for yourself and others.

"Lord, give me grace, so that the times when you refuse to grant my requests may serve to prove and increase the virtues you've planted in me. Please grant your grace and healing to those you've given me, especially . . ." (Continue in your own words.)

Listen to Jesus.

Persist in prayer, even when I seem at first to refuse your request. Trust in me, and trust in my goodness; I will cause all things to work together for good to those who love and believe in me. What else is Jesus saying to you?

Ask God to show you how to live today.

"Help me to pray worthily today, and let me receive your answer, whatever it is, with faith and humility. Amen."

Thursday, August 8, 2019

Know that God is present with you and ready to converse.

"Lord Jesus, you are the Messiah. Reveal yourself to me in your Word."

Read the gospel: Matthew 16:13–23.

Now when Jesus came into the district of Caesarea Philippi, he asked his disciples, "Who do people say that the Son of Man is?" And they said, "Some say John the Baptist, but others Elijah, and still others Jeremiah or one of the prophets." He said to them, "But who do you say that I am?" Simon Peter answered, "You are the Messiah, the Son of the living God." And Jesus answered him, "Blessed are you, Simon son of Jonah! For flesh and blood has not revealed this to you, but my Father in heaven. And I tell you, you are Peter, and on this rock I will build my church, and the gates of Hades will not prevail against it. I will give you the keys of the kingdom of heaven, and whatever you bind on earth will be bound in heaven, and whatever you loose on earth will be loosed in heaven." Then he sternly ordered the disciples not to tell anyone that he was the Messiah.

From that time on, Jesus began to show his disciples that he must go to Jerusalem and undergo great suffering at the hands of the elders and chief priests and scribes, and be killed, and on the third day be raised. And Peter took him aside and began to rebuke him, saying, "God forbid it, Lord! This must never happen to you." But he turned and said to Peter, "Get behind me, Satan! You are a stumbling block to me; for you are setting your mind not on divine things but on human things."

Notice what you think and feel as you read the gospel.

Jesus tests his disciples about his identity. When Peter proclaims him the Messiah, Jesus teaches them that he will have to undergo great suffering. Peter doesn't understand that power is not without suffering.

Pray as you are led for yourself and others.

"Lord, you suffered, died, and rose again so that I might follow you. I unite my sufferings to yours, including . . ." (Continue in your own words.)

Listen to Jesus.

I have liberated you from sin and death, beloved disciple. Your life has profound meaning for you and those I have given you. What else is Jesus saying to you?

Ask God to show you how to live today.

"Let me live and work today with my mind tuned to yours, my heart tuned to heaven. Thank you, Savior. Amen."

Friday, August 9, 2019

Know that God is present with you and ready to converse.

"Stir up my spirit, Lord, and refresh me as I ponder your Word."

Read the gospel: Matthew 16:24–28.

Then Jesus told his disciples, "If any want to become my followers, let them deny themselves and take up their cross and follow me. For those who want to save their life will lose it, and those who lose their life for my sake will find it. For what will it profit them if they gain the whole world but forfeit their life? Or what will they give in return for their life?

   "For the Son of Man is to come with his angels in the glory of his Father, and then he will repay everyone for what has been done. Truly I tell you, there are some standing here who will not taste death before they see the Son of Man coming in his kingdom."

Notice what you think and feel as you read the gospel.

Jesus expresses the paradox of life: those who seek to save their lives will lose them while those who seek to lose their lives will save them. Gaining the whole world is not worth losing your life. Judgment is coming, and some will enter into eternal life.

Pray as you are led for yourself and others.

"Teach me how to lose my life for the sake of your kingdom, Lord. Open the eyes of many to your mystery of life . . ." (Continue in your own words.)

Listen to Jesus.

I will do as you ask, child. Come to me and stay with me a long while, and I will show you wonderful things. What else is Jesus saying to you?

Ask God to show you how to live today.

"Give me the gift of prayer, Lord, for it is the key to our love for one another, and your love will lead me in my work and prayer. Amen."

Saturday, August 10, 2019

Know that God is present with you and ready to converse.

"You know the hearts of all, my God. You are here with me now to search me by your Word."

Read the gospel: John 12:24–26.

Jesus said, "Very truly, I tell you, unless a grain of wheat falls into the earth and dies, it remains just a single grain; but if it dies, it bears much fruit. Those who love their life lose it, and those who hate their life in this world will keep it for eternal life. Whoever serves me must follow me, and where I am, there will my servant be also. Whoever serves me, the Father will honor."

Notice what you think and feel as you read the gospel.

Jesus illustrates the paradox of life with a grain of wheat. It must fall to the ground and die in order for new life to sprout. Knowing this, we will detach ourselves from our lives in this world so that we can have eternal life in the next. If we serve him in this life, the Father will honor us.

Pray as you are led for yourself and others.

"Lord, I pray to serve you well. Let many come to serve you . . ." (Continue in your own words.)

Listen to Jesus.

Do not be afraid to put yourself at risk in my service. My work is not easy and you will be hated and persecuted at times. Other times you will recognize a great many brothers and sisters. What else is Jesus saying to you?

Ask God to show you how to live today.

"Show me how to die to self today, Lord, so that I can grow closer to you. Amen."

Sunday, August 11, 2019
Nineteenth Sunday in Ordinary Time

Know that God is present with you and ready to converse.

"Let your Word awaken my heart and keep me ever watchful for you, Lord."

Read the gospel: Luke 12:35–40 (Lk 12:32–48).

Jesus said, "Be dressed for action and have your lamps lit; be like those who are waiting for their master to return from the wedding banquet, so that they may open the door for him as soon as he comes and knocks. Blessed are those slaves whom the master finds alert when he comes; truly I tell you, he will fasten his belt and have them sit down to eat, and he will come and serve them. If he comes during the middle of the night, or near dawn, and finds them so, blessed are those slaves.

"But know this: if the owner of the house had known at what hour the thief was coming, he would not have let his house be broken into. You also must be ready, for the Son of Man is coming at an unexpected hour."

Notice what you think and feel as you read the gospel.

Jesus speaks of the end, when he will return and gather his flock into the eternal kingdom of God. Watch, pray, and work for the kingdom until he returns. If he seems to delay, do not despair, for he will return and bring judgment. The judgment is coming.

Pray as you are led for yourself and others.

"I wait for you, too, Jesus, for your return in all your power and glory. Lord, keep me faithful to you . . ." (Continue in your own words.)

Listen to Jesus.

You desire me, and I desire you, dear child. You are beloved of God, and God seeks your love in return. Do you love me? What else is Jesus saying to you?

Ask God to show you how to live today.

"Lord, I do love you. Show me how to serve you today. Amen."

Monday, August 12, 2019

Know that God is present with you and ready to converse.

"Lord, in you I have all I need. You give yourself to me by your Spirit and your Word. I praise you!"

Read the gospel: Matthew 17:22–27.

As they were gathering in Galilee, Jesus said to them, "The Son of Man is going to be betrayed into human hands, and they will kill him, and on the third day he will be raised." And they were greatly distressed.

When they reached Capernaum, the collectors of the temple tax came to Peter and said, "Does your teacher not pay the temple tax?" He said, "Yes, he does." And when he came home, Jesus spoke of it first, asking, "What do you think, Simon? From whom do kings of the earth take toll or tribute? From their children or from others?" When Peter said, "From others," Jesus said to him, "Then the children are free. However, so that we do not give offence to them, go to the lake and cast a hook; take the first fish that comes up; and when you open its mouth, you will find a coin; take that and give it to them for you and me."

Notice what you think and feel as you read the gospel.

What does the temple tax have to do with the Passion, Death, and Resurrection of Jesus? In the Resurrection, we are made children of God, we are made free; and our Father, the king of heaven, does not collect taxes. He demands that we love him and one another. And so Jesus, not wanting to offend his Jewish brethren, divinely provides the means to pay the tax. If we show love and respect to our neighbors, God will provide for us.

Pray as you are led for yourself and others.

"Lord, your providence is miraculous. Please provide for those you've given me, especially . . ." (Continue in your own words.)

Listen to Jesus.

Rest in me, dear child. Follow me with complete confidence. Your trust in me will be your peace. Serve one another in love and keep your mind and heart focused on me, and I will take care of the rest. What else is Jesus saying to you?

Ask God to show you how to live today.

"Let no shadow or fear block me from you today, Lord. Let your peace go with me always. Amen."

Tuesday, August 13, 2019

Know that God is present with you and ready to converse.

"Almighty Father, you are the source of faith, which comes to me by hearing the Word of God. Refresh my faith today. Be real to me now."

Read the gospel: Matthew 18:1–5, 10, 12–14.

At that time the disciples came to Jesus and asked, "Who is the greatest in the kingdom of heaven?" He called a child, whom he put among them, and said, "Truly I tell you, unless you change and become like children, you will never enter the kingdom of heaven. Whoever becomes humble like this child is the greatest in the kingdom of heaven. Whoever welcomes one such child in my name welcomes me. . . .

"Take care that you do not despise one of these little ones; for, I tell you, in heaven their angels continually see the face of my Father in heaven. . . ."

"What do you think? If a shepherd has a hundred sheep, and one of them has gone astray, does he not leave the ninety-nine on the mountains and go in search of the one that went astray? And if he finds it, truly I tell you, he rejoices over it more than over the ninety-nine that never went astray. So it is not the will of your Father in heaven that one of these little ones should be lost."

Notice what you think and feel as you read the gospel.
The small, the lost, the humble are all treasured and sought after in the kingdom of heaven.

Pray as you are led for yourself and others.
"Lord, make me your child. Give me true humility and joyful acceptance of your care. I place all these in your care . . ." (Continue in your own words.)

Listen to Jesus.
I love you. Give me your gratitude, obedience, acceptance, and love, for these are my treasures. What else is Jesus saying to you?

Ask God to show you how to live today.
"Lord, when I try to take control today, when I try to do it all myself, when I worry and stray, call me back to you and give me your peace and your joy. Amen."

Wednesday, August 14, 2019

Know that God is present with you and ready to converse.
"God, you are present in all things. Let me see and know you in your holy Word."

Read the gospel: Matthew 18:15–20.
Jesus said, "If another member of the church sins against you, go and point out the fault when the two of you are alone. If the member listens to you, you have regained that one. But if you are not listened to, take one or two others along with you, so that every word may be confirmed by the evidence of two or three witnesses. If the member refuses to listen to them, tell it to the church; and if the offender refuses to listen even to the church, let such a one be to you as a Gentile and a tax collector. Truly I tell you, whatever you bind on earth will be bound in heaven, and whatever you loose on earth will be loosed in heaven. Again, truly I tell you, if two of you agree on earth about anything you ask, it will be done for you by my Father in heaven. For where two or three are gathered in my name, I am there among them."

Notice what you think and feel as you read the gospel.

Jesus gives practical advice regarding disputes among believers: seek mediation from others in the church, seek reconciliation, and remember that final judgment will come from the Father.

Pray as you are led for yourself and others.

"Lord, let me be fair and honest with my adversaries, both believers and nonbelievers. I pray for those you have given me . . ." (Continue in your own words.)

Listen to Jesus.

I hear your prayers, beloved disciple. I grant you what you have asked. What else may I do for you? What else is Jesus saying to you?

Ask God to show you how to live today.

"Let today be another small step in my life toward you and with you. I love you, praise you, and worship you for allowing me to walk with you today. Amen."

Thursday, August 15, 2019
Assumption of the Blessed Virgin Mary

Know that God is present with you and ready to converse.

"Lord, your servant is here with you. I come to do your will."

Read the gospel: Luke 1:39–56.

In those days Mary set out and went with haste to a Judean town in the hill country, where she entered the house of Zechariah and greeted Elizabeth. When Elizabeth heard Mary's greeting, the child leapt in her womb. And Elizabeth was filled with the Holy Spirit and exclaimed with a loud cry, "Blessed are you among women, and blessed is the fruit of your womb. And why has this happened to me, that the mother of my Lord comes to me? For as soon as I heard the sound of your greeting, the child in my womb leapt for joy. And blessed is she who believed that there would be a fulfillment of what was spoken to her by the Lord."

And Mary said,

> "My soul magnifies the Lord,
>   and my spirit rejoices in God my Savior,
> for he has looked with favor on the lowliness of his servant.

> Surely, from now on all generations will call me blessed;
> for the Mighty One has done great things for me,
>   and holy is his name.
> His mercy is for those who fear him
>   from generation to generation.
> He has shown strength with his arm;
>   he has scattered the proud in the thoughts of their hearts.
> He has brought down the powerful from their thrones,
>   and lifted up the lowly;
> he has filled the hungry with good things,
>   and sent the rich away empty.
> He has helped his servant Israel,
>   in remembrance of his mercy,
> according to the promise he made to our ancestors,
>   to Abraham and to his descendants for ever."

And Mary remained with her for about three months and then returned to her home.

Notice what you think and feel as you read the gospel.

Mary goes to visit her cousin Elizabeth while both women are pregnant. Elizabeth congratulates Mary, and Mary turns all praise and attention to God. Mary is just a humble servant; her blessedness is because of God's might and mercy.

Pray as you are led for yourself and others.

"Lord, help me to keep you always in the forefront of my mind, as Mary did, so that I may turn to you and praise you in every moment and direct others to you as well, especially . . ." (Continue in your own words.)

Listen to Jesus.

Even in her Assumption, even in her role as Queen of Heaven, my Mother points all Christians to me. Follow her and let her bring you to me. What else is Jesus saying to you?

Ask God to show you how to live today.

"What aspect of my life needs to be redirected to you? Show me, and give me the grace to say yes to you and to surrender that part of me to your will. Amen."

Friday, August 16, 2019

Know that God is present with you and ready to converse.
"Lord of Life, you loved me before the foundation of the world and give me life in this moment. Give me wisdom to live it as you will."

Read the gospel: Matthew 19:3–12.
Some Pharisees came to Jesus, and to test him they asked, "Is it lawful for a man to divorce his wife for any cause?" He answered, "Have you not read that the one who made them at the beginning 'made them male and female,' and said, 'For this reason a man shall leave his father and mother and be joined to his wife, and the two shall become one flesh'? So they are no longer two, but one flesh. Therefore what God has joined together, let no one separate." They said to him, "Why then did Moses command us to give a certificate of dismissal and to divorce her?" He said to them, "It was because you were so hard-hearted that Moses allowed you to divorce your wives, but at the beginning it was not so. And I say to you, whoever divorces his wife, except for unchastity, and marries another commits adultery."

His disciples said to him, "If such is the case of a man with his wife, it is better not to marry." But he said to them, "Not everyone can accept this teaching, but only those to whom it is given. For there are eunuchs who have been so from birth, and there are eunuchs who have been made eunuchs by others, and there are eunuchs who have made themselves eunuchs for the sake of the kingdom of heaven. Let anyone accept this who can."

Notice what you think and feel as you read the gospel.
Jesus asserts the sanctity of marriage, deploring divorce as ungodly. Marriage is not for everyone; those who cannot accept marriage on these terms should, for the sake of the kingdom of heaven, refrain from marrying.

Pray as you are led for yourself and others.
"Lord, many are divorced. Let me not judge them, because I cannot know their hearts. I pray for those who struggle in marriage. I pray for those who are divorced . . ." (Continue in your own words.)

Listen to Jesus.

You are right not to judge. People do not always understand what they are doing when they make decisions to divorce, and many who are divorced are not fully culpable. What else is Jesus saying to you?

Ask God to show you how to live today.

"Let me see you today in others, Lord, and show them sincere love in words and in action, for I value only the things of God, who is Love. Amen."

Saturday, August 17, 2019

Know that God is present with you and ready to converse.

"Mysterious God, you are the great I AM, eternal, present everywhere at all times, even with me now. Let me respond to you in faith."

Read the gospel: Matthew 19:13–15.

Then little children were being brought to him in order that he might lay his hands on them and pray. The disciples spoke sternly to those who brought them; but Jesus said, "Let the little children come to me, and do not stop them; for it is to such as these that the kingdom of heaven belongs." And he laid his hands on them and went on his way.

Notice what you think and feel as you read the gospel.

Jesus receives, loves, and prays for the little children, who show us how to enter the kingdom of heaven.

Pray as you are led for yourself and others.

"Lord, I pray to be a child of God in your eternal kingdom. I pray now for these children . . ." (Continue in your own words.)

Listen to Jesus.

I grant you the faith you need, my child. I know your struggles. I love those I have given you. I have them in my care. What else is Jesus saying to you?

Ask God to show you how to live today.

"Let me be simple and loving with all I encounter today. Make me conscious of you all day, Lord. Thank you. Amen."

Sunday, August 18, 2019
Twentieth Sunday in Ordinary Time

Know that God is present with you and ready to converse.

"O eternal God of love and power, I believe in you. Help my unbelief as I encounter your holy Word today."

Read the gospel: Luke 12:49–53.

Jesus said, "I came to bring fire to the earth, and how I wish it were already kindled! I have a baptism with which to be baptized, and what stress I am under until it is completed! Do you think that I have come to bring peace to the earth? No, I tell you, but rather division! From now on, five in one household will be divided, three against two and two against three; they will be divided:

> father against son
>   and son against father,
> mother against daughter
>   and daughter against mother,
> mother-in-law against her daughter-in-law
>   and daughter-in-law against mother-in-law."

Notice what you think and feel as you read the gospel.

Jesus understands that his Gospel, that he himself, is divisive and will lead to violence on the earth. We have seen violence and division, even in our families.

Pray as you are led for yourself and others.

"Lord, I pray for peace in the world and in families. I pray for those you have given me . . ." (Continue in your own words.)

Listen to Jesus.

My peace surpasses understanding, for while violence rages, you can find perfect peace in me. What else is Jesus saying to you?

Ask God to show you how to live today.

"Let me walk in your peace today, Lord. Let me trust you to see me through it all. I thank you, dear Lord. Amen."

Monday, August 19, 2019

Know that God is present with you and ready to converse.

"Lord of All, I long to enter into your life. I will listen to your Word with all my heart."

Read the gospel: Matthew 19:16–22.

Then someone came to Jesus and said, "Teacher, what good deed must I do to have eternal life?" And he said to him, "Why do you ask me about what is good? There is only one who is good. If you wish to enter into life, keep the commandments." He said to him, "Which ones?" And Jesus said, "You shall not murder; You shall not commit adultery; You shall not steal; You shall not bear false witness; Honor your father and mother; also, You shall love your neighbour as yourself." The young man said to him, "I have kept all these; what do I still lack?" Jesus said to him, "If you wish to be perfect, go, sell your possessions, and give the money to the poor, and you will have treasure in heaven; then come, follow me." When the young man heard this word, he went away grieving, for he had many possessions.

Notice what you think and feel as you read the gospel.

Jesus reminds the rich young man of the commandments but says perfection requires more than just keeping them: the young man must give up everything and follow Jesus—and his reward will be great. The young man cannot receive Jesus' words.

Pray as you are led for yourself and others.

"Jesus, please do not allow possessions or pursuit of possessions to come between us. Let me be generous with my wealth and follow you. I pray for these needs . . ." (Continue in your own words.)

Listen to Jesus.

Be a spiritual person, dear disciple, so that you can grow in the love and knowledge of God, which is your sole duty and the only lasting good. What else is Jesus saying to you?

Ask God to show you how to live today.

"Let me be responsible in my earthly affairs, Lord, but keep my focus on you and heavenly things all day long. You are my everything, Jesus. Amen."

Tuesday, August 20, 2019

Know that God is present with you and ready to converse.

"For you, Lord, all things are possible. Bring me to you by your Word."

Read the gospel: Matthew 19:23–30.

Then Jesus said to his disciples, "Truly I tell you, it will be hard for a rich person to enter the kingdom of heaven. Again I tell you, it is easier for a camel to go through the eye of a needle than for someone who is rich to enter the kingdom of God." When the disciples heard this, they were greatly astounded and said, "Then who can be saved?" But Jesus looked at them and said, "For mortals it is impossible, but for God all things are possible."

Then Peter said in reply, "Look, we have left everything and followed you. What then will we have?" Jesus said to them, "Truly I tell you, at the renewal of all things, when the Son of Man is seated on the throne of his glory, you who have followed me will also sit on twelve thrones, judging the twelve tribes of Israel. And everyone who has left houses or brothers or sisters or father or mother or children or fields, for my name's sake, will receive a hundredfold, and will inherit eternal life. But many who are first will be last, and the last will be first."

Notice what you think and feel as you read the gospel.

Jesus speaks of the dangers of wealth, how they hinder entry into the kingdom of God. Yet with God all things are possible. Peter asks Jesus what they will receive for leaving everything and following him. Jesus promises they will receive a hundredfold in return and inherit eternal life.

Pray as you are led for yourself and others.

"God, your ways are perfect. I aspire to eternal life. May this be the focus of my whole being. I give myself to you to manage my life, today and always. I also give you the lives of those you wish me to pray for . . ." (Continue in your own words.)

Listen to Jesus.

You are mine, beloved. Because you have given yourself to God, you are included in God's family. We love those you love. What else is Jesus saying to you?

Ask God to show you how to live today.

"I thank you for accepting me, loving me, and forming me according to your good pleasure. Help me to cooperate with you today and please you. Amen."

Wednesday, August 21, 2019

Know that God is present with you and ready to converse.

"Lord Jesus, Wisdom of the Father, you lived among us to tell us the truth. You are here with me now to teach me by your Word."

Read the gospel: Matthew 20:1–16.

Jesus said, "For the kingdom of heaven is like a landowner who went out early in the morning to hire laborers for his vineyard. After agreeing with the laborers for the usual daily wage, he sent them into his vineyard. When he went out about nine o'clock, he saw others standing idle in the marketplace; and he said to them, 'You also go into the vineyard, and I will pay you whatever is right.' So they went. When he went out again about noon and about three o'clock, he did the same. And about five o'clock he went out and found others standing around; and he said to them, 'Why are you standing here idle all day?' They said to him, 'Because no one has hired us.' He said to them, 'You also go into the vineyard.' When evening came, the owner of the vineyard said to his manager, 'Call the laborers and give them their pay, beginning with the last and then going to the first.' When those hired about five o'clock came, each of them received the usual daily wage. Now when the first came, they thought they would receive more; but each of them also received the usual daily wage. And when they received it, they grumbled against the landowner, saying, 'These last worked only one hour, and you have made them equal to us who have borne the burden of the day and the scorching heat.' But he replied to one of them, 'Friend, I am doing you no wrong; did you not agree with me for the usual daily wage? Take what belongs to you and go; I choose to give to this last the same as I give to you. Am I not allowed to do what I choose with what belongs to me? Or are you envious because I am generous?' So the last will be first, and the first will be last."

Notice what you think and feel as you read the gospel.

Jesus tells a parable about hired field hands who agree to work for the daily wage. At the end of the day the landowner gives them all the same pay, whether they worked all day or just for an hour. Those who worked all day complain, and the landowner says they appear envious because he is generous. So, too, in the kingdom of heaven, God will be generous to whomever he chooses.

Pray as you are led for yourself and others.

"Lord, let me work in your service and not count the cost. I will not compare myself with others. I pray now for these . . ." (Continue in your own words.)

Listen to Jesus.

You are easy to love, dear one. I created you to love you; I also created the people you struggle to love so I could love them. What else is Jesus saying to you?

Ask God to show you how to live today.

"Guide my steps today, God, and let my mind return often to you. Amen."

Thursday, August 22, 2019

Know that God is present with you and ready to converse.

"Merciful Father, I wish to understand your mercy. Teach me, and form me in your likeness."

Read the gospel: Matthew 22:1–14.

Once more Jesus spoke to them in parables, saying: "The kingdom of heaven may be compared to a king who gave a wedding banquet for his son. He sent his slaves to call those who had been invited to the wedding banquet, but they would not come. Again he sent other slaves, saying, 'Tell those who have been invited: Look, I have prepared my dinner, my oxen and my fat calves have been slaughtered, and everything is ready; come to the wedding banquet.' But they made light of it and went away, one to his farm, another to his business, while the rest seized his slaves, maltreated them, and killed them. The king was enraged. He sent his troops, destroyed those murderers, and burned their city. Then he said to his slaves, 'The wedding is ready, but those invited were not worthy. Go therefore into the main streets, and invite everyone you find to the wedding banquet.' Those slaves went out into the streets and gathered all whom they found, both good and bad; so the wedding hall was filled with guests.

"But when the king came in to see the guests, he noticed a man there who was not wearing a wedding robe, and he said to him, 'Friend, how did you get in here without a wedding robe?' And he was speechless. Then the king said to the attendants, 'Bind him hand and foot, and throw him into the outer darkness, where there will be weeping and gnashing of teeth.' For many are called, but few are chosen."

Notice what you think and feel as you read the gospel.

This is the parable of the wedding banquet, which represents the kingdom of heaven. Many are invited, but few accept the invitation. So the king has his servant go out into the streets and invite everyone, the good and the bad. They come to the banquet. One man is not wearing a wedding garment, so he is thrown out.

Pray as you are led for yourself and others.

"Lord, I pray to be among the chosen at your banquet. Robe me in righteousness. Let me be loving in all I do. I think of . . ." (Continue in your own words.)

Listen to Jesus.

I grant you what you seek, beloved. Regard all people with mercy, and our hearts will be one. What else is Jesus saying to you?

Ask God to show you how to live today.

"Open me to opportunities today to regard others in the light of your love. Thank you, loving God. I adore you. Amen."

Friday, August 23, 2019

Know that God is present with you and ready to converse.

"Lord, I come to you in the midst of the complications of life. Inscribe your precepts upon my heart that I may walk justly in your ways."

Read the gospel: Matthew 22:34–40.

When the Pharisees heard that Jesus had silenced the Sadducees, they gathered together, and one of them, a lawyer, asked him a question to test him. "Teacher, which commandment in the law is the greatest?" He said to him, "'You shall love the Lord your God with all your heart, and with all your soul, and with all your mind.' This is the greatest and first commandment. And a second is like it: 'You shall love your neighbor as yourself.' On these two commandments hang all the law and the prophets."

Notice what you think and feel as you read the gospel.

The lawyer, thinking he already know the answers, quizzes Jesus. But he asks a question we all might honestly put to Jesus: What's the most important thing I need to do? Jesus preaches that the two great commandments are to love God and love one's neighbor.

Pray as you are led for yourself and others.

"Lord, help me not to obey your commandments. Guide me and those you have given me to make loving choices . . ." (Continue in your own words.)

Listen to Jesus.

Bring me all your questions, even when you think you already know the answer. I will tell you the truth. What else is Jesus saying to you?

Ask God to show you how to live today.

"Help me to be authentic today in all my dealings with others, beginning with you. Teach me to speak the truth in love. Amen."

Saturday, August 24, 2019
St. Bartholomew, Apostle

Know that God is present with you and ready to converse.

"Lord, you know me. Let me know you and love you better by the hearing of your Word."

Read the gospel: John 1:45–51.

Philip found Nathanael and said to him, "We have found him about whom Moses in the law and also the prophets wrote, Jesus son of Joseph from Nazareth." Nathanael said to him, "Can anything good come out of Nazareth?" Philip said to him, "Come and see." When Jesus saw Nathanael coming towards him, he said of him, "Here is truly an Israelite in whom there is no deceit!" Nathanael asked him, "Where did you come to know me?" Jesus answered, "I saw you under the fig tree before Philip called you." Nathanael replied, "Rabbi, you are the Son of God! You are the King of Israel!" Jesus answered, "Do you believe because I told you that I saw you under the fig tree? You will see greater things than these."

And he said to him, "Very truly, I tell you, you will see heaven opened and the angels of God ascending and descending upon the Son of Man."

Notice what you think and feel as you read the gospel.

Nathanael is a good man, but he is skeptical about Jesus being the great prophet Moses and the prophets foretold. After all, Jesus is from Nazareth. When Jesus sees him approaching, he calls him a man without deceit. Nathanael, still skeptical, asks Jesus how he could know that. That's when Jesus tells Nathanael that he saw him under the fig tree even before Philip called him. Nathanael immediately believes that Jesus is the Son of God.

Pray as you are led for yourself and others.

"Glorious Lord and King, I long to see you as you are. I praise you and thank you for all your love and mercy to me and those you have given me . . ." (Continue in your own words.)

Listen to Jesus.

You shall see me and know me as I am, beloved disciple. Set your heart on heaven. What else is Jesus saying to you?

Ask God to show you how to live today.

"When you call me today, Lord, give me the grace to hear you and answer your call. Amen."

Sunday, August 25, 2019
Twenty-First Sunday in Ordinary Time

Know that God is present with you and ready to converse.

"Lord, I am ready to listen to your voice. Teach me your way."

Read the gospel: Luke 13:22–30.

Jesus went through one town and village after another, teaching as he made his way to Jerusalem. Someone asked him, "Lord, will only a few be saved?" He said to them, "Strive to enter through the narrow door; for many, I tell you, will try to enter and will not be able. When once the owner of the house has got up and shut the door, and you begin to stand outside and to knock at the door, saying, 'Lord, open to us,' then in reply he will say to you, 'I do not know where you come from.' Then you will begin to say, 'We ate and drank with you, and you taught in our streets.' But he will say, 'I do not know where you come from; go away from me, all you evildoers!' There will be weeping and gnashing of teeth when you see Abraham and Isaac and Jacob and all the prophets in the kingdom of God, and you yourselves thrown out. Then people will come from east and west, from north and south, and will eat in the kingdom of God. Indeed, some are last who will be first, and some are first who will be last."

Notice what you think and feel as you read the gospel.

Jesus talks about going through the narrow door to get to heaven. We cannot take salvation for granted. If we do not know and love Jesus with our whole heart and mind, we risk eternal separation from God.

Pray as you are led for yourself and others.

"Let my faith become a long and fruitful faithfulness, Lord, for you have given me much. I pray for those I serve . . ." (Continue in your own words.)

Listen to Jesus.

Do not be afraid, beloved disciple, friend, and servant. I am with you now and I will be with you always. God is faithful. What else is Jesus saying to you?

Ask God to show you how to live today.

"How may I serve today, Lord? Give me ways to please you. Amen."

Monday, August 26, 2019

Know that God is present with you and ready to converse.

"Lord, your servant is here with you now. I am ready to learn what you would have me do to inherit eternal life."

Read the gospel: Matthew 23:13–22.

Jesus said, "But woe to you, scribes and Pharisees, hypocrites! For you lock people out of the kingdom of heaven. For you do not go in yourselves, and when others are going in, you stop them. Woe to you, scribes and Pharisees, hypocrites! For you cross sea and land to make a single convert, and you make the new convert twice as much a child of hell as yourselves.

"Woe to you, blind guides, who say, 'Whoever swears by the sanctuary is bound by nothing, but whoever swears by the gold of the sanctuary is bound by the oath.' You blind fools! For which is greater, the gold or the sanctuary that has made the gold sacred? And you say, 'Whoever swears by the altar is bound by nothing, but whoever swears by the gift that is on the altar is bound by the oath.' How blind you are! For which is greater, the gift or the altar that makes the gift sacred? So whoever swears by the altar, swears by it and by everything on it; and whoever swears by the sanctuary, swears by it and by the one who dwells in it; and whoever swears by heaven, swears by the throne of God and by the one who is seated upon it."

Notice what you think and feel as you read the gospel.

Jesus preaches against hypocrisy and religious legalism. He rebukes the religious leaders who impose human laws in God's name.

Pray as you are led for yourself and others.

"Jesus, let me turn away from hypocrisy in all things. I pray for the integrity of religious leaders . . ." (Continue in your own words.)

Listen to Jesus.

The way to God is the way of Truth. Cling to me, for I am humble and real. Beloved disciple, my way is good. What else is Jesus saying to you?

Ask God to show you how to live today.

"Reveal to me the falseness in my own heart, Lord, and let me turn from that darkness to follow you more closely. Good Master, give me the power to do this. I give myself to you today. Amen."

Tuesday, August 27, 2019

Know that God is present with you and ready to converse.

"Savior, I need saving every day. Save me from myself and from the traps around me. I welcome you into my day through the power of your holy Word."

Read the gospel: Matthew 23:23–26.

Jesus said, "Woe to you, scribes and Pharisees, hypocrites! For you tithe mint, dill, and cumin, and have neglected the weightier matters of the law: justice and mercy and faith. It is these you ought to have practiced without neglecting the others. You blind guides! You strain out a gnat but swallow a camel!

"Woe to you, scribes and Pharisees, hypocrites! For you clean the outside of the cup and of the plate, but inside they are full of greed and self-indulgence. You blind Pharisee! First clean the inside of the cup, so that the outside also may become clean."

Notice what you think and feel as you read the gospel.

Jesus condemns the hypocrisy of the scribes and Pharisees, for they observe little rules of their own but neglect what's important to God, namely justice, mercy, and faith. They care about appearances, but inside they are full of greed and self-indulgence.

Pray as you are led for yourself and others.

"Lord, give me hatred for my own hypocrisy, so that I may be true to you. Let me know you more and more as I follow you. I pray for these things and these people . . ." (Continue in your own words.)

Listen to Jesus.

Beloved, I have you in my hand. Come to me often, love me, and I will care for you until the end. What else is Jesus saying to you?

Ask God to show you how to live today.

"I love you, Jesus Christ, my Redeemer and King. Let me walk in your loving way. Show me authenticity, Lord. Amen."

Wednesday, August 28, 2019

Know that God is present with you and ready to converse.

"Eternal Father, you have given us the gift of eternal life through your Son, Jesus, who paid it all on the Cross. I receive your gift with thanksgiving."

Read the gospel: Matthew 23:27–32.

Jesus said, "Woe to you, scribes and Pharisees, hypocrites! For you are like whitewashed tombs, which on the outside look beautiful, but inside they are full of the bones of the dead and of all kinds of filth. So you also on the outside look righteous to others, but inside you are full of hypocrisy and lawlessness.

"Woe to you, scribes and Pharisees, hypocrites! For you build the tombs of the prophets and decorate the graves of the righteous, and you say, 'If we had lived in the days of our ancestors, we would not have taken part with them in shedding the blood of the prophets.' Thus you testify against yourselves that you are descendants of those who murdered the prophets. Fill up, then, the measure of your ancestors."

Notice what you think and feel as you read the gospel.

Jesus speaks often against the hypocrisy of religious leaders. He is trying to jolt them out of their complacency. They are the children of those who murdered the prophets of old. Jesus, knowing what is to come, says they will do as their ancestors did, and worse.

Pray as you are led for yourself and others.

"Lord, for all the times I have disregarded your messengers and your commandments, I beg forgiveness. Fill me with your life that I may be truly beautiful, as you are. I pray also for . . ." (Continue in your own words.)

Listen to Jesus.

Life is what I offer you, dear friend. You have it now, and following me, you will extend your life into eternity with God. Do the work I have given you to do, and you will inherit the kingdom of God. What else is Jesus saying to you?

Ask God to show you how to live today.

"Let me work today for you, Lord. I offer you all my thoughts, words, and deeds—all my joy and all my suffering. Let everything I do serve you, Jesus. Amen."

Thursday, August 29, 2019
Martyrdom of John the Baptist

Know that God is present with you and ready to converse.

"I come into your presence today, Lord God of hosts. I am blessed by your Holy Spirit's teaching me by your Word."

Read the gospel: Mark 6:17–29.

For Herod himself had sent men who arrested John, bound him, and put him in prison on account of Herodias, his brother Philip's wife, because Herod had married her. For John had been telling Herod, "It is not lawful for you to have your brother's wife." And Herodias had a grudge against him, and wanted to kill him. But she could not, for Herod feared John, knowing that he was a righteous and holy man, and he protected him. When he heard him, he was greatly perplexed; and yet he liked to listen to him. But an opportunity came when Herod on his birthday gave a banquet for his courtiers and officers and for the leaders of Galilee. When his daughter Herodias came in and danced, she pleased Herod and his guests; and the king said to the girl, "Ask me for whatever you wish, and I will give it." And he solemnly swore to her, "Whatever you ask me, I will give you, even half of my kingdom." She went out and said to her mother, "What should I ask for?" She replied, "The head of John the baptizer." Immediately she rushed back to the king and requested, "I want you to give me at once the head of John the Baptist on a platter." The king was deeply grieved; yet out of regard for his oaths and for the guests, he did not want to refuse her. Immediately the king sent a soldier of the guard with orders to bring John's head. He went and beheaded him in the prison, brought his head on a platter, and gave it to the girl. Then the girl gave it to her mother. When his disciples heard about it, they came and took his body, and laid it in a tomb.

Notice what you think and feel as you read the gospel.

John the Baptist spoke truth to power and was martyred for it in an absurd and grotesque way.

Pray as you are led for yourself and others.

"Lord, let me be fearless in proclaiming you. Keep my mind and my heart on you, and save me from evil. Keep safe also those you have given me . . ." (Continue in your own words.)

Listen to Jesus.

There is sin and evil in the world, but I have conquered sin. I am your victory. Cling to me, and I will bring you safely to your eternal home. What else is Jesus saying to you?

Ask God to show you how to live today.

"Help me remember, when I face evil and the consequences of sin today, that you are Lord. Amen."

Friday, August 30, 2019

Know that God is present with you and ready to converse.

"Sweep away all my distraction, Lord, as I listen to you."

Read the gospel: Matthew 25:1–13.

Jesus said, "Then the kingdom of heaven will be like this. Ten brides-maids took their lamps and went to meet the bridegroom. Five of them were foolish, and five were wise. When the foolish took their lamps, they took no oil with them; but the wise took flasks of oil with their lamps.

As the bridegroom was delayed, all of them became drowsy and slept. But at midnight there was a shout, 'Look! Here is the bridegroom! Come out to meet him.' Then all those bridesmaids got up and trimmed their lamps. The foolish said to the wise, 'Give us some of your oil, for our lamps are going out.' But the wise replied, 'No! there will not be enough for you and for us; you had better go to the dealers and buy some for yourselves.' And while they went to buy it, the bridegroom came, and those who were ready went with him into the wedding banquet; and the door was shut. Later the other bridesmaids came also, saying, 'Lord, lord, open to us.' But he replied, 'Truly I tell you, I do not know you.' Keep awake therefore, for you know neither the day nor the hour."

Notice what you think and feel as you read the gospel.

Jesus uses the parable of the ten bridesmaids to help us be ready for his return. Five of the ten are wise and keep oil with their lamps. The other five are foolish and have no oil. The bridegroom has tarried so long they neglected their lamps. When they beg entrance to the wedding banquet, the Lord says, "I do not know you."

Pray as you are led for yourself and others.

"Lord, help me to be ready, expecting your return even in my own life-time, even today. Do not let my heart stray from longing for you. I pray for . . ." (Continue in your own words.)

Listen to Jesus.

Your love for God and others can grow infinitely. This is the oil in your lamp. This is the joy of living, to increase in the knowledge and love of God. Come often in prayer. What else is Jesus saying to you?

Ask God to show you how to live today.

"Teach me to pray, Lord, for I am eager to know you, love you, and please you more and more. How may I return your love? Amen."

Saturday, August 31, 2019

Know that God is present with you and ready to converse.

"Most High Lord of heaven and earth, I bow before you. Instruct me by your Word."

Read the gospel: Matthew 25:14–30.

Jesus said, "For it is as if a man, going on a journey, summoned his slaves and entrusted his property to them; to one he gave five talents, to another two, to another one, to each according to his ability. Then he went away. The one who had received the five talents went off at once and traded with them, and made five more talents. In the same way, the one who had the two talents made two more talents. But the one who had received the one talent went off and dug a hole in the ground and hid his master's money. After a long time the master of those slaves came and settled accounts with them. Then the one who had received the five talents came forward, bringing five more talents, saying, 'Master, you handed over to me five talents; see, I have made five more talents.' His master said to him, 'Well done, good and trustworthy slave; you have been trustworthy in a few things, I will put you in charge of many things; enter into the joy of your master.' And the one with the two talents also came forward, saying, 'Master, you handed over to me two talents; see, I have made two more talents.' His master said to him, 'Well done, good and trustworthy slave; you have been trustworthy in a few things, I will put you in charge of many things; enter into the joy of your master.' Then the one who had received the one talent also came forward, saying, 'Master, I knew that you were a harsh man, reaping where you did not sow, and gathering where you did not scatter seed; so I was afraid, and I went and hid your talent in the ground. Here you have what is yours.' But his master replied, 'You wicked and lazy slave! You knew, did you, that I reap where I did not sow, and gather where I did not scatter? Then you ought to have invested my money with the bankers, and on my return I would have received what was my own with interest. So take the talent from him, and give it to the one with the ten talents. For to all those who have, more will be given, and they will have an abundance; but from those who have nothing, even what they have will be taken away. As for this worthless slave, throw him into the outer darkness, where there will be weeping and gnashing of teeth.'"

Notice what you think and feel as you read the gospel.

Jesus tells a parable about faithful stewardship of the master's resources. The master is God, and we are the servants, each of us with different gifts or talents. Those who use them, who invest them in service of the master, will be welcomed into the joy of the master. Those who bury them will be rejected.

Pray as you are led for yourself and others.

"I thank you, Lord, for the talents you have given me, however simple. I give them to you and to the world in your service. Let me serve in your joy . . ." (Continue in your own words.)

Listen to Jesus.

I see your heart, my beloved. I thank you for serving me in love. I give you power to follow me. What else is Jesus saying to you?

Ask God to show you how to live today.

"Thank you for being with me, leading me all day long. I have so much to learn about being your servant. Stay near me, Lord. Amen."

THE POPE'S MONTHLY PRAYER INTENTION FOR SEPTEMBER 2019

That politicians, scientists, and economists work together to protect the world's seas and oceans.

Sunday, September 1, 2019
Twenty-Second Sunday in Ordinary Time

Know that God is present with you and ready to converse.

"Lord Jesus Christ, I long to follow you, to know God the Father, Son, and Holy Spirit. I open myself now to your Word."

Read the gospel: Luke 14:1, 7–14.

On one occasion when Jesus was going to the house of a leader of the Pharisees to eat a meal on the sabbath, they were watching him closely. . . .

When he noticed how the guests chose the places of honor, he told them a parable. "When you are invited by someone to a wedding banquet, do not sit down at the place of honor, in case someone more distinguished than you has been invited by your host; and the host who invited both of you may come and say to you, 'Give this person your place,' and then in disgrace you would start to take the lowest place. But when you are invited, go and sit down at the lowest place, so that when your host comes, he may say to you, 'Friend, move up higher'; then you will be honored in the presence of all who sit at the table with you. For all who exalt themselves will be humbled, and those who humble themselves will be exalted."

He said also to the one who had invited him, "When you give a luncheon or a dinner, do not invite your friends or your brothers or your relatives or rich neighbors, in case they may invite you in return, and you would be repaid. But when you give a banquet, invite the poor, the crippled, the lame, and the blind. And you will be blessed, because they cannot repay you, for you will be repaid at the resurrection of the righteous."

Notice what you think and feel as you read the gospel.

Through parables, Jesus teaches his followers humility and generosity. We are not to look for rewards, but do everything for the love of God, in imitation of our Savior.

Pray as you are led for yourself and others.

"Lord, thank you for your teachings. They keep me grounded in truth and virtue. I pray for those you have given me . . ." (Continue in your own words.)

Listen to Jesus.

I have invited you to my banquet. Go out and invite others, then come and sit near me. What else is Jesus saying to you?

Ask God to show you how to live today.

"Son of God, be near me now and always. In you I place all my trust. Amen."

Monday, September 2, 2019

Know that God is present with you and ready to converse.

"Jesus, you are the long-promised Messiah, come to bring salvation to all. Let me receive you now by the power of your Word."

Read the gospel: Luke 4:16–22 (Lk 4:16–30).

When Jesus came to Nazareth, where he had been brought up, he went to the synagogue on the sabbath day, as was his custom. He stood up to read, and the scroll of the prophet Isaiah was given to him. He unrolled the scroll and found the place where it was written:

> "The Spirit of the Lord is upon me,
>   because he has anointed me
>   to bring good news to the poor.
> He has sent me to proclaim release to the captives
>   and recovery of sight to the blind,
>   to let the oppressed go free,
> to proclaim the year of the Lord's favor."

And he rolled up the scroll, gave it back to the attendant, and sat down. The eyes of all in the synagogue were fixed on him. Then he began to say to them, "Today this scripture has been fulfilled in your hearing." All spoke well of him and were amazed at the gracious words that came from his mouth. They said, "Is not this Joseph's son?"

Notice what you think and feel as you read the gospel.

Jesus has a close call in his hometown because the people do not accept him as a prophet. Somehow he passes through the midst of them untouched and leaves. They are enraged because he attributes Isaiah's words about the Messiah to himself. At first they speak well of him, but then they realize they know him, Joseph's son. How can he be the Messiah?

Pray as you are led for yourself and others.

"Lord, I believe in you. You heal and restore the world. Heal my wounds and restore me to joy. Show God's favor also to those I love . . ." (Continue in your own words.)

Listen to Jesus.

I am present with you today, tomorrow, and always. I will release you from the oppression of sin, so you can love me and my people and proclaim freedom in my name. What else is Jesus saying to you?

Ask God to show you how to live today.

"In every moment today, let me praise God for his wonderful goodness to all his people. Amen."

Tuesday, September 3, 2019

Know that God is present with you and ready to converse.

"Almighty God, your Word speaks of the authority of your Son, authority he uses in the service of your love. Let me sit at the feet of your Son and learn from him."

Read the gospel: Luke 4:31–37.

He went down to Capernaum, a city in Galilee, and was teaching them on the sabbath. They were astounded at his teaching, because he spoke with authority. In the synagogue there was a man who had the spirit of an unclean demon, and he cried out with a loud voice, "Let us alone! What have you to do with us, Jesus of Nazareth? Have you come to destroy us? I know who you are, the Holy One of God." But Jesus rebuked him, saying, "Be silent, and come out of him!" When the demon had thrown him down before them, he came out of him without having done him any harm. They were all amazed and kept saying to one another, "What kind of utterance is this? For with authority and power he commands the unclean spirits, and out they come!" And a report about him began to reach every place in the region.

Notice what you think and feel as you read the gospel.

People are amazed by Jesus' words and deeds, as he speaks and acts with unprecedented power. His words and deeds continue to reign in power over these many centuries since he walked the earth.

Pray as you are led for yourself and others.

"Lord, let me never doubt your word and your power. You are the living God. Help me trust your goodness and love, come what may . . ." (Continue in your own words.)

Listen to Jesus.

Walk in light, my beloved, for the darkness is wide. I have made a way for you. What else is Jesus saying to you?

Ask God to show you how to live today.

"I will seek to love others as you do, Lord. Give me your grace. Amen."

Wednesday, September 4, 2019

Know that God is present with you and ready to converse.
"Lord, you came to defeat evil on earth, and your work continues until you establish your everlasting kingdom among us. Work in me by your Word today."

Read the gospel: Luke 4:38–44.
After leaving the synagogue he entered Simon's house. Now Simon's mother-in-law was suffering from a high fever, and they asked him about her. Then he stood over her and rebuked the fever, and it left her. Immediately she got up and began to serve them.

As the sun was setting, all those who had any who were sick with various kinds of diseases brought them to him; and he laid his hands on each of them and cured them. Demons also came out of many, shouting, "You are the Son of God!" But he rebuked them and would not allow them to speak, because they knew that he was the Messiah.

At daybreak he departed and went into a deserted place. And the crowds were looking for him; and when they reached him, they wanted to prevent him from leaving them. But he said to them, "I must proclaim the good news of the kingdom of God to the other cities also; for I was sent for this purpose." So he continued proclaiming the message in the synagogues of Judea.

Notice what you think and feel as you read the gospel.
Jesus shows his powerful love for people. This is the Good News he brings. This is the purpose for which he was sent.

Pray as you are led for yourself and others.
"You were a servant of all who came to you, whatever their need. You are healing and the embodiment of the infinite Love of God. I pray that I may serve others in your Spirit . . ." (Continue in your own words.)

Listen to Jesus.
I will give you power to serve, beloved servant. Seek me in all your thoughts and ways, and I will let you know what to do and how to do it. What else is Jesus saying to you?

Ask God to show you how to live today.
"Let me be ready to receive your light, Lord, that my darkness may be cast out and I may serve in your grace. Thank you, Savior. Amen."

Thursday, September 5, 2019

Know that God is present with you and ready to converse.

"Lord, let me awaken now to you. You speak in so many ways—words, actions, parables, and your holy presence. You are here with me. I ask for your blessing as I give myself to your Word."

Read the gospel: Luke 5:1–11.

Once while Jesus was standing beside the lake of Gennesaret, and the crowd was pressing in on him to hear the word of God, he saw two boats there at the shore of the lake; the fishermen had gone out of them and were washing their nets. He got into one of the boats, the one belonging to Simon, and asked him to put out a little way from the shore. Then he sat down and taught the crowds from the boat. When he had finished speaking, he said to Simon, "Put out into the deep water and let down your nets for a catch." Simon answered, "Master, we have worked all night long but have caught nothing. Yet if you say so, I will let down the nets." When they had done this, they caught so many fish that their nets were beginning to break. So they signalled to their partners in the other boat to come and help them. And they came and filled both boats, so that they began to sink. But when Simon Peter saw it, he fell down at Jesus' knees, saying, "Go away from me, Lord, for I am a sinful man!" For he and all who were with him were amazed at the catch of fish that they had taken; and so also were James and John, sons of Zebedee, who were partners with Simon. Then Jesus said to Simon, "Do not be afraid; from now on you will be catching people." When they had brought their boats to shore, they left everything and followed him.

Notice what you think and feel as you read the gospel.

Jesus is a fisherman among fishermen. He preaches from the boat to the people on the shore. Then he orders his disciples to put out into the deep water, where they catch so many fish they can hardly pull up their nets. The meaning of this miracle is not about fish but about people and their new commission to gather people for God.

Pray as you are led for yourself and others.

"Lord, let me be faithful to you, to others, to my work. I pray for your help especially in these areas and with these people . . ." (Continue in your own words.)

Listen to Jesus.

Do a small thing well for me today, dear servant. That thing you have done will make it easier to do another small thing well. Fill up your time doing small things well. I will love you and reward you. What else is Jesus saying to you?

Ask God to show you how to live today.

"Let me receive your words to me today with utmost seriousness. Let me do some small thing to please you. Let me fish for you. Amen."

Friday, September 6, 2019

Know that God is present with you and ready to converse.

"Lord, you sometimes speak mysteriously. Let your Word enter into me and lead me in your ways."

Read the gospel: Luke 5:33–39.

Then they said to him, "John's disciples, like the disciples of the Pharisees, frequently fast and pray, but your disciples eat and drink." Jesus said to them, "You cannot make wedding guests fast while the bridegroom is with them, can you? The days will come when the bridegroom will be taken away from them, and then they will fast in those days." He also told them a parable: "No one tears a piece from a new garment and sews it on an old garment; otherwise the new will be torn, and the piece from the new will not match the old. And no one puts new wine into old wineskins; otherwise the new wine will burst the skins and will be spilled, and the skins will be destroyed. But new wine must be put into fresh wineskins. And no one after drinking old wine desires new wine, but says, 'The old is good.'"

Notice what you think and feel as you read the gospel.

Jesus speaks of fasting and feasting. Why don't his disciples fast like John's? Because he is the Bridegroom and remains with them. Later they will fast. Jesus' metaphors of the torn cloth and the old wineskins mysteriously speak of something new and different in religious practice. His coming changes everything.

Pray as you are led for yourself and others.

"Jesus, I am here today with you to love you and know you more and more; I want to be ready. I pray for myself and those you have given me . . ." (Continue in your own words.)

Listen to Jesus.
To keep your love for me fresh and new, pray. Pray until you know my peace and love. Then nothing can keep us apart. What else is Jesus saying to you?

Ask God to show you how to live today.
"I offer you all that I have, all that I do, and all that I am today. Use me as you will. I give you glory, Lord. Amen."

Saturday, September 7, 2019

Know that God is present with you and ready to converse.
"You came to reveal God and the ways of God to all. You are here to teach me now. Let me hear."

Read the gospel: Luke 6:1–5.
One sabbath while Jesus was going through the cornfields, his disciples plucked some heads of grain, rubbed them in their hands, and ate them. But some of the Pharisees said, "Why are you doing what is not lawful on the sabbath?" Jesus answered, "Have you not read what David did when he and his companions were hungry? He entered the house of God and took and ate the bread of the Presence, which it is not lawful for any but the priests to eat, and gave some to his companions?" Then he said to them, "The Son of Man is lord of the sabbath."

Notice what you think and feel as you read the gospel.
Jesus finds another way to show his power and glory as the Son of God, the Lord of all. He refutes the reasoning of the Pharisees by the power of scripture.

Pray as you are led for yourself and others.
"Master, help me to put you before all religious observance, for I want to serve you out of love and not obligation. I pray also for others who serve you . . ." (Continue in your own words.)

Listen to Jesus.
I give you the will and the grace to serve my people, beloved disciple. Come to me daily and tell me what you need. I love you. What else is Jesus saying to you?

Ask God to show you how to live today.

"I love you, too, dear Lord. Let me do one thing today—one of many things—that pleases you and glorifies you. Lead me, Lord. Amen."

Sunday, September 8, 2019
Twenty-Third Sunday in Ordinary Time

Know that God is present with you and ready to converse.

"Lord, I welcome you today. Sometimes I struggle in my service to you and to others. Give me your Spirit that I may pray well today."

Read the gospel: Luke 14:25–33.

Now large crowds were traveling with him; and he turned and said to them, "Whoever comes to me and does not hate father and mother, wife and children, brothers and sisters, yes, and even life itself, cannot be my disciple. Whoever does not carry the cross and follow me cannot be my disciple. For which of you, intending to build a tower, does not first sit down and estimate the cost, to see whether he has enough to complete it? Otherwise, when he has laid a foundation and is not able to finish, all who see it will begin to ridicule him, saying, 'This fellow began to build and was not able to finish.' Or what king, going out to wage war against another king, will not sit down first and consider whether he is able with ten thousand to oppose the one who comes against him with twenty thousand? If he cannot, then, while the other is still far away, he sends a delegation and asks for the terms of peace. So therefore, none of you can become my disciple if you do not give up all your possessions."

Notice what you think and feel as you read the gospel.

Jesus teaches the crowd what is the cost of discipleship—everything, including their possessions and their closest relationships. A disciple must be willing to abandon all and follow him in service, wherever that may lead.

Pray as you are led for yourself and others.

"Jesus, you ask from me what you gave: everything. I offer to you my life today and always. It is yours to use as you will . . ." (Continue in your own words.)

Listen to Jesus.

I will give you grace to persevere in all I ask you to do, my dear servant. I will turn your sorrow to joy. I am abiding in you and will never leave you. What else is Jesus saying to you?

Ask God to show you how to live today.

"What is my cross today, Jesus? Do not allow me to look past it, but instead, by your grace, help me to pick it up and carry it, following you. Let your kingdom come soon, my God. Amen."

Monday, September 9, 2019

Know that God is present with you and ready to converse.

"Lord, I receive you here and now; send your Spirit to heal me and teach me. You are the Word of the Father."

Read the gospel: Luke 6:6–11.

On another sabbath he entered the synagogue and taught, and there was a man there whose right hand was withered. The scribes and the Pharisees watched him to see whether he would cure on the sabbath, so that they might find an accusation against him. Even though he knew what they were thinking, he said to the man who had the withered hand, "Come and stand here." He got up and stood there. Then Jesus said to them, "I ask you, is it lawful to do good or to do harm on the sabbath, to save life or to destroy it?" After looking around at all of them, he said to him, "Stretch out your hand." He did so, and his hand was restored. But they were filled with fury and discussed with one another what they might do to Jesus.

Notice what you think and feel as you read the gospel.

Jesus angers the scribes and Pharisees by healing a man on the Sabbath. They are blind to who he is because their hearts are jealous, and their anger makes them want to do him harm.

Pray as you are led for yourself and others.

"Son of God, your coming among us is a great marvel, difficult to comprehend. Help me to believe in you more and more. I pray also for the faith of those who reject you . . ." (Continue in your own words.)

Listen to Jesus.

Beloved disciple, I know everything about you and love you dearly. Seek to know me, and you will be healed and fulfilled beyond your most marvelous imagination. What else is Jesus saying to you?

Ask God to show you how to live today.

"Interrupt me today, Jesus, with moments of awareness of your knowing me, loving me, and helping me serve and do your bidding. Amen."

Tuesday, September 10, 2019

Know that God is present with you and ready to converse.

"Jesus, you have chosen me—you love me and speak to me. Make me your disciple by your Word."

Read the gospel: Luke 6:12–19.

Now during those days he went out to the mountain to pray; and he spent the night in prayer to God. And when day came, he called his disciples and chose twelve of them, whom he also named apostles: Simon, whom he named Peter, and his brother Andrew, and James, and John, and Philip, and Bartholomew, and Matthew, and Thomas, and James son of Alphaeus, and Simon, who was called the Zealot, and Judas son of James, and Judas Iscariot, who became a traitor.

He came down with them and stood on a level place, with a great crowd of his disciples and a great multitude of people from all Judea, Jerusalem, and the coast of Tyre and Sidon. They had come to hear him and to be healed of their diseases; and those who were troubled with unclean spirits were cured. And all in the crowd were trying to touch him, for power came out from him and healed all of them.

Notice what you think and feel as you read the gospel.

Jesus prays all night, then chooses twelve disciples to be his apostles, including Judas. Then he goes down to the great multitude and heals all of them.

Pray as you are led for yourself and others.

"All are in need of healing, Lord, inside and outside. I pray especially for those who need spiritual and psychological healing . . ." (Continue in your own words.)

Listen to Jesus.

I am healing you, too, beloved, making you whole. I am the fountain of holiness, and I give you this pure water to drink. Pray with me. Stay with me as long as you can. We need our time together. What else is Jesus saying to you?

Ask God to show you how to live today.

"Give me this water, Lord, and keep me close by you everywhere I go. Amen."

Wednesday, September 11, 2019

Know that God is present with you and ready to converse.

"Jesus, you did only the will of your Father on earth. Let your spirit of obedience fill me as I seek you in your Word."

Read the gospel: Luke 6:20–26.

Then Jesus looked up at his disciples and said:

> "Blessed are you who are poor,
>> for yours is the kingdom of God.
> "Blessed are you who are hungry now,
>> for you will be filled.
> "Blessed are you who weep now,
>> for you will laugh.

"Blessed are you when people hate you, and when they exclude you, revile you, and defame you on account of the Son of Man. Rejoice in that day and leap for joy, for surely your reward is great in heaven; for that is what their ancestors did to the prophets.

> "But woe to you who are rich,
>> for you have received your consolation.
> "Woe to you who are full now,
>> for you will be hungry.
> "Woe to you who are laughing now,
>> for you will mourn and weep.

"Woe to you when all speak well of you, for that is what their ancestors did to the false prophets."

Notice what you think and feel as you read the gospel.

Jesus speaks blessing to those in misery of all kinds, and he pronounces woe upon those who are living in good circumstances. Life in God is moral, not circumstantial, so we must act in accordance with God's will and not according to human measures.

Pray as you are lead for yourself and for others.

"Jesus, you turned the world upside down. Let me see and live my life through your eyes. Let me find wisdom and strength in my time with you . . ." (Continue in your own words.)

Listen to Jesus.

You may rest in me, beloved disciple. I am in your joy, and I am in your suffering. What else is Jesus saying to you?

Ask God to show you how to live today.

"You are good, dear Lord. I praise you for your goodness. Let it spread through all the earth and glorify God. I offer myself for your purposes. Amen."

Thursday, September 12, 2019

Know that God is present with you and ready to converse.

"Maker of heaven and earth, you rule over all, yet you have made me free to hear your Word. I choose to do so now."

Read the gospel: Luke 6:27–38.

Jesus said, "But I say to you that listen, Love your enemies, do good to those who hate you, bless those who curse you, pray for those who abuse you. If anyone strikes you on the cheek, offer the other also; and from anyone who takes away your coat do not withhold even your shirt. Give to everyone who begs from you; and if anyone takes away your goods, do not ask for them again. Do to others as you would have them do to you.

"If you love those who love you, what credit is that to you? For even sinners love those who love them. If you do good to those who do good to you, what credit is that to you? For even sinners do the same. If you lend to those from whom you hope to receive, what credit is that to you? Even sinners lend to sinners, to receive as much again. But love your enemies, do good, and lend, expecting nothing in return. Your reward will be great, and you will be children of the Most High; for he is kind to the ungrateful and the wicked. Be merciful, just as your Father is merciful.

"Do not judge, and you will not be judged; do not condemn, and you will not be condemned. Forgive, and you will be forgiven; give, and it will be given to you. A good measure, pressed down, shaken together, running over, will be put into your lap; for the measure you give will be the measure you get back."

Notice what you think and feel as you read the gospel.

Jesus clearly asks us to love our enemies, those who hate, curse, and abuse us. Who else has ever spoken like this?

Pray as you are led for yourself and others.

"Fill me with your love, Lord, for I do not have the power in myself to love as you ask. But with you I can do it . . ." (Continue in your own words.)

Listen to Jesus.

I want you to know me as I know you, to love me as I love you. As you love me, you will have infinite power to love others, even your enemies. What else is Jesus saying to you?

Ask God to show you how to live today.

"Whatever I do today, Lord, let it be motivated by your love. Let your loving words and actions flow through me to others. Amen."

Friday, September 13, 2019

Know that God is present with you and ready to converse.

"God, you are Lord of all the peoples of the earth, and you accomplish your purposes through us. Be with me now and work in me by your Word."

Read the gospel: Luke 6:39–42.

Jesus also told them a parable: "Can a blind person guide a blind person? Will not both fall into a pit? A disciple is not above the teacher, but everyone who is fully qualified will be like the teacher. Why do you see the speck in your neighbor's eye, but do not notice the log in your own eye? Or how can you say to your neighbor, 'Friend, let me take out the speck in your eye,' when you yourself do not see the log in your own eye? You hypocrite, first take the log out of your own eye, and then you will see clearly to take the speck out of your neighbor's eye."

Notice what you think and feel as you read the gospel.

Jesus teaches about judging others with a parable about the error of trying to remove a speck from a neighbor's eye without attending to the log in your own eye. First take out your log, and then you will see clearly to take the speck out of your neighbor's eye.

Pray as you are led for yourself and others.

"Lord, teach me not to judge others. Let me just love all people, especially those you have given me . . ." (Continue in your own words.)

Listen to Jesus.

Give me your blind eyes today, and I will let you use mine, so that you can see your neighbors with eyes of love. What else is Jesus saying to you?

Ask God to show you how to live today.

"Lord, I offer you all I am today so that you may animate me by your Spirit. I am at your service. Thank you for this assignment. Amen."

Saturday, September 14, 2019
Exaltation of the Holy Cross

Know that God is present with you and ready to converse.

"Almighty Father, Son, and Holy Spirit, your nature is to love. I choose to receive you now. Let your Word free me to love."

Read the gospel: John 3:13–17.

Jesus said, "No one has ascended into heaven except the one who descended from heaven, the Son of Man. And just as Moses lifted up the serpent in the wilderness, so must the Son of Man be lifted up, that whoever believes in him may have eternal life.

"For God so loved the world that he gave his only Son, so that everyone who believes in him may not perish but may have eternal life.

"Indeed, God did not send the Son into the world to condemn the world, but in order that the world might be saved through him."

Notice what you think and feel as you read the gospel.

Jesus foretells his crucifixion and explains its motive, power, and method. Its motive is God's love, its power is salvation, and its method is one's belief in Jesus.

Pray as you are led for yourself and others.

"Lord, I believe in you, and I exalt your Holy Cross. I thank you for saving me from sin and death and for promising me eternal life in your kingdom of love. I pray for all those who do not believe . . ." (Continue in your own words.)

Listen to Jesus.

I receive you today, beloved. When you need me, I am always here for you, for I know you have crosses of your own. What else is Jesus saying to you?

Ask God to show you how to live today.

"Lord, I lay down my freedom before you and ask only that I may serve you as you will. Lead me to do acts of love. Amen."

Sunday, September 15, 2019
Twenty-Fourth Sunday in Ordinary Time

Know that God is present with you and ready to converse.

"Lord, I am among those who follow you. I open myself to your Word."

Read the gospel: Luke 15:1–10 (Lk 15:1–32).

Now all the tax collectors and sinners were coming near to listen to Jesus. And the Pharisees and the scribes were grumbling and saying, "This fellow welcomes sinners and eats with them."

So he told them this parable: "Which one of you, having a hundred sheep and losing one of them, does not leave the ninety-nine in the wilderness and go after the one that is lost until he finds it? When he has found it, he lays it on his shoulders and rejoices. And when he comes home, he calls together his friends and neighbors, saying to them, 'Rejoice with me, for I have found my sheep that was lost.' Just so, I tell you, there will be more joy in heaven over one sinner who repents than over ninety-nine righteous people who need no repentance.

"Or what woman having ten silver coins, if she loses one of them, does not light a lamp, sweep the house, and search carefully until she finds it? When she has found it, she calls together her friends and neighbors, saying, 'Rejoice with me, for I have found the coin that I had lost.' Just so, I tell you, there is joy in the presence of the angels of God over one sinner who repents."

Notice what you think and feel as you read the gospel.

Jesus tells richly instructive stories about ordinary people, shepherds and women. They are all about the love and joy of God.

Pray as you are led for yourself and others.

"Lord, pour your meanings into my heart and guide my life. Let me begin by praying for all those you have given me . . ." (Continue in your own words.)

Listen to Jesus.

God is at work in little things as well as great, dear servant. Attend closely to little things, and great things will come out of them. What else is Jesus saying to you?

Ask God to show you how to live today.

"Give me small things to do today, Lord. Let God be glorified in the small things I do. Thank you for giving my life holy purpose. Amen."

Monday, September 16, 2019

Know that God is present with you and ready to converse.

"Father in heaven, you gave us Jesus so that we can know and love you. Let your Word help me to do that now."

Read the gospel: Luke 7:1–10.

After Jesus had finished all his sayings in the hearing of the people, he entered Capernaum. A centurion there had a slave whom he valued highly, and who was ill and close to death. When he heard about Jesus, he sent some Jewish elders to him, asking him to come and heal his slave. When they came to Jesus, they appealed to him earnestly, saying, "He is worthy of having you do this for him, for he loves our people, and it is he who built our synagogue for us." And Jesus went with them, but when he was not far from the house, the centurion sent friends to say to him, "Lord, do not trouble yourself, for I am not worthy to have you come under my roof; therefore I did not presume to come to you. But only speak the word, and let my servant be healed. For I also am a man set under authority, with soldiers under me; and I say to one, 'Go,' and he goes, and to another, 'Come,' and he comes, and to my slave, 'Do this,' and the slave does it." When Jesus heard this he was amazed at him, and turning to the crowd that followed him, he said, "I tell you, not even in Israel have I found such faith." When those who had been sent returned to the house, they found the slave in good health.

Notice what you think and feel as you read the gospel.

In a bold demonstration of faith, the centurion asks Jesus to heal his slave. He recognizes in Jesus the same kind of authority he himself both has and answers to: if Jesus gives the command, the servant will be well. Jesus commends his faith and heals the slave.

Pray as you are led for yourself and others.

"Lord, let me find truths about you in my everyday life, so that when you come, I, too, like the centurion, will recognize you and believe. I pray that all people may find your fingerprints everywhere in the world you've created and come to faith in you . . ." (Continue in your own words.)

Listen to Jesus.

Seek me always, in the world and in my Word. Seek me, and you will find me, and I will come to you. What else is Jesus saying to you?

Ask God to show you how to live today.

"Keep my eyes open today, Lord, that I may see you in all, and hear and respond to your commands. Amen."

Tuesday, September 17, 2019

Know that God is present with you and ready to converse.

"Let your Word increase my love and service of you, Lord."

Read the gospel: Luke 7:11–17.

Soon afterwards Jesus went to a town called Nain, and his disciples and a large crowd went with him. As he approached the gate of the town, a man who had died was being carried out. He was his mother's only son, and she was a widow; and with her was a large crowd from the town. When the Lord saw her, he had compassion for her and said to her, "Do not weep." Then he came forward and touched the bier, and the bearers stood still. And he said, "Young man, I say to you, rise!" The dead man sat up and began to speak, and Jesus gave him to his mother. Fear seized all of them; and they glorified God, saying, "A great prophet has risen among us!" and "God has looked favorably on his people!" This word about him spread throughout Judea and all the surrounding country.

Notice what you think and feel as you read the gospel.

Jesus raises the widow's son from the dead; understandably, his fame spreads rapidly and widely.

Pray as you are led for yourself and others.

"Jesus, you call people to life in you. I pray that many answer your call and come to you for forgiveness and healing . . ." (Continue in your own words.)

Listen to Jesus.

By my Spirit, I continue to do the works of God among people. Be filled with my Spirit and join us in this holy work, my child. What else is Jesus saying to you?

Ask God to show you how to live today.

"Today let me walk closely in the light and power of your Spirit, Lord. When I step off the path, set me straight. I love you, Jesus. Amen."

Wednesday, September 18, 2019

Know that God is present with you and ready to converse.

"God, you know me thoroughly. You know my need for you. I am ready for your touch."

Read the gospel: Luke 7:31–35.

Jesus said, "To what then will I compare the people of this generation, and what are they like? They are like children sitting in the marketplace and calling to one another,

> 'We played the flute for you, and you did not dance;
>   we wailed, and you did not weep.'

For John the Baptist has come eating no bread and drinking no wine, and you say, 'He has a demon'; the Son of Man has come eating and drinking, and you say, 'Look, a glutton and a drunkard, a friend of tax collectors and sinners!' Nevertheless, wisdom is vindicated by all her children."

Notice what you think and feel as you read the gospel.
Jesus criticizes those who turn a blind eye to the prophets who come to them, who use any excuse to complain about the ones who don't play according to their rules.

Pray as you are led for yourself and others.
"Lord, I ask for the wisdom to follow you wherever you lead today. Open my eyes and ears to your truth . . ." (Continue in your own words.)

Listen to Jesus.
Dearly beloved disciple, I want to spend this time with you. This is your time to experience heaven, to taste the wine of the kingdom. I give you my blessing. What else is Jesus saying to you?

Ask God to show you how to live today.
"Do not depart from me, Jesus. Be my companion throughout this day and night. I love you. Amen."

Thursday, September 19, 2019

Know that God is present with you and ready to converse.
"Heavenly king, you came down from heaven to show us the love of God. You are here with me to do the same. Alleluia."

Read the gospel: Luke 7:36–50.
One of the Pharisees asked Jesus to eat with him, and he went into the Pharisee's house and took his place at the table. And a woman in the city, who was a sinner, having learned that he was eating in the Pharisee's house, brought an alabaster jar of ointment. She stood behind him at his feet, weeping, and began to bathe his feet with her tears and to dry them with her hair. Then she continued kissing his feet and anointing them with the ointment. Now when the Pharisee who had invited him saw it, he said to himself, "If this man were a prophet, he would have known who and what kind of woman this is who is touching him—that she is a sinner." Jesus spoke up and said to him, "Simon, I have something to say to you." "Teacher," he replied, "speak." "A certain creditor had two debtors; one owed five hundred denarii, and the other fifty. When they could not pay, he cancelled the debts for both of them. Now which of them will love him more?" Simon answered, "I suppose the one for whom he cancelled the greater debt." And Jesus said to him, "You have

judged rightly." Then turning towards the woman, he said to Simon, "Do you see this woman? I entered your house; you gave me no water for my feet, but she has bathed my feet with her tears and dried them with her hair. You gave me no kiss, but from the time I came in she has not stopped kissing my feet. You did not anoint my head with oil, but she has anointed my feet with ointment. Therefore, I tell you, her sins, which were many, have been forgiven; hence she has shown great love. But the one to whom little is forgiven, loves little." Then he said to her, "Your sins are forgiven." But those who were at the table with him began to say among themselves, "Who is this who even forgives sins?" And he said to the woman, "Your faith has saved you; go in peace."

Notice what you think and feel as you read the gospel.

Jesus accepts a Pharisee's invitation to dine at his house, and while he is at the table, a notorious sinner enters and anoints Jesus' feet, kissing them. The Pharisee thinks Jesus should know better and not allow this. Knowing his thoughts, Jesus points out that those who are forgiven more, love more. Then he forgives the woman's sins, again shocking the Pharisees present.

Pray as you are led for yourself and others.

"Thank you for your forgiveness, Lord. Make me truly grateful. Help me to forgive others . . ." (Continue in your own words.)

Listen to Jesus.

I am blessed by those who embrace my forgiveness. Beloved, your sins are forgiven. Enter into my joy. What else is Jesus saying to you?

Ask God to show you how to live today.

"Let me be mindful of your mercy and understand what it means for my life, today, tomorrow, and always. I follow you. Amen."

Friday, September 20, 2019

Know that God is present with you and ready to converse.

"Father in heaven, save us, for they have crucified the Lord."

Read the gospel: Luke 8:1–3.

Soon afterwards Jesus went on through cities and villages, proclaiming and bringing the good news of the kingdom of God. The twelve were with him, as well as some women who had been cured of evil spirits and infirmities: Mary, called Magdalene, from whom seven demons had gone out, and Joanna, the wife of Herod's steward Chuza, and Susanna, and many others, who provided for them out of their resources.

Notice what you think and feel as you read the gospel.

Jesus allows women to follow him and travel with him and the apostles. The women serve them.

Pray as you are led for yourself and others.

"I, too, want to accompany Jesus. I respect the women who love Jesus and serve him. I, too, offer myself to serve . . ." (Continue in your own words.)

Listen to Jesus.

All those who serve me help me bring the Good News of the kingdom of heaven. Will you join us? What else is Jesus saying to you?

Ask God to show you how to live today.

"Lord, show me how I may provide for you and your people out of the resources that I have. Amen."

Saturday, September 21, 2019
St. Matthew, Apostle and Evangelist

Know that God is present with you and ready to converse.

"I call upon you, Lord, for I know I need you. You are always here for me. Thank you for your Word."

Read the gospel: Matthew 9:9–13.

As Jesus was walking along, he saw a man called Matthew sitting at the tax booth; and he said to him, "Follow me." And he got up and followed him.

And as he sat at dinner in the house, many tax collectors and sinners came and were sitting with him and his disciples. When the Pharisees saw this, they said to his disciples, "Why does your teacher eat with tax collectors and sinners?" But when he heard this, he said, "Those who are well have no need of a physician, but those who are sick. Go and learn what this means, 'I desire mercy, not sacrifice.' For I have come to call not the righteous but sinners."

Notice what you think and feel as you read the gospel.

Jesus calls Matthew. Many tax collectors and sinners join them at dinner. The Pharisees disapprove. Jesus points out that those who are sick need a doctor; the well do not. He has come to call not the righteous but sinners.

Pray as you are led for yourself and others.

"Lord, teach me to value mercy over sacrifice. I offer myself to you anew today. Help me give my all . . ." (Continue in your own words.)

Listen to Jesus.

Every day is a gift to you. Every day I ask you to give your day to me. You may not see it, but the day you give to me bears fruit for your good and for the good of those I have given you. What else is Jesus saying to you?

Ask God to show you how to live today.

"Lord, come into my heart that I may truly know you and speak out of the abundance you provide. What do you want me to do today? Amen."

Sunday, September 22, 2019
Twenty-Fifth Sunday in Ordinary Time

Know that God is present with you and ready to converse.

"Lord, I long to hear your Good News in the depth of my heart, in the bottom of my soul. Speak to me."

Read the gospel: Luke 16:1–13.

Then Jesus said to the disciples, "There was a rich man who had a manager, and charges were brought to him that this man was squandering his property. So he summoned him and said to him, 'What is this that I hear about you? Give me an account of your management, because you cannot be my manager any longer.' Then the manager said to himself, 'What will I do, now that my master is taking the position away from me? I am not strong enough to dig, and I am ashamed to beg. I have decided what to do so that, when I am dismissed as manager, people may welcome me into their homes.' So, summoning his master's debtors one by one, he asked the first, 'How much do you owe my master?' He answered, 'A hundred jugs of olive oil.' He said to him, 'Take your bill, sit down quickly, and make it fifty.' Then he asked another, 'And how much do you owe?' He replied, 'A hundred containers of wheat.' He said to him, 'Take your bill and make it eighty.' And his master commended the dishonest manager because he had acted shrewdly; for the children of this age are more shrewd in dealing with their own generation than are the children of light. And I tell you, make friends for yourselves by means of dishonest wealth so that when it is gone, they may welcome you into the eternal homes.

"Whoever is faithful in a very little is faithful also in much; and whoever is dishonest in a very little is dishonest also in much. If then you have not been faithful with the dishonest wealth, who will entrust to you the true riches? And if you have not been faithful with what belongs to another, who will give you what is your own? No slave can serve two masters; for a slave will either hate the one and love the other, or be devoted to the one and despise the other. You cannot serve God and wealth."

Notice what you think and feel as you read the gospel.

Jesus teaches about faithful, single-minded service, using a parable about a dishonest servant. He makes his moral clear at the end. Was the parable about the dishonest servant Jesus' way of grabbing attention?

Pray as you are led for yourself and others.

"God, thank you for your faithful love of me. Let me serve you and those you have given me with godly faithfulness. I pray for . . ." (Continue in your own words.)

Listen to Jesus.

Be faithful with what belongs to me—with all my beloved children—and I will give you eternal life. What else is Jesus saying to you?

Ask God to show you how to live today.

"You must help me, Lord. Take all evil from my heart and give me your faithfulness. Amen."

Monday, September 23, 2019

Know that God is present with you and ready to converse.

"Lord, I am here to listen to your holy Word. Glory to you, Almighty."

Read the gospel: Luke 8:16–18.

Jesus said, "No one after lighting a lamp hides it under a jar, or puts it under a bed, but puts it on a lampstand, so that those who enter may see the light. For nothing is hidden that will not be disclosed, nor is anything secret that will not become known and come to light. Then pay attention to how you listen; for to those who have, more will be given; and from those who do not have, even what they seem to have will be taken away."

Notice what you think and feel as you read the gospel.

Jesus advises us to pay attention to how we listen that we may receive more wisdom and more light with which to live our lives. If we shut God out of our lives, we will lose those graces he provides.

Pray as you are led for yourself and others.

"Lord, I am not worthy of you, but I seek you and your graces that my life may be pleasing to you . . ." (Continue in your own words.)

Listen to Jesus.

It is good for you to pray with faith in me, beloved. Without faith, how can you know me? With faith, you live and move in the power of God. What else is Jesus saying to you?

Ask God to show you how to live today.

"Help me find a way to please you with my faith today, Jesus. I want to please you, and I want to help others in need. Thank you. Amen."

Tuesday, September 24, 2019

Know that God is present with you and ready to converse.

"Wisdom of the Father, I cast aside all my own understanding and intelligence so that I can gain the highest knowledge, the knowledge of God."

Read the gospel: Luke 8:19–21.

Then Jesus' mother and his brothers came to him, but they could not reach him because of the crowd. And he was told, "Your mother and your brothers are standing outside, wanting to see you." But he said to them, "My mother and my brothers are those who hear the word of God and do it."

Notice what you think and feel as you read the gospel.

Jesus loves his family, but here he extends membership in his family to all who hear the Word of God and do it. Our relationship to God, our receiving God's Word, and our obedience make us members of God's holy family.

Pray as you are led for yourself and others.

"Lord, I hear your Word; let me do it in my thoughts, words, and deeds. I pray now for those who struggle to obey you . . ." (Continue in your own words.)

Listen to Jesus.

This is entry into the kingdom of heaven: to love others not of your own family, to serve others, to work with others to alleviate suffering, and to share the Good News of God's complete salvation. What else is Jesus saying to you?

Ask God to show you how to live today.

"Help me keep my ears and eyes open as I move through the day today, so that I can discern the will of God in each moment; then give me the grace to do his will. Amen."

Wednesday, September 25, 2019

Know that God is present with you and ready to converse.

"Here I am, Lord; I come to do your will."

Read the gospel: Luke 9:1–6.

Then Jesus called the twelve together and gave them power and authority over all demons and to cure diseases, and he sent them out to proclaim the kingdom of God and to heal. He said to them, "Take nothing for your journey, no staff, nor bag, nor bread, nor money—not even an extra tunic. Whatever house you enter, stay there, and leave from there. Wherever they do not welcome you, as you are leaving that town shake the dust off your feet as a testimony against them." They departed and went through the villages, bringing the good news and curing diseases everywhere.

Notice what you think and feel as you read the gospel.

Jesus puts his disciples to work, giving them authority and power to proclaim the kingdom and to heal. He asks them to trust God for everything; they should just do the work and move on, regardless of what happens.

Pray as you are led for yourself and others.

"Let me throw myself into your service, Lord. Do you want me to do the good works that you did? Give me power to do them and then send me . . ." (Continue in your own words.)

Listen to Jesus.

I do give you power, servant. I set before you the things that you can do for others. To please me, serve them. What else is Jesus saying to you?

Ask God to show you how to live today.

"Help me to transform my desire to please you into concrete action. That is the power I ask of you today. I am grateful, Lord. Amen."

Thursday, September 26, 2019

Know that God is present with you and ready to converse.

"Who can know you, Lord, except you reveal yourself? Would you show yourself to me? I long to know you."

Read the gospel: Luke 9:7–9.

Now Herod the ruler heard about all that had taken place, and he was perplexed, because it was said by some that John had been raised from the dead, by some that Elijah had appeared, and by others that one of the ancient prophets had arisen. Herod said, "John I beheaded; but who is this about whom I hear such things?" And he tried to see him.

Notice what you think and feel as you read the gospel.

Hearing about Jesus, Herod is perplexed, despite his power and his attempts to control things. Why does he want to see Jesus?

Pray as you are led for yourself and others.

"Lord, I pray for the powerful. You give power to do good and to do evil. I pray that those in power do good . . ." (Continue in your own words.)

Listen to Jesus.

All power is mine. The power of this world comes to nothing. I give you my power to do my will, dear servant. Our good work shall endure. What else is Jesus saying to you?

Ask God to show you how to live today.

"I will not seek earthly power, Lord. I serve by your grace and power. Amen."

Friday, September 27, 2019

Know that God is present with you and ready to converse.
"Lord, I wish to know you as you are. Lead me by your Word."

Read the gospel: Luke 9:18–22.
Once when Jesus was praying alone, with only the disciples near him, he asked them, "Who do the crowds say that I am?" They answered, "John the Baptist; but others, Elijah; and still others, that one of the ancient prophets has arisen." He said to them, "But who do you say that I am?" Peter answered, "The Messiah of God."

He sternly ordered and commanded them not to tell anyone, saying, "The Son of Man must undergo great suffering, and be rejected by the elders, chief priests, and scribes, and be killed, and on the third day be raised."

Notice what you think and feel as you read the gospel.
Jesus knows that our acceptance of his identity as the Messiah, the Son of God, is most important for our salvation. Once Peter identifies him as such, Jesus foretells his own suffering and death. The disciples, not understanding that his crucifixion is also essential for salvation, must have been mystified.

Pray as you are led for yourself and others.
"Lord, thank you for suffering and dying for me. How may I console you across the centuries?"

Listen to Jesus.
Those who follow me are free. You are free from sin and death. You are free from the judgment of others. You are free in me. What else is Jesus saying to you?

Ask God to show you how to live today.
"Let me exercise my freedom from the judgment of others, Lord, following you without reservation or shame. For you have done great things for me. Glory be to the Father, the Son, and the Holy Spirit. Amen."

Saturday, September 28, 2019

Know that God is present with you and ready to converse.
"You are high, my God, and I am low. How can I understand you? Yet you are speaking to me in your Word."

Read the gospel: Luke 9:43b–45.
While everyone was amazed at all that Jesus was doing, he said to his disciples, "Let these words sink into your ears: The Son of Man is going to be betrayed into human hands." But they did not understand this saying; its meaning was concealed from them, so that they could not perceive it. And they were afraid to ask him about this saying.

Notice what you think and feel as you read the gospel.
In the midst of his mighty works of healing, Jesus injects a dose of reality. He predicts his betrayal, but his disciples do not understand, and they are afraid to ask him to explain himself.

Pray as you are led for yourself and others.
"Lord, keep me grounded in reality, in your truth. Let your words sink into my ears. I pray for others, too, that they may understand your words . . ." (Continue in your own words.)

Listen to Jesus.
Follow me in the way of the Cross, beloved. Do so willingly and without fear, for I go before you, and I am with you to the end. This way is life. What else is Jesus saying to you?

Ask God to show you how to live today.
"Give me courage to accept your truth, my God. Let me persevere on my way into your kingdom. Amen."

Sunday, September 29, 2019
Twenty-Sixth Sunday in Ordinary Time

Know that God is present with you and ready to converse.
"Lord, you intervened in human history to save us from ourselves. Let me respond to your Word in the manner you would have me. Let me learn from you."

Read the gospel: Luke 16:19–31.

Jesus said, "There was a rich man who was dressed in purple and fine linen and who feasted sumptuously every day. And at his gate lay a poor man named Lazarus, covered with sores, who longed to satisfy his hunger with what fell from the rich man's table; even the dogs would come and lick his sores. The poor man died and was carried away by the angels to be with Abraham. The rich man also died and was buried. In Hades, where he was being tormented, he looked up and saw Abraham far away with Lazarus by his side. He called out, 'Father Abraham, have mercy on me, and send Lazarus to dip the tip of his finger in water and cool my tongue; for I am in agony in these flames.' But Abraham said, 'Child, remember that during your lifetime you received your good things, and Lazarus in like manner evil things; but now he is comforted here, and you are in agony. Besides all this, between you and us a great chasm has been fixed, so that those who might want to pass from here to you cannot do so, and no one can cross from there to us.' He said, 'Then, father, I beg you to send him to my father's house—for I have five brothers—that he may warn them, so that they will not also come into this place of torment.' Abraham replied, 'They have Moses and the prophets; they should listen to them.' He said, 'No, father Abraham; but if someone goes to them from the dead, they will repent.' He said to him, 'If they do not listen to Moses and the prophets, neither will they be convinced even if someone rises from the dead.'"

Notice what you think and feel as you read the gospel.

By this parable Jesus shows how blind the rich can be to those suffering nearby. Their blindness is a moral failing for which they will be judged and sentenced at death. The rich man discovers it's too late for him now. Abraham tells him that many who are alive will not repent even if they hear from one who has risen from the dead.

Pray as you are led for yourself and others.

"Lord, many do not believe that you have risen from the dead, and they do not see any need to repent. I pray for mercy, repentance, and conversion for them today, including . . ." (Continue in your own words.)

Listen to Jesus.

Your growth in grace is a progression of belief, faith, conviction, assurance. Ask for deepening in faith, hope, and love. This is the way to joy. What else is Jesus saying to you?

Ask God to show you how to live today.

"As I pray for others, Lord, let me deepen in my understanding of you, that I may be truly useful to you and your works of grace. Amen."

Monday, September 30, 2019

Know that God is present with you and ready to converse.

"Lord, I welcome you in your Word."

Read the gospel: Luke 9:46–48 (Lk 9:46–50).

An argument arose among the disciples as to which one of them was the greatest. But Jesus, aware of their inner thoughts, took a little child and put it by his side, and said to them, "Whoever welcomes this child in my name welcomes me, and whoever welcomes me welcomes the one who sent me; for the least among all of you is the greatest."

Notice what you think and feel as you read the gospel.

The apostles are trying to figure out which of them is best, most important, and closest to Jesus. But Jesus turns their argument on its head: Whose definition of "greatest" are you using? Jesus tells us to treat every person the world considers insignificant as we would treat the king of heaven.

Pray as you are led for yourself and others.

"Lord, you show me your priorities, so different from the world's; help me to embrace them. I pray for all your children, especially . . ." (Continue in your own words.)

Listen to Jesus.

Welcome the small, the poor and lowly, the insignificant, the sinners—welcome them in my name so that I can come to you also. What else is Jesus saying to you?

Ask God to show you how to live today.

"I want to be with you, Lord. Remind me, throughout the day, that each small, unimportant thing I am asked to do is an invitation to spend time with you. Amen."

THE POPE'S MONTHLY PRAYER INTENTION FOR OCTOBER 2019

That the breath of the Holy Spirit engenders a new missionary spring in the Church.

Tuesday, October 1, 2019

Know that God is present with you and ready to converse.

"Lord, you give your love and mercy unmerited. I am grateful for that because I do not deserve your blessings. I open myself to your Word now."

Read the gospel: Luke 9:51–56.

When the days drew near for him to be taken up, Jesus set his face to go to Jerusalem. And he sent messengers ahead of him. On their way they entered a village of the Samaritans to make ready for him; but they did not receive him, because his face was set towards Jerusalem. When his disciples James and John saw it, they said, "Lord, do you want us to command fire to come down from heaven and consume them?" But he turned and rebuked them. Then they went on to another village.

Notice what you think and feel as you read the gospel.

Humble and compassionate, Jesus simply goes on his way when the Samaritan village does not receive him. He is not angry at them, and he rebukes James and John for suggesting violence.

Pray as you are led for yourself and others.

"Be in me Spirit of Jesus Christ, and I will resent no one, even those who have hurt me. I pray for them . . ." (Continue in your own words.)

Listen to Jesus.

My virtues belong to you, beloved. Exercise them and grow strong. What else is Jesus saying to you?

Ask God to show you how to live today.

"Lord, your face is set for Jerusalem. Let me walk with you today. Amen."

Wednesday, October 2, 2019
The Guardian Angels

Know that God is present with you and ready to converse.

"Lord of Hosts, how many love you and serve you throughout the universe and in heaven? Here I am, Lord, use me."

Read the gospel: Matthew 18:1–5, 10.

At that time the disciples came to Jesus and asked, "Who is the greatest in the kingdom of heaven?" He called a child, whom he put among them, and said, "Truly I tell you, unless you change and become like children, you will never enter the kingdom of heaven. Whoever becomes humble like this child is the greatest in the kingdom of heaven. Whoever welcomes one such child in my name welcomes me. . . .

"Take care that you do not despise one of these little ones; for, I tell you, in heaven their angels continually see the face of my Father in heaven."

Notice what you think and feel as you read the gospel.

Jesus asks his followers to become humble like children. Those shall be greatest in his kingdom, for even though they are humble, the children have angels in heaven.

Pray as you are led for yourself and others.

"Lord, set your guard of angels around me and all those you have given me, especially the children . . ." (Continue in your own words.)

Listen to Jesus.

Come to me, child. I care for you and those for whom you pray. You are all mine, for you have given them to me with yourself. What else is Jesus saying to you?

Ask God to show you how to live today.

"You ask me to change, Lord, to become like a child. Show me what I need to change in my life, in myself, and give me power to do it. I seek to do your will. Amen."

Thursday, October 3, 2019

Know that God is present with you and ready to converse.

"Lord, I get distracted and overwhelmed sometimes. Wake me up to your presence in my life and in your Word."

Read the gospel: Luke 10:1–12.

After this the Lord appointed seventy others and sent them on ahead of him in pairs to every town and place where he himself intended to go. He said to them, "The harvest is plentiful, but the laborers are few; therefore ask the Lord of the harvest to send out laborers into his harvest. Go on your way. See, I am sending you out like lambs into the midst of wolves. Carry no purse, no bag, no sandals; and greet no one on the road. Whatever house you enter, first say, 'Peace to this house!' And if anyone is there who shares in peace, your peace will rest on that person; but if not, it will return to you. Remain in the same house, eating and drinking whatever they provide, for the laborer deserves to be paid. Do not move about from house to house. Whenever you enter a town and its people welcome you, eat what is set before you; cure the sick who are there, and say to them, 'The kingdom of God has come near to you.' But whenever you enter a town and they do not welcome you, go out into its streets and say, 'Even the dust of your town that clings to our feet, we wipe off in protest against you. Yet know this: the kingdom of God has come near.' I tell you, on that day it will be more tolerable for Sodom than for that town."

Notice what you think and feel as you read the gospel.

Jesus makes the work of the kingdom seem simple, yet he calls people to realize the radical change required.

Pray as you are led for yourself and others.

"The unharvested fields are vast, Lord. Send laborers to bring in the harvest. I offer you myself . . ." (Continue in your own words.)

Listen to Jesus.

When you go to do my work, I go with you, beloved. Do what you can do and leave the rest for me. What else is Jesus saying to you?

Ask God to show you how to live today.

"Give me wisdom and grace to do your work well, Lord. Thank you for working alongside of me. Amen."

Friday, October 4, 2019

Know that God is present with you and ready to converse.
"My God, I am listening to you. Open my ears to your voice."

Read the gospel: Luke 10:13–16.

Jesus said, "Woe to you, Chorazin! Woe to you, Bethsaida! For if the deeds of power done in you had been done in Tyre and Sidon, they would have repented long ago, sitting in sackcloth and ashes. But at the judgment it will be more tolerable for Tyre and Sidon than for you. And you, Capernaum,

> will you be exalted to heaven?
> No, you will be brought down to Hades.

"Whoever listens to you listens to me, and whoever rejects you rejects me, and whoever rejects me rejects the one who sent me."

Notice what you think and feel as you read the gospel.
Jesus pronounces woe upon the towns that reject him. He is among them doing mighty deeds, and they still refuse to repent. Jesus tells his disciples that they are speaking for and as him; those who hear them, hear Jesus.

Pray as you are led for yourself and others.
"Let me hear your voice in others, Lord. And let me speak of your kingdom as you would. I pray for all who bear your message and your name . . ." (Continue in your own words.)

Listen to Jesus.
The Gospel of the kingdom is yours to proclaim, beloved disciple. When you speak of it, speak from your heart to the heart of those who hear you. Some will hear you now. Some will hear you later. What else is Jesus saying to you?

Ask God to show you how to live today.
"Let me speak with your love, Jesus, Master. I do not wish to dishonor your good name. Amen."

Saturday, October 5, 2019

Know that God is present with you and ready to converse.
"Lord of heaven and earth, I thank you. I am happy to be with you again."

Read the gospel: Luke 10:17–24.

The seventy returned with joy, saying, "Lord, in your name even the demons submit to us!" Jesus said to them, "I watched Satan fall from heaven like a flash of lightning. See, I have given you authority to tread on snakes and scorpions, and over all the power of the enemy; and nothing will hurt you. Nevertheless, do not rejoice at this, that the spirits submit to you, but rejoice that your names are written in heaven."

At that same hour Jesus rejoiced in the Holy Spirit and said, "I thank you, Father, Lord of heaven and earth, because you have hidden these things from the wise and the intelligent and have revealed them to infants; yes, Father, for such was your gracious will. All things have been handed over to me by my Father; and no one knows who the Son is except the Father, or who the Father is except the Son and anyone to whom the Son chooses to reveal him."

Then turning to the disciples, Jesus said to them privately, "Blessed are the eyes that see what you see! For I tell you that many prophets and kings desired to see what you see, but did not see it, and to hear what you hear, but did not hear it."

Notice what you think and feel as you read the gospel.
When the disciples rejoice over the power Jesus has given them, Jesus says that what's really worth rejoicing about is that their names are written in heaven. Then he rejoices and thanks his Father that he reveals his truths to infants, not to the intelligent. Only the Father can reveal the Son to someone; only the Son can reveal the Father. Knowing God is the ultimate blessing.

Pray as you are led for yourself and others.
"Let me know you more and more, Lord: Father, Son, and Holy Spirit. I rejoice in you and pray that many, many come to know you as you are . . ." (Continue in your own words.)

Listen to Jesus.

This is what matters, beloved. God desires souls who love God as God loves them. This is the time of mercy. Come to the Son and love the Father. What else is Jesus saying to you?

Ask God to show you how to live today.

"Lord, I come. Thank you for your words and your grace. Amen."

Sunday, October 6, 2019
Twenty-Seventh Sunday in Ordinary Time

Know that God is present with you and ready to converse.

"Jesus, I enter your kingdom today as I follow you into the Word of God."

Read the gospel: Luke 17:5–10.

The apostles said to the Lord, "Increase our faith!" The Lord replied, "If you had faith the size of a mustard seed, you could say to this mulberry tree, 'Be uprooted and planted in the sea,' and it would obey you.

"Who among you would say to your slave who has just come in from ploughing or tending sheep in the field, 'Come here at once and take your place at the table'? Would you not rather say to him, 'Prepare supper for me, put on your apron and serve me while I eat and drink; later you may eat and drink'? Do you thank the slave for doing what was commanded? So you also, when you have done all that you were ordered to do, say, 'We are worthless slaves; we have done only what we ought to have done!'"

Notice what you think and feel as you read the gospel.

The disciples ask Jesus to increase their faith. Jesus compares faith to a mustard seed, saying that is enough faith to do wonders. Then he teaches them about humble service. They are called to serve as he does. We show our faith in faithful service.

Pray as you are led for yourself and others.

"Lord, increase my faith so that I may serve you more faithfully. Let me turn the hearts of people to you . . ." (Continue in your own words.)

Listen to Jesus.
Some wish to be served. You will find joy in serving others. Look to me for grace each day, my beloved. What else is Jesus saying to you?

Ask God to show you how to live today.
"Help me to serve you and others, Savior, for I have received the salvation of God. Amen."

Monday, October 7, 2019

Know that God is present with you and ready to converse.
"The love of God surrounds me here. I taste eternal life."

Read the gospel: Luke 10:25–37.
Just then a lawyer stood up to test Jesus. "Teacher," he said, "what must I do to inherit eternal life?" He said to him, "What is written in the law? What do you read there?" He answered, "You shall love the Lord your God with all your heart, and with all your soul, and with all your strength, and with all your mind; and your neighbor as yourself." And he said to him, "You have given the right answer; do this, and you will live."

But wanting to justify himself, he asked Jesus, "And who is my neighbor?" Jesus replied, "A man was going down from Jerusalem to Jericho, and fell into the hands of robbers, who stripped him, beat him, and went away, leaving him half dead. Now by chance a priest was going down that road; and when he saw him, he passed by on the other side. So likewise a Levite, when he came to the place and saw him, passed by on the other side. But a Samaritan while travelling came near him; and when he saw him, he was moved with pity. He went to him and bandaged his wounds, having poured oil and wine on them. Then he put him on his own animal, brought him to an inn, and took care of him. The next day he took out two denarii, gave them to the innkeeper, and said, 'Take care of him; and when I come back, I will repay you whatever more you spend.' Which of these three, do you think, was a neighbor to the man who fell into the hands of the robbers?" He said, "The one who showed him mercy." Jesus said to him, "Go and do likewise."

Notice what you think and feel as you read the gospel.
The lawyer answers his own question correctly: love God, love your neighbor, and you will inherit eternal life. The parable identifies who our neighbor is: everyone. Who may receive eternal life? Everyone who

shows mercy to a neighbor—in this case, the Samaritan shows love of neighbor, but the priest and the Levite, who profess to keep the commandments, do not. Praising the example of the good Samaritan, Jesus commands us to "go and do likewise" and show mercy to our neighbors.

Pray as you are led for yourself and others.

"I know some who suffer, Lord. I pray for them now as you lead me . . ." (Continue in your own words.)

Listen to Jesus.

I hear your prayers, my friend. Are there ways you can show mercy to any of those you have prayed for? What else is Jesus saying to you?

Ask God to show you how to live today.

"You will help me find ways to love my neighbor, Teacher. Let my heart be moved with pity as I stop to help whoever is in need, for I long to inherit eternal life. Amen."

Tuesday, October 8, 2019

Know that God is present with you and ready to converse.

"When I am overwhelmed, calm me and simplify my life with your presence. Be with me now, Lord."

Read the gospel: Luke 10:38–42.

Now as they went on their way, he entered a certain village, where a woman named Martha welcomed him into her home. She had a sister named Mary, who sat at the Lord's feet and listened to what he was saying. But Martha was distracted by her many tasks; so she came to him and asked, "Lord, do you not care that my sister has left me to do all the work by myself? Tell her then to help me." But the Lord answered her, "Martha, Martha, you are worried and distracted by many things; there is need of only one thing. Mary has chosen the better part, which will not be taken away from her."

Notice what you think and feel as you read the gospel.

Martha is being a good hostess as people visit her house to hear Jesus. Martha's sister, Mary, is among those listening to Jesus. Martha points out to Jesus that her sister isn't helping her. Jesus gently puts the situation in perspective for Martha. The better part is to sit at Jesus' feet and listen to him.

Pray as you are led for yourself and others.
"You are present, Lord, so I am listening now. I love to hear you. Then let me serve others . . ." (Continue in your own words.)

Listen to Jesus.
Prayer is spending time with God, sharing your whole heart, soul, and mind. Out of that comes service and the best results. What else is Jesus saying to you?

Ask God to show you how to live today.
"Jesus, I offer you my day of service as a prayer of thanks for all those you have given me. Thank you for staying by me today. Amen."

Wednesday, October 9, 2019

Know that God is present with you and ready to converse.
"I turn to you today, my God, and ask you to lead me in prayer, for I need you to teach me."

Read the gospel: Luke 11:1–4.
Jesus was praying in a certain place, and after he had finished, one of his disciples said to him, "Lord, teach us to pray, as John taught his disciples." He said to them, "When you pray, say:

> Father, hallowed be your name.
> > Your kingdom come.
> > Give us each day our daily bread.
> > And forgive us our sins,
> > > for we ourselves forgive everyone indebted to us.
> > And do not bring us to the time of trial."

Notice what you think and feel as you read the gospel.
Luke records this short prayer that begins by praising the Father and then immediately asks for the coming of the kingdom of God. The prayer ends differently from the one Matthew records, asking God not to bring us to the time of trial. To what does this refer?

Pray as you are led for yourself and others.
"I fear I will fail in trial. If I must undergo trial, Lord, as you yourself did, give me grace to accept it and to do your will. I can do it in your

strength. I pray for all who are undergoing trials . . ." (Continue in your own words.)

Listen to Jesus.

All are tested by trials, but trials are in the nature of things, not brought on by God. Often they are brought on by oneself. You learn obedience by trials. What else is Jesus saying to you?

Ask God to show you how to live today.

"Lord, I abandon myself to your providence. You know what is best for me. You love me. I trust you. Amen."

Thursday, October 10, 2019

Know that God is present with you and ready to converse.

"Lord, I seek you in your Word; give me the gift of yourself."

Read the gospel: Luke 11:5–13.

And Jesus said to them, "Suppose one of you has a friend, and you go to him at midnight and say to him, 'Friend, lend me three loaves of bread; for a friend of mine has arrived, and I have nothing to set before him.' And he answers from within, 'Do not bother me; the door has already been locked, and my children are with me in bed; I cannot get up and give you anything.' I tell you, even though he will not get up and give him anything because he is his friend, at least because of his persistence he will get up and give him whatever he needs.

"So I say to you, Ask, and it will be given to you; search, and you will find; knock, and the door will be opened for you. For everyone who asks receives, and everyone who searches finds, and for everyone who knocks, the door will be opened. Is there anyone among you who, if your child asks for a fish, will give a snake instead of a fish? Or if the child asks for an egg, will give a scorpion? If you then, who are evil, know how to give good gifts to your children, how much more will the heavenly Father give the Holy Spirit to those who ask him!"

Notice what you think and feel as you read the gospel.

Jesus tells his disciples to persist in asking, searching, and knocking, saying that God will give what we ask. God wants to give us the Holy Spirit, the best gift of all.

Pray as you are led for yourself and others.

"You put desire for you in my heart, Lord. Let this hunger grow not just in me but in all those you have given me . . ." (Continue in your own words.)

Listen to Jesus.

I will satisfy your hunger for God, beloved disciple. God hears your prayers and is filling you with the fullness of God. What else is Jesus saying to you?

Ask God to show you how to live today.

"By your grace, my God, I will walk in your Spirit today, doing small acts of love whenever I can. Glory to you, O Lord. Amen."

Friday, October 11, 2019

Know that God is present with you and ready to converse.

"Lord, you come to me as invisible Spirit to teach me about Jesus and his way. You give me the Word of God."

Read the gospel: Luke 11:15–26.

But some of the crowd said, "He casts out demons by Beelzebul, the ruler of the demons." Others, to test Jesus, kept demanding from him a sign from heaven. But he knew what they were thinking and said to them, "Every kingdom divided against itself becomes a desert, and house falls on house. If Satan also is divided against himself, how will his kingdom stand?—for you say that I cast out the demons by Beelzebul. Now if I cast out the demons by Beelzebul, by whom do your exorcists cast them out? Therefore they will be your judges. But if it is by the finger of God that I cast out the demons, then the kingdom of God has come to you. When a strong man, fully armed, guards his castle, his property is safe. But when one stronger than he attacks him and overpowers him, he takes away his armor in which he trusted and divides his plunder. Whoever is not with me is against me, and whoever does not gather with me scatters.

"When the unclean spirit has gone out of a person, it wanders through waterless regions looking for a resting-place, but not finding any, it says, 'I will return to my house from which I came.' When it comes, it finds it swept and put in order. Then it goes and brings seven other spirits more evil than itself, and they enter and live there; and the last state of that person is worse than the first."

Notice what you think and feel as you read the gospel.

In response to being accused of being in league with the devil, Jesus speaks about the nature of evil spirits as they work in the world. He has power over them, for he is the Lord of all. He can cast them out, but the unclean spirit can return to the person in which it once was and, with other spirits, make it even worse for the person.

Pray as you are led for yourself and others.

"Lord, protect me and those I love from all the powers of evil, for there is spiritual warfare going on. Place your Holy Spirit upon us so that no evil can remain in us . . ." (Continue in your own words.)

Listen to Jesus.

There is a struggle between light and darkness, good and evil, in the world and in every person's soul. I have power, and I give you power to resist and defeat evil. Be careful and stay nearby, my child. What else is Jesus saying to you?

Ask God to show you how to live today.

"By your power I am enemy to all the evil I encounter. Give me wisdom to do what I should do in opposing it, and let God be victorious. Amen."

Saturday, October 12, 2019

Know that God is present with you and ready to converse.

"Blessed Lord, I welcome you. Let me hear your Word in the deepest regions of my soul."

Read the gospel: Luke 11:27–28.

While Jesus was saying this, a woman in the crowd raised her voice and said to him, "Blessed is the womb that bore you and the breasts that nursed you!" But he said, "Blessed rather are those who hear the word of God and obey it!"

Notice what you think and feel as you read the gospel.

A woman in the crowd raises her voice in praise of Jesus' mother, calling her blessed. Jesus turns her blessing back upon the whole crowd by proclaiming that the truly blessed are those who hear and obey the Word of God.

Pray as you are led for yourself and others.

"I seek to obey your Word, dear Savior, for I want your blessedness for me and for those you have given me . . ." (Continue in your own words.)

Listen to Jesus.

You are one of the holy family, with all the saints of all time. We love you and watch over you as you journey through this world. We will welcome you into the kingdom, beloved disciple. What else is Jesus saying to you?

Ask God to show you how to live today.

"You are wonderful to me, my God. If I should face some difficulty or sorrow today, remind me of your goodness to me and your promises. Glory be to the Father, the Son, and the Holy Spirit. Amen."

Sunday, October 13, 2019
Twenty-Eighth Sunday in Ordinary Time

Know that God is present with you and ready to converse.

"Lord, in your Word is healing and life. Thank you!"

Read the gospel: Luke 17:11–19.

On the way to Jerusalem Jesus was going through the region between Samaria and Galilee. As he entered a village, ten lepers approached him. Keeping their distance, they called out, saying, "Jesus, Master, have mercy on us!" When he saw them, he said to them, "Go and show your-selves to the priests." And as they went, they were made clean. Then one of them, when he saw that he was healed, turned back, praising God with a loud voice. He prostrated himself at Jesus' feet and thanked him. And he was a Samaritan. Then Jesus asked, "Were not ten made clean? But the other nine, where are they? Was none of them found to return and give praise to God except this foreigner?" Then he said to him, "Get up and go on your way; your faith has made you well."

Notice what you think and feel as you read the gospel.

With the healing of the ten lepers, Jesus teaches gratitude to God. He also comments on human nature—we tend to take our blessings for granted. He praises the one who shows thanks, because the one who is thankful is also joyful, basking in the love of God.

Pray as you are led for yourself and others.

"I know many people who are far from you, Lord, and do not seem to
want you in their lives. I pray for them. Send your Holy Spirit and revive
in their hearts a desire for you . . ." (Continue in your own words.)

Listen to Jesus.

*People are free to come to me. Many do. Many do not. Many more will. I con-
tinue to call.* What else is Jesus saying to you?

Ask God to show you how to live today.

"Lord, what can I do? Send me out to praise you before others. Give me
the words. Amen."

Monday, October 14, 2019

Know that God is present with you and ready to converse.

"You are here, Lord. Cut through my darkness with the light of your
Word."

Read the gospel: Luke 11:29–32.

When the crowds were increasing, Jesus began to say, "This generation
is an evil generation; it asks for a sign, but no sign will be given to it
except the sign of Jonah. For just as Jonah became a sign to the people of
Nineveh, so the Son of Man will be to this generation. The queen of the
South will rise at the judgment with the people of this generation and
condemn them, because she came from the ends of the earth to listen
to the wisdom of Solomon, and see, something greater than Solomon
is here! The people of Nineveh will rise up at the judgment with this
generation and condemn it, because they repented at the proclamation
of Jonah, and see, something greater than Jonah is here!"

Notice what you think and feel as you read the gospel.

Jesus condemns those who ask him for signs. He has performed many
mighty works and has spoken with authority about his Father and the
kingdom of heaven, and yet they still want a sign. The only sign they
will get is the sign of Jonah, Jesus says, for Jonah was three days in the
belly of a fish. When he appeared in Nineveh, the people repented. At the
final judgment, they will rise and condemn this generation for refusing
to repent despite the warnings of the Son of God.

Pray as you are led for yourself and others.

"Lord, give me true repentance for my sins. I pray for those you have given me, that they will come to you seeking your forgiveness . . ." (Continue in your own words.)

Listen to Jesus.

Every generation is the same, beloved. My heart longs for them to come to me and to know the blessedness of God. Would you share my longing? What else is Jesus saying to you?

Ask God to show you how to live today.

"Lord, you work in many ways behind the scenes, often in ways I cannot see at the time. Let me see and understand how I can help. Your kingdom come and your will be done on earth. Amen."

Tuesday, October 15, 2019

Know that God is present with you and ready to converse.

"I am a sinner, Lord, but you are here with me to save me by your Word."

Read the gospel: Luke 11:37–41.

While Jesus was speaking, a Pharisee invited him to dine with him; so he went in and took his place at the table. The Pharisee was amazed to see that he did not first wash before dinner. Then the Lord said to him, "Now you Pharisees clean the outside of the cup and of the dish, but inside you are full of greed and wickedness. You fools! Did not the one who made the outside make the inside also? So give for alms those things that are within; and see, everything will be clean for you."

Notice what you think and feel as you read the gospel.

Jesus asks for inner cleanliness, not a show of outer cleanliness. He says that, inside, the Pharisees are full of greed and wickedness. If the Pharisees can instead give of themselves in true charity, then they need not worry about external cleanliness.

Pray as you are led for yourself and others.

"Lord, I seek to abandon my own greed and wickedness so that I will be clean in your sight. Cleanse me, Lord, and make clean the hearts of all those you have given me . . ." (Continue in your own words.)

Listen to Jesus.
You are clean, my beloved. I wash you in the water of my Word and put my Holy Spirit within you. Let us walk together. What else is Jesus saying to you?

Ask God to show you how to live today.
"I rejoice in you, my God. All things are possible for you, mighty Savior of the world. Let me do what you want me to do today. Amen."

Wednesday, October 16, 2019

Know that God is present with you and ready to converse.
"Your voice is truth, Jesus. Let me hear it now in your Word."

Read the gospel: Luke 11:42–46.
Jesus said, "But woe to you Pharisees! For you tithe mint and rue and herbs of all kinds, and neglect justice and the love of God; it is these you ought to have practiced, without neglecting the others. Woe to you Pharisees! For you love to have the seat of honor in the synagogues and to be greeted with respect in the market places. Woe to you! For you are like unmarked graves, and people walk over them without realizing it."

One of the lawyers answered him, "Teacher, when you say these things, you insult us too." And he said, "Woe also to you lawyers! For you load people with burdens hard to bear, and you yourselves do not lift a finger to ease them."

Notice what you think and feel as you read the gospel.
Jesus condemns religious hypocrites and legalists, saying they are dead.

Pray as you are led for yourself and others.
"Keep me from religious sins, Lord. Let me know your grace in all I think, do, and say. I pray for those who speak your words and for those who hear them, that all may come into your blessed kingdom . . ." (Continue in your own words.)

Listen to Jesus.
Let us stay close, you and I, for I want to go with you. We must work together for the coming of the kingdom. What else is Jesus saying to you?

Ask God to show you how to live today.

"I know you ask us to do good things for others, Lord. I offer myself to do good today. Thank you for being near me. Amen."

Thursday, October 17, 2019

Know that God is present with you and ready to converse.

"You are holy, O Lord, and the fountain of all holiness, present with me now as I turn to your Word."

Read the gospel: Luke 11:47–54.

Jesus said, "Woe to you! For you build the tombs of the prophets whom your ancestors killed. So you are witnesses and approve of the deeds of your ancestors; for they killed them, and you build their tombs. Therefore also the Wisdom of God said, 'I will send them prophets and apostles, some of whom they will kill and persecute,' so that this generation may be charged with the blood of all the prophets shed since the foundation of the world, from the blood of Abel to the blood of Zechariah, who perished between the altar and the sanctuary. Yes, I tell you, it will be charged against this generation. Woe to you lawyers! For you have taken away the key of knowledge; you did not enter yourselves, and you hindered those who were entering."

When he went outside, the scribes and the Pharisees began to be very hostile towards him and to cross-examine him about many things, lying in wait for him, to catch him in something he might say.

Notice what you think and feel as you read the gospel.

Jesus opposes the scribes and Pharisees, accusing them of killing God's prophets as their ancestors did. He condemns the lawyers for taking away the "key of knowledge," not entering themselves and hindering others from entering. How should the scribes and Pharisees react to his harsh correction? They lack the humility to accept it, so they try to trip him up, to negate his teaching.

Pray as you are led for yourself and others.

"Jesus, no one can trap you in your words. You are the Word of God and speak only truth. I pray for those who are hostile toward you, that they may see your truth and goodness . . ." (Continue in your own words.)

Listen to Jesus.

My Word rings forth throughout the earth and captures hearts and minds. Let those who have ears to hear, hear. What else is Jesus saying to you?

Ask God to show you how to live today.

"Let your words remain in me today as I do what you have given me to do. Make holy the works of my hands, dear Lord. Amen."

Friday, October 18, 2019
St. Luke, Evangelist

Know that God is present with you and ready to converse.

"Teacher, Friend, Savior, I come before you with an open, humble heart."

Read the gospel: Luke 10:1–9.

After this the Lord appointed seventy others and sent them on ahead of him in pairs to every town and place where he himself intended to go. He said to them, "The harvest is plentiful, but the laborers are few; therefore ask the Lord of the harvest to send out laborers into his harvest. Go on your way. See, I am sending you out like lambs into the midst of wolves. Carry no purse, no bag, no sandals; and greet no one on the road. Whatever house you enter, first say, 'Peace to this house!' And if anyone is there who shares in peace, your peace will rest on that person; but if not, it will return to you. Remain in the same house, eating and drinking whatever they provide, for the laborer deserves to be paid. Do not move about from house to house. Whenever you enter a town and its people welcome you, eat what is set before you; cure the sick who are there, and say to them, 'The kingdom of God has come near to you.'"

Notice what you think and feel as you read the gospel.

Jesus sends out his disciples to do his works. He gives them a message and an approach. Some of those they encounter will believe, some will not.

Pray as you are led for yourself and others.

"I pray for the conversion of souls and for grace for those who bear the words and works of God. I think of these . . ." (Continue in your own words.)

Listen to Jesus.

Keep your heart open, child, and I will fill it with my love for others. It is my love that gives you power to do good. What else is Jesus saying to you?

Ask God to show you how to live today.

"I receive your love, Lord. Lead me on my way to love and serve others. Amen."

Saturday, October 19, 2019

Know that God is present with you and ready to converse.

"Holy Spirit, you are present in the Word of God to teach us about Jesus Christ. Be present within me so that I may receive him as my Lord."

Read the gospel: Luke 12:8–12.

Jesus said, "And I tell you, everyone who acknowledges me before others, the Son of Man also will acknowledge before the angels of God; but whoever denies me before others will be denied before the angels of God. And everyone who speaks a word against the Son of Man will be forgiven; but whoever blasphemes against the Holy Spirit will not be forgiven. When they bring you before the synagogues, the rulers, and the authorities, do not worry about how you are to defend yourselves or what you are to say; for the Holy Spirit will teach you at that very hour what you ought to say."

Notice what you think and feel as you read the gospel.

Jesus asks that we acknowledge him before others and not deny him. When others oppose you, don't worry about defending yourself, for the Holy Spirit will show you what to say in that hour.

Pray as you are led for yourself and others.

"Lord, give me your Spirit without measure so that I can serve you and others fearlessly and well . . ." (Continue in your own words.)

Listen to Jesus.

I love you, child, and I thank you for turning to me. Know that no matter how others treat you because of me, I will be with you always. What else is Jesus saying to you?

Ask God to show you how to live today.

"Jesus, I want to know God and love God more and more, in part so I can speak confidently when others question my faith. Tell me how to do that today and tomorrow and always. I praise you for your great glory. Amen."

Sunday, October 20, 2019
Twenty-Ninth Sunday in Ordinary Time

Know that God is present with you and ready to converse.

"Let my prayer come before you, Lord, and let me hear your Word."

Read the gospel: Luke 18:1–8.

Then Jesus told them a parable about their need to pray always and not to lose heart. He said, "In a certain city there was a judge who neither feared God nor had respect for people. In that city there was a widow who kept coming to him and saying, 'Grant me justice against my opponent.' For a while he refused; but later he said to himself, 'Though I have no fear of God and no respect for anyone, yet because this widow keeps bothering me, I will grant her justice, so that she may not wear me out by continually coming.'" And the Lord said, "Listen to what the unjust judge says. And will not God grant justice to his chosen ones who cry to him day and night? Will he delay long in helping them? I tell you, he will quickly grant justice to them. And yet, when the Son of Man comes, will he find faith on earth?"

Notice what you think and feel as you read the gospel.

Jesus teaches persistence in prayer, likening God to a judge and his chosen ones to a widow who continues to appeal to the judge for justice against her opponent. The judge eventually gives in to her just to be free of her. How much more will God grant justice to his chosen ones who cry to him day and night?

Pray as you are led for yourself and others.

"Lord, you are coming to establish justice. I pray that you will find faith on earth when you come . . ." (Continue in your own words.)

Listen to Jesus.

Seeing the great injustices that continue in every community everywhere, you can get discouraged. You can look past injustices and refuse to acknowledge them because of your own helplessness to set them right. Don't give up on justice. Cry to God day and night. I am the just Judge of all, and justice will be done. What else is Jesus saying to you?

Ask God to show you how to live today.

"Lord, how may I work for justice in my own community? Open my eyes, Lord, and show me what to do. Amen."

Monday, October 21, 2019

Know that God is present with you and ready to converse.

"Jesus, you know me from the inside. Purify my heart by your holy Word."

Read the gospel: Luke 12:13–21.

Someone in the crowd said to Jesus, "Teacher, tell my brother to divide the family inheritance with me." But he said to him, "Friend, who set me to be a judge or arbitrator over you?" And he said to them, "Take care! Be on your guard against all kinds of greed; for one's life does not consist in the abundance of possessions." Then he told them a parable: "The land of a rich man produced abundantly. And he thought to himself, 'What should I do, for I have no place to store my crops?' Then he said, 'I will do this: I will pull down my barns and build larger ones, and there I will store all my grain and my goods. And I will say to my soul, Soul, you have ample goods laid up for many years; relax, eat, drink, be merry.' But God said to him, 'You fool! This very night your life is being demanded of you. And the things you have prepared, whose will they be?' So it is with those who store up treasures for themselves but are not rich toward God."

Notice what you think and feel as you read the gospel.

Jesus warns against greed, teaching that life does not consist in possessions. We tend to think it does, like the man who builds bigger barns to store all his grain and goods while he eats, drinks, and is merry. But possessions mean nothing in eternal life, so Jesus teaches the crowd to be rich toward God, instead.

Pray as you are led for yourself and others.

"Direct my eyes to the things of God, Lord, and away from all greed. Be my treasure, Jesus, for your love I can carry with me into the eternal kingdom of heaven. I pray for all who are slaves of greed . . ." (Continue in your own words.)

Listen to Jesus.

I know that you need things, child, and I will continue to provide for you. Do not allow things to distract you from me. Do not compare what you have with what others have. Do not judge others. You are mine and are heir to all the treasures of heaven. Follow me. What else is Jesus saying to you?

Ask God to show you how to live today.

"Jesus, what material thing can I let go of today, to make more room for you in my heart? Show me, Lord. Amen."

Tuesday, October 22, 2019

Know that God is present with you and ready to converse.

"Lord, I watch and wait for your coming. I am ready now."

Read the gospel: Luke 12:35–38.

Jesus said, "Be dressed for action and have your lamps lit; be like those who are waiting for their master to return from the wedding banquet, so that they may open the door for him as soon as he comes and knocks. Blessed are those slaves whom the master finds alert when he comes; truly I tell you, he will fasten his belt and have them sit down to eat, and he will come and serve them. If he comes during the middle of the night, or near dawn, and finds them so, blessed are those slaves."

Notice what you think and feel as you read the gospel.

Jesus bids his disciples to be ready for his return. When he returns, he says, he will have us sit down and will serve us. Blessed are those who are ready.

Pray as you are led for yourself and others.

"Lord, I am ready now. Keep me faithful all my life, every day. I pray for all who have grown impatient with waiting . . ." (Continue in your own words.)

Listen to Jesus.

Your time is short, beloved. In the end your whole life will be compressed into a single moment. Yet while the days stretch before you, look forward to my coming. You will be with me in eternity. What else is Jesus saying to you?

Ask God to show you how to live today.

"This day, this moment, I look to you, Lord. Let your Holy Spirit be my lamp, burning brightly within me to keep me awake and show me your coming. I know you will keep your promises to me. Amen."

Wednesday, October 23, 2019

Know that God is present with you and ready to converse.

"Lord, you have come. Please return soon and establish justice."

Read the gospel: Luke 12:41–48 (Lk 12:39–48).

And the Lord said, "Who then is the faithful and prudent manager whom his master will put in charge of his slaves, to give them their allowance of food at the proper time? Blessed is that slave whom his master will find at work when he arrives. Truly I tell you, he will put that one in charge of all his possessions. But if that slave says to himself, 'My master is delayed in coming,' and if he begins to beat the other slaves, men and women, and to eat and drink and get drunk, the master of that slave will come on a day when he does not expect him and at an hour that he does not know, and will cut him in pieces, and put him with the unfaithful. That slave who knew what his master wanted, but did not prepare himself or do what was wanted, will receive a severe beating. But the one who did not know and did what deserved a beating will receive a light beating. From everyone to whom much has been given, much will be required; and from the one to whom much has been entrusted, even more will be demanded."

Notice what you think and feel as you read the gospel.

Jesus predicts his coming at an unexpected hour. He asks us to be faithful and prudent until he returns.

Pray as you are led for yourself and others.

"Lord, I have not been as faithful and prudent as you would like. Forgive me. By your grace I will do better. Help me to know your will, that I may do it and may help others to do so also . . ." (Continue in your own words.)

Listen to Jesus.

Beloved, I speak to you. You listen. You know what I ask of you, that you take care of what I have given you. I also ask you to look beyond to see what else needs doing. I will reward your efforts to act in love for the good of those in need. What else is Jesus saying to you?

Ask God to show you how to live today.

"Open my eyes to the needs of others, Lord, the needs I would not see on my own, and let me act, manifesting your love. Amen."

Thursday, October 24, 2019

Know that God is present with you and ready to converse.

"Lord, be my peace now, for the world is often violent."

Read the gospel: Luke 12:49–53.

Jesus said, "I came to bring fire to the earth, and how I wish it were already kindled! I have a baptism with which to be baptized, and what stress I am under until it is completed! Do you think that I have come to bring peace to the earth? No, I tell you, but rather division! From now on five in one household will be divided, three against two and two against three; they will be divided:

> father against son
>   and son against father,
> mother against daughter
>   and daughter against mother,
> mother-in-law against her daughter-in-law
>   and daughter-in-law against mother-in-law."

Notice what you think and feel as you read the gospel.

Jesus understands that his coming among us will lead to dissension, even within families. He does not lament this, because everyone must make a personal decision whether to believe in Jesus.

Pray as you are led for yourself and others.

"Lord, I believe, even in the midst of strife and dissension among those I love. Let me persist in prayer for them . . ." (Continue in your own words.)

Listen to Jesus.

I am pleased by your faith, my child. I know it is not easy. But it is better for you to continue with me by your side than to go forward without me. With me you can do anything. *You can pray in genuine hope for those you love.* What else is Jesus saying to you?

Ask God to show you how to live today.

"Lord, give me the grace to live in hope, praying even for situations that may seem hopeless. Thank you for this power, Lord. Amen."

Friday, October 25, 2019

Know that God is present with you and ready to converse.

"Lord, I will search the scriptures for your truth, that I may act in obedience to you."

Read the gospel: Luke 12:54–59.

Jesus also said to the crowds, "When you see a cloud rising in the west, you immediately say, 'It is going to rain'; and so it happens. And when you see the south wind blowing, you say, 'There will be scorching heat'; and it happens. You hypocrites! You know how to interpret the appearance of earth and sky, but why do you not know how to interpret the present time?

"And why do you not judge for yourselves what is right? Thus, when you go with your accuser before a magistrate, on the way make an effort to settle the case, or you may be dragged before the judge, and the judge hand you over to the officer, and the officer throw you in prison. I tell you, you will never get out until you have paid the very last penny."

Notice what you think and feel as you read the gospel.

Jesus tells the crowds that they should recognize that this is the time of salvation, for he is among them. This is the time to get right with God.

Pray as you are led for yourself and others.

"Lord, I hear you say that the situation is urgent. I throw myself upon you, trusting you to save me. I forgive all who have hurt me . . ." (Continue in your own words.)

Listen to Jesus.

In the span of a life, there are many times of urgency. Moments of danger should drive you back to me. I want you to trust me in danger and trust me in tranquility. You will find me faithful at all times. You are dear to me. What else is Jesus saying to you?

Ask God to show you how to live today.

"Lord, in danger or tranquility today, I will trust in you. Amen."

Saturday, October 26, 2019

Know that God is present with you and ready to converse.

"Lord, I look out at the world and see what I see. I come to your Word to see what you see."

Read the gospel: Luke 13:1–5 (Lk 13:1–9).

At that very time there were some present who told him about the Galileans whose blood Pilate had mingled with their sacrifices. He asked them, "Do you think that because these Galileans suffered in this way they were worse sinners than all other Galileans? No, I tell you; but unless you repent, you will all perish as they did. Or those eighteen who were killed when the tower of Siloam fell on them—do you think that they were worse offenders than all the others living in Jerusalem? No, I tell you; but unless you repent, you will all perish just as they did."

Notice what you think and feel as you read the gospel.

Jesus says we cannot consider the demise of others as the judgment of God. We are all susceptible to judgment, and we all need to repent.

Pray as you are led for yourself and others.

"Lord, so many horrific things happen in the world—not because of anyone's specific sin but because of our shared sinful nature. Heal me, Lord, help me overcome sin. I pray for healing for the whole world, especially . . ." (Continue in your own words.)

Listen to Jesus.

I mourn with you for all the harm, all the evil in the world. But remember, I have conquered sin. Bring all your sins to me and I will cast them away from you. What else is Jesus saying to you?

Ask God to show you how to live today.

"Lord, let me seek you in the sacrament of Reconciliation, and then send me out to bring your healing to the world. Amen."

Sunday, October 27, 2019
Thirtieth Sunday in Ordinary Time

Know that God is present with you and ready to converse.

"Lord, I seek your righteousness. Show me how to obtain it by your holy Word."

Read the gospel: Luke 18:9–14.

Jesus also told this parable to some who trusted in themselves that they were righteous and regarded others with contempt: "Two men went up to the temple to pray, one a Pharisee and the other a tax collector. The Pharisee, standing by himself, was praying thus, 'God, I thank you that I am not like other people: thieves, rogues, adulterers, or even like this tax collector. I fast twice a week; I give a tenth of all my income.' But the tax collector, standing far off, would not even look up to heaven, but was beating his breast and saying, 'God, be merciful to me, a sinner!' I tell you, this man went down to his home justified rather than the other; for all who exalt themselves will be humbled, but all who humble themselves will be exalted."

Notice what you think and feel as you read the gospel.

Jesus tells this thinly veiled parable to the self-righteous. One might wonder how they received this lesson.

Pray as you are led for yourself and others.

"Lord, give me the humility I need to hear and accept correction when you give it, and give me the grace to submit myself, with all my flaws, to your mercy . . ." (Continue in your own words.)

Listen to Jesus.

I see you, my beloved, with eyes of mercy. Raise your eyes to heaven, and look at me. What else is Jesus saying to you?

Ask God to show you how to live today.

"Let me raise my eyes to see you on the Cross, Lord, where you suffered for me and because of me, and let me fall down in worship. Amen."

Monday, October 28, 2019

Know that God is present with you and ready to converse.
"God, your Word is Truth. Let it speak to me."

Read the gospel: Luke 13:10–17.

Now Jesus was teaching in one of the synagogues on the sabbath. And just then there appeared a woman with a spirit that had crippled her for eighteen years. She was bent over and was quite unable to stand up straight. When Jesus saw her, he called her over and said, "Woman, you are set free from your ailment." When he laid his hands on her, immediately she stood up straight and began praising God. But the leader of the synagogue, indignant because Jesus had cured on the sabbath, kept saying to the crowd, "There are six days on which work ought to be done; come on those days and be cured, and not on the sabbath day." But the Lord answered him and said, "You hypocrites! Does not each of you on the sabbath untie his ox or his donkey from the manger, and lead it away to give it water? And ought not this woman, a daughter of Abraham whom Satan bound for eighteen long years, be set free from this bondage on the sabbath day?" When he said this, all his opponents were put to shame; and the entire crowd was rejoicing at all the wonderful things that he was doing.

Notice what you think and feel as you read the gospel.

Jesus heals the crippled woman and is criticized by the leader of the synagogue for doing it on the Sabbath. Jesus puts all his accusers to shame, and the crowd rejoices.

Pray as you are led for yourself and others.

"Forgive me for my own small-mindedness, Lord. Let me rejoice in the good fortune of others. I pray for all those who are critical, that they may receive and be freed by your mercy . . ." (Continue in your own words.)

Listen to Jesus.

I work in you to purify your heart, to sanctify your motives. This is the work of my Spirit within you. Beloved disciple, give yourself to God's work within you. What else is Jesus saying to you?

Ask God to show you how to live today.

"I bow before you, Lord God of Hosts. Light my way today as I walk into the kingdom of heaven, focusing on the riches of your kingdom and not those of this earth. Amen."

Tuesday, October 29, 2019

Know that God is present with you and ready to converse.

"Wherever you are, Lord, mercy and truth abounds. You grant peace to troubled souls. I turn to you now, my God."

Read the gospel: Luke 13:18–21.

Jesus said therefore, "What is the kingdom of God like? And to what should I compare it? It is like a mustard seed that someone took and sowed in the garden; it grew and became a tree, and the birds of the air made nests in its branches."

And again he said, "To what should I compare the kingdom of God? It is like yeast that a woman took and mixed in with three measures of flour until all of it was leavened."

Notice what you think and feel as you read the gospel.

The kingdom of God starts small but grows large by its own energy. That energy must be the Holy Spirit. May the kingdom grow large on earth. May the kingdom grow large within us.

Pray as you are led for yourself and others.

"I pray for the coming of the kingdom of heaven. May it leaven every nation and every person, that God may be glorified for God's goodness and might . . ." (Continue in your own words.)

Listen to Jesus.

You don't need to do anything, beloved disciple. I have already done everything, and the Spirit is working within you, renewing your life. What else is Jesus saying to you?

Ask God to show you how to live today.

"Let me behave as one who lives by the life of God. Let me honor and never disgrace you, Lord Jesus Christ, for I am called by your name. Amen."

Wednesday, October 30, 2019

Know that God is present with you and ready to converse.
"Lord, you condescend to speak to us. Let me hear and obey your Word."

Read the gospel: Luke 13:22–30.

Jesus went through one town and village after another, teaching as he made his way to Jerusalem. Someone asked him, "Lord, will only a few be saved?" He said to them, "Strive to enter through the narrow door; for many, I tell you, will try to enter and will not be able. When once the owner of the house has got up and shut the door, and you begin to stand outside and to knock at the door, saying, 'Lord, open to us,' then in reply he will say to you, 'I do not know where you come from.' Then you will begin to say, 'We ate and drank with you, and you taught in our streets.' But he will say, 'I do not know where you come from; go away from me, all you evildoers!' There will be weeping and gnashing of teeth when you see Abraham and Isaac and Jacob and all the prophets in the kingdom of God, and you yourselves thrown out. Then people will come from east and west, from north and south, and will eat in the kingdom of God. Indeed, some are last who will be first, and some are first who will be last."

Notice what you think and feel as you read the gospel.

Someone asks Jesus how many people will be saved; but the question he's perhaps really asking is "will I be saved"? Jesus answers both questions, giving a command and a warning.

Pray as you are led for yourself and others.

"To be saved is to know you, Jesus, and to know you is to do your will. Help me, and those you've given me, seek to know and to do your will in this life, that we may be with you in the next one . . ." (Continue in your own words.)

Listen to Jesus.

Strive to enter by the narrow door; and remember, "I am the gate. Whoever enters by me will be saved." Come to me and enter into my love. What else is Jesus saying to you?

Ask God to show you how to live today.

"Lord Jesus, be my safety today. Direct my eyes to your will for me in this moment. Amen."

Thursday, October 31, 2019

Know that God is present with you and ready to converse.
"You are Lord of all the earth, Almighty God. Open my understanding to walk in your way."

Read the gospel: Luke 13:31–35.
At that very hour some Pharisees came and said to Jesus, "Get away from here, for Herod wants to kill you." He said to them, "Go and tell that fox for me, 'Listen, I am casting out demons and performing cures today and tomorrow, and on the third day I finish my work. Yet today, tomorrow, and the next day I must be on my way, because it is impossible for a prophet to be killed away from Jerusalem.' Jerusalem, Jerusalem, the city that kills the prophets and stones those who are sent to it! How often have I desired to gather your children together as a hen gathers her brood under her wings, and you were not willing! See, your house is left to you. And I tell you, you will not see me until the time comes when you say, 'Blessed is the one who comes in the name of the Lord.'"

Notice what you think and feel as you read the gospel.
Jesus knows Herod wants to kill him, but he continues to Jerusalem to meet his destiny—suffering and death. He laments that the people are set against God and resist his grace.

Pray as you are led for yourself and others.
"I pray that people throughout the earth, who are torn apart by religious differences, may be open to God. Let us be one in God. I pray for those in my own family . . ." (Continue in your own words.)

Listen to Jesus.
I know you suffer as I suffer, wanting peace and love to reign over all. That day is coming, beloved. In the meantime, there are things to do. What else is Jesus saying to you?

Ask God to show you how to live today.
"I offer myself to you today to serve. Thank you for this privilege. Amen."

THE POPE'S MONTHLY PRAYER INTENTION FOR NOVEMBER 2019

That the spirit of dialogue, encounter, and reconciliation emerge in the Near East, where diverse religious communities share their lives together.

Friday, November 1, 2019
All Saints Day

Know that God is present with you and ready to converse.
"You come to me in Word and in Spirit, my God. Help me to interpret and apply your Word."

Read the gospel: Matthew 5:1–12a.
When Jesus saw the crowds, he went up the mountain; and after he sat down, his disciples came to him. Then he began to speak, and taught them, saying:

"Blessed are the poor in spirit, for theirs is the kingdom of heaven.

"Blessed are those who mourn, for they will be comforted.

"Blessed are the meek, for they will inherit the earth.

"Blessed are those who hunger and thirst for righteousness, for they will be filled.

"Blessed are the merciful, for they will receive mercy.

"Blessed are the pure in heart, for they will see God.

"Blessed are the peacemakers, for they will be called children of God.

"Blessed are those who are persecuted for righteousness' sake, for theirs is the kingdom of heaven.

"Blessed are you when people revile you and persecute you and utter all kinds of evil against you falsely on my account. Rejoice and be glad, for your reward is great in heaven, for in the same way they persecuted the prophets who were before you."

Notice what you think and feel as you read the gospel.
Jesus teaches the way of happiness through the spiritual qualities of humility, simplicity, peacefulness, gentleness, righteousness, and so forth. He wants us to be happy.

Pray as you are led for yourself and others.
"Lord, I pray for those who accuse me or dispute with me. Let me forgive them from my heart . . ." (Continue in your own words.)

Listen to Jesus.
Take care that the things and the struggles of this life do not distract you from the goal of heaven. Come to me and I will show you the treasures of heaven. What else is Jesus saying to you?

Ask God to show you how to live today.
"Help me not to engage in pointless disputes with others, Lord. Put a guard on my lips until I can speak a word of peace in season. Amen."

Saturday, November 2, 2019
The Commemoration of All the Faithful Departed (All Souls)

Know that God is present with you and ready to converse.
"Many have died and are with you, Lord. When I die, let me join that great company, praising you for eternity, and let me join them in praising you here and now."

Read the gospel: John 6:37–40.
Jesus said, "Everything that the Father gives me will come to me, and anyone who comes to me I will never drive away; for I have come down from heaven, not to do my own will, but the will of him who sent me. And this is the will of him who sent me, that I should lose nothing of all that he has given me, but raise it up on the last day. This is indeed the will of my Father, that all who see the Son and believe in him may have eternal life; and I will raise them up on the last day."

Notice what you think and feel as you read the gospel.
Jesus says he will never drive away anyone who comes to him. The Father wills that Jesus lose no one, and he will raise us up to eternal life on the last day.

Pray as you are led for yourself and others.

"Who can imagine the fulfillment of that promise? Jesus describes God as generous, mighty, and faithful. May all those you have given me come to believe in God . . ." (Continue in your own words.)

Listen to Jesus.

My Father is glorious, and he has given glory to me. You, too, live and move in the glory of God. We love you because you are ours. What else is Jesus saying to you?

Ask God to show you how to live today.

"If I am a beloved child of God, I will find ways to honor and serve God today. What shall I do? Amen."

Sunday, November 3, 2019
Thirty-First Sunday in Ordinary Time

Know that God is present with you and ready to converse.

"Jesus, you are always aware of whoever wants you. You have stopped here for me this moment. Thank you, Jesus."

Read the gospel: Luke 19:1–10.

Jesus entered Jericho and was passing through it. A man was there named Zacchaeus; he was a chief tax collector and was rich. He was trying to see who Jesus was, but on account of the crowd he could not, because he was short in stature. So he ran ahead and climbed a sycamore tree to see him, because he was going to pass that way. When Jesus came to the place, he looked up and said to him, "Zacchaeus, hurry and come down; for I must stay at your house today." So he hurried down and was happy to welcome him. All who saw it began to grumble and said, "He has gone to be the guest of one who is a sinner." Zacchaeus stood there and said to the Lord, "Look, half of my possessions, Lord, I will give to the poor; and if I have defrauded anyone of anything, I will pay back four times as much." Then Jesus said to him, "Today salvation has come to this house, because he too is a son of Abraham. For the Son of Man came to seek out and to save the lost."

Notice what you think and feel as you read the gospel.

Zacchaeus, a sinner, desires to see Jesus, and Jesus changes his life. Jesus sought him and saved him. Zacchaeus promises to make full amends for his sins.

Pray as you are led for yourself and others.

"Lord, I, too, wish to make amends for my sins. Lead me in doing so, and let it be on behalf of those you have given me . . ." (Continue in your own words.)

Listen to Jesus.

Whatever you give to another in my name, I will return sevenfold. I will load you with blessings because you are my child, my beloved, my friend, my disciple. What else is Jesus saying to you?

Ask God to show you how to live today.

"Let me remember my resolve to make amends for my sins today. By your grace, I will do it. Thank you, Savior. Amen."

Monday, November 4, 2019

Know that God is present with you and ready to converse.

"God, you are the object of all my longing. Instruct me by your Word so that I may know you and love you more and more."

Read the gospel: Luke 14:12–14.

Jesus said also to the one who had invited him, "When you give a luncheon or a dinner, do not invite your friends or your brothers or your relatives or rich neighbors, in case they may invite you in return, and you would be repaid. But when you give a banquet, invite the poor, the crippled, the lame, and the blind. And you will be blessed, because they cannot repay you, for you will be repaid at the resurrection of the righteous."

Notice what you think and feel as you read the gospel.

Jesus turns human social gatherings upside down. Do not invite the people you want to impress and who will invite you in return. Instead, invite the poor, the disabled, the blind—those people who cannot pay you back. You will be repaid at the resurrection.

Pray as you are led for yourself and others.

"Lord, I, too, have wanted to impress others. Turn my attention to caring for the poor, the hungry, the hurting. I pray for them . . ." (Continue in your own words.)

Listen to Jesus.

To serve my people is a blessing, beloved disciple, more than you can know. Look for me among them. What else is Jesus saying to you?

Ask God to show you how to live today.

"Lord, when I look past a person, redirect my line of sight. Let me see you in every person I meet. Amen."

Tuesday, November 5, 2019

Know that God is present with you and ready to converse.

"Lord, I know you are here with me; let me not take you for granted. Let your Spirit rest upon me as I ponder your Word."

Read the gospel: Luke 14:15–24.

One of the dinner guests, on hearing this, said to Jesus, "Blessed is anyone who will eat bread in the kingdom of God!" Then Jesus said to him, "Someone gave a great dinner and invited many. At the time for the dinner he sent his slave to say to those who had been invited, 'Come; for everything is ready now.' But they all alike began to make excuses. The first said to him, 'I have bought a piece of land, and I must go out and see it; please accept my apologies.' Another said, 'I have bought five yoke of oxen, and I am going to try them out; please accept my apologies.' Another said, 'I have just been married, and therefore I cannot come.' So the slave returned and reported this to his master. Then the owner of the house became angry and said to his slave, 'Go out at once into the streets and lanes of the town and bring in the poor, the crippled, the blind, and the lame.' And the slave said, 'Sir, what you ordered has been done, and there is still room.' Then the master said to the slave, 'Go out into the roads and lanes, and compel people to come in, so that my house may be filled. For I tell you, none of those who were invited will taste my dinner.'"

Notice what you think and feel as you read the gospel.

Jesus speaks of all the excuses people give instead of coming into the kingdom of God. Because the invited guests will not come to the dinner, the master of the house sends his servants to bring in the poor, the disabled, and the blind. They will eat his dinner.

Pray as you are led for yourself and others.

"Lord, knock down all my defenses and everything that hinders me from loving and serving you completely. I place myself in your loving care. I also place in your care all those you have given me . . ." (Continue in your own words.)

Listen to Jesus.

Have no fear of the future, dear friend, and make no excuses to not follow me. You will always find me near you, and I will help you prepare for the marriage supper of the Lamb. What else is Jesus saying to you?

Ask God to show you how to live today.

"Make me mindful of the excuses I make, Master, and give me courage simply to act as one who follows you. I am yours, Lord. Amen."

Wednesday, November 6, 2019

Know that God is present with you and ready to converse.

"Lord of Hosts, Creator and Savior, your servants love you and learn your virtues. Teach me."

Read the gospel: Luke 14:25–33.

Now large crowds were travelling with him; and Jesus turned and said to them, "Whoever comes to me and does not hate father and mother, wife and children, brothers and sisters, yes, and even life itself, cannot be my disciple. Whoever does not carry the cross and follow me cannot be my disciple. For which of you, intending to build a tower, does not first sit down and estimate the cost, to see whether he has enough to complete it? Otherwise, when he has laid a foundation and is not able to finish, all who see it will begin to ridicule him, saying, 'This fellow began to build and was not able to finish.' Or what king, going out to wage war against another king, will not sit down first and consider whether he is able with ten thousand to oppose the one who comes against him with twenty thousand? If he cannot, then, while the other is still far away, he sends a delegation and asks for the terms of peace. So therefore, none of you can become my disciple if you do not give up all your possessions."

Notice what you think and feel as you read the gospel.

Jesus seeks followers who are completely committed to him and his way of the Cross. He exhorts us to be realistic about it, to count the cost, which includes forsaking people, possessions, and even life itself to follow him.

Pray as you are led for yourself and others.

"Lord, I am still learning to forsake all. Today I give you everything— those I love, those you have given me, all I possess, my talents, my thoughts, my words, and my deeds . . ." (Continue in your own words.)

Listen to Jesus.

I can use you, beloved disciple, and teach you to forsake all. Come with me. What else is Jesus saying to you?

Ask God to show you how to live today.

"If you lead me, Lord, I will follow. Let me venture into the unknown with holy expectations. What lies ahead? Amen."

Thursday, November 7, 2019

Know that God is present with you and ready to converse.

"Lord, I come joyfully into your presence."

Read the gospel: Luke 15:1–10.

Now all the tax collectors and sinners were coming near to listen to Jesus. And the Pharisees and the scribes were grumbling and saying, "This fellow welcomes sinners and eats with them."

So he told them this parable: "Which one of you, having a hundred sheep and losing one of them, does not leave the ninety-nine in the wilderness and go after the one that is lost until he finds it? When he has found it, he lays it on his shoulders and rejoices. And when he comes home, he calls together his friends and neighbors, saying to them, 'Rejoice with me, for I have found my sheep that was lost.' Just so, I tell you, there will be more joy in heaven over one sinner who repents than over ninety-nine righteous people who need no repentance.

"Or what woman having ten silver coins, if she loses one of them, does not light a lamp, sweep the house, and search carefully until she finds it? When she has found it, she calls together her friends and neighbors, saying, 'Rejoice with me, for I have found the coin that I had lost.' Just so, I tell you, there is joy in the presence of the angels of God over one sinner who repents."

Notice what you think and feel as you read the gospel.

Jesus tells parables of joy at finding what was lost. He is the embodiment of the Good Shepherd. Rejoice with him.

Pray as you are led for yourself and others.

"Lord, teach me to rejoice with you over all the souls you find; use me to seek them out. And bring all your lost sheep back to the fold, especially . . ." (Continue in your own words.)

Listen to Jesus.

Your desire to be with me also gives me joy. Stay close to me and you will share my joy. What else is Jesus saying to you?

Ask God to show you how to live today.

"Let me return to you again and again today, in prayer and mindfulness, and you will show me the way to go. Amen."

Friday, November 8, 2019

Know that God is present with you and ready to converse.

"Lord, write your Word in my heart. I come joyfully into your presence and receive you here."

Read the gospel: Luke 16:1–8.

Then Jesus said to the disciples, "There was a rich man who had a manager, and charges were brought to him that this man was squandering his property. So he summoned him and said to him, 'What is this that I hear about you? Give me an account of your management, because you cannot be my manager any longer.' Then the manager said to himself, 'What will I do, now that my master is taking the position away from me? I am not strong enough to dig, and I am ashamed to beg. I have decided what to do so that, when I am dismissed as manager, people may welcome me into their homes.' So, summoning his master's debtors one by one, he asked the first, 'How much do you owe my master?' He answered, 'A hundred jugs of olive oil.' He said to him, 'Take your bill, sit down quickly, and make it fifty.' Then he asked another, 'And how much do you owe?' He replied, 'A hundred containers of wheat.' He said to him, 'Take your bill and make it eighty.' And his master commended the dishonest manager because he had acted shrewdly; for the children of this age are more shrewd in dealing with their own generation than are the children of light."

Notice what you think and feel as you read the gospel.

Jesus uses this unusual parable of the dishonest manager to teach his disciples a spiritual lesson. What is he teaching? That the children of light should be as shrewd in spiritual things as the ungodly are in worldly things. As the children of light, we, too, will have to account to our Master how we have used the resources we have been given.

Pray as you are led for yourself and others.

"Lord, let your meaning and your message go deep in me. I pray for the dishonest and the wasteful, especially those in positions of authority. I pray also for those you have given me . . ." (Continue in your own words.)

Listen to Jesus.

Being a child of the light requires awareness. Take time with me to learn my ways. Be prudent. Do what you know is right. What else is Jesus saying to you?

Ask God to show you how to live today.

"Lord, let me be a serious disciple, prudent in my service of you and others. Let me bring honor to you, Father in heaven. Amen."

Saturday, November 9, 2019
Dedication of the Lateran Basilica in Rome

Know that God is present with you and ready to converse.

"Our Father, heaven cannot contain you. You are Spirit, the very Spirit that raised Jesus Christ from the dead, present with me now."

Read the gospel: John 2:13–22.

The Passover of the Jews was near, and Jesus went up to Jerusalem. In the temple he found people selling cattle, sheep, and doves, and the money changers seated at their tables. Making a whip of cords, he drove all of them out of the temple, both the sheep and the cattle. He also poured out the coins of the money changers and overturned their tables. He told those who were selling the doves, "Take these things out of here! Stop making my Father's house a marketplace!" His disciples remembered that it was written, "Zeal for your house will consume me." The Jews then said to him, "What sign can you show us for doing this?" Jesus answered them, "Destroy this temple, and in three days I will raise it up." The Jews then said, "This temple has been under construction for forty-six years, and will you raise it up in three days?" But he was speaking of the temple of his body. After he was raised from the dead, his disciples remembered that he had said this; and they believed the scripture and the word that Jesus had spoken.

Notice what you think and feel as you read the gospel.

Jesus shows anger in this passage because people are using God to make money and enrich themselves. He drives the animals out of the temple and overturns the tables, for his Father's house is not a marketplace. Then he speaks of the temple of his body, how it will be raised from the dead in three days. Only later would his disciples understand.

Pray as you are led for yourself and others.

"Lord, let me serve you without greed or selfishness. I don't trust my own motives. Shine your light in me . . ." (Continue in your own words.)

Listen to Jesus.

I have many things to tell you, beloved. Come to me with the matters that weigh on your heart, all your desires, all your secrets. I will sanctify your way. What else is Jesus saying to you?

Ask God to show you how to live today.

"Risen Jesus, I surrender to you. Help me to trust you in everything, for you love me, know me, and will guide me as is best. Thank you, my God. Amen."

Sunday, November 10, 2019
Thirty-Second Sunday in Ordinary Time

Know that God is present with you and ready to converse.

"Jesus, my constant companion, I am here to encounter you by your Spirit and your Word. Lead me, Lord."

Read the gospel: Luke 20:27–38.

Some Sadducees, those who say there is no resurrection, came to him and asked him a question, "Teacher, Moses wrote for us that if a man's brother dies, leaving a wife but no children, the man shall marry the widow and raise up children for his brother. Now there were seven brothers; the first married, and died childless; then the second and the third married her, and so in the same way all seven died childless. Finally the woman also died. In the resurrection, therefore, whose wife will the woman be? For the seven had married her."

Jesus said to them, "Those who belong to this age marry and are given in marriage; but those who are considered worthy of a place in that age and in the resurrection from the dead neither marry nor are given in marriage. Indeed they cannot die any more, because they are like angels and are children of God, being children of the resurrection. And the fact that the dead are raised Moses himself showed, in the story about the bush, where he speaks of the Lord as the God of Abraham, the God of Isaac, and the God of Jacob. Now he is God not of the dead, but of the living; for to him all of them are alive."

Notice what you think and feel as you read this gospel.

In response to the Pharisees' trapping question about marriage in the afterlife, Jesus explains that their hypothetical is irrelevant because life in heaven is not like life on earth. People won't be married there. They are deathless, like angels, and are the children of God, who is God not of the dead but of the living.

Pray as you are led for yourself and others.

"Lord, I ask you to keep me on the path to inheriting eternal life. Let God alone be my treasure. I pray the same for all those you have given me . . ." (Continue in your own words.)

Listen to Jesus.

I am glad that my Father has given you to me, beloved. Know that I love you always and will never abandon you on the road. What else is Jesus saying to you?

Ask God to show you how to live today.

"If I am tempted to sin in any way today, Lord, arrest me by your Spirit and let me receive your grace to resist. Thank you for loving me. Amen."

Monday, November 11, 2019

Know that God is present with you and ready to converse.
"Lord, speak plainly to your disciple, for I am here to understand you and obey."

Read the gospel: Luke 17:1–6.
Jesus said to his disciples, "Occasions for stumbling are bound to come, but woe to anyone by whom they come! It would be better for you if a millstone were hung around your neck and you were thrown into the sea than for you to cause one of these little ones to stumble. Be on your guard! If another disciple sins, you must rebuke the offender, and if there is repentance, you must forgive. And if the same person sins against you seven times a day, and turns back to you seven times and says, 'I repent,' you must forgive."

The apostles said to the Lord, "Increase our faith!" The Lord replied, "If you had faith the size of a mustard seed, you could say to this mulberry tree, 'Be uprooted and planted in the sea,' and it would obey you."

Notice what you think and feel as you read the gospel.
Jesus warns his disciples to avoid being the occasion of stumbling for others. We are to be on our guard and full of forgiveness. Jesus does not talk about the power of much faith. He talks about the power of a little faith acted upon.

Pray as you are led for yourself and others.
"Lord, let me act on my little faith. Let me accomplish through prayer and action great things for those you have given me . . ." (Continue in your own words.)

Listen to Jesus.
My way of love always involves others, dear disciple. Love the others in your life and widen the circle of love. Let your love go deeper than before. Act on it. What else is Jesus saying to you?

Ask God to show you how to live today.
"Lord, make me an instrument of your love. Give me occasions to support, lift up, and help others. Amen."

Tuesday, November 12, 2019

Know that God is present with you and ready to converse.

"Lord, I welcome you into my heart. What word have you for me today?"

Read the gospel: Luke 17:7–10.

Jesus said, "Who among you would say to your slave who has just come in from ploughing or tending sheep in the field, 'Come here at once and take your place at the table'? Would you not rather say to him, 'Prepare supper for me, put on your apron and serve me while I eat and drink; later you may eat and drink'? Do you thank the slave for doing what was commanded? So you also, when you have done all that you were ordered to do, say, 'We are worthless slaves; we have done only what we ought to have done!'"

Notice what you think and feel as you read the gospel.

These words of Jesus strip us of all pride in our accomplishments. Our assignment and our job is simply to serve. If we have done that, we have done only what we ought to do. What's the merit in that?

Pray as you are led for yourself and others.

"Lord, you teach faithful service in humility. Let me serve you and others humbly. I pray for . . ." (Continue in your own words.)

Listen to Jesus.

I love the humble, beloved, and give to them my greatest blessings. Learn humility. Follow me. What else is Jesus saying to you?

Ask God to show you how to live today.

"Nothing I do for you today is my doing alone. You work in me and through me. I give you all the glory and thank you for letting me do anything for you. Amen."

Wednesday, November 13, 2019

Know that God is present with you and ready to converse.

"Merciful God, show me your glory, your power by your Word."

Read the gospel: Luke 17:11–19.

On the way to Jerusalem Jesus was going through the region between Samaria and Galilee. As he entered a village, ten lepers approached him. Keeping their distance, they called out, saying, "Jesus, Master, have mercy on us!" When he saw them, he said to them, "Go and show yourselves to the priests." And as they went, they were made clean. Then one of them, when he saw that he was healed, turned back, praising God with a loud voice. He prostrated himself at Jesus' feet and thanked him. And he was a Samaritan. Then Jesus asked, "Were not ten made clean? But the other nine, where are they? Was none of them found to return and give praise to God except this foreigner?" Then he said to him, "Get up and go on your way; your faith has made you well."

Notice what you think and feel as you read the gospel.

Jesus shows mercy to the ten lepers, healing them. One of them returns and throws himself on his face to thank Jesus. Jesus asks about the other nine. Aren't they grateful for their healing?

Pray as you are led for yourself and others.

"Lord, you give me everything. I thank you for all you have given me . . ." (Continue in your own words.)

Listen to Jesus.

You are a jewel in my sight, beloved. I love to shower you with favors. Thank you for taking time with me. What else is Jesus saying to you?

Ask God to show you how to live today.

"What can I do today to show gratitude to you and to others? Prompt me, Lord, with praise and thanksgiving, for I am your own. Amen."

Thursday, November 14, 2019

Know that God is present with you and ready to converse.

"Lord, gather me into your kingdom. I seek you in your Word."

Read the gospel: Luke 17:20–25.

Once Jesus was asked by the Pharisees when the kingdom of God was coming, and he answered, "The kingdom of God is not coming with things that can be observed; nor will they say, 'Look, here it is!' or 'There it is!' For, in fact, the kingdom of God is among you."

Then he said to the disciples, "The days are coming when you will long to see one of the days of the Son of Man, and you will not see it. They will say to you, 'Look there!' or 'Look here!' Do not go, do not set off in pursuit. For as the lightning flashes and lights up the sky from one side to the other, so will the Son of Man be in his day. But first he must endure much suffering and be rejected by this generation."

Notice what you think and feel as you read the gospel.

Jesus says the coming of the kingdom is not observable. It is not here or there. It is present now among us. Others will claim it is here or there, but we shouldn't fall for it. Jesus, rejected in this world by those he came to save, will return like a flash of lightning, visible to all.

Pray as you are led for yourself and others.

"I long to see you, Jesus. Come quickly, Lord. Prepare me and those you have given me for your glorious return . . ." (Continue in your own words.)

Listen to Jesus.

In the meantime, servant, occupy your time in the work of the kingdom of God. It is pleasant work for it is my work and the work of our Father. It is the work of love. What else is Jesus saying to you?

Ask God to show you how to live today.

"Give me that work, Lord, and let me rejoice in doing it with you by my side. Thank you. Amen."

Friday, November 15, 2019

Know that God is present with you and ready to converse.

"Lord, you are mystery and you speak of mysteries to me. Help me to understand what you would have me understand."

Read the gospel: Luke 17:26–37.

Jesus said, "Just as it was in the days of Noah, so too it will be in the days of the Son of Man. They were eating and drinking, and marrying and being given in marriage, until the day Noah entered the ark, and the flood came and destroyed all of them. Likewise, just as it was in the days of Lot: they were eating and drinking, buying and selling, planting and building, but on the day that Lot left Sodom, it rained fire and sulphur from heaven and destroyed all of them—it will be like that on the day that the Son of Man is revealed. On that day, anyone on the housetop who has belongings in the house must not come down to take them away; and likewise anyone in the field must not turn back. Remember Lot's wife. Those who try to make their life secure will lose it, but those who lose their life will keep it. I tell you, on that night there will be two in one bed; one will be taken and the other left. There will be two women grinding meal together; one will be taken and the other left." Then they asked him, "Where, Lord?" He said to them, "Where the corpse is, there the vultures will gather."

Notice what you think and feel as you read the gospel.

It will be business as usual the day the Lord returns. When he does, it will be too late to prepare or get away. Those who try to save their lives will lose them; those who lose their lives will save them. When? Where? How?

Pray as you are led for yourself and others.

"I give you my life, my Jesus. Do with it what you will. I offer you this day not for myself but for the good of those you have given me . . ." (Continue in your own words.)

Listen to Jesus.

I gave my life for love of others, beloved. That is the only way to live. Come enter into my life, child. What else is Jesus saying to you?

Ask God to show you how to live today.

"Let your mysteries swirl around me today, Lord. Let me serve you unafraid, for you are my faithful friend. Glory be to the Father, to the Son, and to the Holy Spirit. Amen."

Saturday, November 16, 2019

Know that God is present with you and ready to converse.

"Jesus, do you have a word for me today? Refresh me in your Spirit."

Read the gospel: Luke 18:1–8.

Then Jesus told them a parable about their need to pray always and not to lose heart. He said, "In a certain city there was a judge who neither feared God nor had respect for people. In that city there was a widow who kept coming to him and saying, 'Grant me justice against my opponent.' For a while he refused; but later he said to himself, 'Though I have no fear of God and no respect for anyone, yet because this widow keeps bothering me, I will grant her justice, so that she may not wear me out by continually coming.'" And the Lord said, "Listen to what the unjust judge says. And will not God grant justice to his chosen ones who cry to him day and night? Will he delay long in helping them? I tell you, he will quickly grant justice to them. And yet, when the Son of Man comes, will he find faith on earth?"

Notice what you think and feel as you read the gospel.

Jesus speaks about persisting in prayer, which requires faith and heart. God will do justice on earth, and quickly. Jesus ends with this haunting thought, "Yet, when the Son of Man comes, will he find faith on earth?"

Pray as you are led for yourself and others.

"Lord, why do I have doubts? I am flesh and blood. Help me to walk to you by faith, not doubting, praying continuously. I pray also for faith for those you have given me. Jesus, save us . . ." (Continue in your own words.)

Listen to Jesus.

I am with you, beloved. Because you are mine, I am your savior in all your circumstances. Look to God in prayer. Look to me. What else is Jesus saying to you?

Ask God to show you how to live today.

"Lord, be with me today and be a light to my feet. Let me come to you. Amen."

Sunday, November 17, 2019
Thirty-Third Sunday in Ordinary Time

Know that God is present with you and ready to converse.

"Eternal God, Creator, you come to me in time and love me for eternity."

Read the gospel: Luke 21:5–11 (Lk 21:5–19).

When some were speaking about the temple, how it was adorned with beautiful stones and gifts dedicated to God, Jesus said, "As for these things that you see, the days will come when not one stone will be left upon another; all will be thrown down."

They asked him, "Teacher, when will this be, and what will be the sign that this is about to take place?" And he said, "Beware that you are not led astray; for many will come in my name and say, 'I am he!' and, 'The time is near!' Do not go after them.

"When you hear of wars and insurrections, do not be terrified; for these things must take place first, but the end will not follow immediately." Then he said to them, "Nation will rise against nation, and kingdom against kingdom; there will be great earthquakes, and in various places famines and plagues; and there will be dreadful portents and great signs from heaven."

Notice what you think and feel as you read the gospel.

Jesus has the long view. The things of this world, even great things like the temple in Jerusalem, will not remain, yet we should not fear, for he will be with us again.

Pray as you are led for yourself and others.

"Lord, you will bring this age to an end in your own good time. Give me grace to persevere in hope and peace. I pray for those you have given me, asking for grace for them . . ." (Continue in your own words.)

Listen to Jesus.

When you appear before God in the kingdom of heaven, we will show you what a great difference your prayers have made in the lives of those we have given you. Pray with confidence, beloved disciple. What else is Jesus saying to you?

Ask God to show you how to live today.

"Lord, thank you for allowing me to serve in your kingdom. What can I do today? Who needs my prayers? Who needs an act of kindness? Please show me. Amen."

Monday, November 18, 2019

Know that God is present with you and ready to converse.

"Son of God, have mercy on me. Strengthen my faith by your Word."

Read the gospel: Luke 18:35–43.

As Jesus approached Jericho, a blind man was sitting by the roadside begging. When he heard a crowd going by, he asked what was happening. They told him, "Jesus of Nazareth is passing by." Then he shouted, "Jesus, Son of David, have mercy on me!" Those who were in front sternly ordered him to be quiet; but he shouted even more loudly, "Son of David, have mercy on me!" Jesus stood still and ordered the man to be brought to him; and when he came near, he asked him, "What do you want me to do for you?" He said, "Lord, let me see again." Jesus said to him, "Receive your sight; your faith has saved you." Immediately he regained his sight and followed him, glorifying God; and all the people, when they saw it, praised God.

Notice what you think and feel as you read the gospel.
The blind beggar, when he learns that Jesus is passing by, starts shouting and will not be silenced. Jesus hears the cry of the blind beggar, asks what he wants, and heals him. The man immediately follows Jesus, glorifying God. All who see it praise God.

Pray as you are led for yourself and others.
"God, give me persistent faith, for I want to walk hand in hand with you. I entrust to you all these people . . ." (Continue in your own words.)

Listen to Jesus.
How many times have I said, "Your faith has saved you"? Pray in faith, beloved, and I will grant your prayer. Persist in faith and it shall be done for you. Give God the glory. What else is Jesus saying to you?

Ask God to show you how to live today.
"You are glorious, loving God. How may I persevere in loving and praising you today? Amen."

Tuesday, November 19, 2019

Know that God is present with you and ready to converse.
"Lord, you dwell in awesome mystery, yet come to me. Let me hear your voice now in your Word."

Read the gospel: Luke 19:1–10.
Jesus entered Jericho and was passing through it. A man was there named Zacchaeus; he was a chief tax collector and was rich. He was trying to see who Jesus was, but on account of the crowd he could not, because he was short in stature. So he ran ahead and climbed a sycamore tree to see him, because he was going to pass that way. When Jesus came to the place, he looked up and said to him, "Zacchaeus, hurry and come down; for I must stay at your house today." So he hurried down and

was happy to welcome him. All who saw it began to grumble and said, "He has gone to be the guest of one who is a sinner." Zacchaeus stood there and said to the Lord, "Look, half of my possessions, Lord, I will give to the poor; and if I have defrauded anyone of anything, I will pay back four times as much." Then Jesus said to him, "Today salvation has come to this house, because he too is a son of Abraham. For the Son of Man came to seek out and to save the lost."

Notice what you think and feel as you read the gospel.

Jesus seeks out and saves Zacchaeus, who himself sought the Lord. He repents and receives salvation for his whole house.

Pray as you are led for yourself and others.

"Lord, I seek you, but you have already found me. Let me renew my repentance and draw nearer to you. I pray also for those you have given me . . ." (Continue in your own words.)

Listen to Jesus.

Dear one, we have found each other. Let us stay close. Spend time with me every day. What else is Jesus saying to you?

Ask God to show you how to live today.

"How can I help you seek out and save others, Lord? How can I speak of the joy of walking in close friendship with you? Amen."

Wednesday, November 20, 2019

Know that God is present with you and ready to converse.

"Lord, you dwell in awesome majesty and come to me with awesome love. You are holy. I will listen to your voice now, your Word."

Read the gospel: Luke 19:11–28.

As the people were listening to this, Jesus went on to tell a parable, because he was near Jerusalem, and because they supposed that the kingdom of God was to appear immediately. So he said, "A nobleman went to a distant country to get royal power for himself and then return. He summoned ten of his slaves, and gave them ten pounds, and said to them, 'Do business with these until I come back.' But the citizens of his country hated him and sent a delegation after him, saying, 'We do not want this man to rule over us.' When he returned, having received royal power, he ordered these slaves, to whom he had given the money, to be summoned so that he might find out what they had gained by trading. The first came forward and said, 'Lord, your pound has made ten more pounds.' He said to him, 'Well done, good slave! Because you have been trustworthy in a very small thing, take charge of ten cities.' Then the second came, saying, 'Lord, your pound has made five pounds.' He said to him, 'And you, rule over five cities.' Then the other came, saying, 'Lord, here is your pound. I wrapped it up in a piece of cloth, for I was afraid of you, because you are a harsh man; you take what you did not deposit, and reap what you did not sow.' He said to him, 'I will judge you by your own words, you wicked slave! You knew, did you, that I was a harsh man, taking what I did not deposit and reaping what I did not sow? Why then did you not put my money into the bank? Then when I returned, I could have collected it with interest.' He said to the bystanders, 'Take the pound from him and give it to the one who has ten pounds.' (And they said to him, 'Lord, he has ten pounds!') 'I tell you, to all those who have, more will be given; but from those who have nothing, even what they have will be taken away. But as for these enemies of mine who did not want me to be king over them—bring them here and slaughter them in my presence.'"

After he had said this, he went on ahead, going up to Jerusalem.

Notice what you think and feel as you read the gospel.

Jesus judges the wicked slave by his own words. The man's excuses are his undoing. Jesus, the King, shall be the just judge of all.

Pray as you are led for yourself and others.

"Lord, I make excuses. Forgive me. Let me turn away from excuses and use the gifts you have given me for the good of others, especially those you have given me . . ." (Continue in your own words.)

Listen to Jesus.

Beloved disciple, you are right to take my words to heart. I am speaking to you because I love you and want your best both now and hereafter. What else is Jesus saying to you?

Ask God to show you how to live today.

"Call my attention to my phony excuses for not doing my best in my work for you and for others. Let me lean upon your strength to do what you have put before me today and tomorrow. Amen."

Thursday, November 21, 2019

Know that God is present with you and ready to converse.
"Lord, you are with me now. Let me recognize you in your Word and in your Spirit that I may know your peace."

Read the gospel: Luke 19:41–44.
As Jesus came near and saw the city, he wept over it, saying, "If you, even you, had only recognized on this day the things that make for peace! But now they are hidden from your eyes. Indeed, the days will come upon you, when your enemies will set up ramparts around you and surround you, and hem you in on every side. They will crush you to the ground, you and your children within you, and they will not leave within you one stone upon another; because you did not recognize the time of your visitation from God."

Notice what you think and feel as you read the gospel.
Jesus knows what will happen to Jerusalem, that it will be destroyed. He weeps that its inhabitants do not recognize that he is God among them. That failure to recognize him will be the cause of their destruction.

Pray as you are led for yourself and others.
"Lord, you are love and mercy, yet we can be blind to you. Let me take your words deep into my heart and be converted. I pray for all those who do not recognize you . . ." (Continue in your own words.)

Listen to Jesus.
Human history is full of violence, and there is reason to fear destruction in many forms. But you need not fear as long as you cling to me. Love God and you will also love and serve others. What else is Jesus saying to you?

Ask God to show you how to live today.
"Help me to be brave, trusting you for safety for myself and those I love. Let me serve in your peace, Lord. I love you. Amen."

Friday, November 22, 2019

Know that God is present with you and ready to converse.
"Shine your light upon your Word, Holy Spirit. Let it draw me in and transform me."

Read the gospel: Luke 19:45–48.

Then Jesus entered the temple and began to drive out those who were selling things there; and he said, "It is written,

> 'My house shall be a house of prayer';
>> but you have made it a den of robbers."

Every day he was teaching in the temple. The chief priests, the scribes, and the leaders of the people kept looking for a way to kill him; but they did not find anything they could do, for all the people were spellbound by what they heard.

Notice what you think and feel as you read the gospel.

Jesus teaches the people every day, and they love him. Those who oppose him, the religious leaders, cannot do anything to stop him, but they want to kill him.

Pray as you are led for yourself and others.

"Evil lies in human hearts, even in those who profess to be good and holy. Jealousy, revenge, injustice, fear, self-preservation—all these and more cause us to oppose good, to oppose the will of God. Root out the evil in my heart, Lord, so that I can do your will . . ." (Continue in your own words.)

Listen to Jesus.

Make your house a house of prayer, my child. I want to be with you. What else is Jesus saying to you?

Ask God to show you how to live today.

"Interrupt my day, Lord, with opportunities to turn to you, to speak to you, to hear from you. Teach me to pray. Amen."

Saturday, November 23, 2019

Know that God is present with you and ready to converse.

"Teacher, you love me always. I love you, too, and I give myself to your instruction now."

Read the gospel: Luke 20:27–40.

Some Sadducees, those who say there is no resurrection, came to Jesus and asked him a question, "Teacher, Moses wrote for us that if a man's brother dies, leaving a wife but no children, the man shall marry the widow and raise up children for his brother. Now there were seven brothers; the first married, and died childless; then the second and the third married her, and so in the same way all seven died childless. Finally the woman also died. In the resurrection, therefore, whose wife will the woman be? For the seven had married her."

Jesus said to them, "Those who belong to this age marry and are given in marriage; but those who are considered worthy of a place in that age and in the resurrection from the dead neither marry nor are given in marriage. Indeed they cannot die any more, because they are like angels and are children of God, being children of the resurrection. And the fact that the dead are raised Moses himself showed, in the story about the bush, where he speaks of the Lord as the God of Abraham, the God of Isaac, and the God of Jacob. Now he is God not of the dead, but of the living; for to him all of them are alive." Then some of the scribes answered, "Teacher, you have spoken well." For they no longer dared to ask him another question.

Notice what you think and feel as you read the gospel.

The Sadducees have cooked up an impossible question, seeking to confound Jesus on the topic of the resurrection. Jesus rejects their assumptions and affirms, from scripture and from his own knowledge, the resurrection of the dead. We will be like angels in the age to come.

Pray as you are led for yourself and others.

"Jesus, you speak with such confidence. I believe you are the Son of God. Thank you for loving us so much. Let your truth go out to all the world . . ." (Continue in your own words.)

Listen to Jesus.

The present age is subject to time. The age to come will remain forever. Come into the kingdom now, beloved, and spend your time with me. What else is Jesus saying to you?

Ask God to show you how to live today.

"Lord, you are good. How can I express to others that they, too, are beloved of God? Help me do that, please. Amen."

Sunday, November 24, 2019
Christ the King

Know that God is present with you and ready to converse.

"Your Father has made you king of heaven and earth, Jesus Christ. You are my master, Lord. I welcome you now."

Read the gospel: Luke 23:35–43.

And the people stood by, watching; but the leaders scoffed at Jesus, saying, "He saved others; let him save himself if he is the Messiah of God, his chosen one!" The soldiers also mocked him, coming up and offering him sour wine, and saying, "If you are the King of the Jews, save yourself!" There was also an inscription over him, "This is the King of the Jews."

One of the criminals who were hanged there kept deriding him and saying, "Are you not the Messiah? Save yourself and us!" But the other rebuked him, saying, "Do you not fear God, since you are under the same sentence of condemnation? And we indeed have been condemned justly, for we are getting what we deserve for our deeds, but this man has done nothing wrong." Then he said, "Jesus, remember me when you come into your kingdom." He replied, "Truly I tell you, today you will be with me in Paradise."

Notice what you think and feel as you read the gospel.

Jesus, the Messiah of God, is hanging on the Cross, dying. One of the criminals who is being crucified with him challenges him to show his power and save them all. The other criminal rebukes the first, then asks Jesus to remember him when he comes into his kingdom. Jesus promises him paradise.

Pray as you are led for yourself and others.

"Jesus, King, you invite me into your kingdom through the lowly door of service to those in need. There are so many suffering. Let me serve them today, tomorrow, and always . . ." (Continue in your own words.)

Listen to Jesus.

I will give you opportunities to serve the poor. Beloved disciple, look for me in them. I will give you joy. What else is Jesus saying to you?

Ask God to show you how to live today.

"Lord, I have good intentions. Please help me translate them into concrete actions of service. What can I do today? Amen."

Monday, November 25, 2019

Know that God is present with you and ready to converse.

"Lord, you look upon the heart. Come into my heart and speak to me today."

Read the gospel: Luke 21:1–4.

Jesus looked up and saw rich people putting their gifts into the temple treasury; he also saw a poor widow put in two small copper coins. He said, "Truly I tell you, this poor widow has put in more than all of them; for all of them have contributed out of their abundance, but she out of her poverty has put in all she had to live on."

Notice what you think and feel as you read the gospel.

God sees us differently than people do. Jesus commends the poor widow for her generosity even though her gift was very small.

Pray as you are led for yourself and others.

"Jesus, give me the generous heart of the poor widow. I offer all I have and am to you. I offer myself for the good of all those you have given me . . ." (Continue in your own words.)

Listen to Jesus.

Ask God for faith, hope, love, wisdom, peace, and perseverance. Those gifts will manifest themselves in your actions. What else is Jesus saying to you?

Ask God to show you how to live today.

"Jesus, lead me to little acts of love today. Let me please you as the poor widow did. Amen."

Tuesday, November 26, 2019

Know that God is present with you and ready to converse.

"Lord, the world around me is in turmoil. I seek peace in your steadfast Word."

Read the gospel: Luke 21:5–11.

When some were speaking about the temple, how it was adorned with beautiful stones and gifts dedicated to God, Jesus said, "As for these things that you see, the days will come when not one stone will be left upon another; all will be thrown down."

They asked him, "Teacher, when will this be, and what will be the sign that this is about to take place?" And he said, "Beware that you are not led astray; for many will come in my name and say, 'I am he!' and, 'The time is near!' Do not go after them.

"When you hear of wars and insurrections, do not be terrified; for these things must take place first, but the end will not follow immediately." Then he said to them, "Nation will rise against nation, and kingdom against kingdom; there will be great earthquakes, and in various places famines and plagues; and there will be dreadful portents and great signs from heaven."

Notice what you think and feel as you read the gospel.

Terrible things are coming, and Jesus wants his disciples to be forewarned so that fear doesn't separate them from him.

Pray as you are led for yourself and others.

"Lord, your predictions seem to have come true, yet still the end does not come. Send your Spirit to keep me watchful and alert, and let your mercy extend to all in this age . . ." (Continue in your own words.)

Listen to Jesus.

The end will come; when it does, drop everything and look to me. I am the Alpha and the Omega, the beginning and the end, and I love you. Have no fear. What else is Jesus saying to you?

Ask God to show you how to live today.

"My Lord and my God, today let me set aside the world and come to you in prayer, in preparation for the day when this world will fall away and you will be my all in all. Show me how to bring about your kingdom in every moment. Amen."

Wednesday, November 27, 2019

Know that God is present with you and ready to converse.

"Jesus, your name is Wisdom. I rejoice in your presence, Lord. I rejoice in your Word."

Read the gospel: Luke 21:12–19.

Jesus said, "But before all this occurs, they will arrest you and persecute you; they will hand you over to synagogues and prisons, and you will be brought before kings and governors because of my name. This will give you an opportunity to testify. So make up your minds not to prepare your defense in advance; for I will give you words and a wisdom that none of your opponents will be able to withstand or contradict. You will be betrayed even by parents and brothers, by relatives and friends; and they will put some of you to death. You will be hated by all because of my name. But not a hair of your head will perish. By your endurance you will gain your souls."

Notice what you think and feel as you read the gospel.

Jesus prepares us for the terrible times to come before the end. These things will happen and have already begun to happen. You may die, but not a hair of your head will perish, he says. We will gain our souls through enduring this.

Pray as you are led for yourself and others.

"Lord, with you I can do anything, endure anything, for this world and life are just the door to eternal life with you. I pray for the souls of those you have given me . . ." (Continue in your own words.)

Listen to Jesus.

Pray for those who are being persecuted, beloved. Pray that they know that I am with them and thank them for their witness. They will receive glory in the kingdom of my Father. What else is Jesus saying to you?

Ask God to show you how to live today.

"Lord, I offer myself to you, even for persecution, because I am yours. Give me the grace to gladly suffer in your name. Amen."

Thursday, November 28, 2019

Know that God is present with you and ready to converse.

"Lord, stir up my soul to attend to you now, for you have the words of eternal life."

Read the gospel: Luke 21:20–28.

Jesus said, "When you see Jerusalem surrounded by armies, then know that its desolation has come near. Then those in Judea must flee to the mountains, and those inside the city must leave it, and those out in the country must not enter it; for these are days of vengeance, as a fulfillment of all that is written. Woe to those who are pregnant and to those who are nursing infants in those days! For there will be great distress on the earth and wrath against this people; they will fall by the edge of the sword and be taken away as captives among all nations; and Jerusalem will be trampled on by the Gentiles, until the times of the Gentiles are fulfilled.

"There will be signs in the sun, the moon, and the stars, and on the earth distress among nations confused by the roaring of the sea and the waves. People will faint from fear and foreboding of what is coming upon the world, for the powers of the heavens will be shaken. Then they will see 'the Son of Man coming in a cloud' with power and great glory. Now when these things begin to take place, stand up and raise your heads, because your redemption is drawing near."

Notice what you think and feel as you read the gospel.

Jesus describes the terror of the final desolation. Violence among people, displacement, war, disruption in the heavens and in the seas. Then we will see the Son of Man coming in a cloud, our Redeemer.

Pray as you are led for yourself and others.

"Without you, Lord, the world falls apart. Stay with me, Jesus, and with those you have given me . . ." (Continue in your own words.)

Listen to Jesus.

The people of the earth have always believed they could save themselves. The progress of fallen humanity is toward self-destruction. I and all the prophets have spoken the truth about the final devastation. I call out to everyone to turn to God now before the terrible days. What else is Jesus saying to you?

Ask God to show you how to live today.

"Each day has its share of difficulties and distress, Lord, and each day I need you to be the unmoved center. Let me ground myself in you and then carry your peace with me through the storms of the world. Amen."

Friday, November 29, 2019

Know that God is present with you and ready to converse.

"You are near to me, living Word of God. I embrace you."

Read the gospel: Luke 21:29–33.

Then Jesus told them a parable: "Look at the fig tree and all the trees; as soon as they sprout leaves you can see for yourselves and know that summer is already near. So also, when you see these things taking place, you know that the kingdom of God is near. Truly I tell you, this generation will not pass away until all things have taken place. Heaven and earth will pass away, but my words will not pass away."

Notice what you think and feel as you read the gospel.

Do we see the leaves of the fig tree sprouting? How near to us is the coming of the kingdom of God? Jesus says all things will pass away except his words.

Pray as you are led for yourself and others.

"Glory to you, Lord Jesus Christ. All things are under your command. I place myself under your command, and I give you, too, all those you have given to me . . ." (Continue in your own words.)

Listen to Jesus.

Peace to you, beloved. Remain in my peace. What else is Jesus saying to you?

Ask God to show you how to live today.

"Lord, let me be an instrument of your peace today. Amen."

Saturday, November 30, 2019
St. Andrew, Apostle

Know that God is present with you and ready to converse.

"Lord, you seek and find those you have chosen. You have found me today. I praise you."

Read the gospel: Matthew 4:18–22.

As Jesus walked by the Sea of Galilee, he saw two brothers, Simon, who is called Peter, and Andrew his brother, casting a net into the lake—for they were fishermen. And he said to them, "Follow me, and I will make you fish for people." Immediately they left their nets and followed him. As he went from there, he saw two other brothers, James son of Zebedee and his brother John, in the boat with their father Zebedee, mending their nets, and he called them. Immediately they left the boat and their father, and followed him.

Notice what you think and feel as you read the gospel.

Here Jesus calls his chief disciples, some of the apostles. By trade they are fishermen, but Jesus has another job for them—to fish for people. They leave their work, their nets, and their families to follow him.

Pray as you are led for yourself and others.

"Lord, give me that pure, unquestioning commitment in response to your call. I choose to follow you. Let this choice bear good fruit for all those you have given me . . ." (Continue in your own words.)

Listen to Jesus.

We are workers, my child. You do my work, and I do yours. This is the way to redeem the time. Lose yourself in loving and serving others, and find me. What else is Jesus saying to you?

Ask God to show you how to live today.

"Lord, I am grateful to you for simplifying my life with your presence. Stay with me all day as I work your will. Let me do what matters to you. Amen."

The **Pope's Worldwide Prayer Network** is an international ecclesial ministry served by the Jesuits that reaches more than 50 million participants worldwide through its popular website, talks, conferences, radio outreach, publications, and retreats. Each year the Holy Father asks that Christians and non-Christians alike join in praying for his particular intentions on the challenges facing humanity. The regional US–Canadian office can be found at popesprayerusa.net and popesprayercanada.net.

AVE

AVE MARIA PRESS

Founded in 1865, Ave Maria Press,
a ministry of the Congregation of
Holy Cross, is a Catholic publishing
company that serves the spiritual and
formative needs of the Church and its
schools, institutions, and ministers;
Christian individuals and families; and
others seeking spiritual nourishment.

———

For a complete listing of titles from

Ave Maria Press

Sorin Books

Forest of Peace

Christian Classics

visit avemariapress.com